CAGE of EDEN

VOLUME 4

Yoshinobu Yamada

Tran... ...ari Morimoto

...mony

_navigation

KC
KODANSHA
COMICS

Cage of Eden volume 4 is a work of fiction. Names, characters, places, and incidents are the products of the author's imagination or are used fictitiously. Any resemblance to actual events, locales, or persons, living or dead, is entirely coincidental.

A Kodansha Comics Trade Paperback Original

Published in the United States by Kodansha Comics, an imprint of Kodansha USA Publishing, LLC, New York.

Publication rights for this English edition arranged through Kodansha Ltd., Tokyo.

First published in Japan in 2009 by Kodansha Ltd., Tokyo, as *Eden no Ori*, volume 4.

ISBN 978-1-61262-048-0

Printed in the United States of America

www.kodanshacomics.com

9 8 7 6 5 4 3 2 1

Translator: Mari Morimoto
Lettering: Bobby Timony

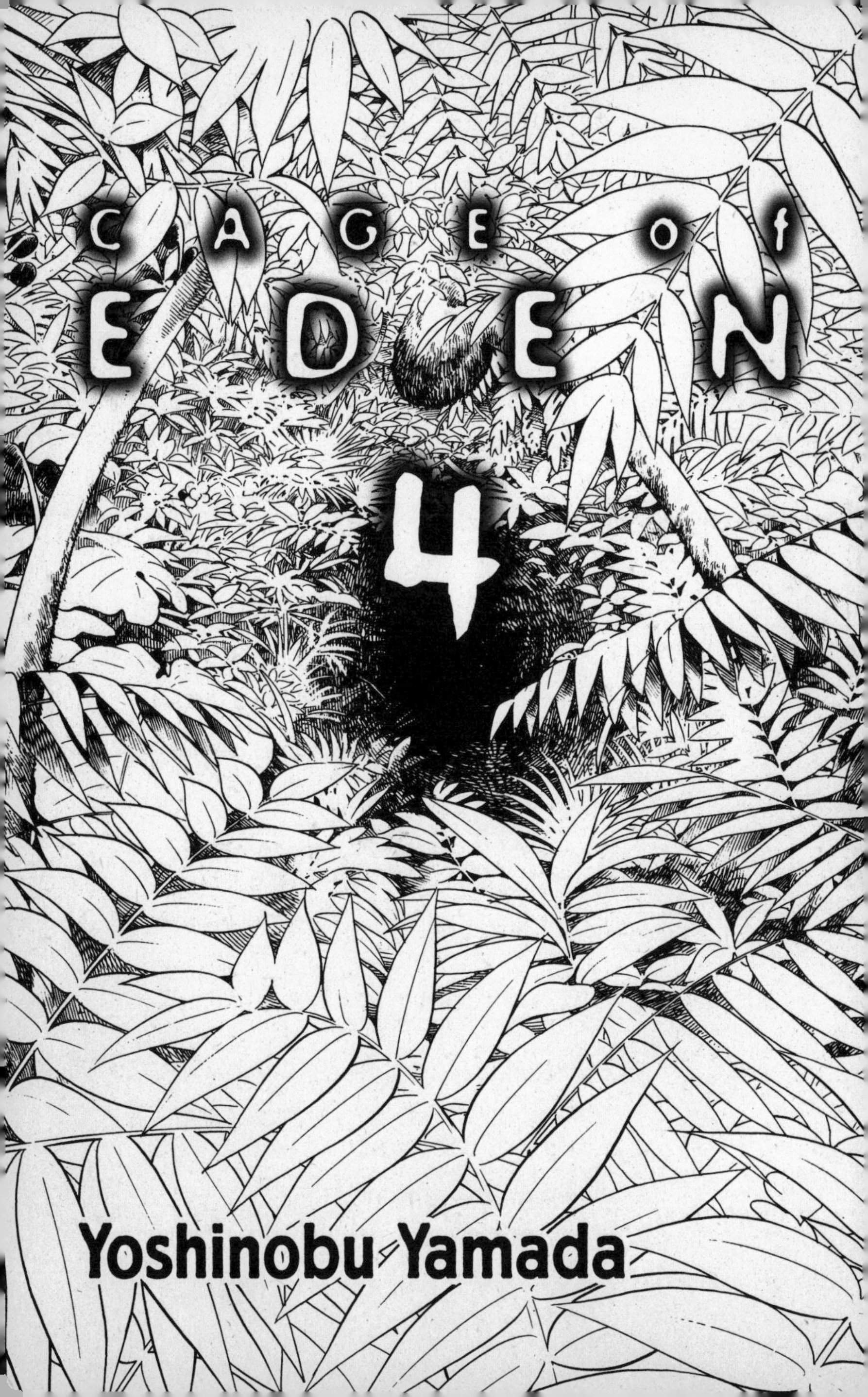
CAGE of
EDEN
4
Yoshinobu Yamada

CAGE of EDEN

Episode 23   THE SECRET MAP -------------------- 3

Episode 24   UPRISING ------------------------------ 23

Episode 25   GOOD PEEPS ------------------------- 43

Episode 26   LIAR, LIAR ------------------------------ 63

Episode 27   THE ARRIVAL OF YUKI
             (BRAIN DAMAGE 1) ---------------- 85

Episode 28   UNDERGROUND WORLD
             (BRAIN DAMAGE 2) -------------- 105

Episode 29   HE WHO FORGES AHEAD
             (BRAIN DAMAGE 3) -------------- 123

Episode 30   RION & YUKI,
             AKIRA & THE GOD OF DEATH
             (BRAIN DAMAGE 4) --------------143

Episode 31   THE VANISHING EYES
             (BRAIN DAMAGE 5) -------------- 163

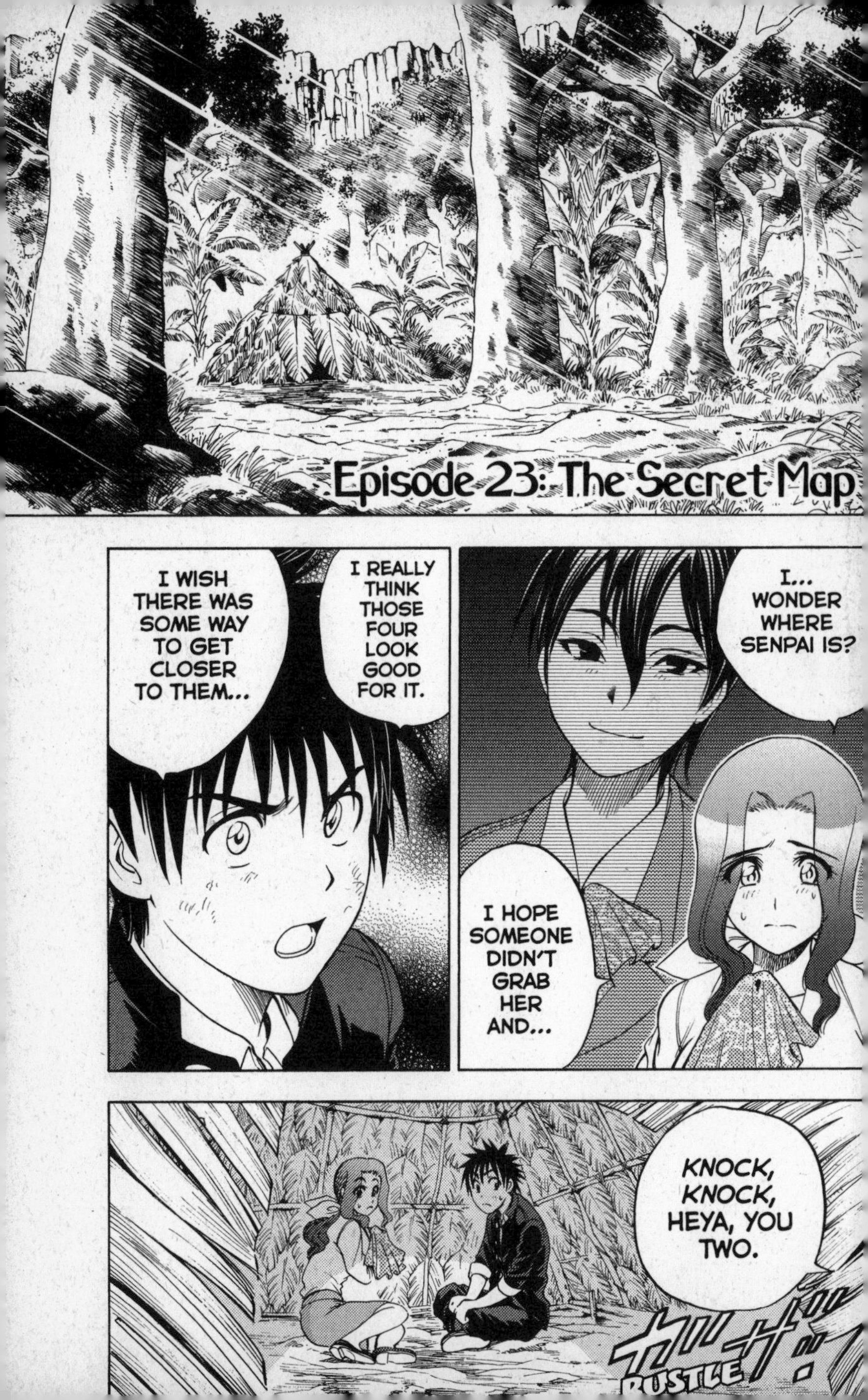
Episode 23: The Secret Map
I... WONDER WHERE SENPAI IS?
I HOPE SOMEONE DIDN'T GRAB HER AND...
I REALLY THINK THOSE FOUR LOOK GOOD FOR IT.
I WISH THERE WAS SOME WAY TO GET CLOSER TO THEM...
KNOCK, KNOCK, HEYA, YOU TWO.
RUSTLE

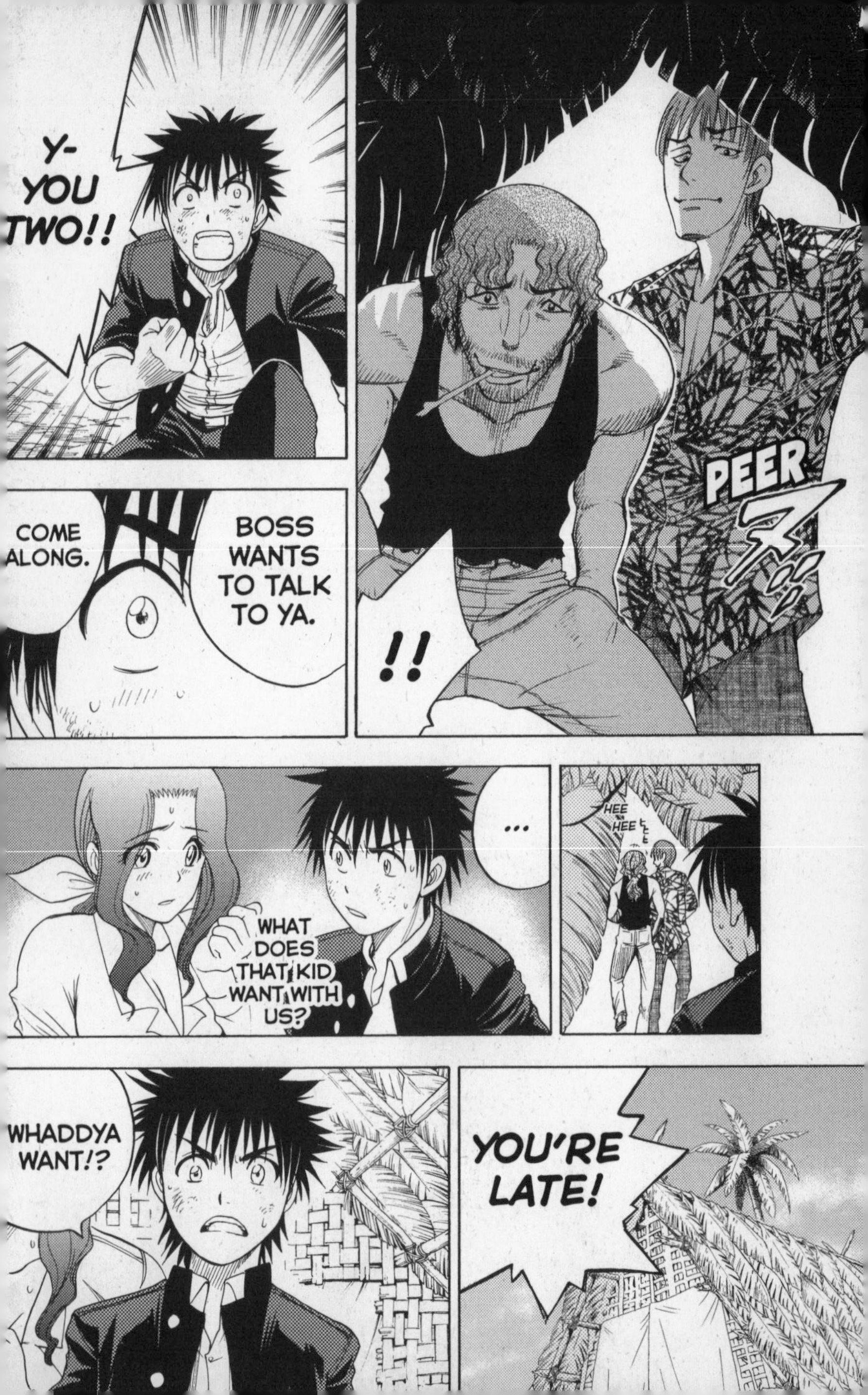
PEER
!!
Y-YOU TWO!!
BOSS WANTS TO TALK TO YA.
COME ALONG.
HEE HEE
...
WHAT DOES THAT KID WANT WITH US?
YOU'RE LATE!
WHADDYA WANT!?

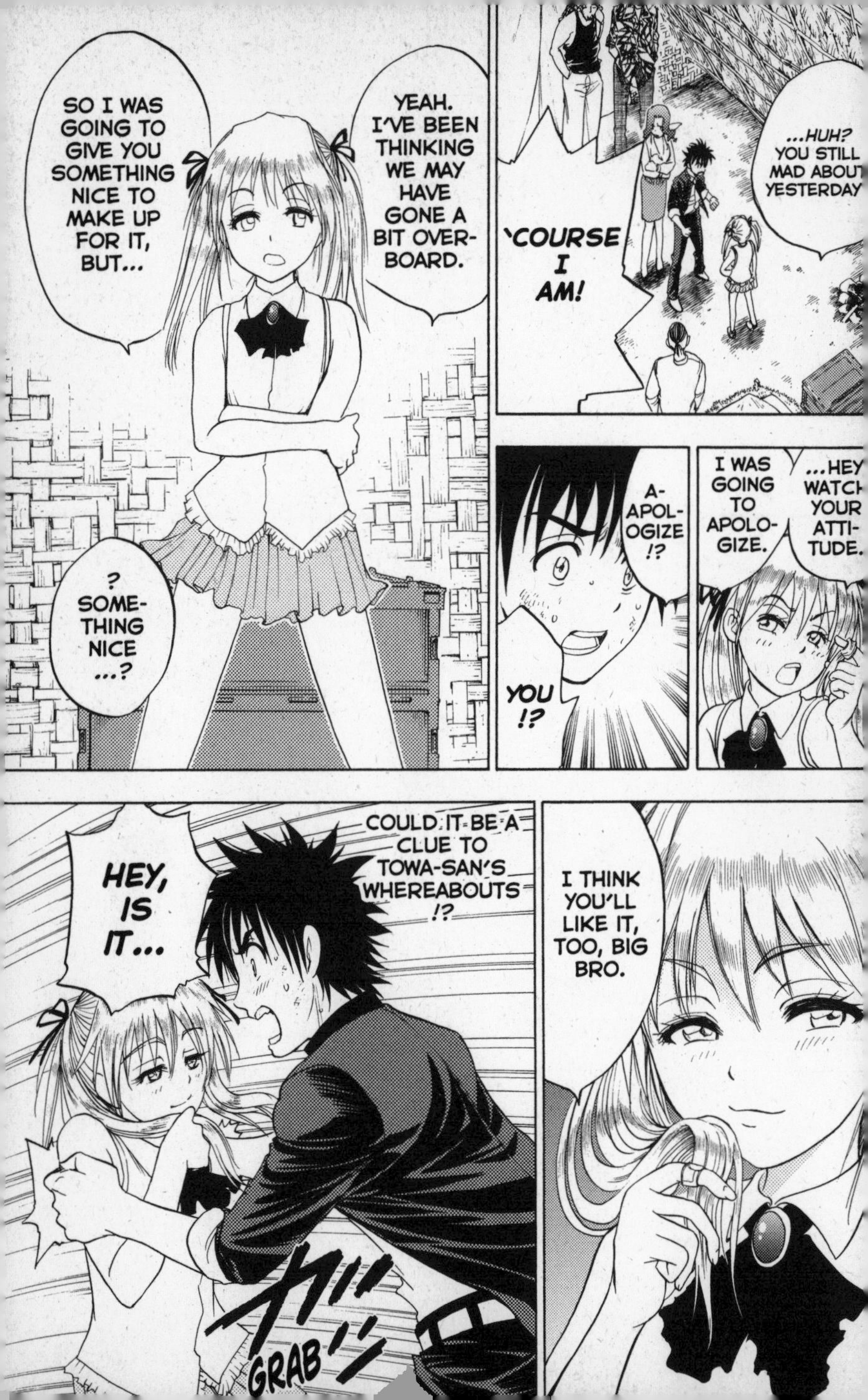
...HUH? YOU STILL MAD ABOUT YESTERDAY
'COURSE I AM!
...HEY WATCH YOUR ATTI-TUDE.
I WAS GOING TO APOLO-GIZE.
A-APOLOGIZE!?
YOU!?
YEAH. I'VE BEEN THINKING WE MAY HAVE GONE A BIT OVER-BOARD.
SO I WAS GOING TO GIVE YOU SOMETHING NICE TO MAKE UP FOR IT, BUT...
? SOME-THING NICE...?
I THINK YOU'LL LIKE IT, TOO, BIG BRO.
COULD IT BE A CLUE TO TOWA-SAN'S WHEREABOUTS!?
HEY, IS IT...
GRAB!!

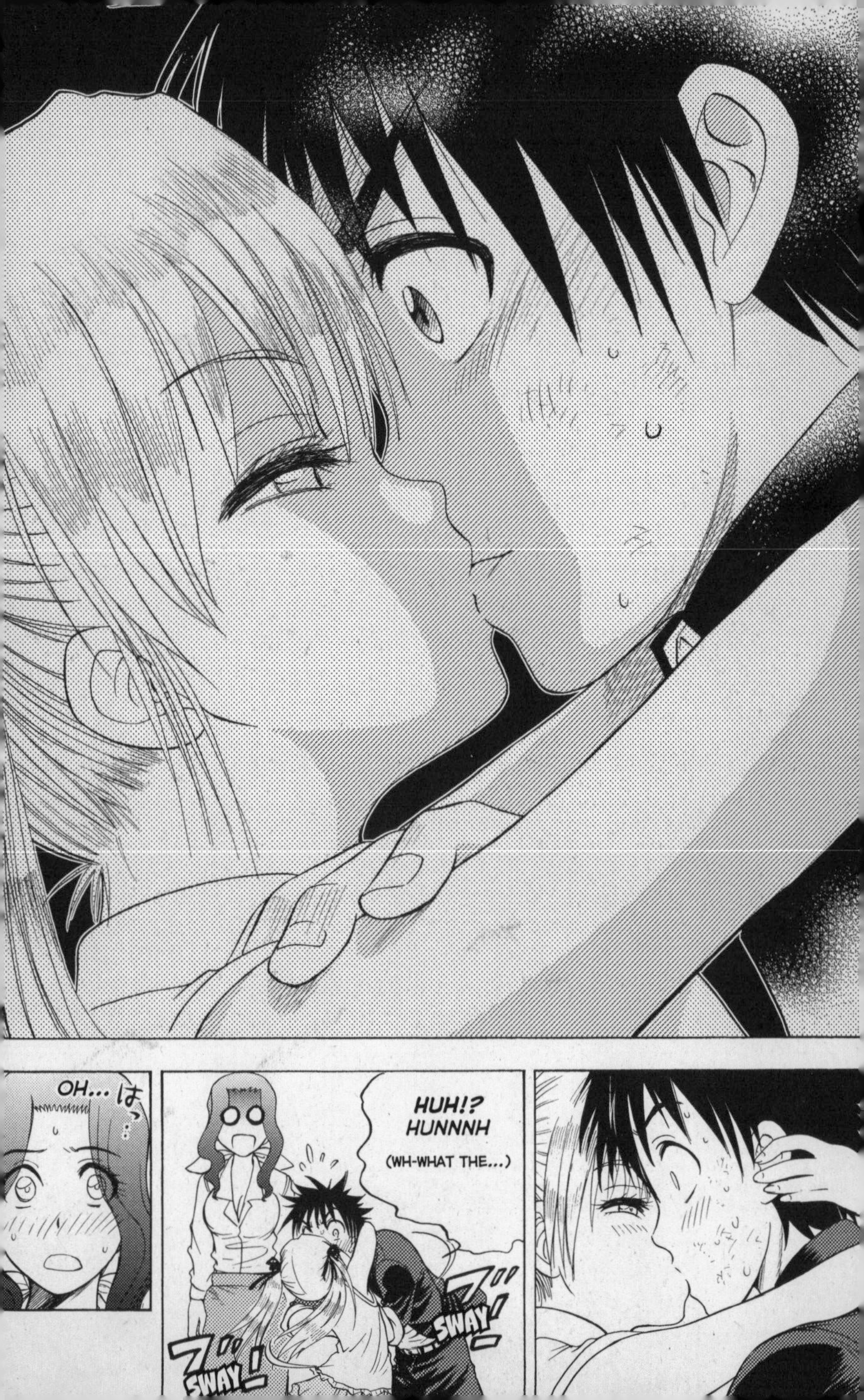
HUH!? HUNNNH
(WH-WHAT THE...)
SWAY!
SWAY!
OH... はっ

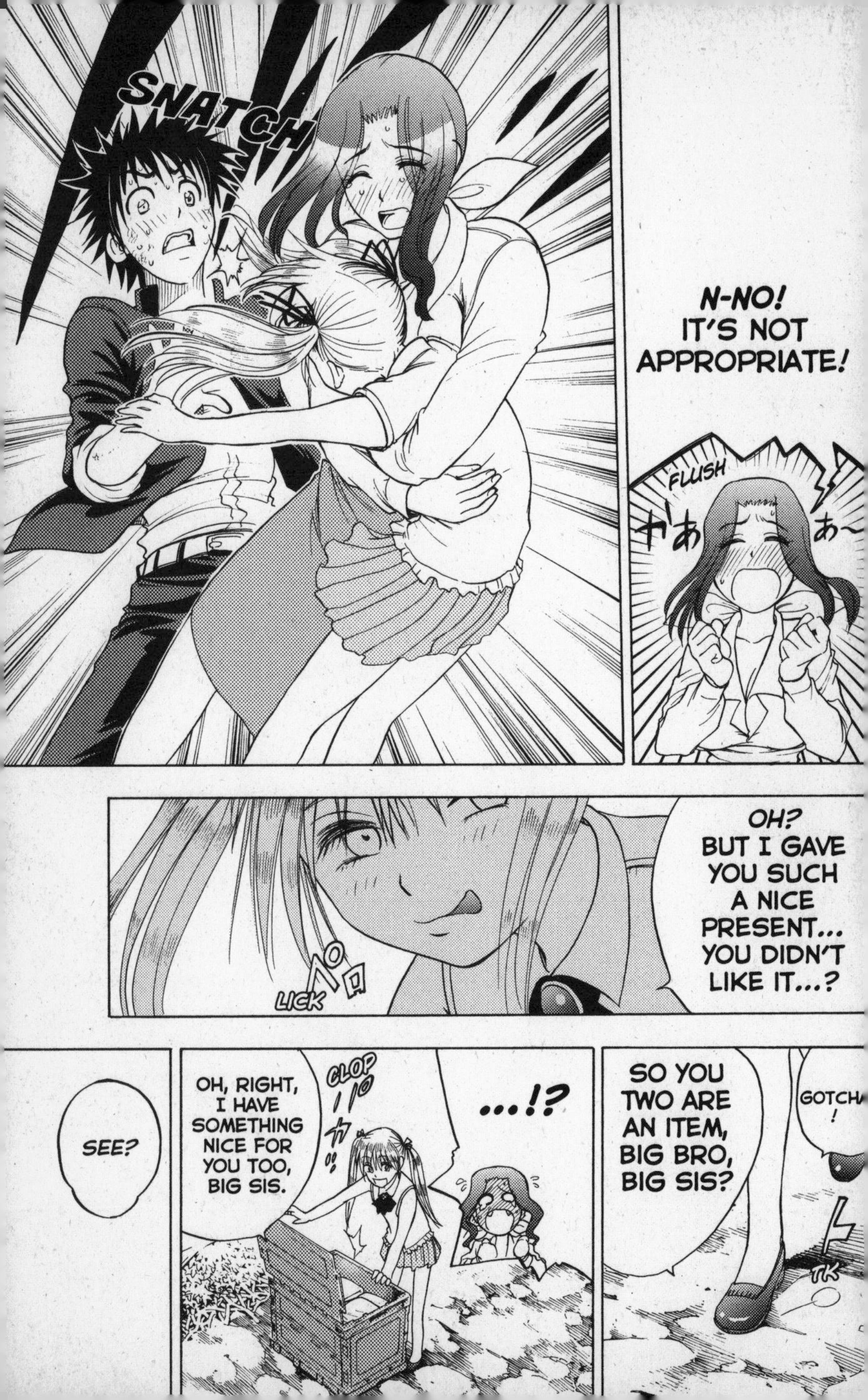
N-NO! IT'S NOT APPROPRIATE!
FLUSH
SNATCH
OH? BUT I GAVE YOU SUCH A NICE PRESENT... YOU DIDN'T LIKE IT...?
LICK
GOTCHA!
SO YOU TWO ARE AN ITEM, BIG BRO, BIG SIS?
TK
...!?
OH, RIGHT, I HAVE SOMETHING NICE FOR YOU TOO, BIG SIS.
CLOP
SEE?

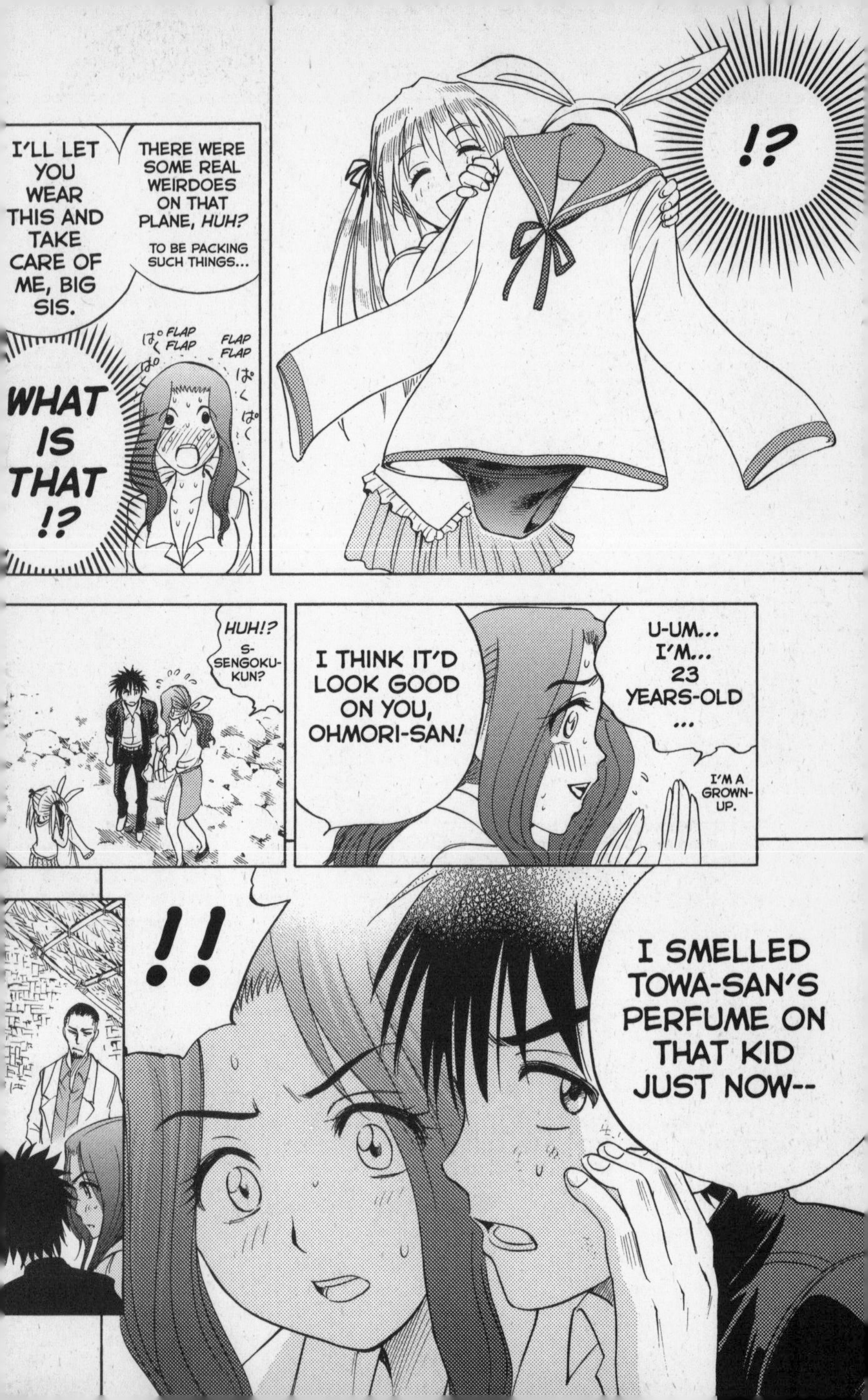
!?
THERE WERE SOME REAL WEIRDOES ON THAT PLANE, *HUH?*
TO BE PACKING SUCH THINGS...
I'LL LET YOU WEAR THIS AND TAKE CARE OF ME, BIG SIS.
ぱくぱく FLAP FLAP
FLAP FLAP ぱくぱく
WHAT IS THAT !?
U-UM... I'M... 23 YEARS-OLD ...
I'M A GROWN-UP.
I THINK IT'D LOOK GOOD ON YOU, OHMORI-SAN!
HUH!?
S-SENGOKU-KUN?
I SMELLED TOWA-SAN'S PERFUME ON THAT KID JUST NOW--
!!

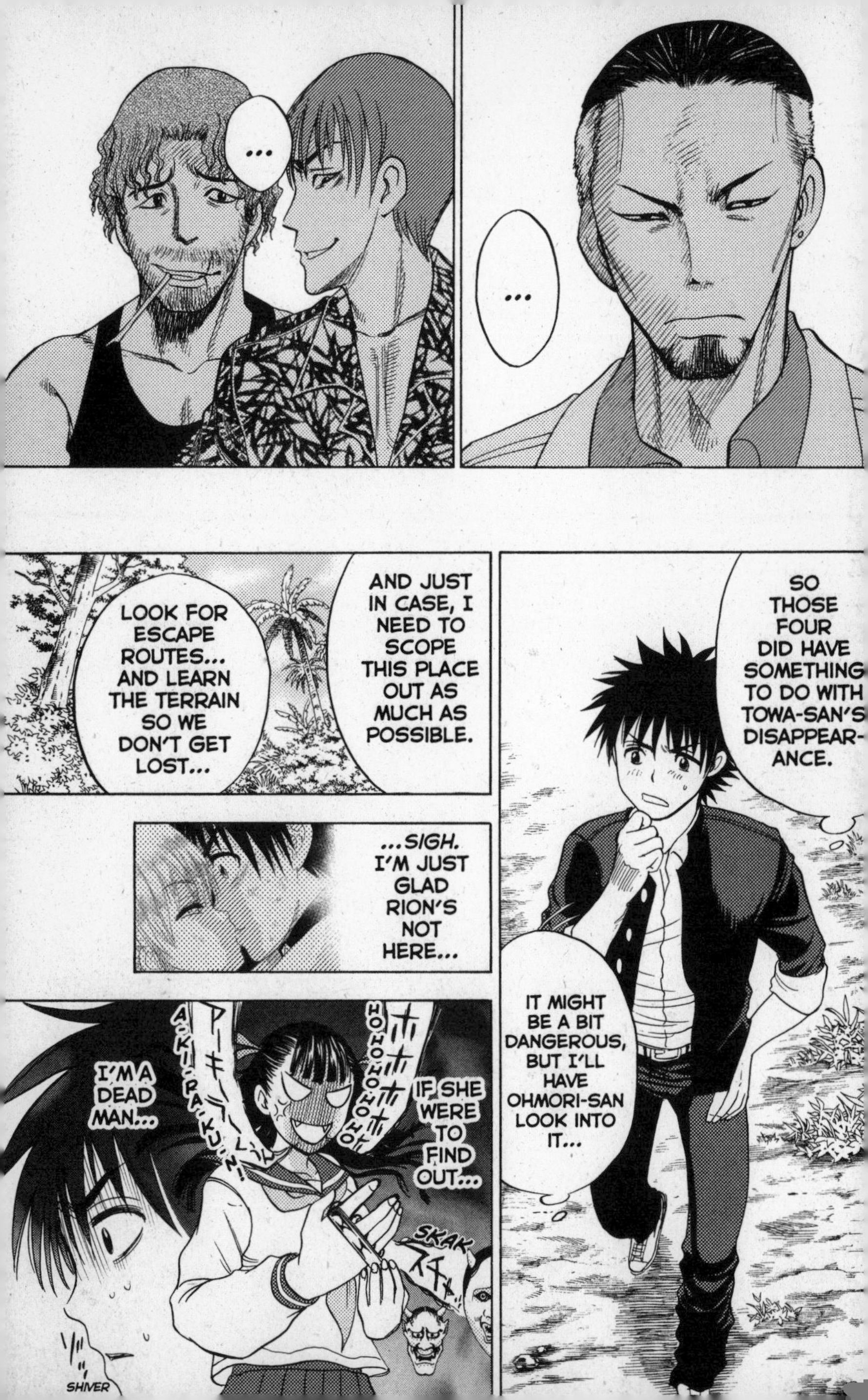
...
...
SO THOSE FOUR DID HAVE SOMETHING TO DO WITH TOWA-SAN'S DISAPPEARANCE.
IT MIGHT BE A BIT DANGEROUS, BUT I'LL HAVE OHMORI-SAN LOOK INTO IT...
AND JUST IN CASE, I NEED TO SCOPE THIS PLACE OUT AS MUCH AS POSSIBLE.
LOOK FOR ESCAPE ROUTES... AND LEARN THE TERRAIN SO WE DON'T GET LOST...
...SIGH. I'M JUST GLAD RION'S NOT HERE...
IF SHE WERE TO FIND OUT...
HOHOHOHOHO
A-KI-RA-KU-N!
SKAK
I'M A DEAD MAN...
SHIVER

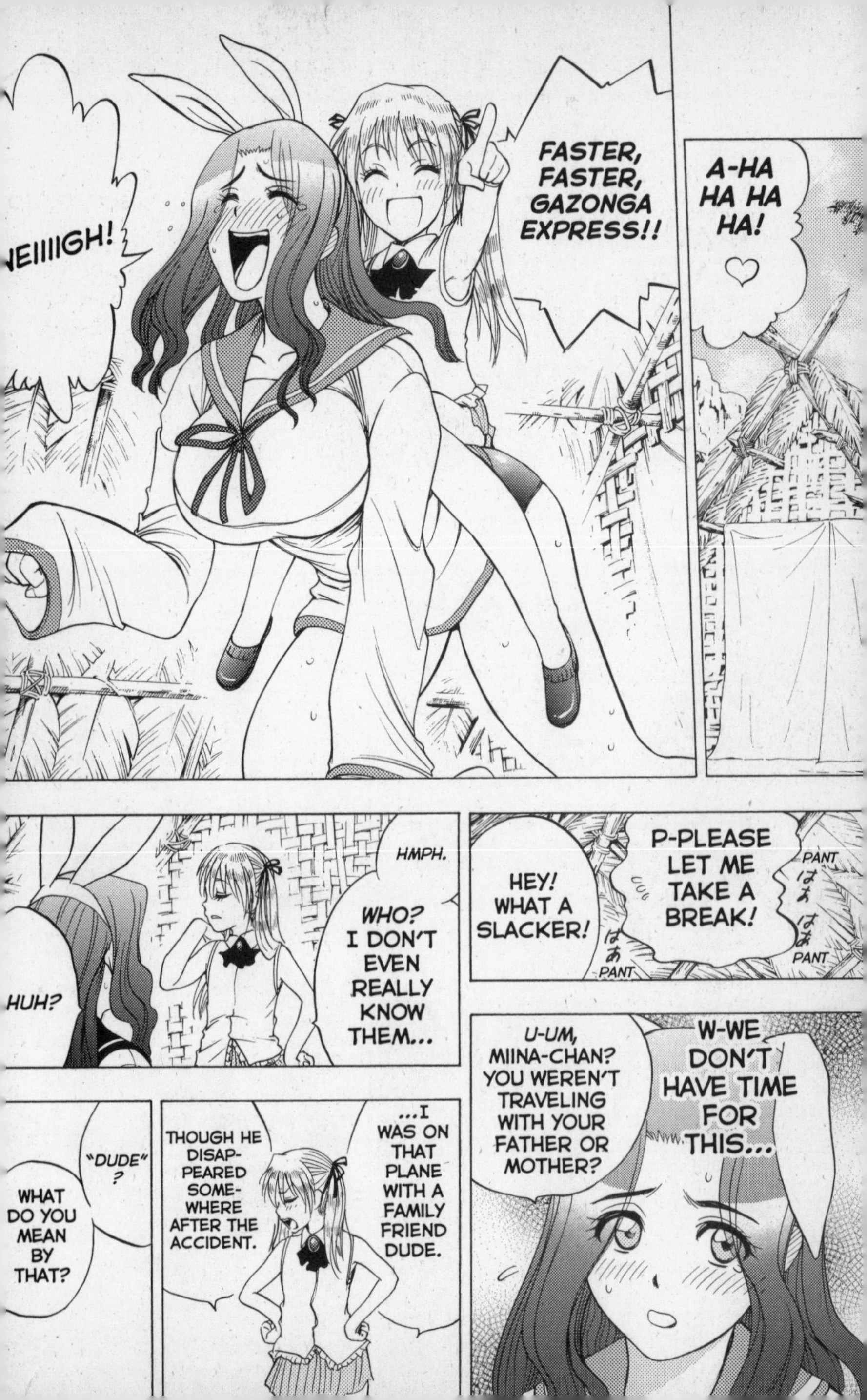

A-HA HA HA HA! ♡
FASTER, FASTER, GAZONGA EXPRESS!!
NEIIIIGH!
P-PLEASE LET ME TAKE A BREAK!
PANT はぁ はぁ PANT
HEY! WHAT A SLACKER!
はぁ PANT
HMPH.
WHO? I DON'T EVEN REALLY KNOW THEM...
HUH?
W-WE DON'T HAVE TIME FOR THIS...
U-UM, MIINA-CHAN? YOU WEREN'T TRAVELING WITH YOUR FATHER OR MOTHER?
...I WAS ON THAT PLANE WITH A FAMILY FRIEND DUDE.
THOUGH HE DISAP-PEARED SOME-WHERE AFTER THE ACCIDENT.
"DUDE"?
WHAT DO YOU MEAN BY THAT?

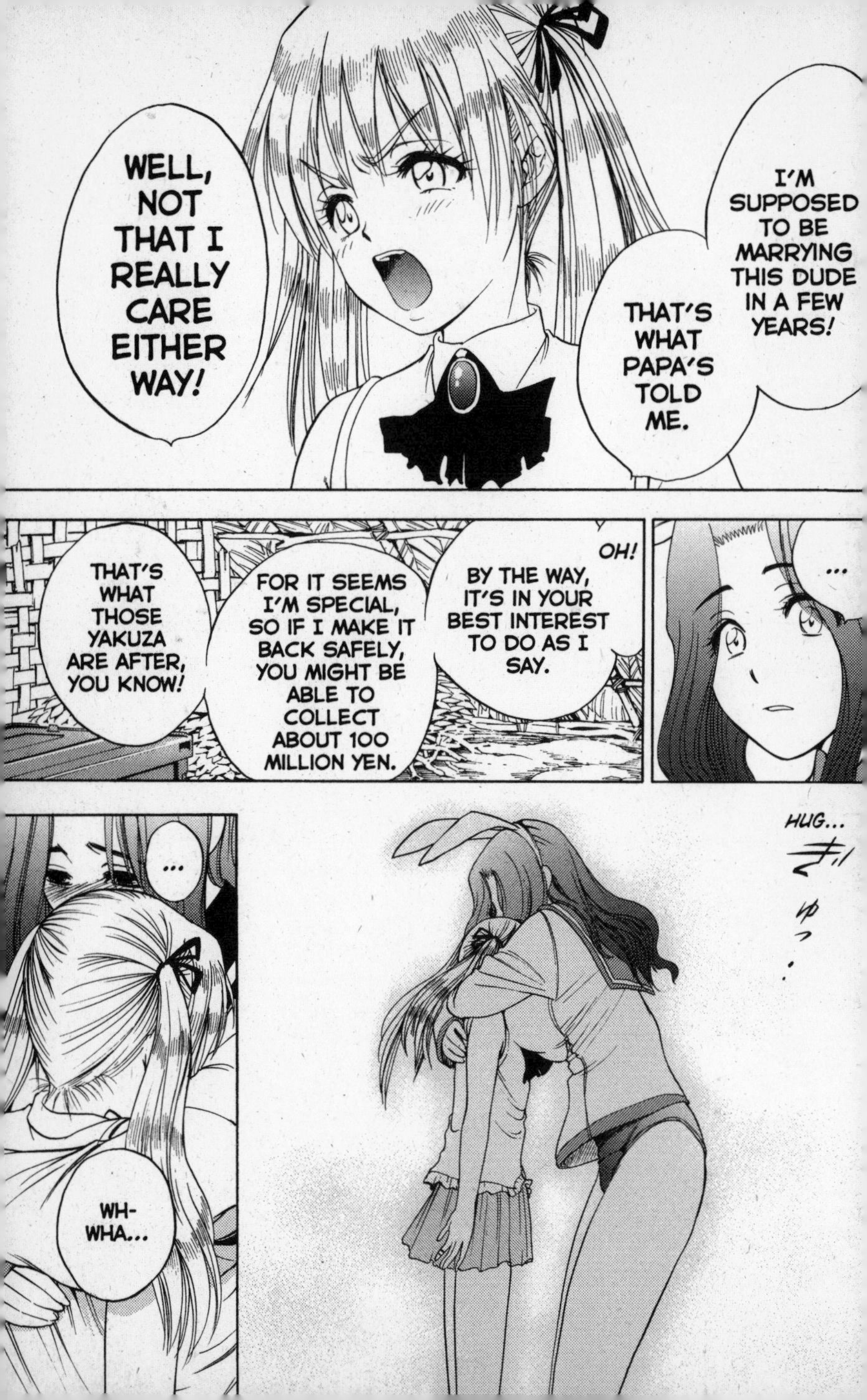
I'M SUPPOSED TO BE MARRYING THIS DUDE IN A FEW YEARS!
THAT'S WHAT PAPA'S TOLD ME.
WELL, NOT THAT I REALLY CARE EITHER WAY!
...
OH!
BY THE WAY, IT'S IN YOUR BEST INTEREST TO DO AS I SAY.
FOR IT SEEMS I'M SPECIAL, SO IF I MAKE IT BACK SAFELY, YOU MIGHT BE ABLE TO COLLECT ABOUT 100 MILLION YEN.
THAT'S WHAT THOSE YAKUZA ARE AFTER, YOU KNOW!
HUG...
ぎゅっ
...
WH-WHA...

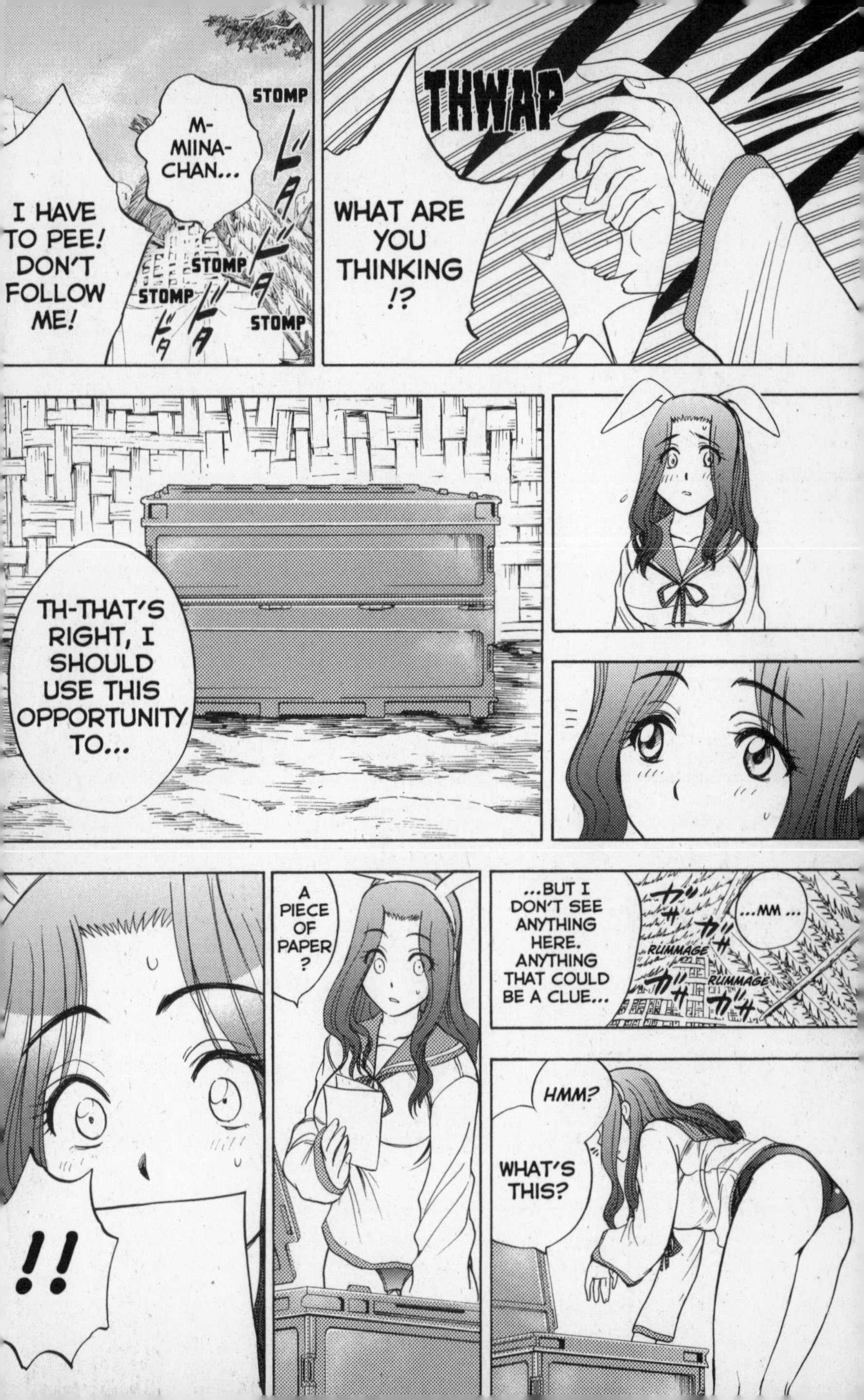
THWAP
WHAT ARE YOU THINKING!?
STOMP
M-MIINA-CHAN...
STOMP
STOMP
STOMP
I HAVE TO PEE! DON'T FOLLOW ME!
TH-THAT'S RIGHT, I SHOULD USE THIS OPPORTUNITY TO...
...MM ...
RUMMAGE
RUMMAGE
...BUT I DON'T SEE ANYTHING HERE. ANYTHING THAT COULD BE A CLUE...
HMM?
WHAT'S THIS?
A PIECE OF PAPER?
!!

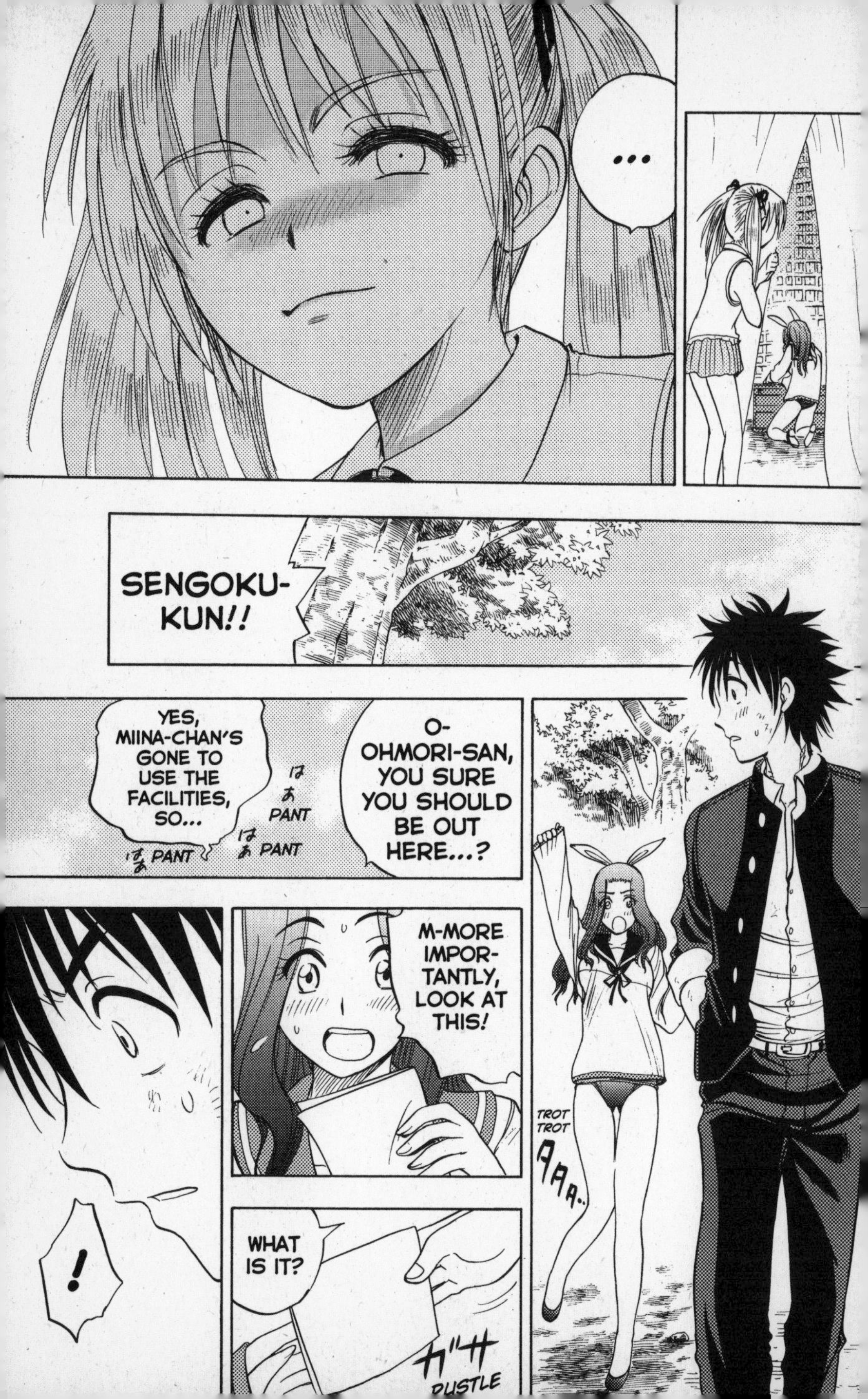
...
SENGOKU-KUN!!
TROT TROT
O-OHMORI-SAN, YOU SURE YOU SHOULD BE OUT HERE...?
はあ PANT
はあ PANT
YES, MIINA-CHAN'S GONE TO USE THE FACILITIES, SO...
はあ PANT
M-MORE IMPORTANTLY, LOOK AT THIS!
WHAT IS IT?
ガサ
RUSTLE
!

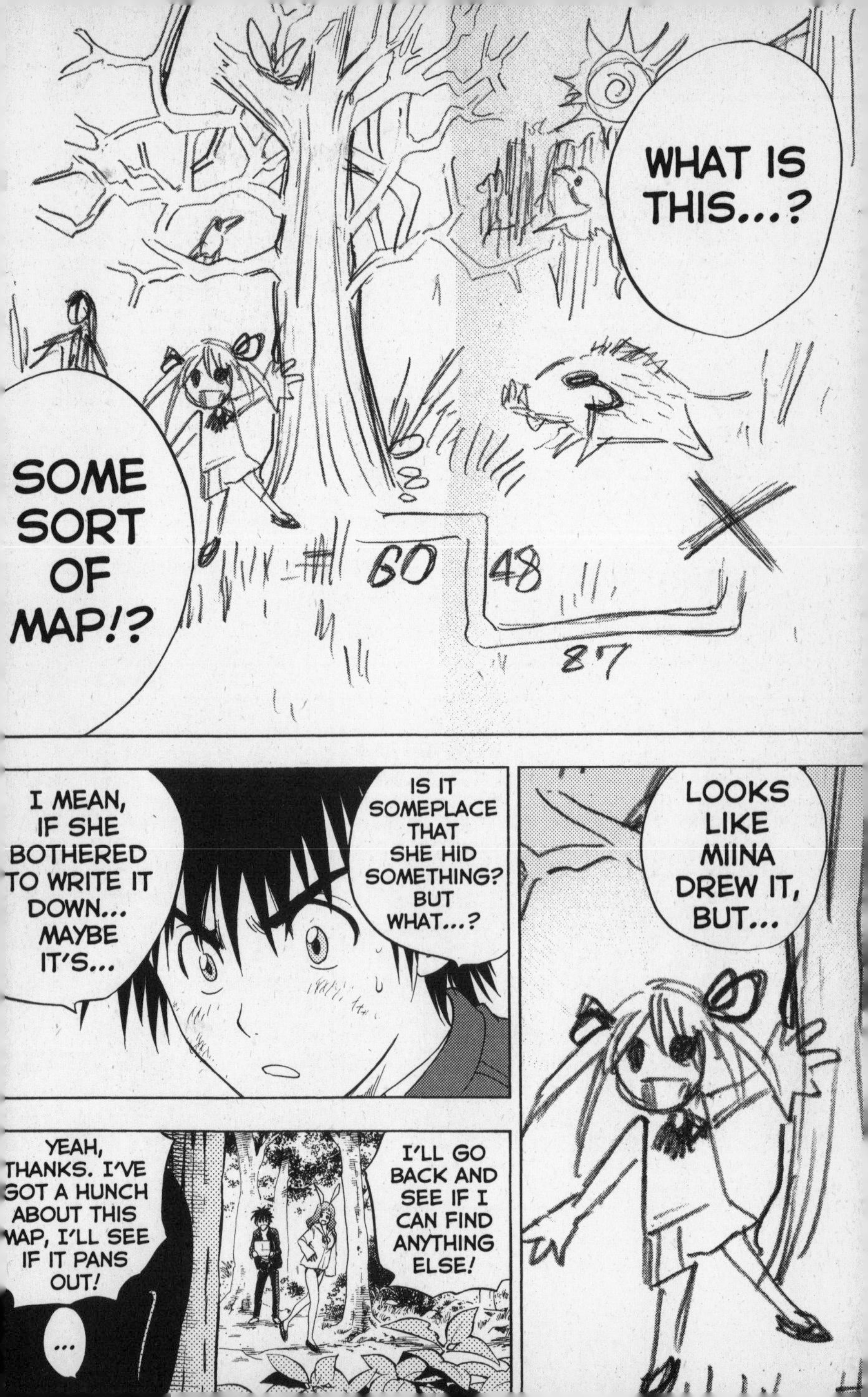
WHAT IS THIS...?
SOME SORT OF MAP!?
60
48
87
LOOKS LIKE MIINA DREW IT, BUT...
IS IT SOMEPLACE THAT SHE HID SOMETHING? BUT WHAT...?
I MEAN, IF SHE BOTHERED TO WRITE IT DOWN... MAYBE IT'S...
I'LL GO BACK AND SEE IF I CAN FIND ANYTHING ELSE!
YEAH, THANKS. I'VE GOT A HUNCH ABOUT THIS MAP, I'LL SEE IF IT PANS OUT!
...

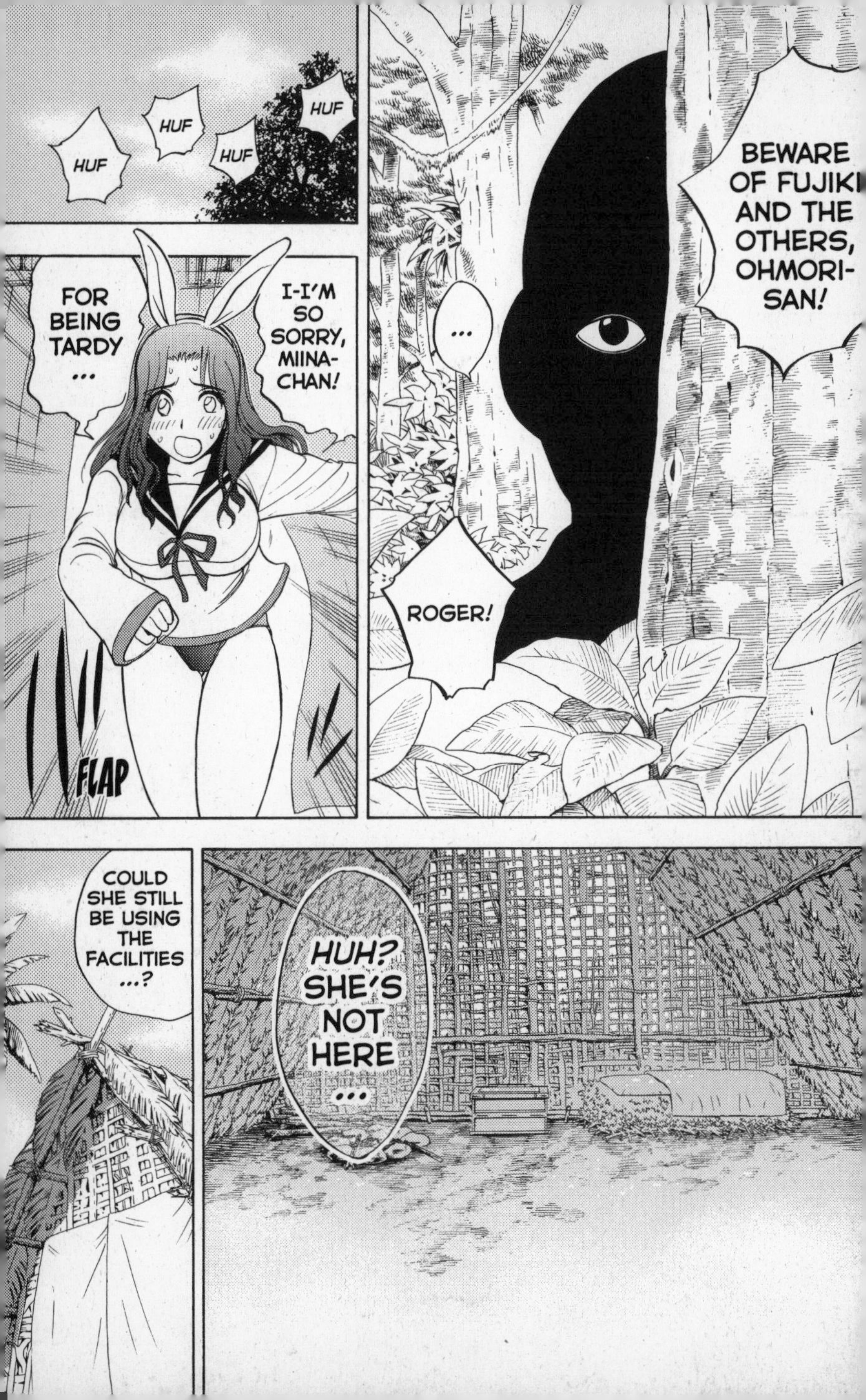
BEWARE OF FUJIKI AND THE OTHERS, OHMORI-SAN!
...
ROGER!
HUF
HUF
HUF
HUF
I-I'M SO SORRY, MIINA-CHAN!
FOR BEING TARDY ...
FLAP
HUH? SHE'S NOT HERE ...
COULD SHE STILL BE USING THE FACILITIES ...?

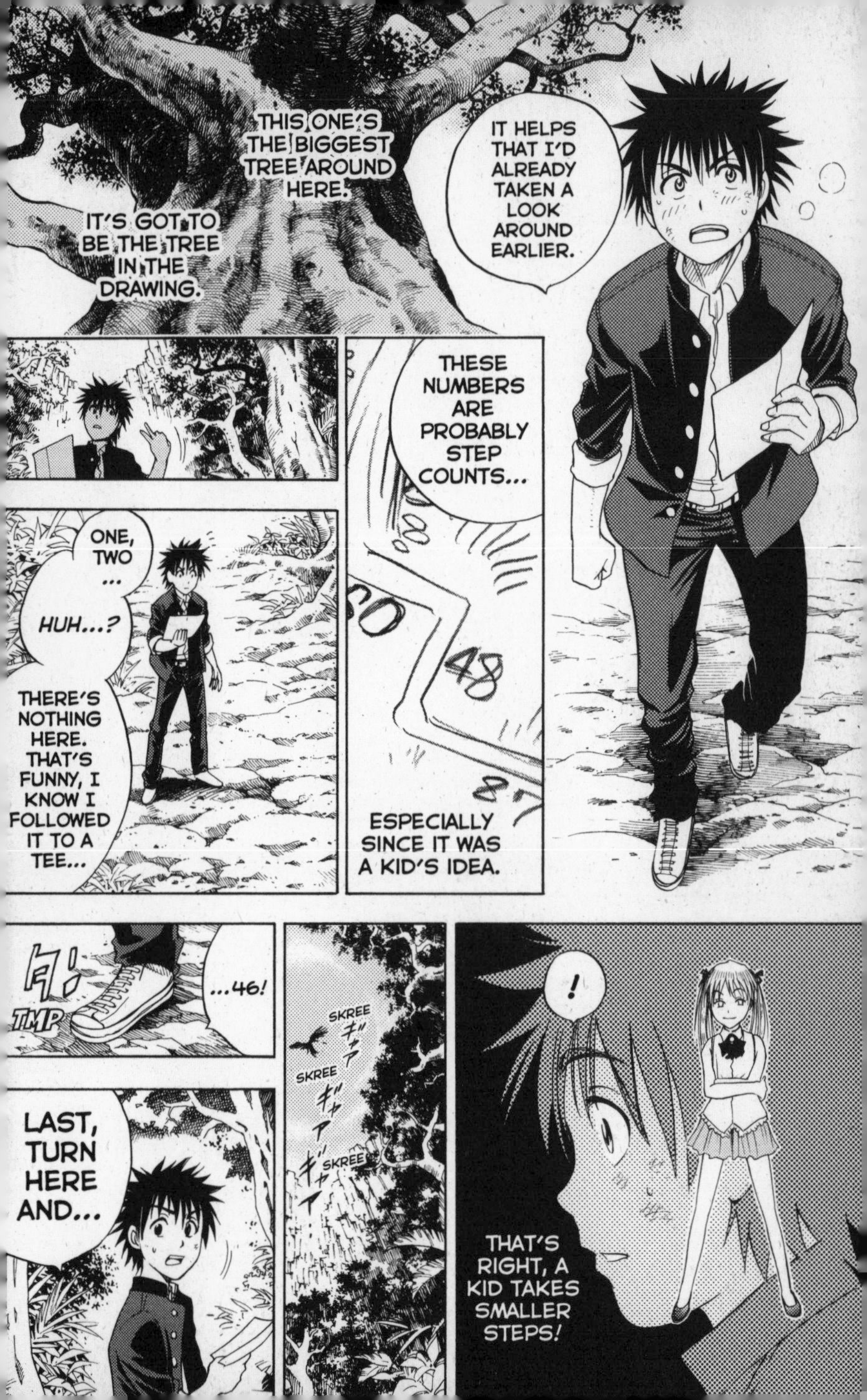
IT HELPS THAT I'D ALREADY TAKEN A LOOK AROUND EARLIER.
THIS ONE'S THE BIGGEST TREE AROUND HERE.
IT'S GOT TO BE THE TREE IN THE DRAWING.
THESE NUMBERS ARE PROBABLY STEP COUNTS...
60
48
87
ESPECIALLY SINCE IT WAS A KID'S IDEA.
ONE, TWO ...
HUH...?
THERE'S NOTHING HERE. THAT'S FUNNY, I KNOW I FOLLOWED IT TO A TEE...
!
THAT'S RIGHT, A KID TAKES SMALLER STEPS!
SKREE
ギャア
SKREE
ギャア
SKREE
ギャア
...46!
TMP
LAST, TURN HERE AND...

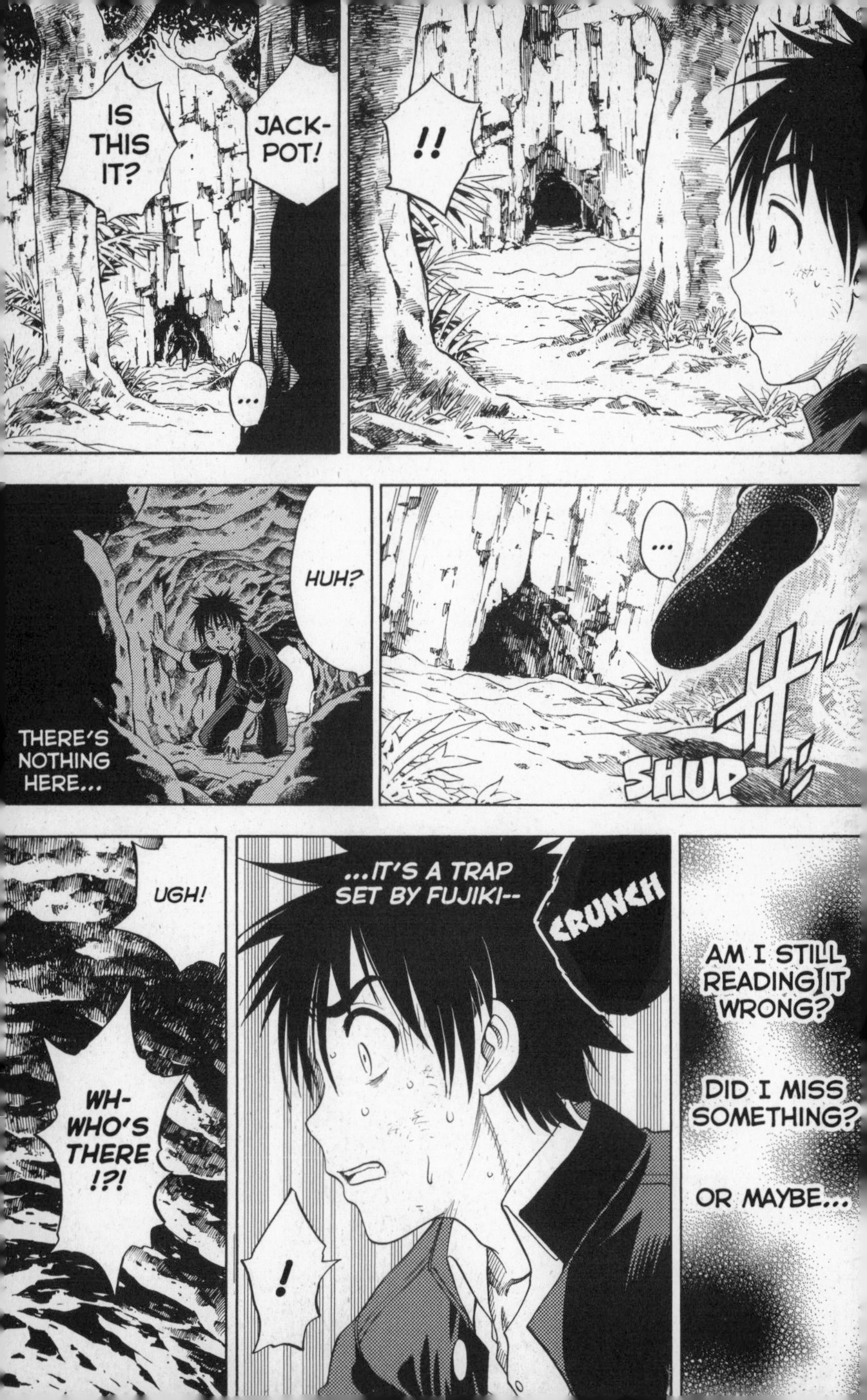
!!
JACK-POT!
IS THIS IT?
...
...
SHUP
HUH?
THERE'S NOTHING HERE...
AM I STILL READING IT WRONG?
DID I MISS SOMETHING?
OR MAYBE...
CRUNCH
...IT'S A TRAP SET BY FUJIKI--
!
UGH!
WH-WHO'S THERE !?!

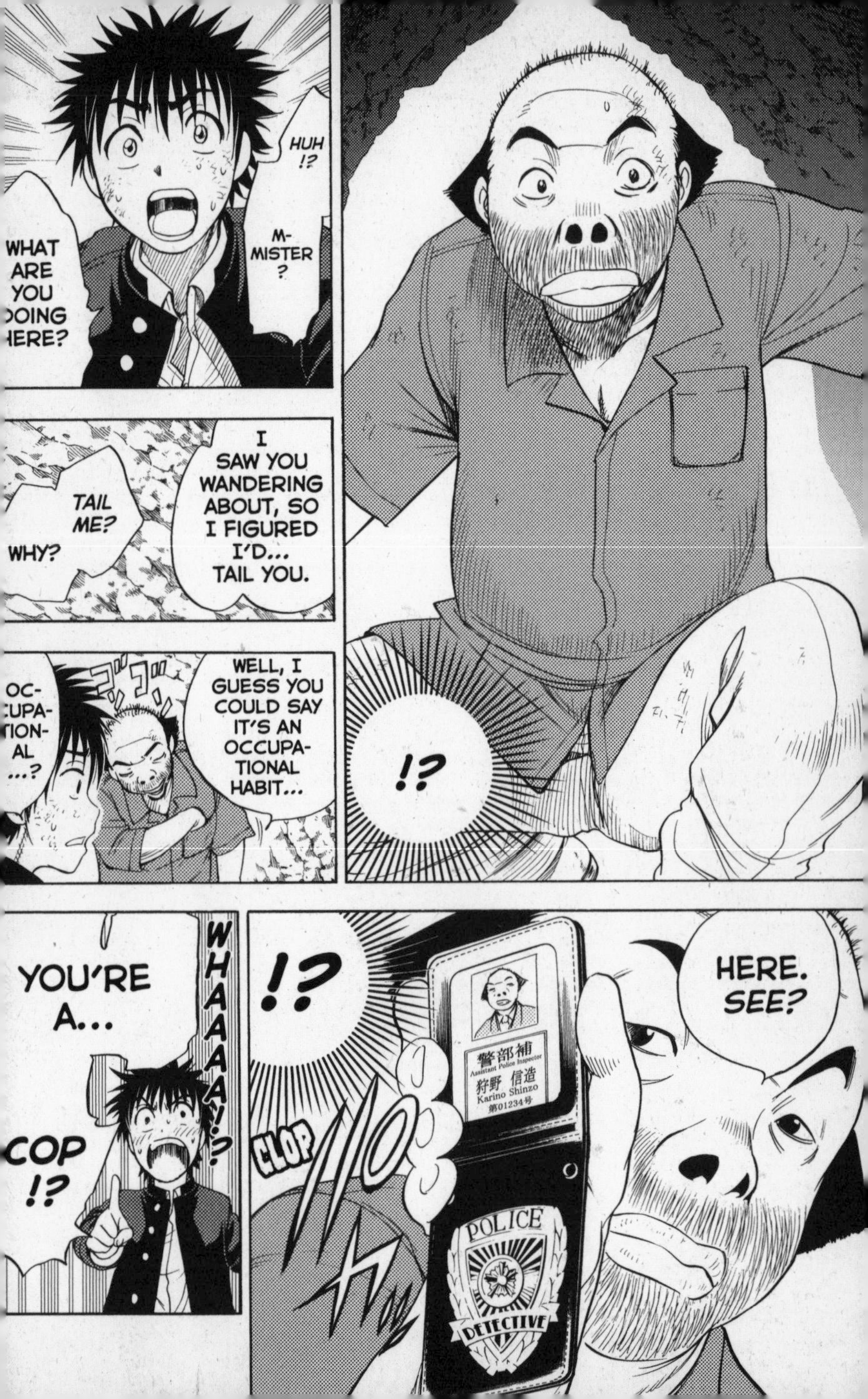
!?
HUH !?
M-MISTER ?
WHAT ARE YOU DOING HERE?
I SAW YOU WANDERING ABOUT, SO I FIGURED I'D... TAIL YOU.
TAIL ME?
WHY?
WELL, I GUESS YOU COULD SAY IT'S AN OCCUPATIONAL HABIT...
OC-CUPA-TION-AL ...?
HERE. SEE?
POLICE
DETECTIVE
警部補
Assistant Police Inspector
狩野 信造
Karino Shinzo
第01234号
CLOP
!?
WHAAAA!?
YOU'RE A...
COP !?

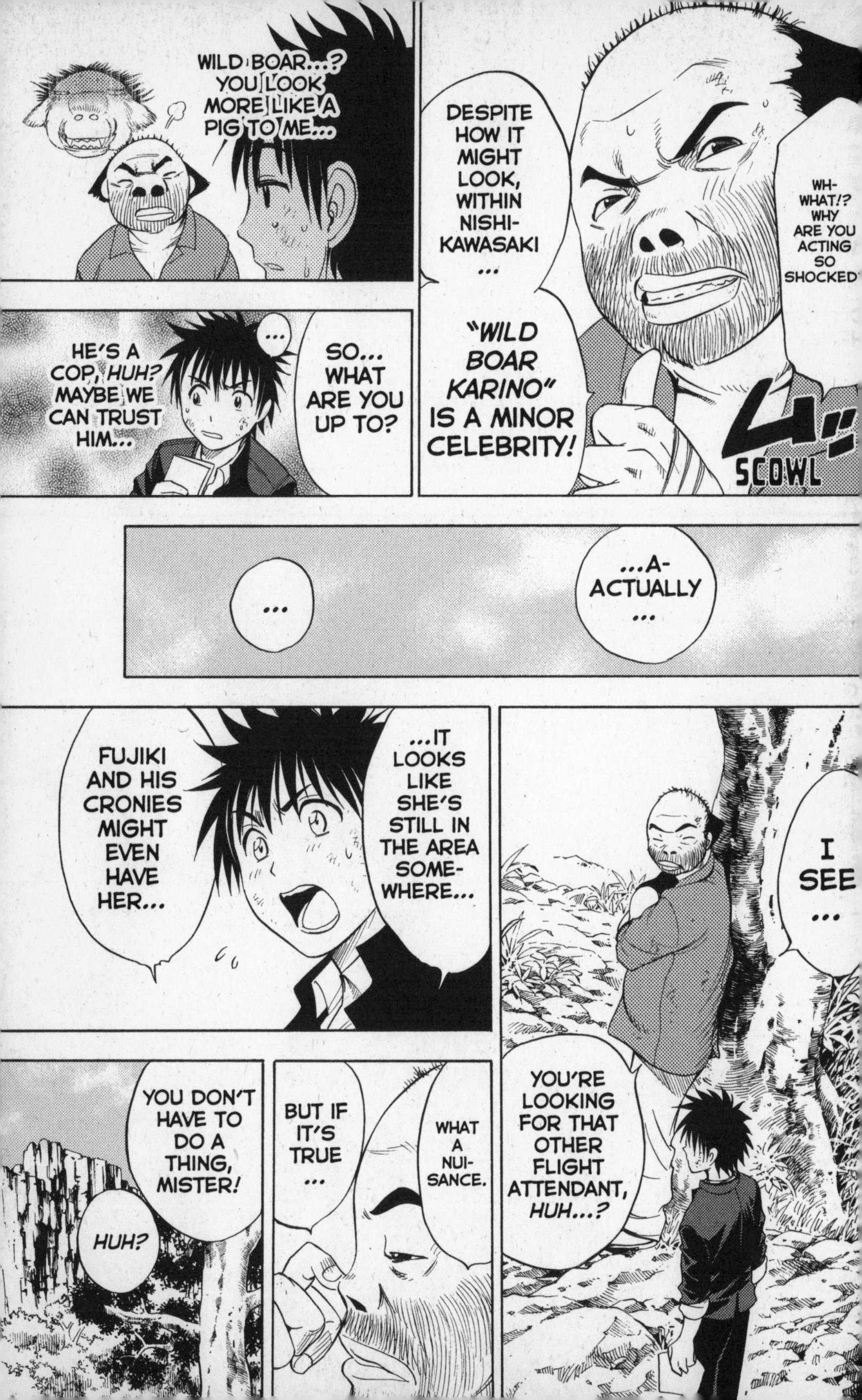
WH-WHAT!? WHY ARE YOU ACTING SO SHOCKED
DESPITE HOW IT MIGHT LOOK, WITHIN NISHI-KAWASAKI ...
"WILD BOAR KARINO" IS A MINOR CELEBRITY!
SCOWL
WILD BOAR...? YOU LOOK MORE LIKE A PIG TO ME...
SO... WHAT ARE YOU UP TO?
...
HE'S A COP, HUH? MAYBE WE CAN TRUST HIM...
...A-ACTUALLY ...
...
I SEE ...
YOU'RE LOOKING FOR THAT OTHER FLIGHT ATTENDANT, HUH...?
...IT LOOKS LIKE SHE'S STILL IN THE AREA SOME-WHERE...
FUJIKI AND HIS CRONIES MIGHT EVEN HAVE HER...
WHAT A NUI-SANCE.
BUT IF IT'S TRUE ...
YOU DON'T HAVE TO DO A THING, MISTER!
HUH?

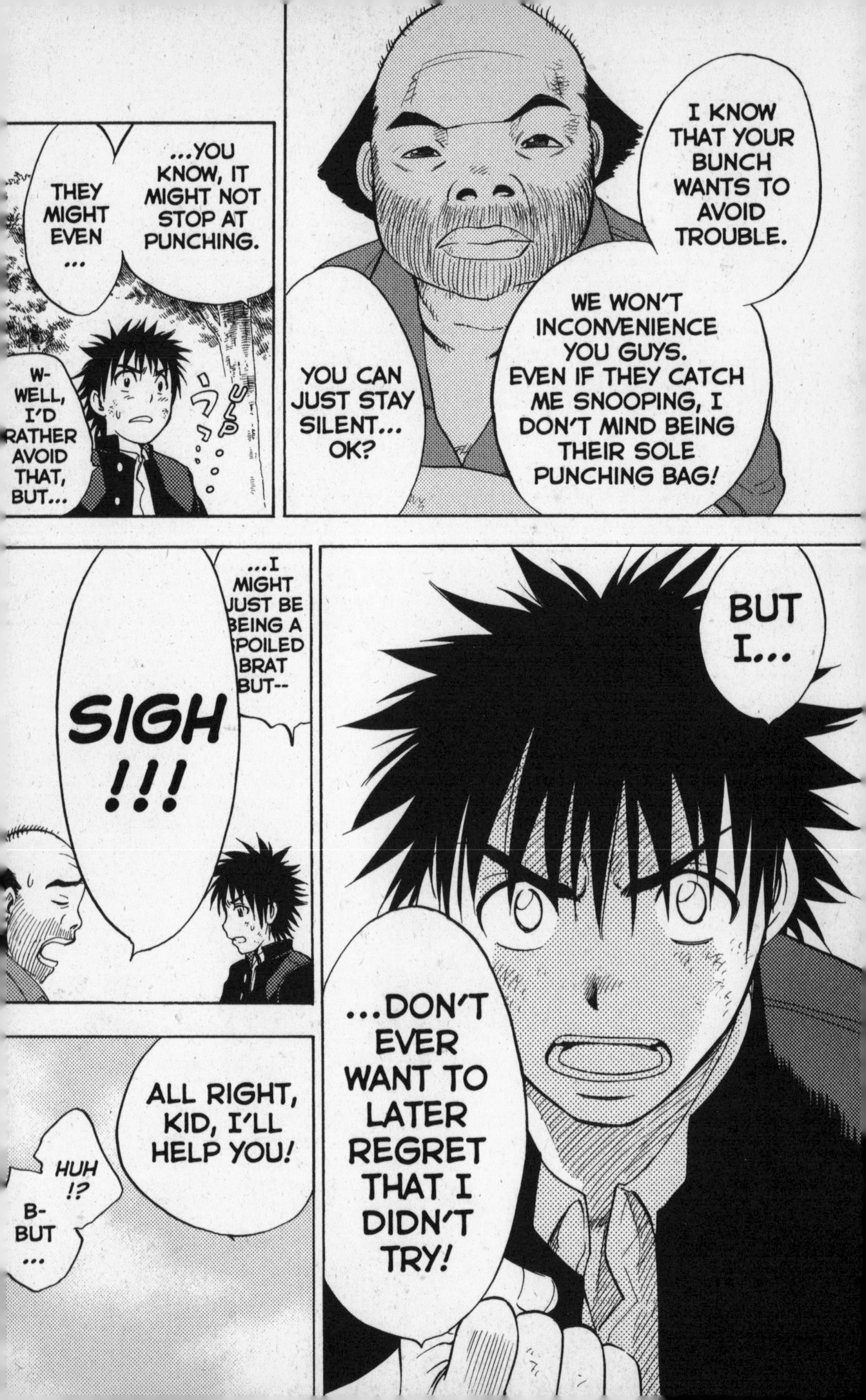
I KNOW THAT YOUR BUNCH WANTS TO AVOID TROUBLE.
WE WON'T INCONVENIENCE YOU GUYS. EVEN IF THEY CATCH ME SNOOPING, I DON'T MIND BEING THEIR SOLE PUNCHING BAG!
YOU CAN JUST STAY SILENT... OK?
...YOU KNOW, IT MIGHT NOT STOP AT PUNCHING.
THEY MIGHT EVEN ...
ULP
W-WELL, I'D RATHER AVOID THAT, BUT...
BUT I...
...DON'T EVER WANT TO LATER REGRET THAT I DIDN'T TRY!
...I MIGHT JUST BE BEING A SPOILED BRAT BUT--
SIGH!!!
ALL RIGHT, KID, I'LL HELP YOU!
HUH!?
B-BUT ...

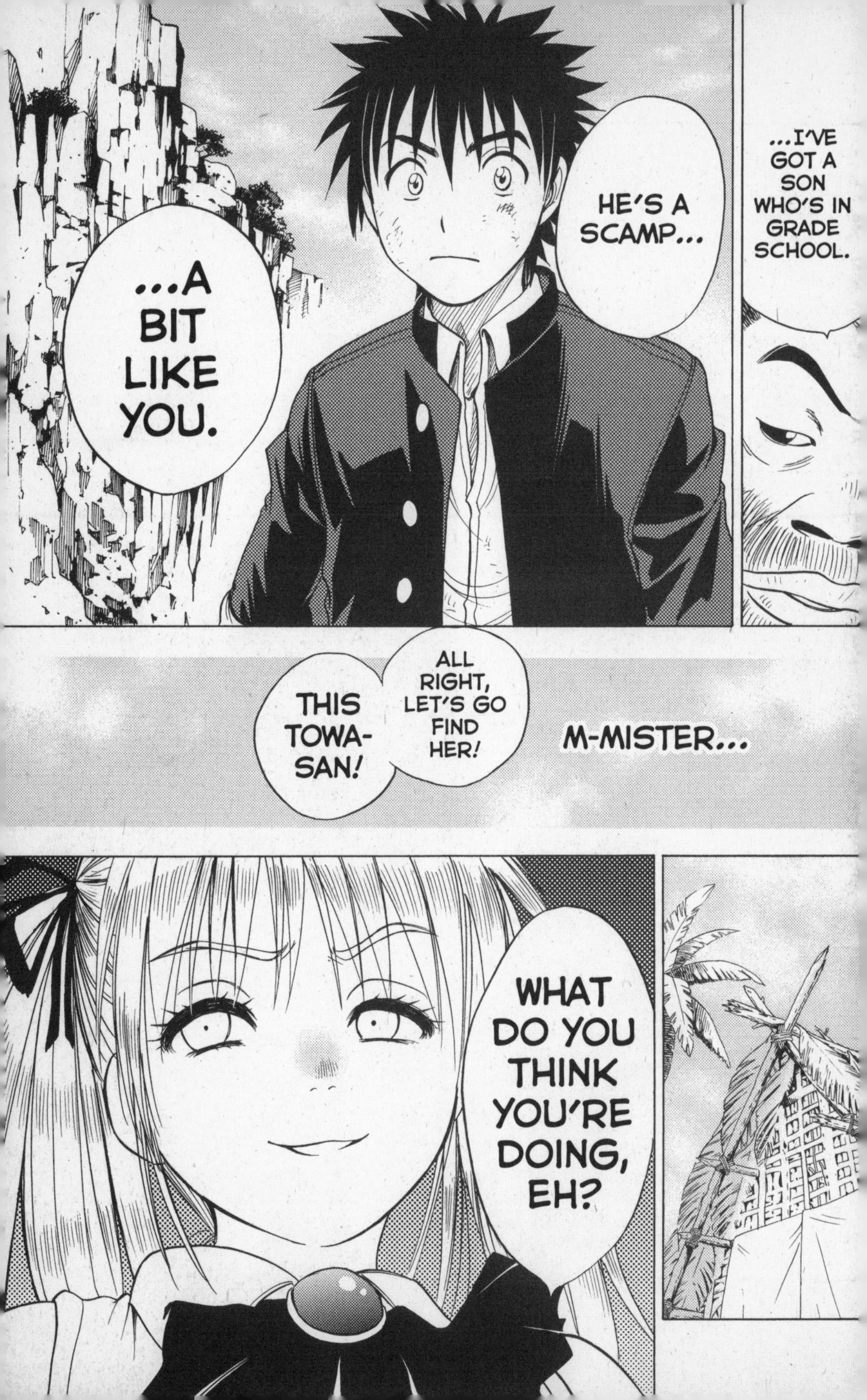
...I'VE GOT A SON WHO'S IN GRADE SCHOOL.
HE'S A SCAMP...
...A BIT LIKE YOU.
M-MISTER...
ALL RIGHT, LET'S GO FIND HER!
THIS TOWA-SAN!
WHAT DO YOU THINK YOU'RE DOING, EH?

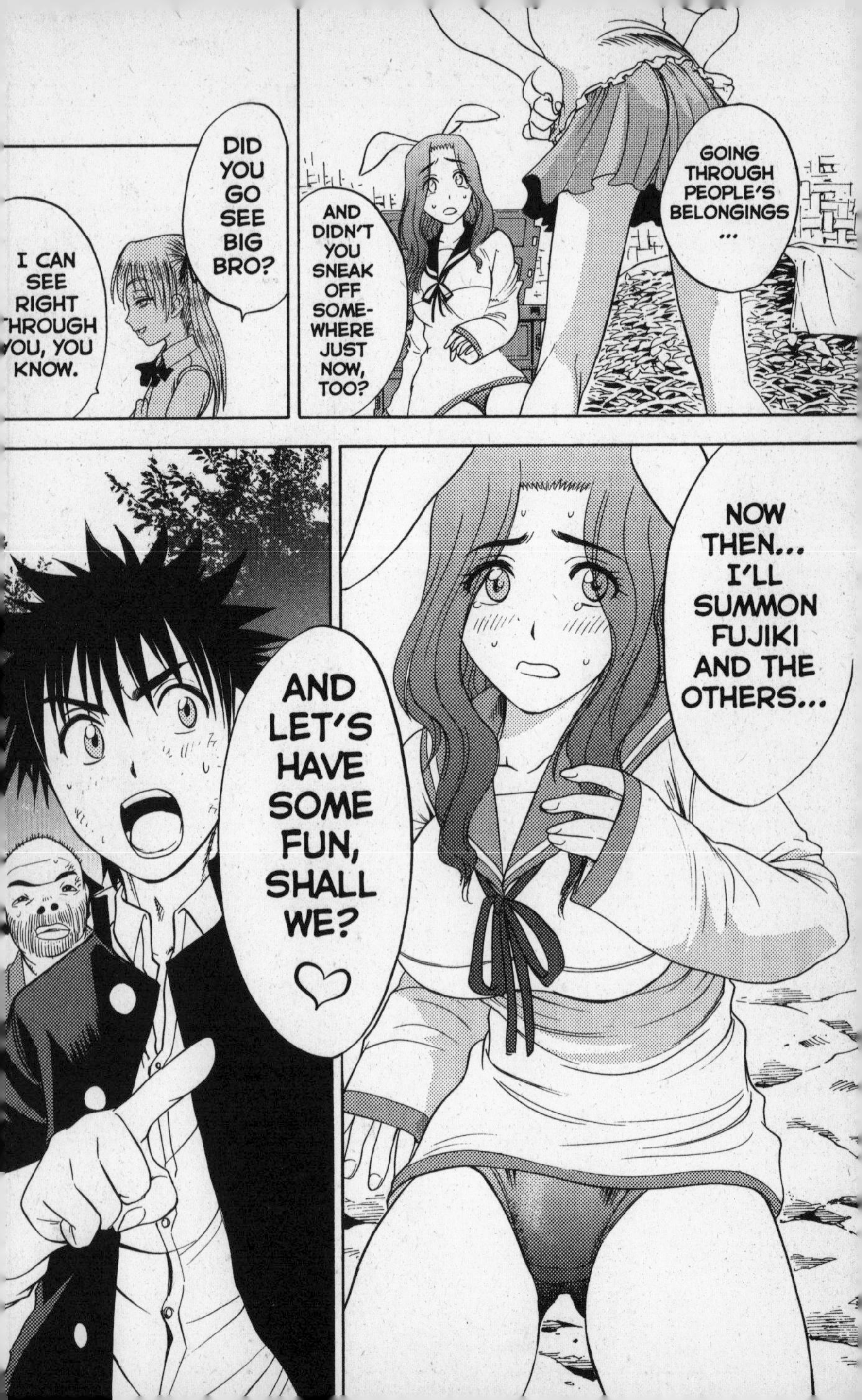
GOING THROUGH PEOPLE'S BELONGINGS...
AND DIDN'T YOU SNEAK OFF SOME-WHERE JUST NOW, TOO?
DID YOU GO SEE BIG BRO?
I CAN SEE RIGHT THROUGH YOU, YOU KNOW.
NOW THEN... I'LL SUMMON FUJIKI AND THE OTHERS...
AND LET'S HAVE SOME FUN, SHALL WE? ♡

Episode 24 Uprising

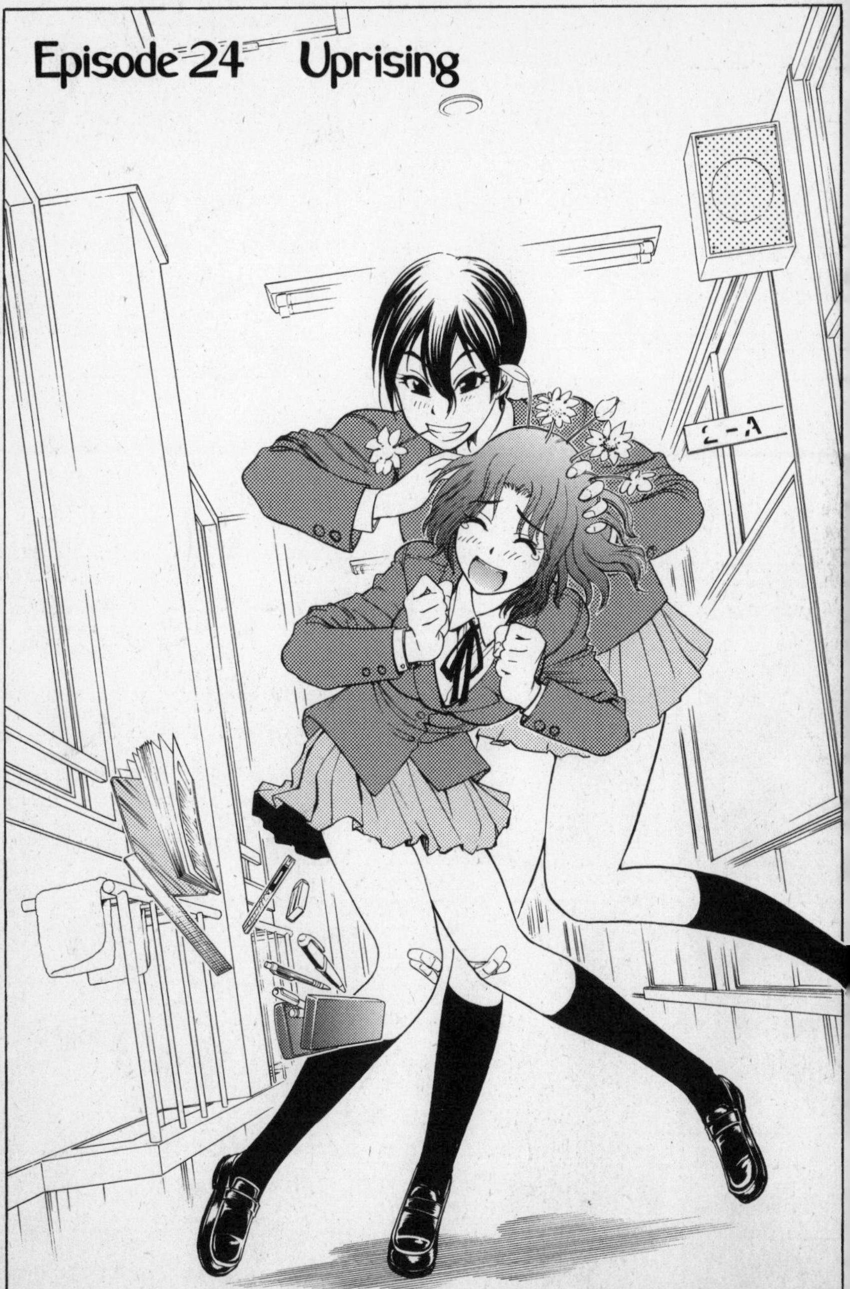
2-A

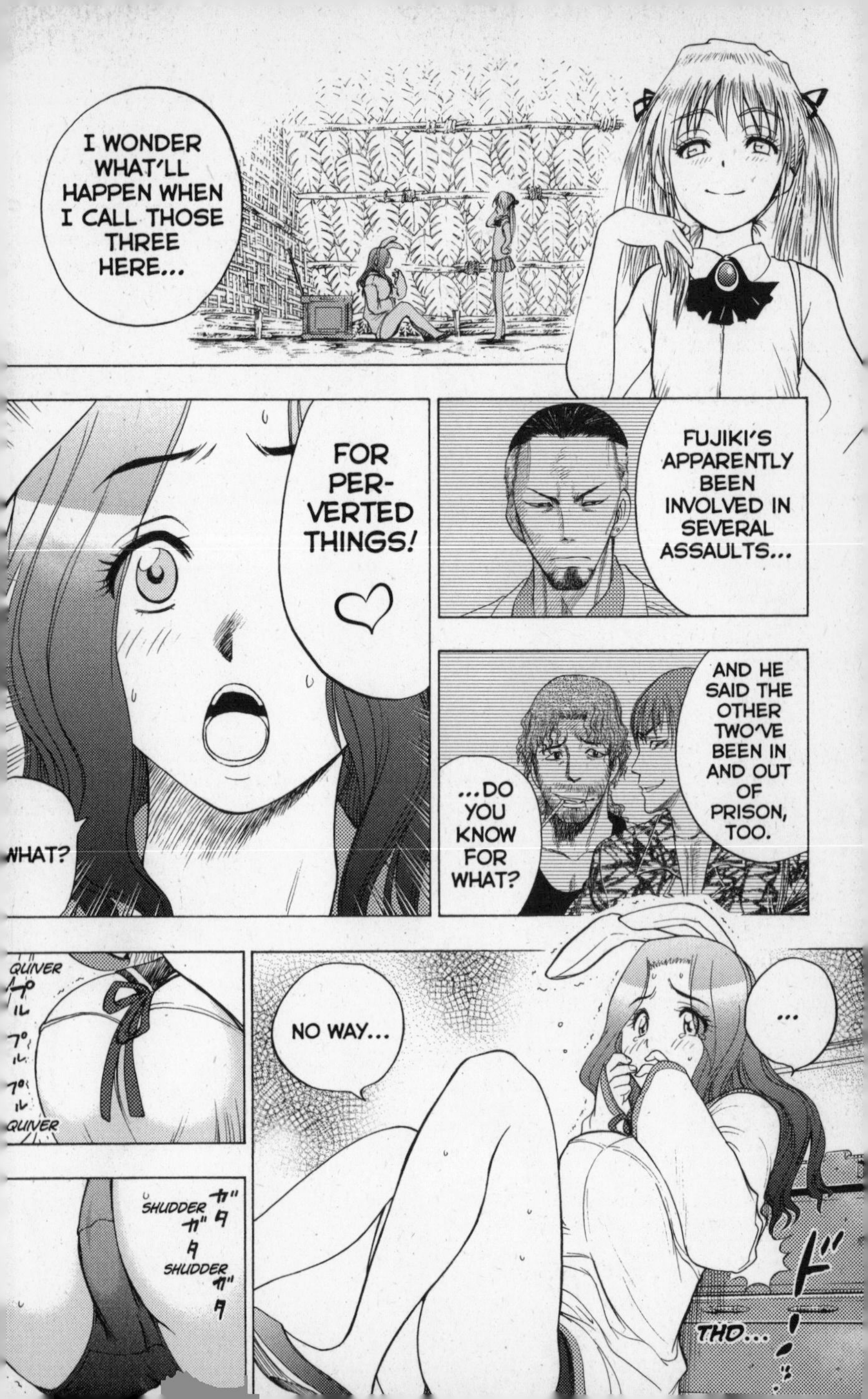
I WONDER WHAT'LL HAPPEN WHEN I CALL THOSE THREE HERE...
FUJIKI'S APPARENTLY BEEN INVOLVED IN SEVERAL ASSAULTS...
AND HE SAID THE OTHER TWO'VE BEEN IN AND OUT OF PRISON, TOO.
...DO YOU KNOW FOR WHAT?
FOR PER-VERTED THINGS! ♡
WHAT?
...
NO WAY...
ドッ
THUD...
QUIVER
プルプルプル
QUIVER
SHUDDER
ガタガタ
SHUDDER
ガタ

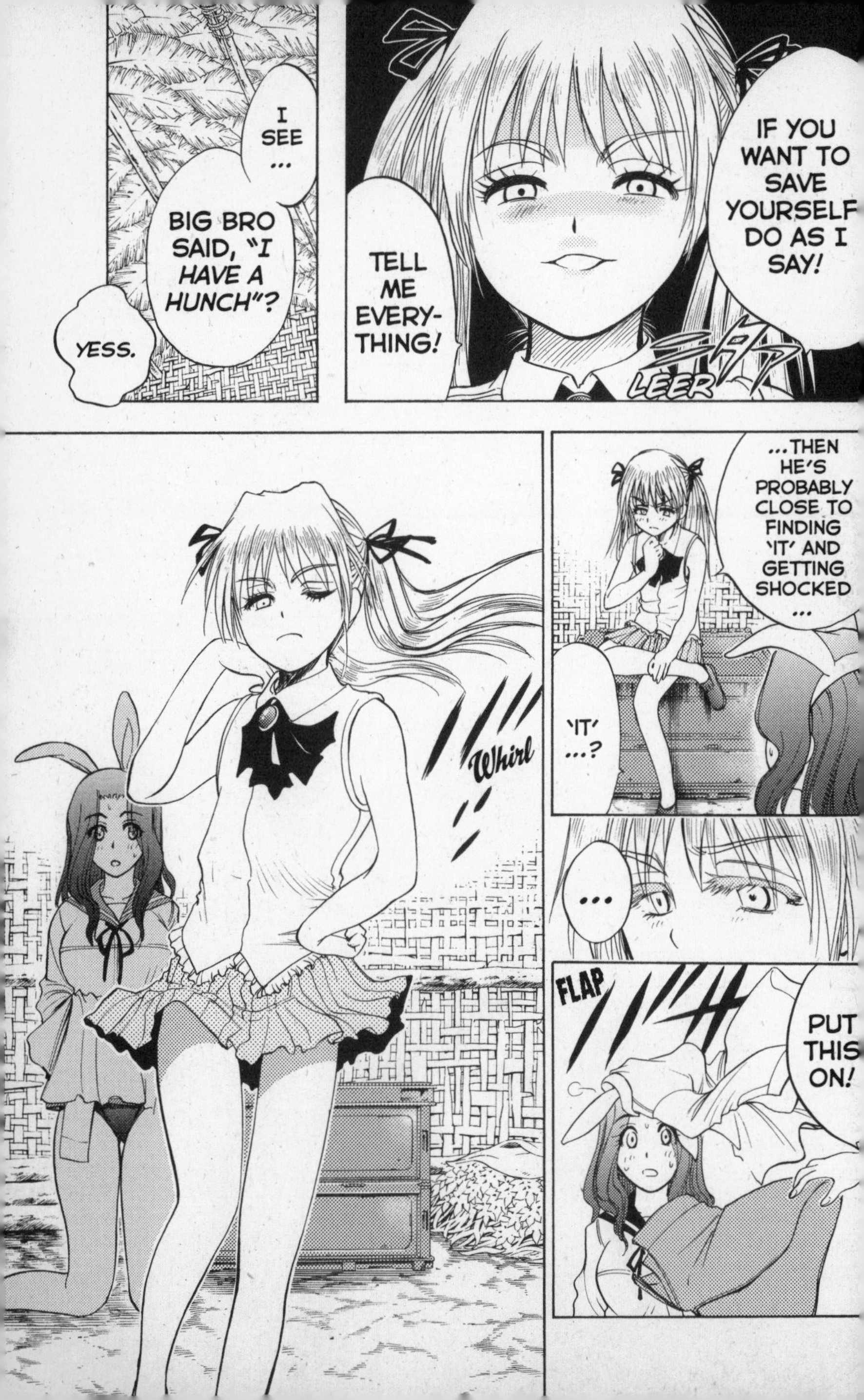
IF YOU WANT TO SAVE YOURSELF DO AS I SAY!
TELL ME EVERY-THING!
LEER
I SEE ...
BIG BRO SAID, "I HAVE A HUNCH"?
YESS.
...THEN HE'S PROBABLY CLOSE TO FINDING 'IT' AND GETTING SHOCKED ...
'IT' ...?
...
FLAP
PUT THIS ON!
Whirl

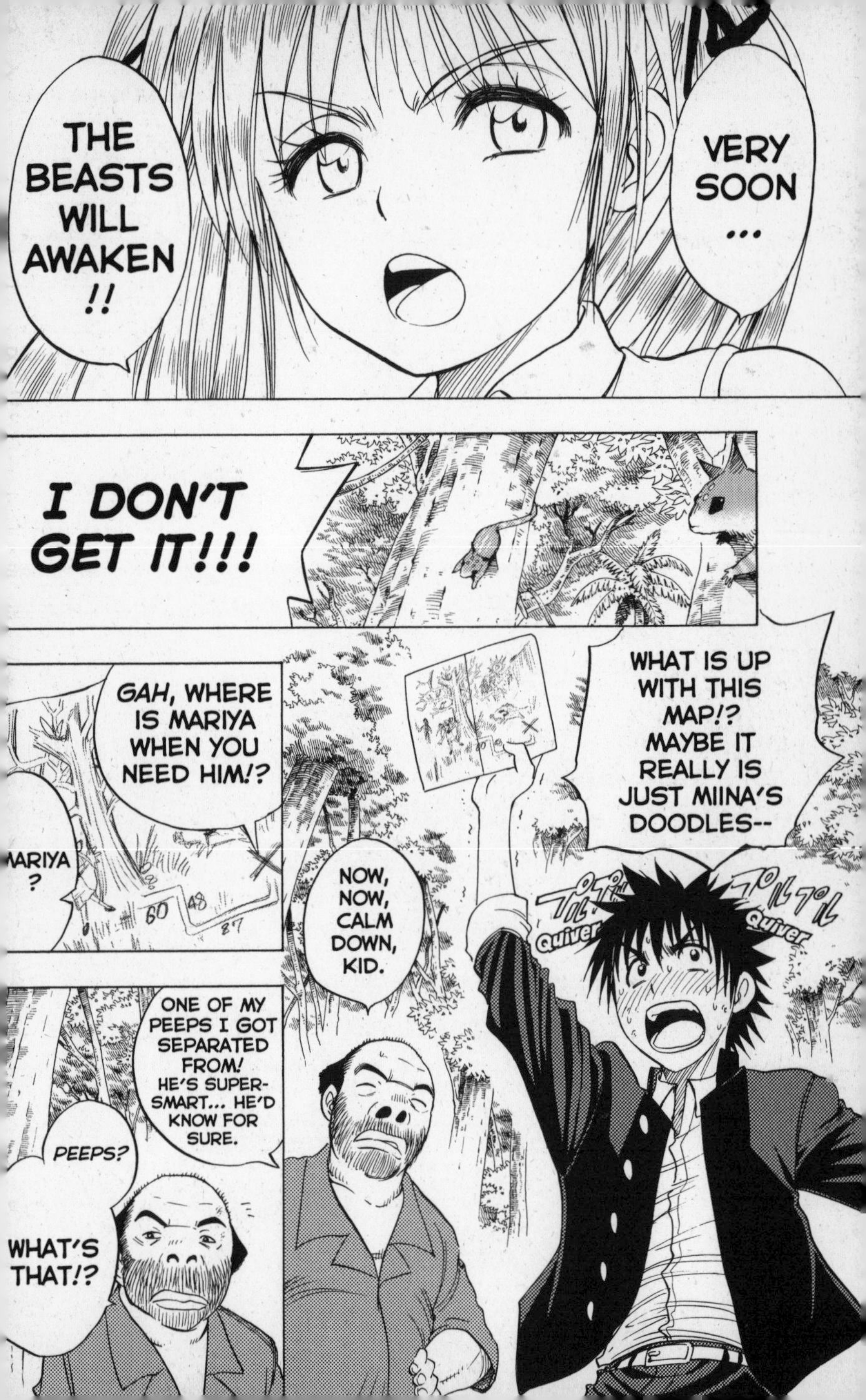
VERY SOON ...
THE BEASTS WILL AWAKEN!!
I DON'T GET IT!!!
WHAT IS UP WITH THIS MAP!? MAYBE IT REALLY IS JUST MIINA'S DOODLES--
Quiver
Quiver
NOW, NOW, CALM DOWN, KID.
GAH, WHERE IS MARIYA WHEN YOU NEED HIM!?
MARIYA?
ONE OF MY PEEPS I GOT SEPARATED FROM! HE'S SUPER-SMART... HE'D KNOW FOR SURE.
PEEPS?
WHAT'S THAT!?

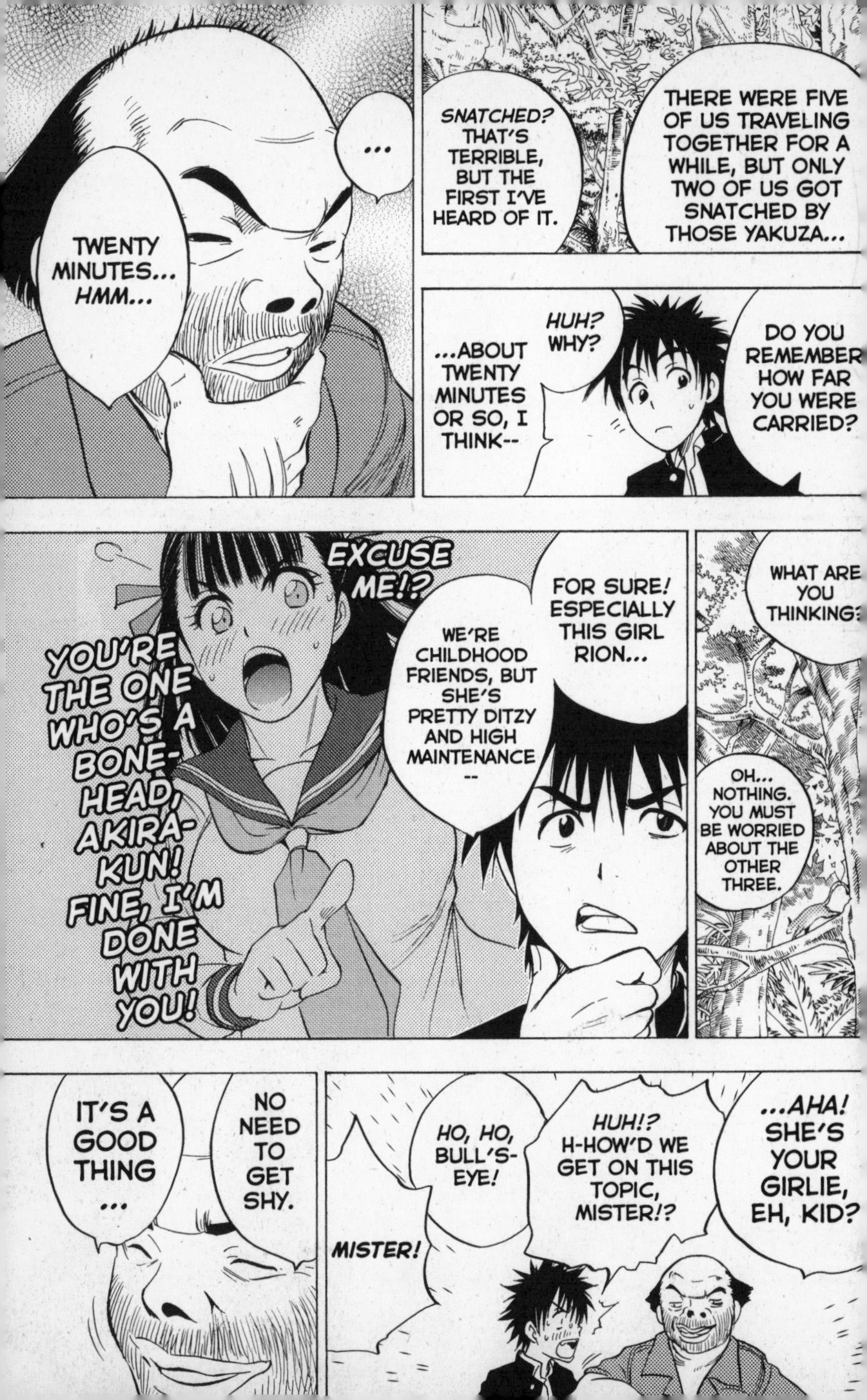
THERE WERE FIVE OF US TRAVELING TOGETHER FOR A WHILE, BUT ONLY TWO OF US GOT SNATCHED BY THOSE YAKUZA...
SNATCHED? THAT'S TERRIBLE, BUT THE FIRST I'VE HEARD OF IT.
DO YOU REMEMBER HOW FAR YOU WERE CARRIED?
HUH? WHY?
...ABOUT TWENTY MINUTES OR SO, I THINK--
...
TWENTY MINUTES... *HMM...*
WHAT ARE YOU THINKING?
OH... NOTHING. YOU MUST BE WORRIED ABOUT THE OTHER THREE.
FOR SURE! ESPECIALLY THIS GIRL RION...
WE'RE CHILDHOOD FRIENDS, BUT SHE'S PRETTY DITZY AND HIGH MAINTENANCE --
EXCUSE ME!?
YOU'RE THE ONE WHO'S A BONE-HEAD, AKIRA-KUN! FINE, I'M DONE WITH YOU!
...AHA! SHE'S YOUR GIRLIE, EH, KID?
HUH!? H-HOW'D WE GET ON THIS TOPIC, MISTER!?
HO, HO, BULL'S-EYE!
MISTER!
NO NEED TO GET SHY.
IT'S A GOOD THING ...

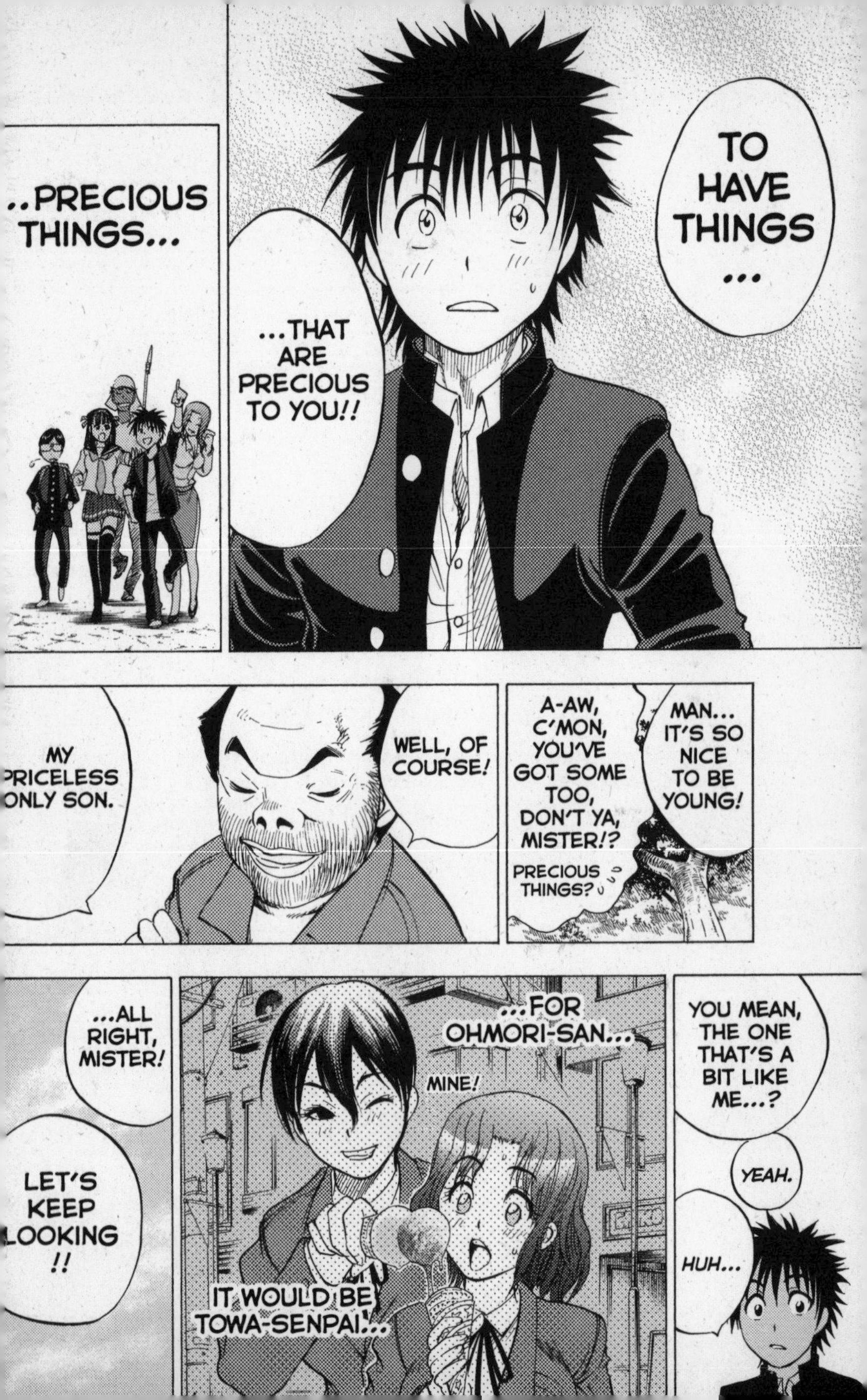
TO HAVE THINGS ...
...THAT ARE PRECIOUS TO YOU!!
..PRECIOUS THINGS...
MAN... IT'S SO NICE TO BE YOUNG!
A-AW, C'MON, YOU'VE GOT SOME TOO, DON'T YA, MISTER!?
PRECIOUS THINGS?
WELL, OF COURSE!
MY PRICELESS ONLY SON.
YOU MEAN, THE ONE THAT'S A BIT LIKE ME...?
YEAH.
HUH...
...FOR OHMORI-SAN...
MINE!
IT WOULD BE TOWA-SENPAI...
...ALL RIGHT, MISTER!
LET'S KEEP LOOKING!!

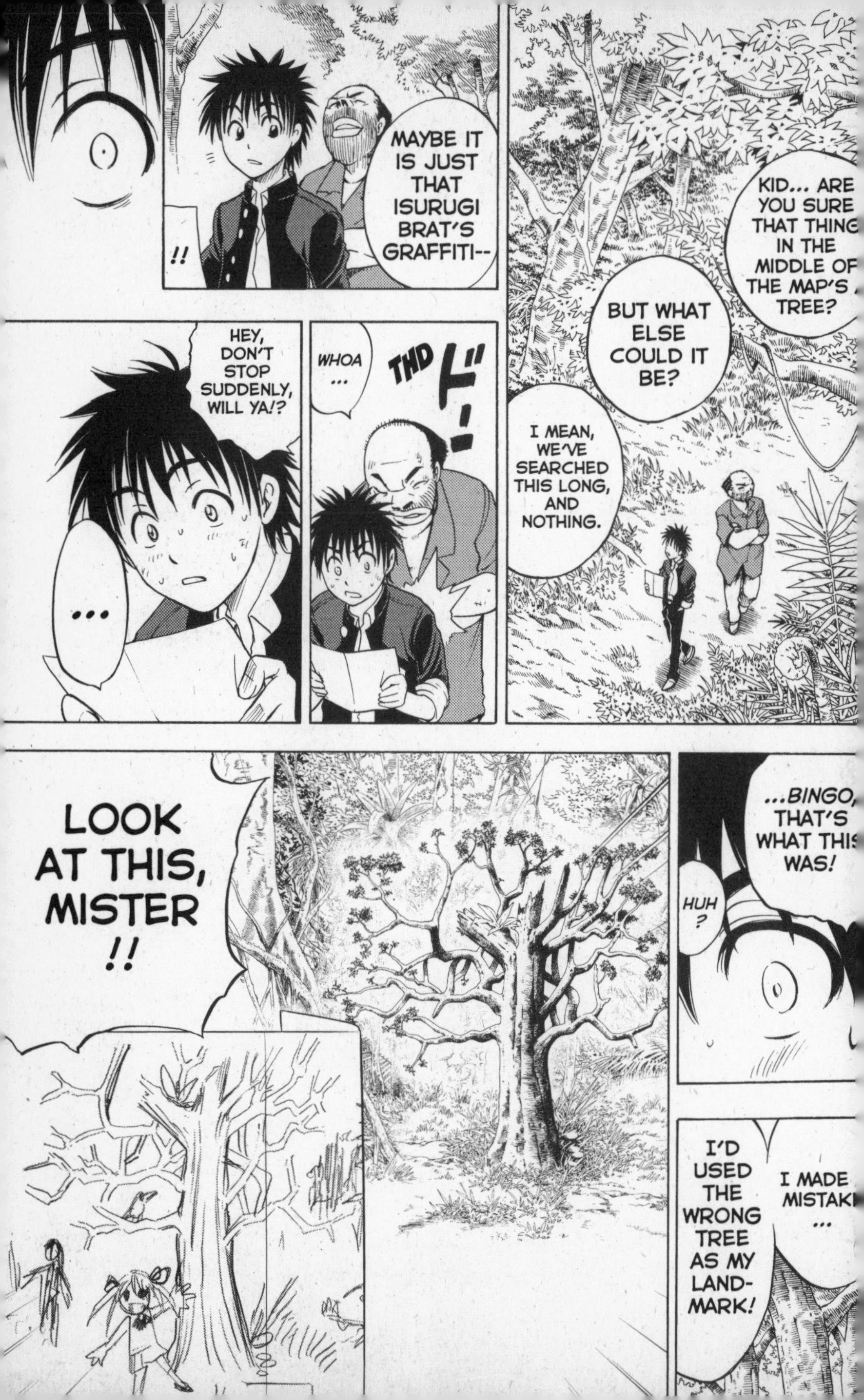

KID... ARE YOU SURE THAT THING IN THE MIDDLE OF THE MAP'S TREE?
BUT WHAT ELSE COULD IT BE?
I MEAN, WE'VE SEARCHED THIS LONG, AND NOTHING.
MAYBE IT IS JUST THAT ISURUGI BRAT'S GRAFFITI--
!!
WHOA ...
THD
HEY, DON'T STOP SUDDENLY, WILL YA!?
...
...BINGO, THAT'S WHAT THIS WAS!
HUH ?
I MADE MISTAK ...
I'D USED THE WRONG TREE AS MY LAND-MARK!
LOOK AT THIS, MISTER !!

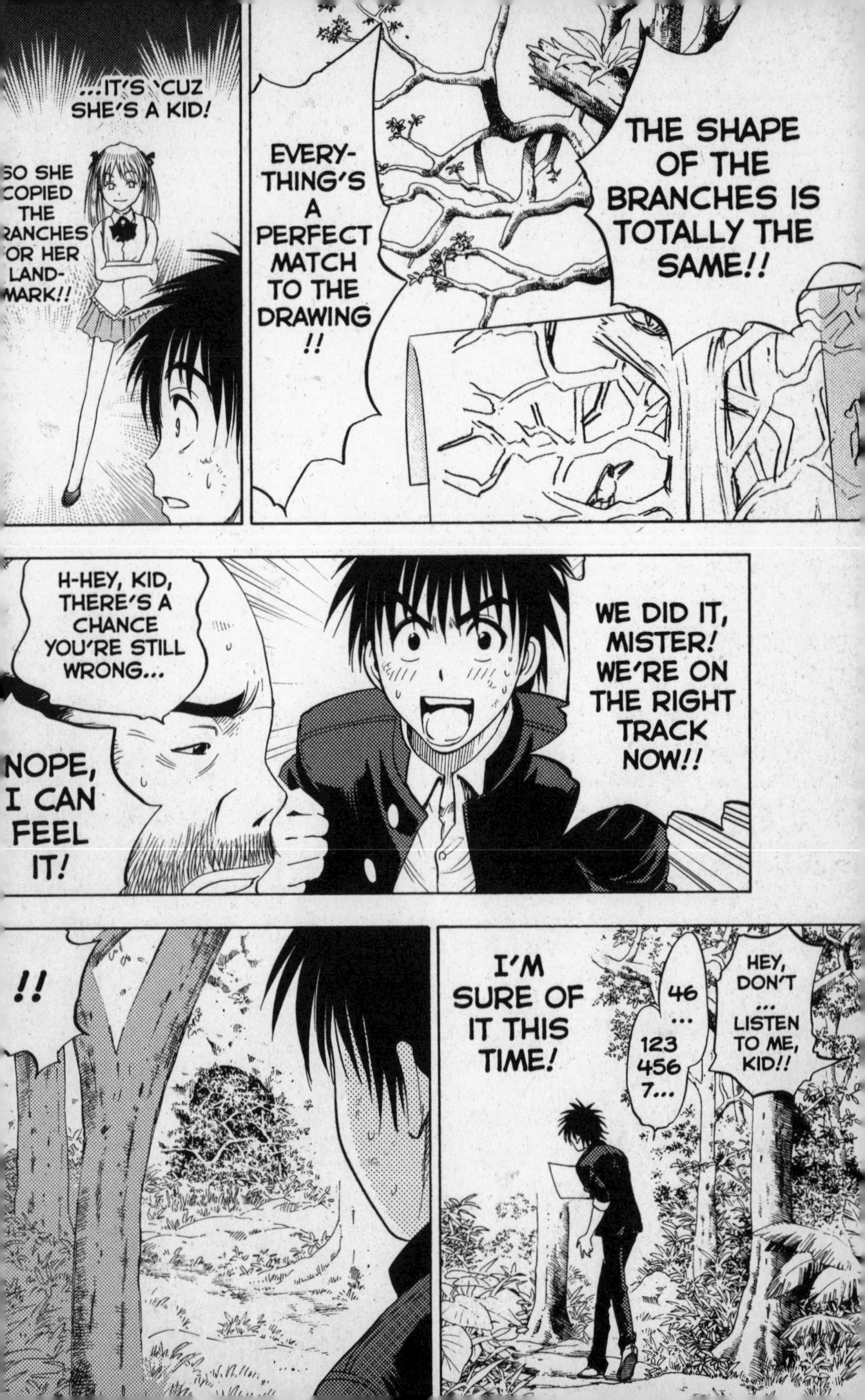
THE SHAPE OF THE BRANCHES IS TOTALLY THE SAME!!
EVERY-THING'S A PERFECT MATCH TO THE DRAWING!!
...IT'S 'CUZ SHE'S A KID!
SO SHE COPIED THE RANCHES OR HER LAND-MARK!!
WE DID IT, MISTER! WE'RE ON THE RIGHT TRACK NOW!!
H-HEY, KID, THERE'S A CHANCE YOU'RE STILL WRONG...
NOPE, I CAN FEEL IT!
HEY, DON'T ... LISTEN TO ME, KID!!
46 ... 123 456 7...
I'M SURE OF IT THIS TIME!
!!

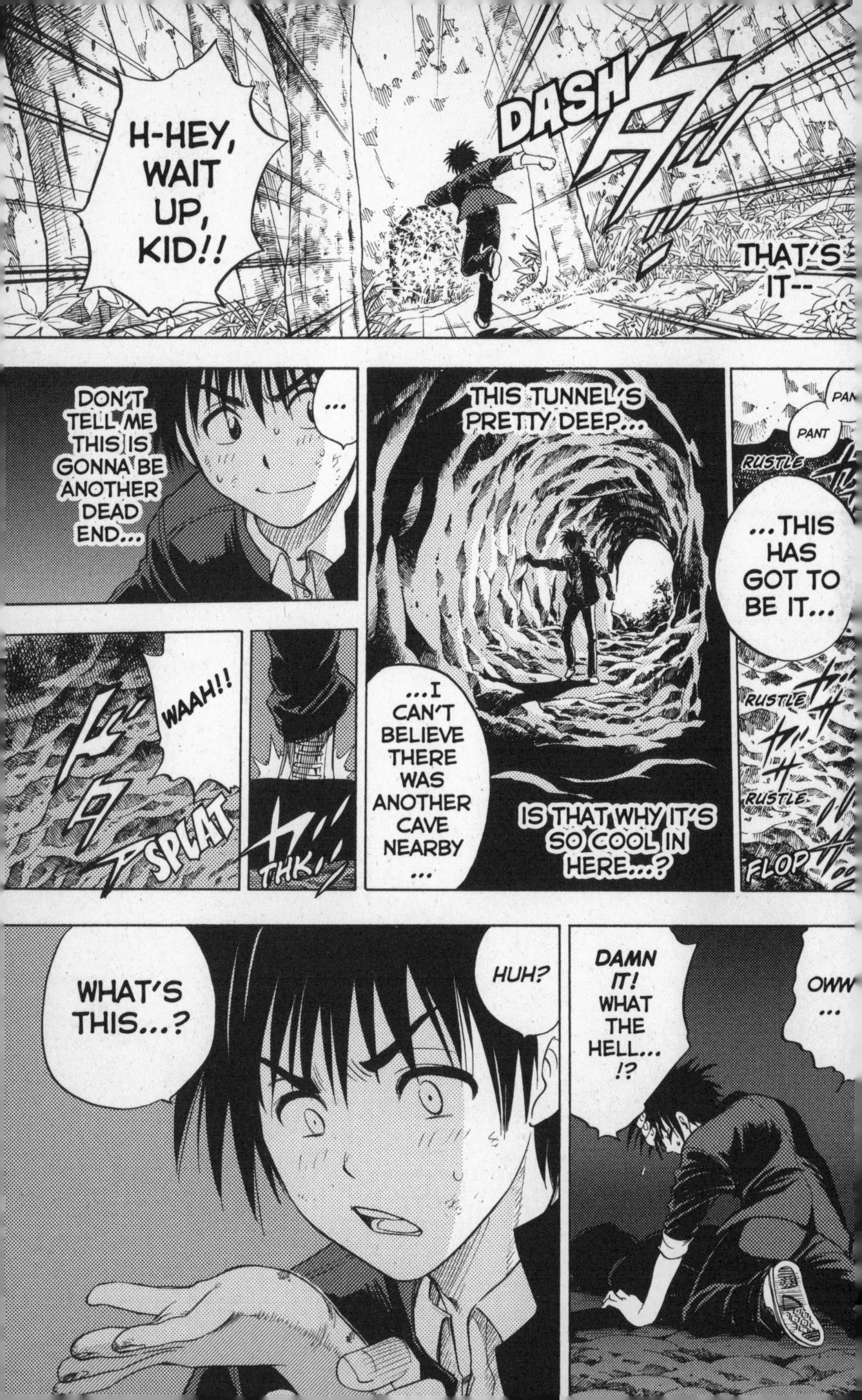
DASH
THAT'S IT--
H-HEY, WAIT UP, KID!!
PANT PANT
RUSTLE
...THIS HAS GOT TO BE IT...
RUSTLE
RUSTLE
FLOP
THIS TUNNEL'S PRETTY DEEP...
...I CAN'T BELIEVE THERE WAS ANOTHER CAVE NEARBY...
IS THAT WHY IT'S SO COOL IN HERE...?
...
DON'T TELL ME THIS IS GONNA BE ANOTHER DEAD END...
THK
WAAH!!
SPLAT
OWW...
DAMN IT! WHAT THE HELL...!?
HUH?
WHAT'S THIS...?

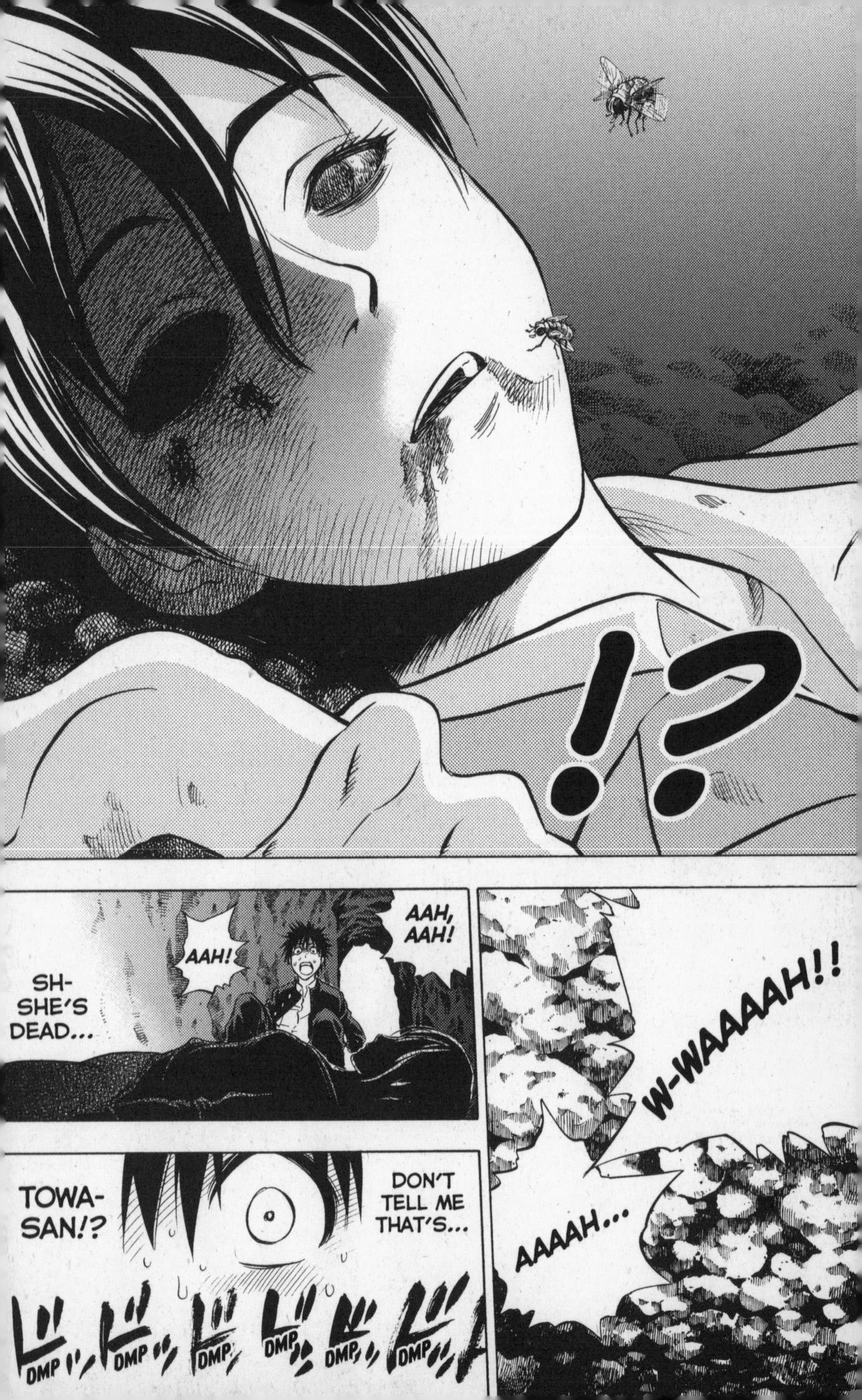
!?
W-WAAAAH!!
AAAAH...
AAH, AAH!
AAH!
SH-SHE'S DEAD...
DON'T TELL ME THAT'S...
TOWA-SAN!?
DMP
DMP
DMP
DMP
DMP
DMP

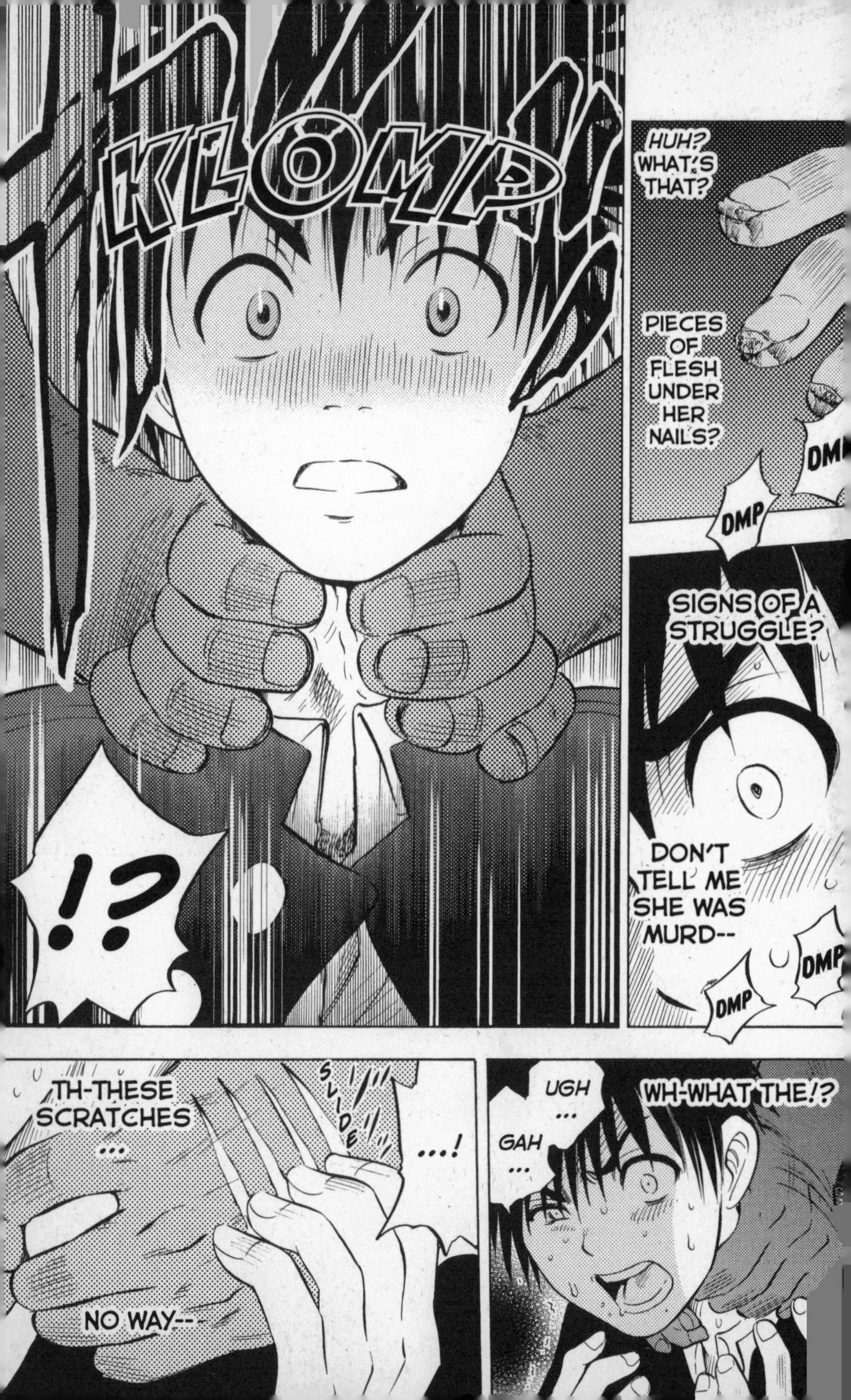
HUH? WHAT'S THAT?
PIECES OF FLESH UNDER HER NAILS?
DMP
DMP
SIGNS OF A STRUGGLE?
DON'T TELL ME SHE WAS MURD--
DMP
DMP
KLOMP
!?
WH-WHAT THE!?
UGH ...
GAH ...
...!
SLIDE
TH-THESE SCRATCHES ...
NO WAY--

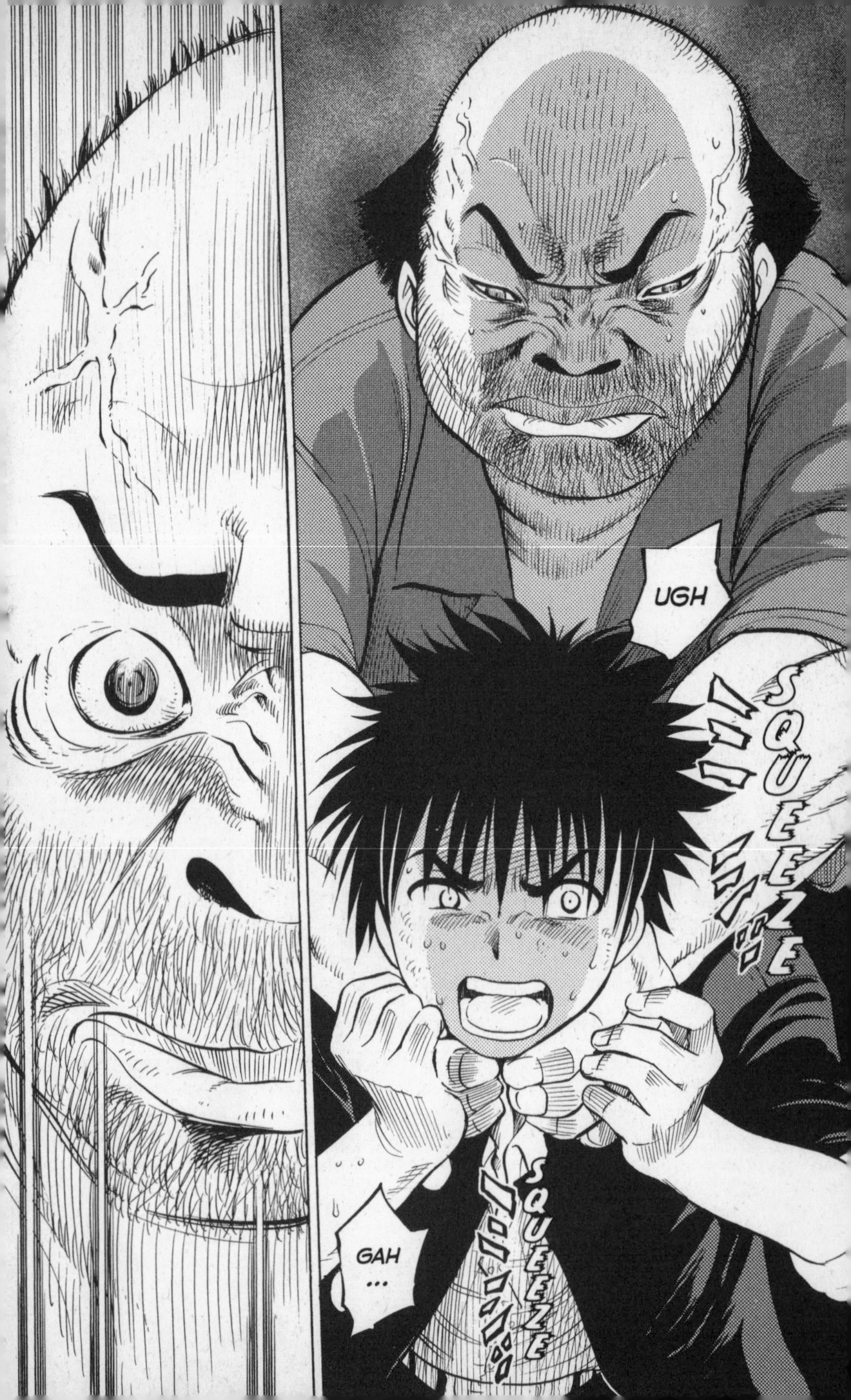
UGH
SQUEEZE
SQUEEZE
GAH ...

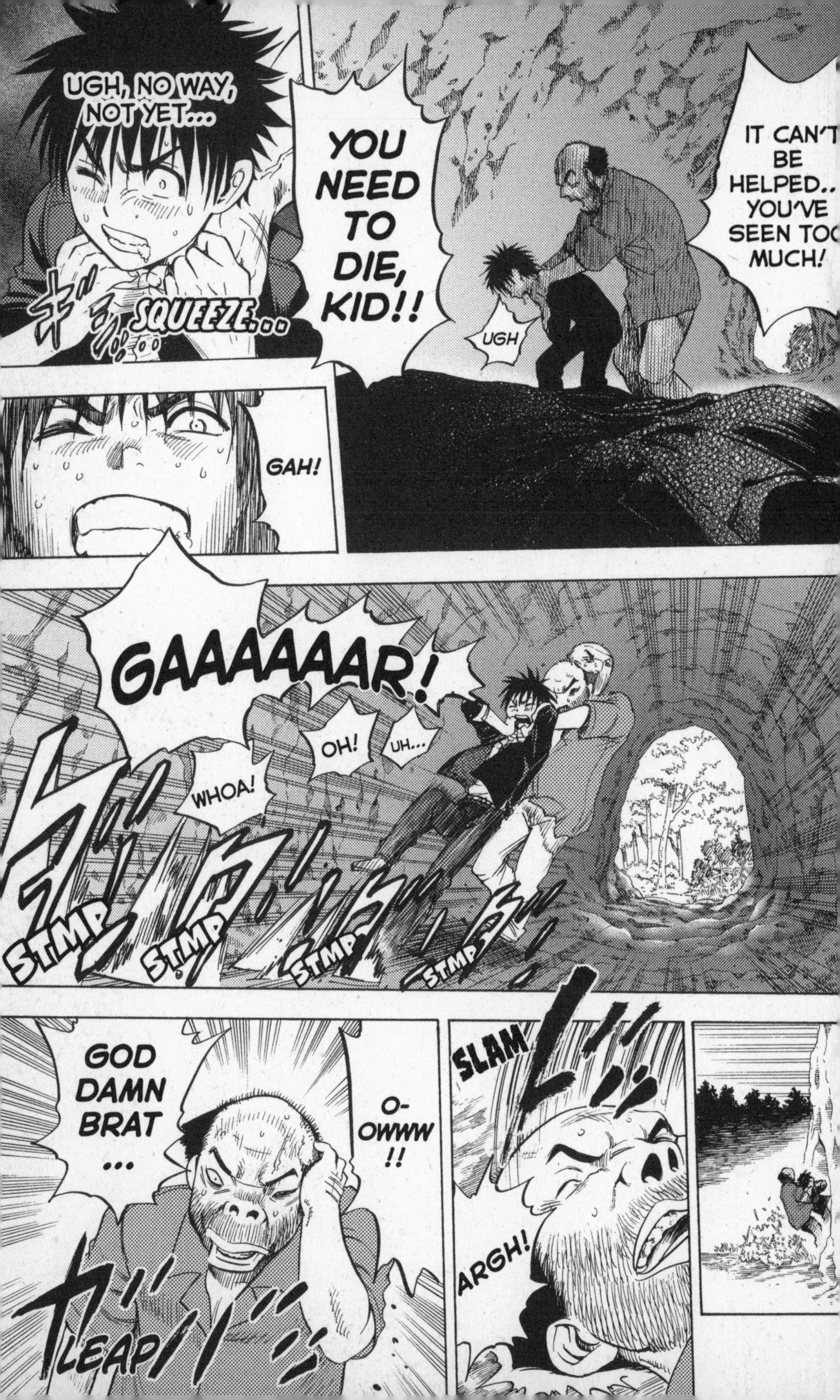
IT CAN'T BE HELPED.. YOU'VE SEEN TOO MUCH!
YOU NEED TO DIE, KID!!
UGH
UGH, NO WAY, NOT YET...
SQUEEZE...
GAH!
GAAAAAAR!
UH...
OH!
WHOA!
STMP
STMP
STMP
STMP
SLAM
ARGH!
O-OWWW!!
GOD DAMN BRAT ...
LEAP!

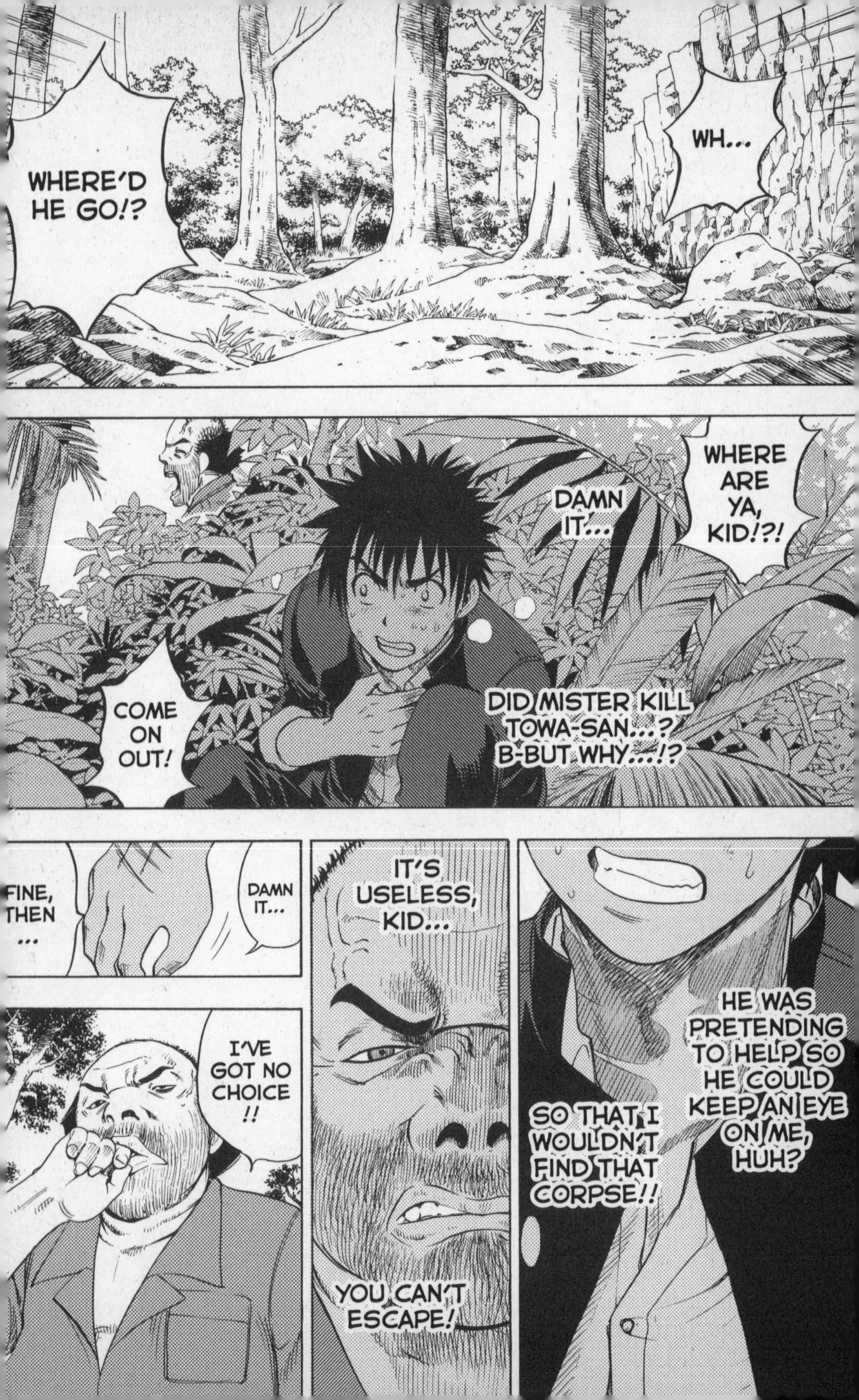
WH...
WHERE'D HE GO!?
WHERE ARE YA, KID!?!
DAMN IT...
DID MISTER KILL TOWA-SAN...? B-BUT WHY...!?
COME ON OUT!
HE WAS PRETENDING TO HELP SO HE COULD KEEP AN EYE ON ME, HUH?
SO THAT I WOULDN'T FIND THAT CORPSE!!
IT'S USELESS, KID...
YOU CAN'T ESCAPE!
DAMN IT...
FINE, THEN ...
I'VE GOT NO CHOICE!!

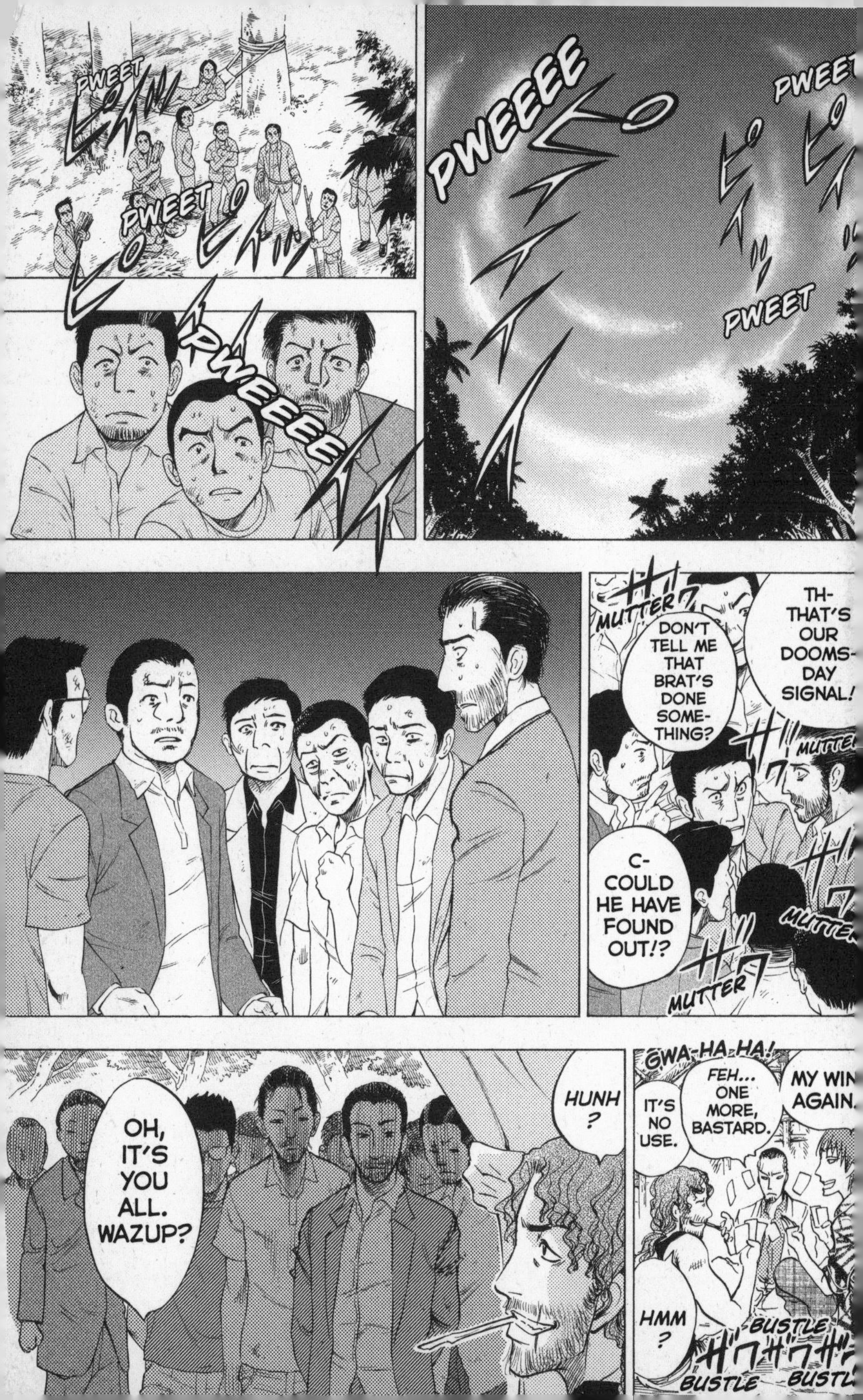

PWEET
PWEEEE
PWEET
PWEET
PWEET
PWEEEE
MUTTER
TH- THAT'S OUR DOOMS-DAY SIGNAL!
DON'T TELL ME THAT BRAT'S DONE SOME-THING?
MUTTER
MUTTER
C- COULD HE HAVE FOUND OUT!?
MUTTER
GWA-HA-HA!
MY WIN AGAIN.
FEH... ONE MORE, BASTARD.
IT'S NO USE.
HMM?
BUSTLE
BUSTLE
BUSTLE
HUNH?
OH, IT'S YOU ALL. WAZUP?

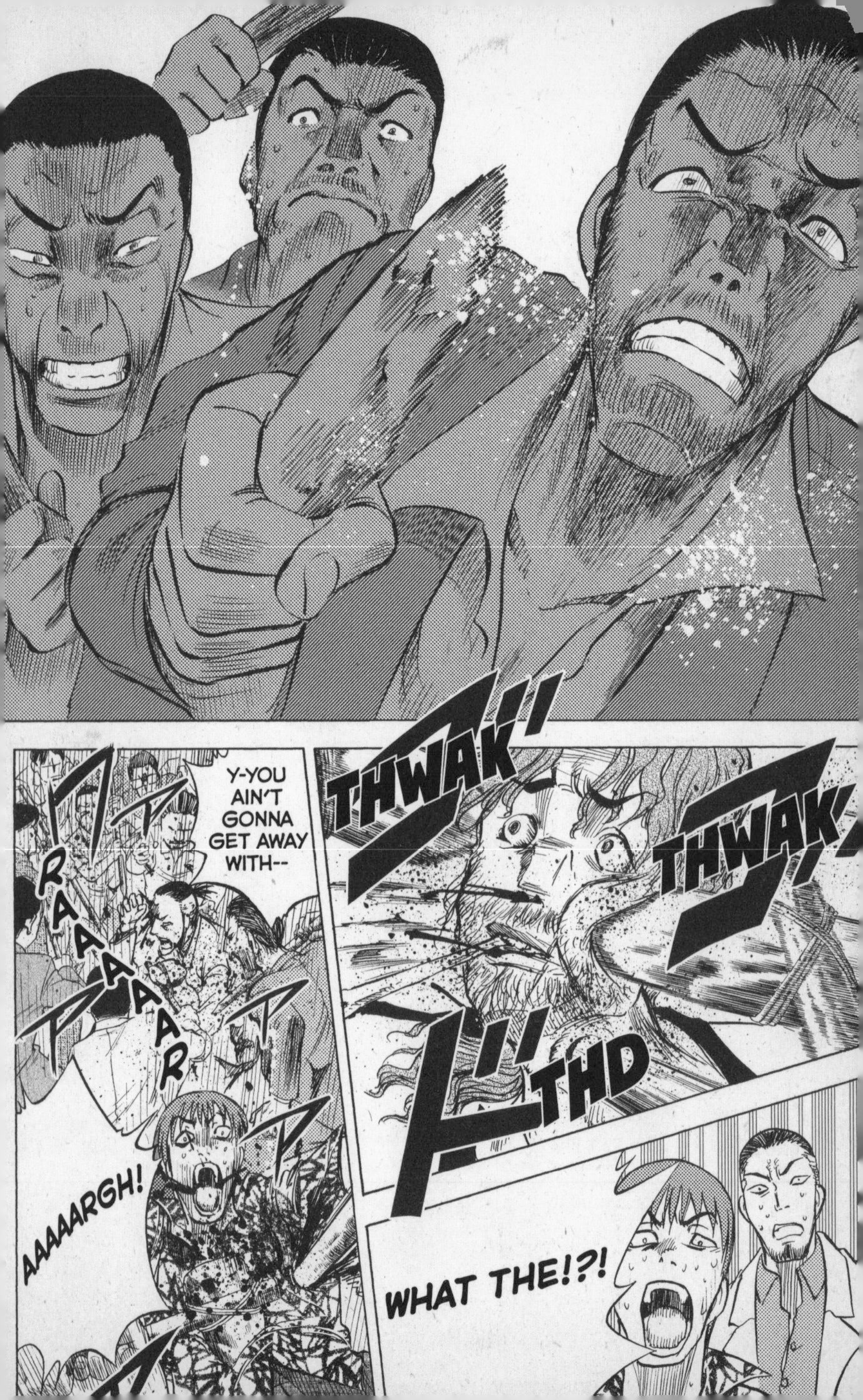
THWAK
THWAK
THD
WHAT THE!?!
Y-YOU AIN'T GONNA GET AWAY WITH--
RAAAAAR
AAAAARGH!

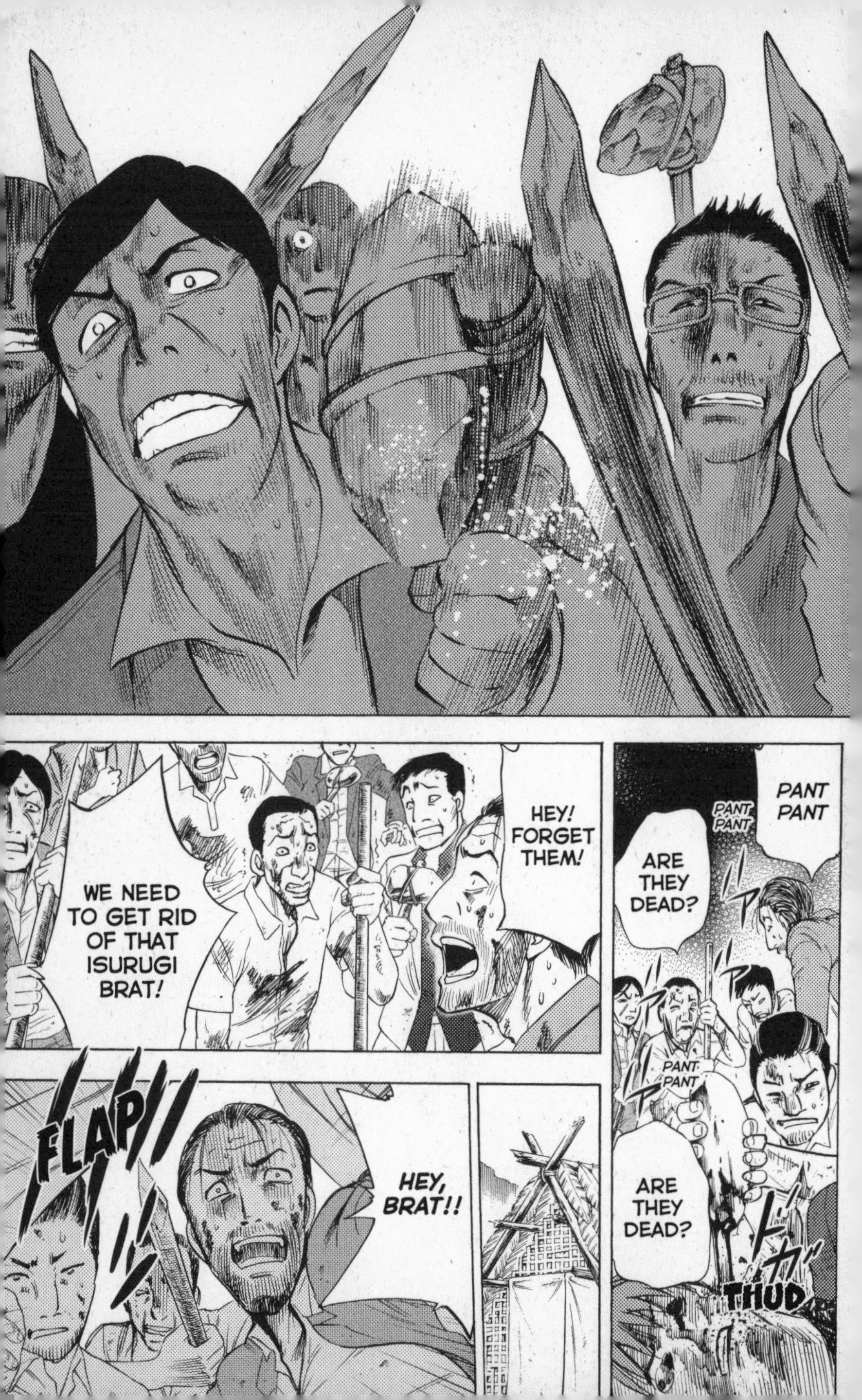
PANT PANT
PANT PANT
ARE THEY DEAD?
PANT PANT
ARE THEY DEAD?
THUD
HEY! FORGET THEM!
WE NEED TO GET RID OF THAT ISURUGI BRAT!
HEY, BRAT!!
FLAP

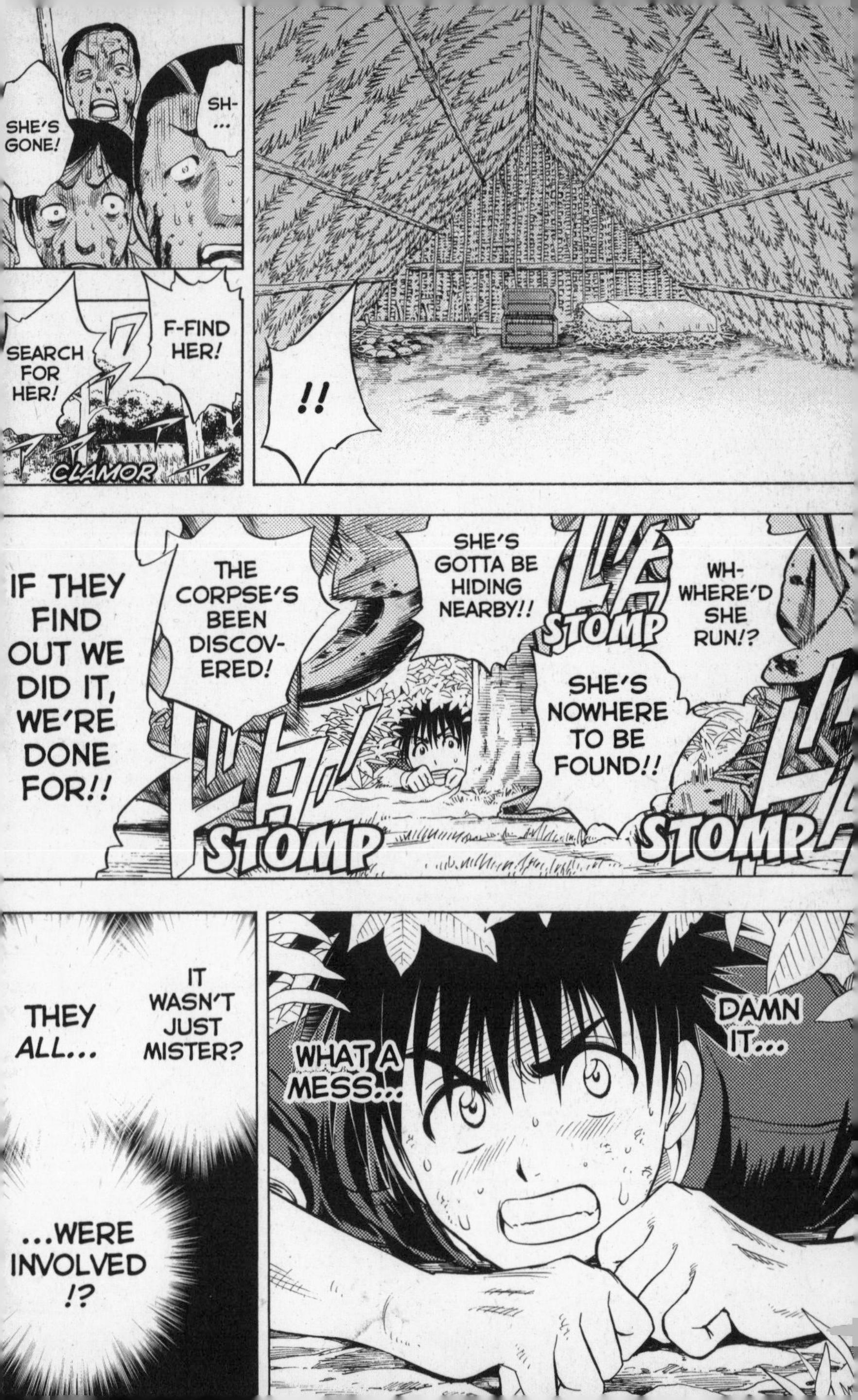
!!
SH-...
SHE'S GONE!
F-FIND HER!
SEARCH FOR HER!
CLAMOR
WH-WHERE'D SHE RUN!?
STOMP
SHE'S GOTTA BE HIDING NEARBY!!
SHE'S NOWHERE TO BE FOUND!!
STOMP
THE CORPSE'S BEEN DISCOVERED!
IF THEY FIND OUT WE DID IT, WE'RE DONE FOR!!
STOMP
DAMN IT...
WHAT A MESS...
IT WASN'T JUST MISTER?
THEY ALL...
...WERE INVOLVED!?

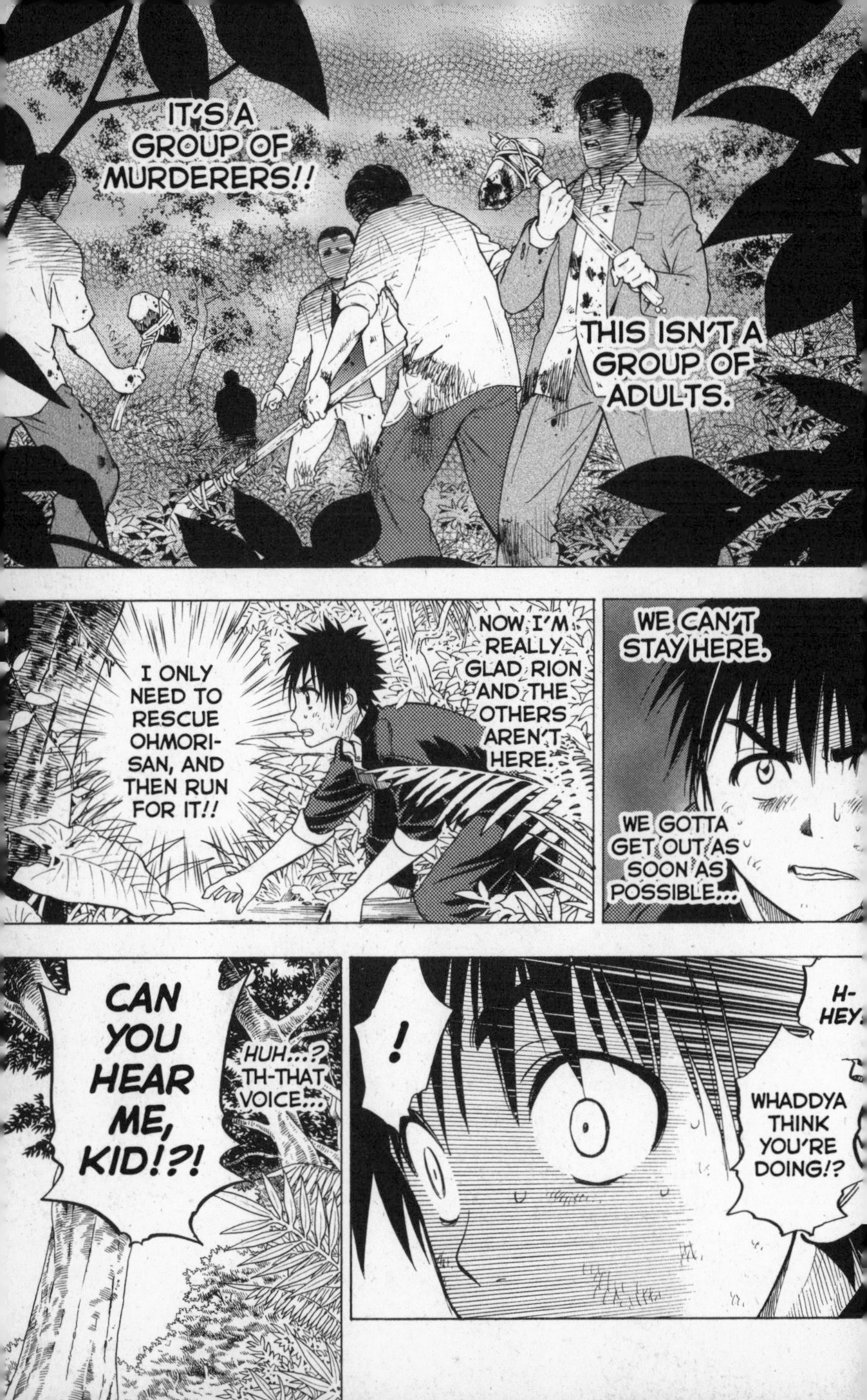
THIS ISN'T A GROUP OF ADULTS.
IT'S A GROUP OF MURDERERS!!
WE CAN'T STAY HERE.
WE GOTTA GET OUT AS SOON AS POSSIBLE...
NOW I'M REALLY GLAD RION AND THE OTHERS AREN'T HERE.
I ONLY NEED TO RESCUE OHMORI-SAN, AND THEN RUN FOR IT!!
H-HEY.
WHADDYA THINK YOU'RE DOING!?
!
CAN YOU HEAR ME, KID!?!
HUH...? TH-THAT VOICE...

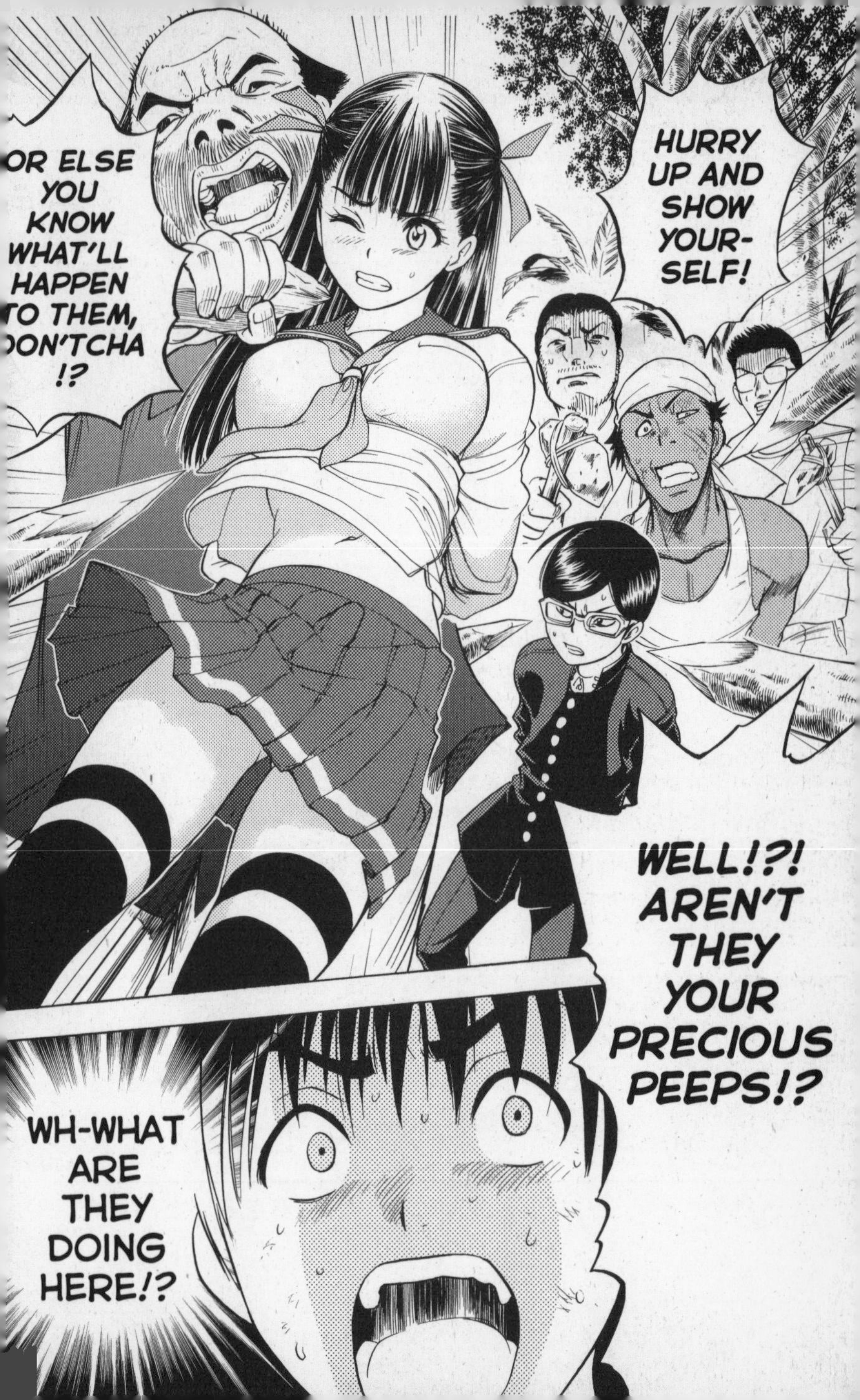
HURRY UP AND SHOW YOUR-SELF!
OR ELSE YOU KNOW WHAT'LL HAPPEN TO THEM, DON'TCHA !?
WELL!?! AREN'T THEY YOUR PRECIOUS PEEPS!?
WH-WHAT ARE THEY DOING HERE!?

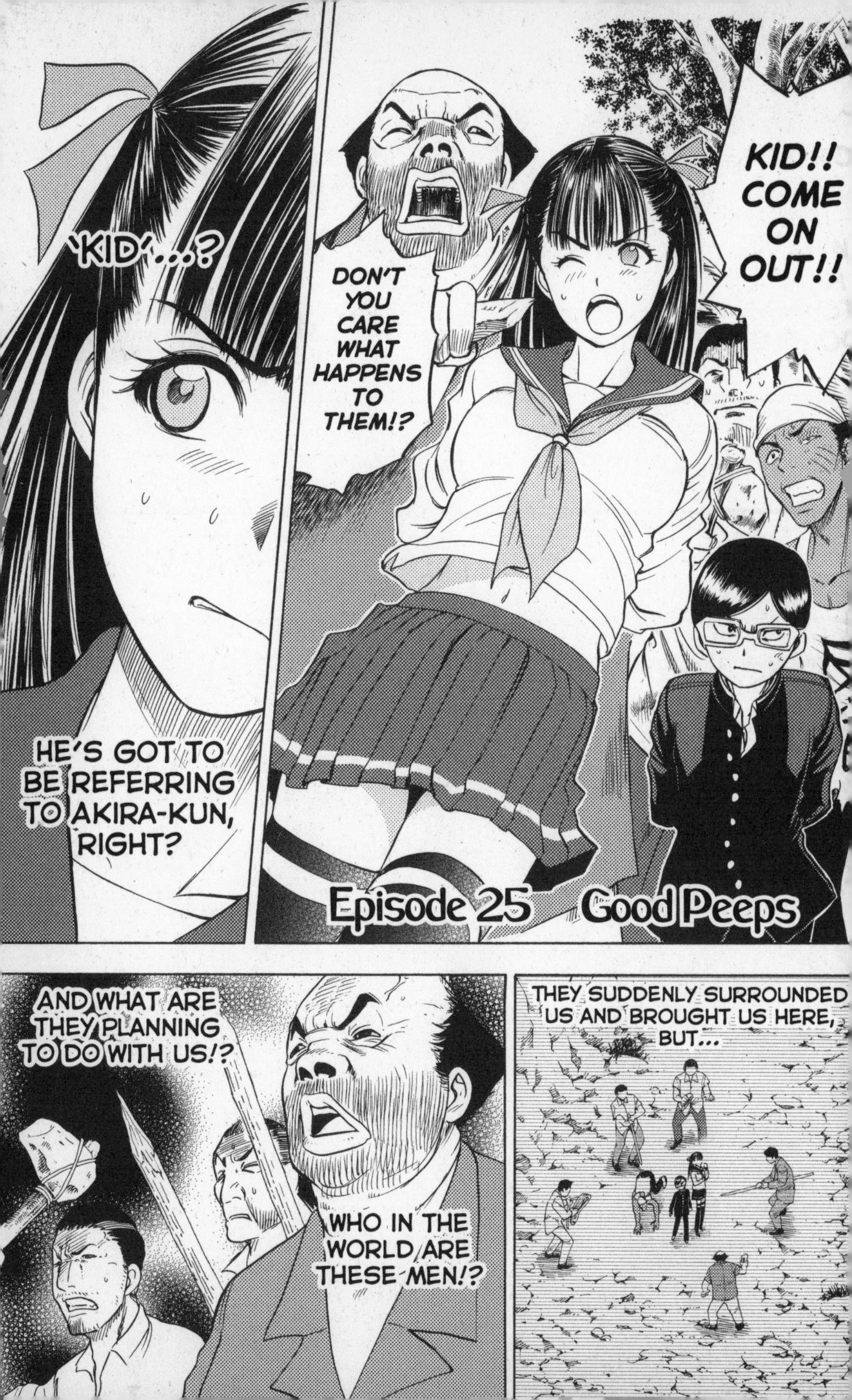
KID!! COME ON OUT!!
DON'T YOU CARE WHAT HAPPENS TO THEM!?
Episode 25 Good Peeps
'KID'...?
HE'S GOT TO BE REFERRING TO AKIRA-KUN, RIGHT?
THEY SUDDENLY SURROUNDED US AND BROUGHT US HERE, BUT...
WHO IN THE WORLD ARE THESE MEN!?
AND WHAT ARE THEY PLANNING TO DO WITH US!?

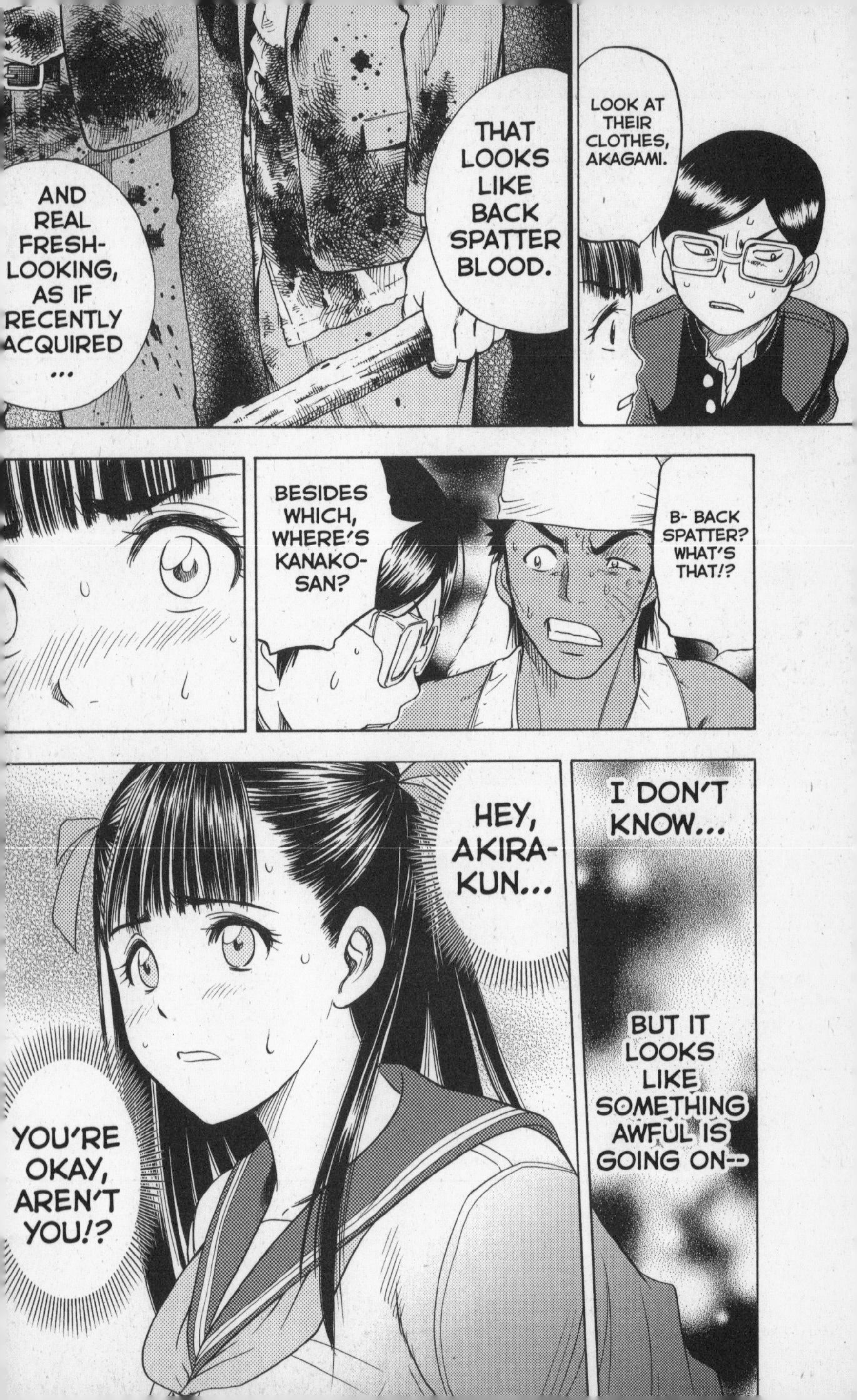
LOOK AT THEIR CLOTHES, AKAGAMI.
THAT LOOKS LIKE BACK SPATTER BLOOD.
AND REAL FRESH-LOOKING, AS IF RECENTLY ACQUIRED...
B- BACK SPATTER? WHAT'S THAT!?
BESIDES WHICH, WHERE'S KANAKO-SAN?
I DON'T KNOW...
BUT IT LOOKS LIKE SOMETHING AWFUL IS GOING ON--
HEY, AKIRA-KUN...
YOU'RE OKAY, AREN'T YOU!?

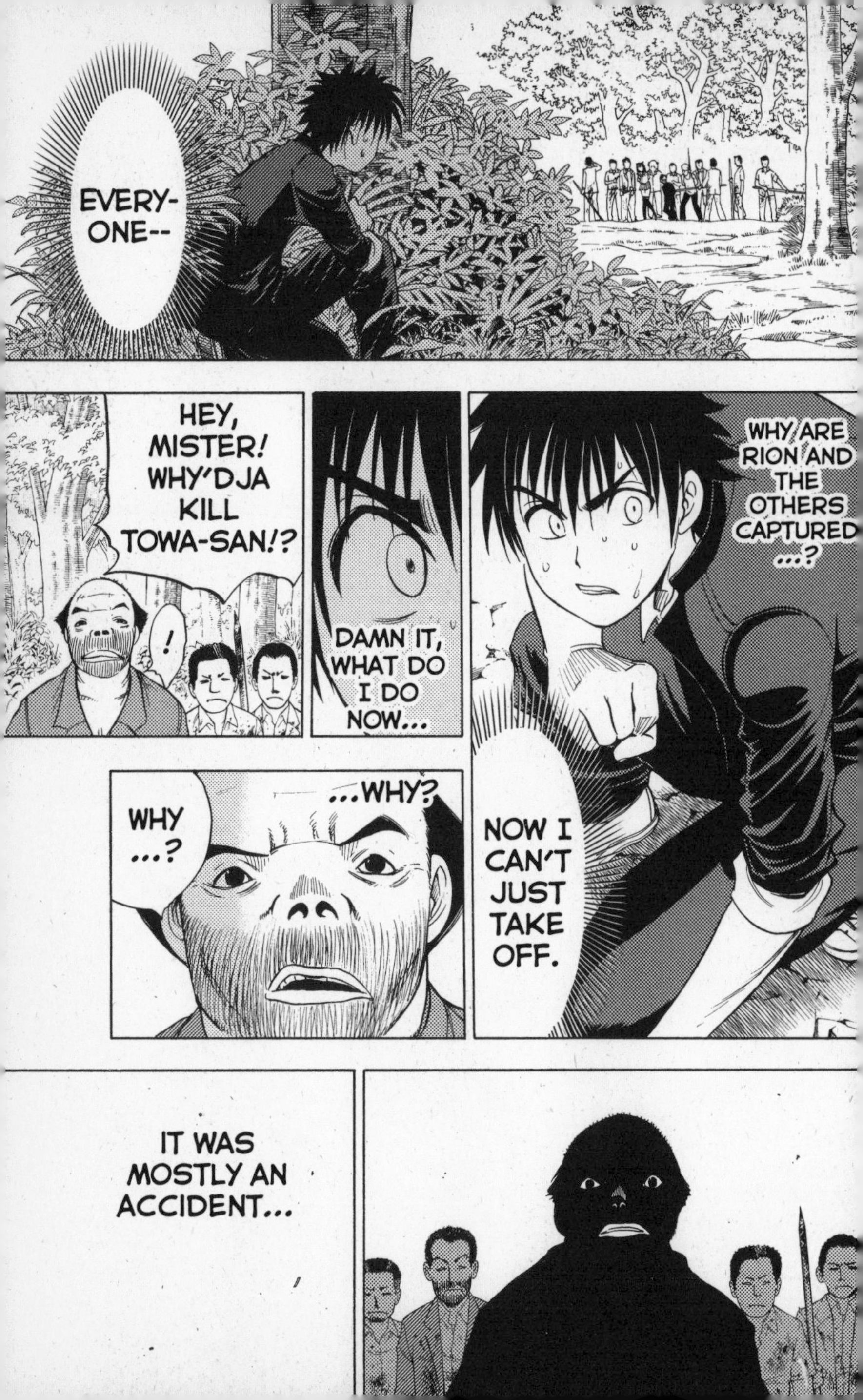
EVERY-ONE--
WHY ARE RION AND THE OTHERS CAPTURED ...?
NOW I CAN'T JUST TAKE OFF.
DAMN IT, WHAT DO I DO NOW...
HEY, MISTER! WHY'DJA KILL TOWA-SAN!?
!
...WHY?
WHY ...?
IT WAS MOSTLY AN ACCIDENT...

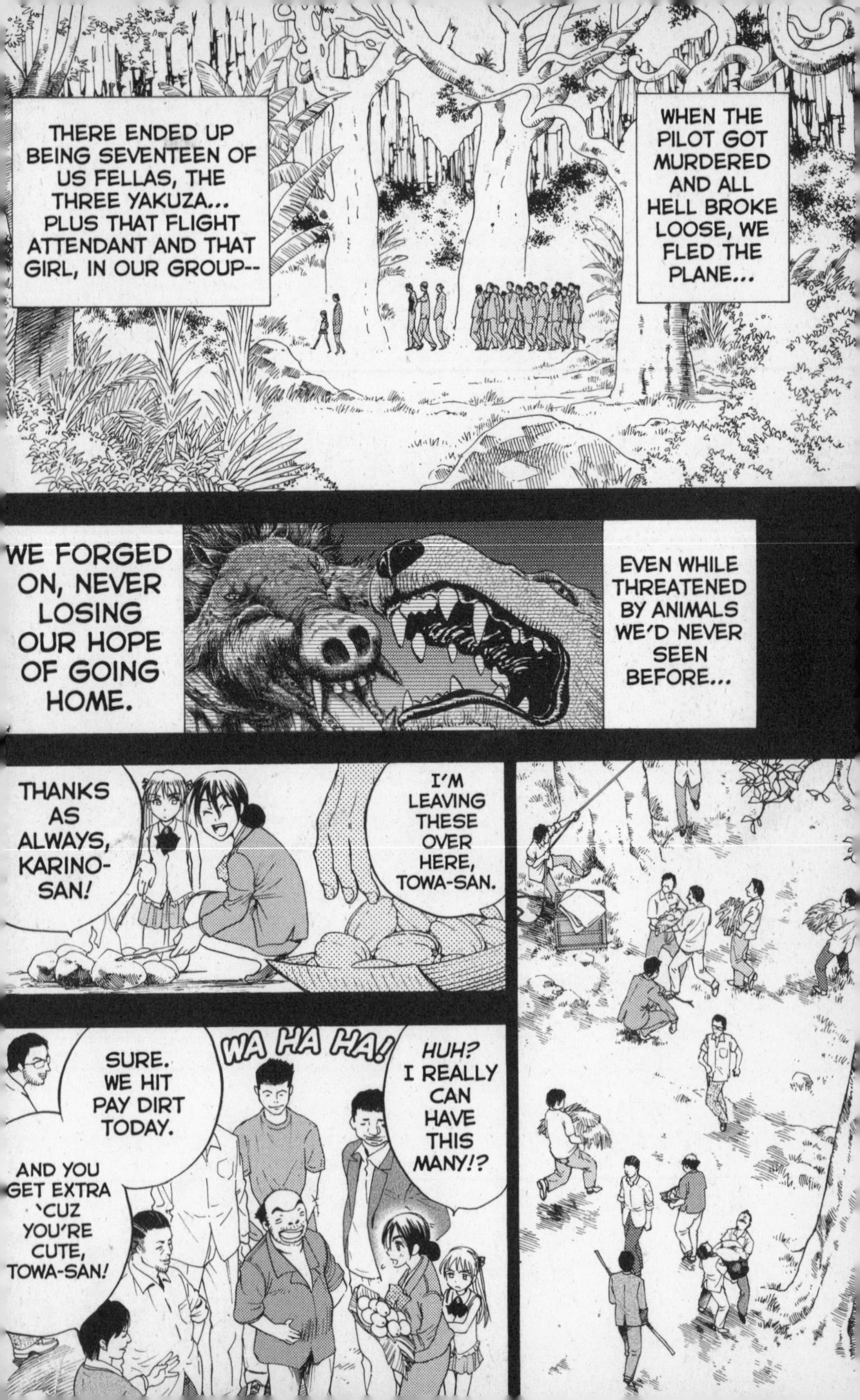
WHEN THE PILOT GOT MURDERED AND ALL HELL BROKE LOOSE, WE FLED THE PLANE...
THERE ENDED UP BEING SEVENTEEN OF US FELLAS, THE THREE YAKUZA... PLUS THAT FLIGHT ATTENDANT AND THAT GIRL, IN OUR GROUP--
EVEN WHILE THREATENED BY ANIMALS WE'D NEVER SEEN BEFORE...
WE FORGED ON, NEVER LOSING OUR HOPE OF GOING HOME.
I'M LEAVING THESE OVER HERE, TOWA-SAN.
THANKS AS ALWAYS, KARINO-SAN!
HUH? I REALLY CAN HAVE THIS MANY!?
WA HA HA!
SURE. WE HIT PAY DIRT TODAY.
AND YOU GET EXTRA 'CUZ YOU'RE CUTE, TOWA-SAN!

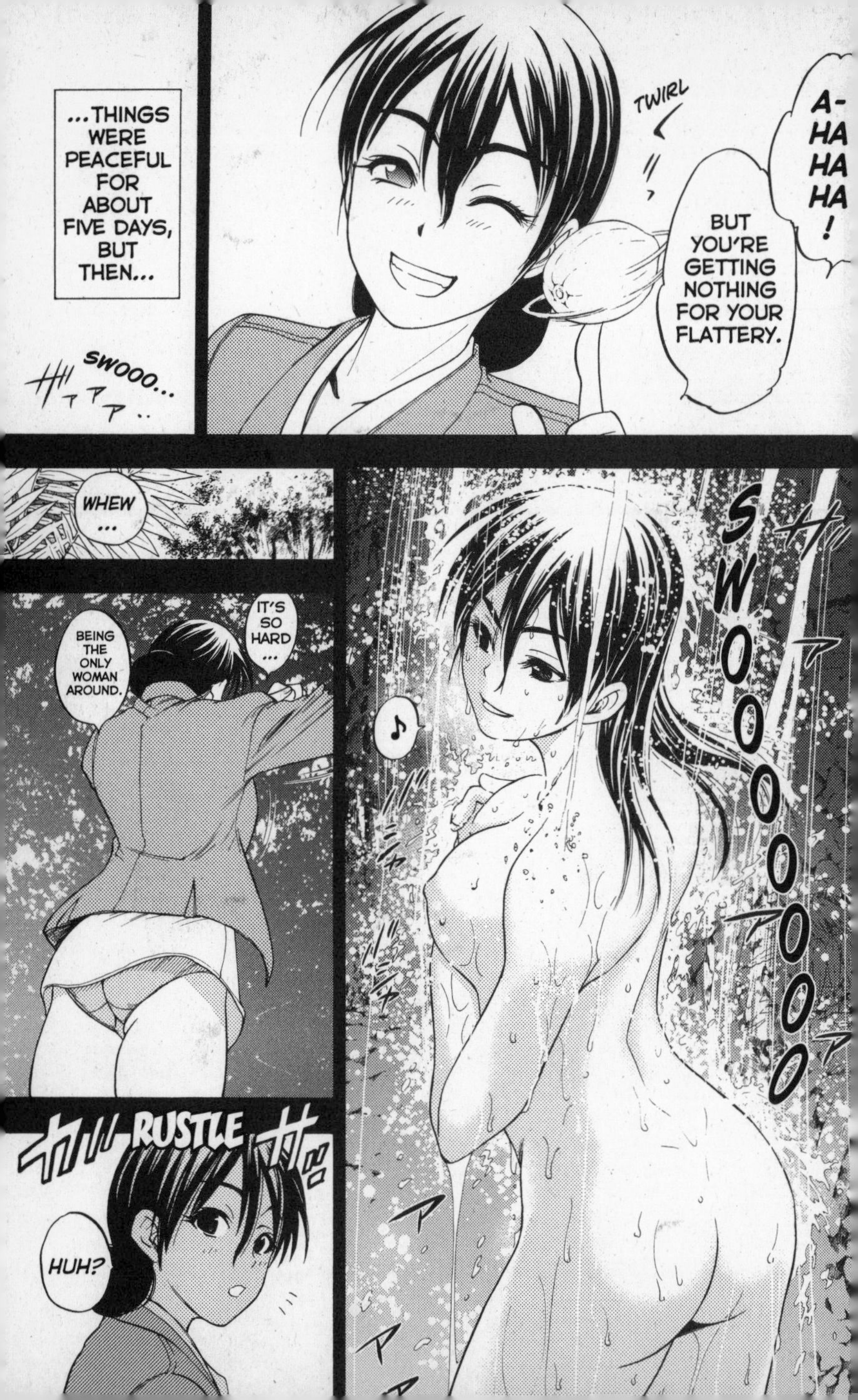
A-HAHAHA!
TWIRL
BUT YOU'RE GETTING NOTHING FOR YOUR FLATTERY.
...THINGS WERE PEACEFUL FOR ABOUT FIVE DAYS, BUT THEN...
SWOOO...
SWOOOOOOOOOO
♪
WHEW...
IT'S SO HARD...
BEING THE ONLY WOMAN AROUND.
RUSTLE
HUH?

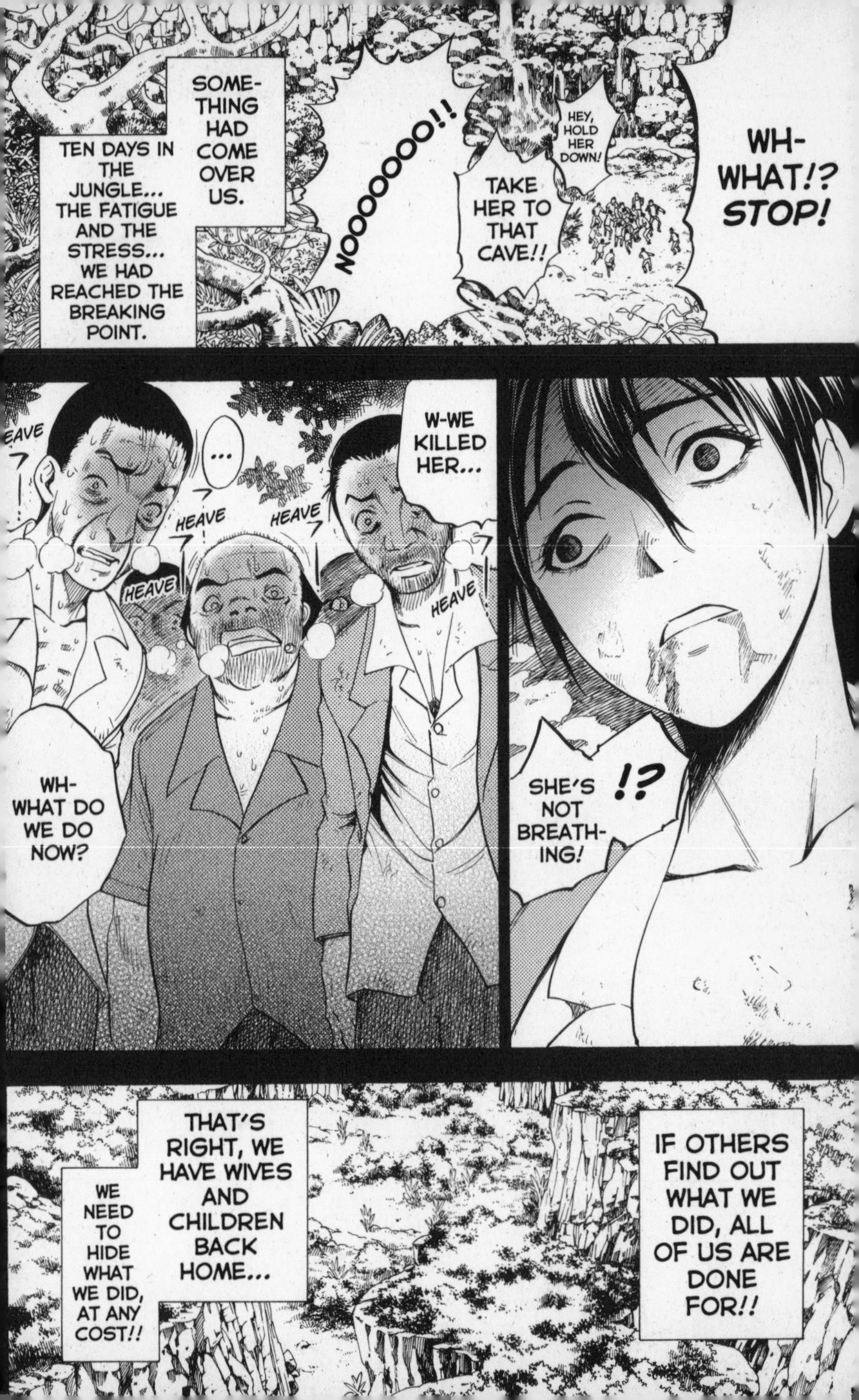
WH-WHAT!? STOP!
HEY, HOLD HER DOWN!
TAKE HER TO THAT CAVE!!
NOOOOOOO!!
SOMETHING HAD COME OVER US.
TEN DAYS IN THE JUNGLE... THE FATIGUE AND THE STRESS... WE HAD REACHED THE BREAKING POINT.
!?
SHE'S NOT BREATHING!
W-WE KILLED HER...
HEAVE
HEAVE
...
HEAVE
HEAVE
EAVE
WH-WHAT DO WE DO NOW?
IF OTHERS FIND OUT WHAT WE DID, ALL OF US ARE DONE FOR!!
THAT'S RIGHT, WE HAVE WIVES AND CHILDREN BACK HOME...
WE NEED TO HIDE WHAT WE DID, AT ANY COST!!

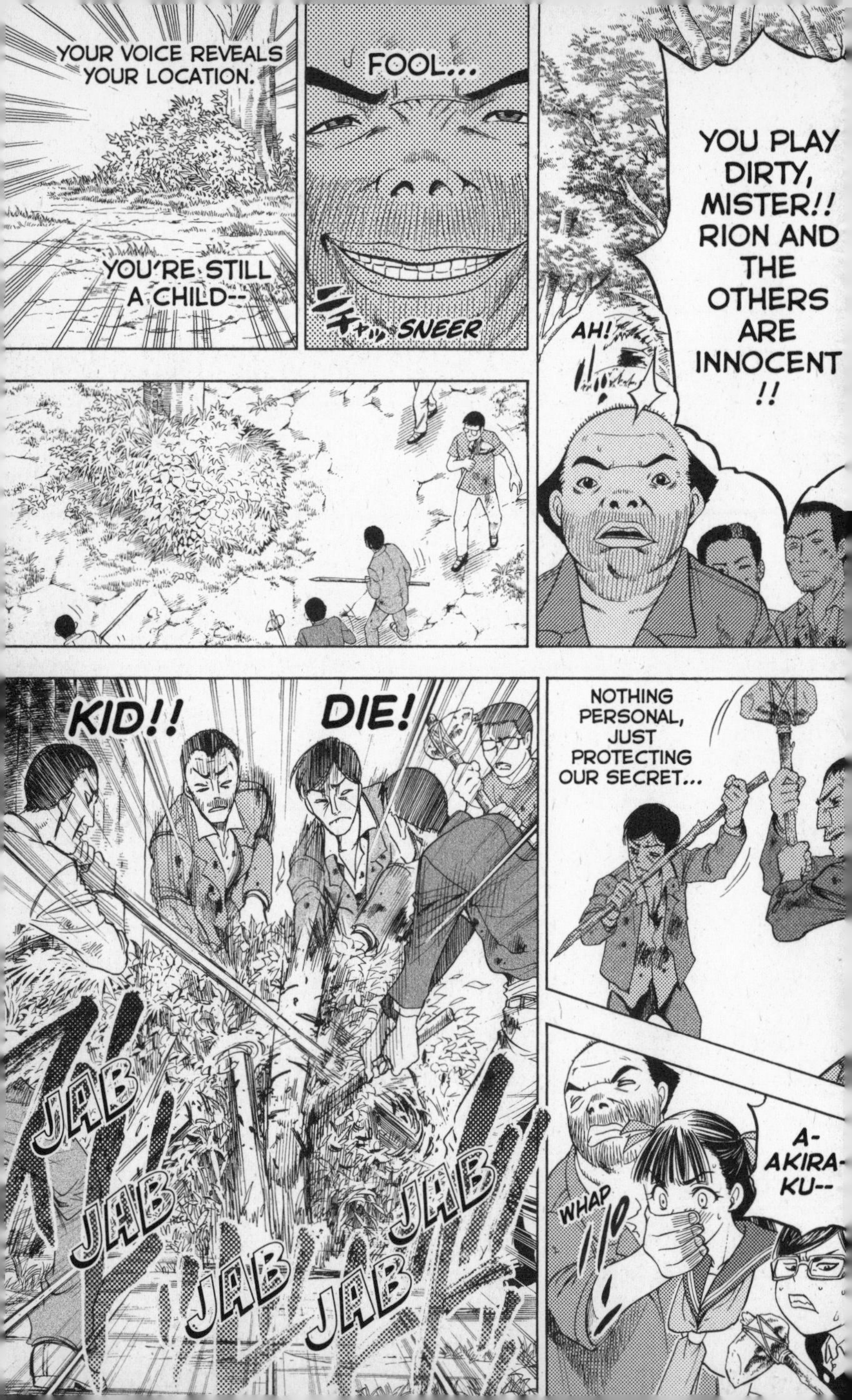
YOU PLAY DIRTY, MISTER!! RION AND THE OTHERS ARE INNOCENT!!
AH!
FOOL...
SNEER
YOUR VOICE REVEALS YOUR LOCATION.
YOU'RE STILL A CHILD--
NOTHING PERSONAL, JUST PROTECTING OUR SECRET...
A- AKIRA-KU--
WHAP
DIE!
KID!!
JAB
JAB
JAB
JAB
JAB
JAB

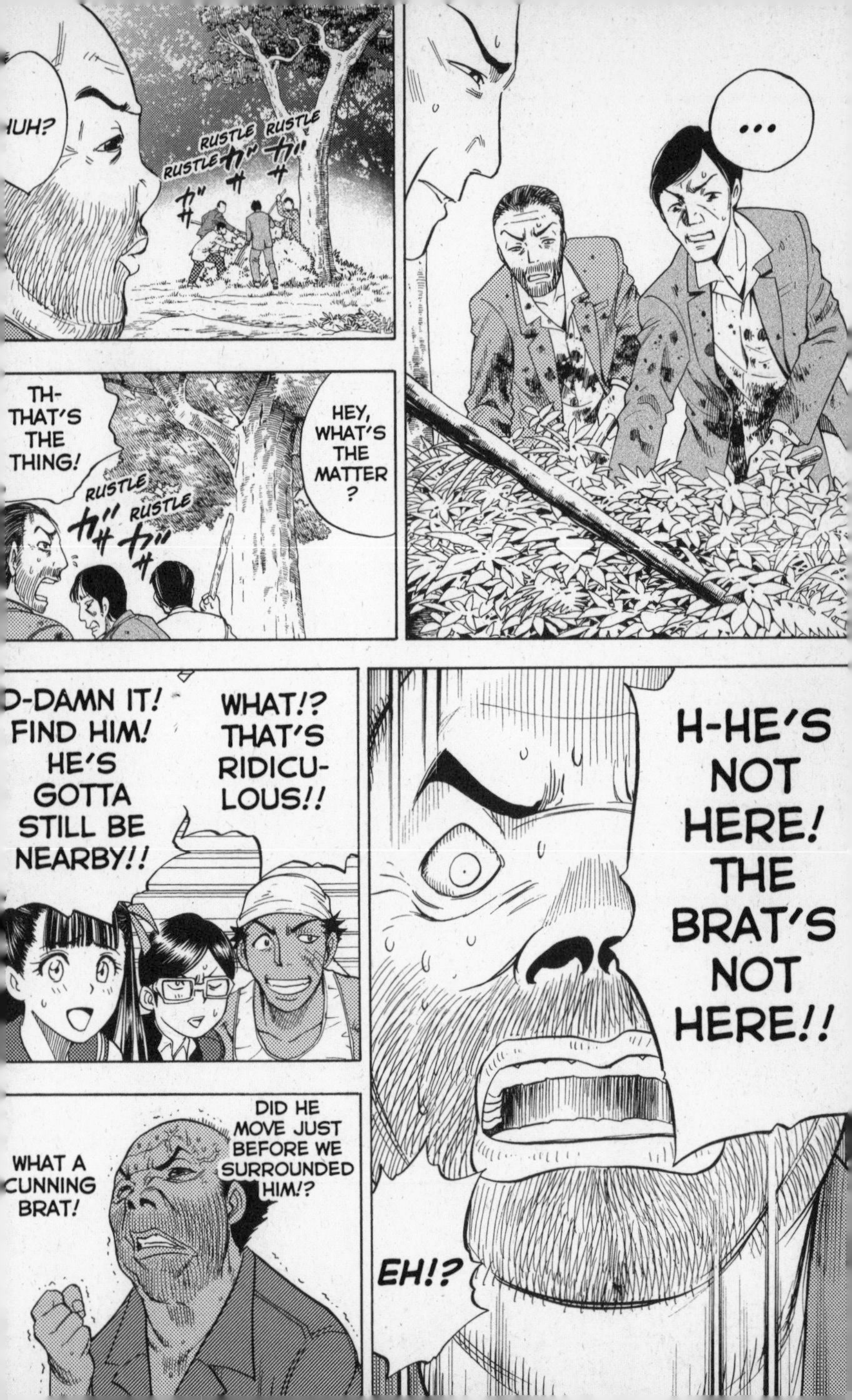
...
HUH?
RUSTLE RUSTLE
RUSTLE RUSTLE
HEY, WHAT'S THE MATTER?
TH- THAT'S THE THING!
RUSTLE RUSTLE
H-HE'S NOT HERE! THE BRAT'S NOT HERE!!
EH!?
WHAT!? THAT'S RIDICULOUS!!
D-DAMN IT! FIND HIM! HE'S GOTTA STILL BE NEARBY!!
DID HE MOVE JUST BEFORE WE SURROUNDED HIM!?
WHAT A CUNNING BRAT!

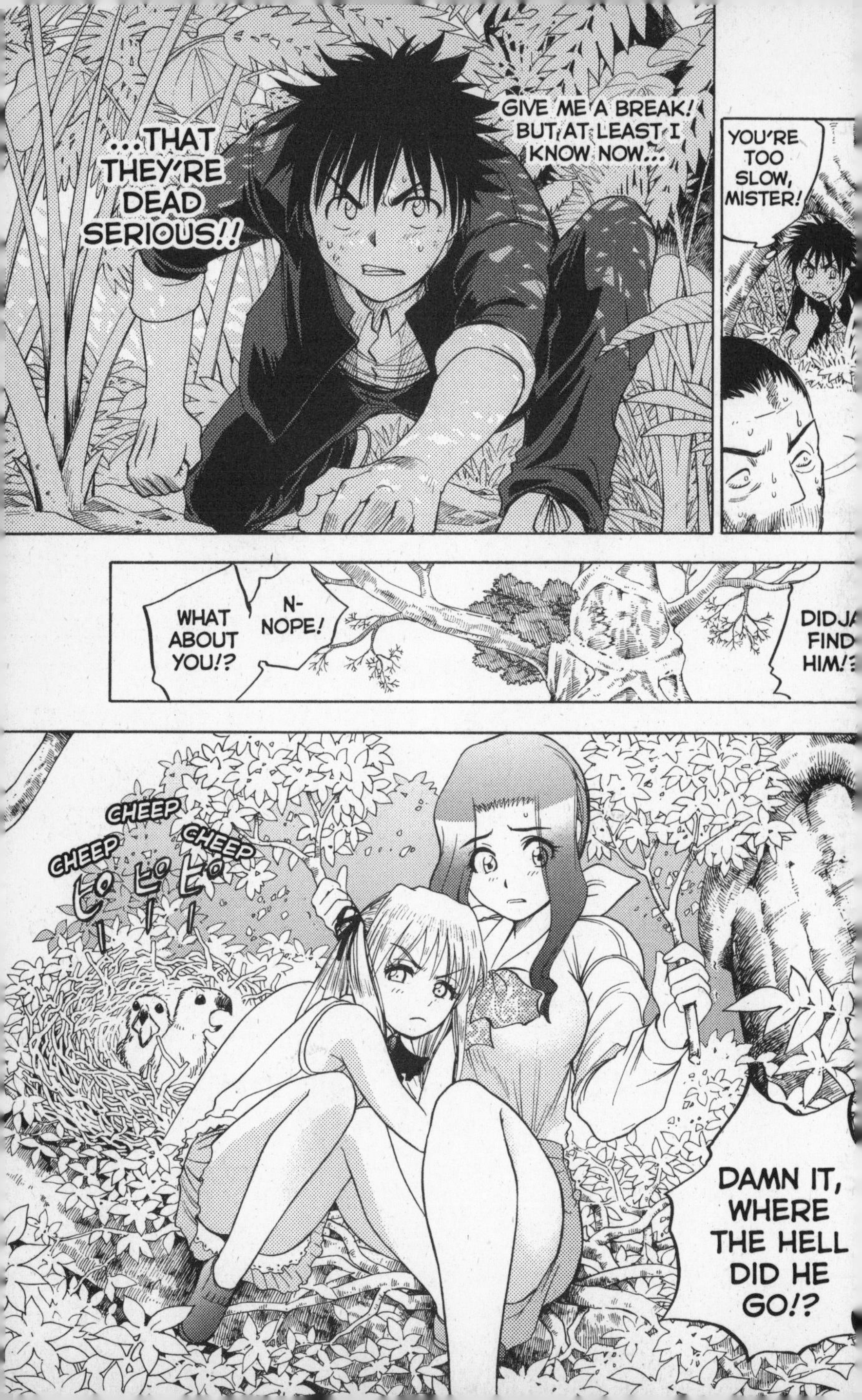
YOU'RE TOO SLOW, MISTER!
GIVE ME A BREAK! BUT AT LEAST I KNOW NOW...
...THAT THEY'RE DEAD SERIOUS!!
DIDJA FIND HIM!?
N-NOPE!
WHAT ABOUT YOU!?
DAMN IT, WHERE THE HELL DID HE GO!?
CHEEP
ピー
CHEEP
ピー
CHEEP
ピー

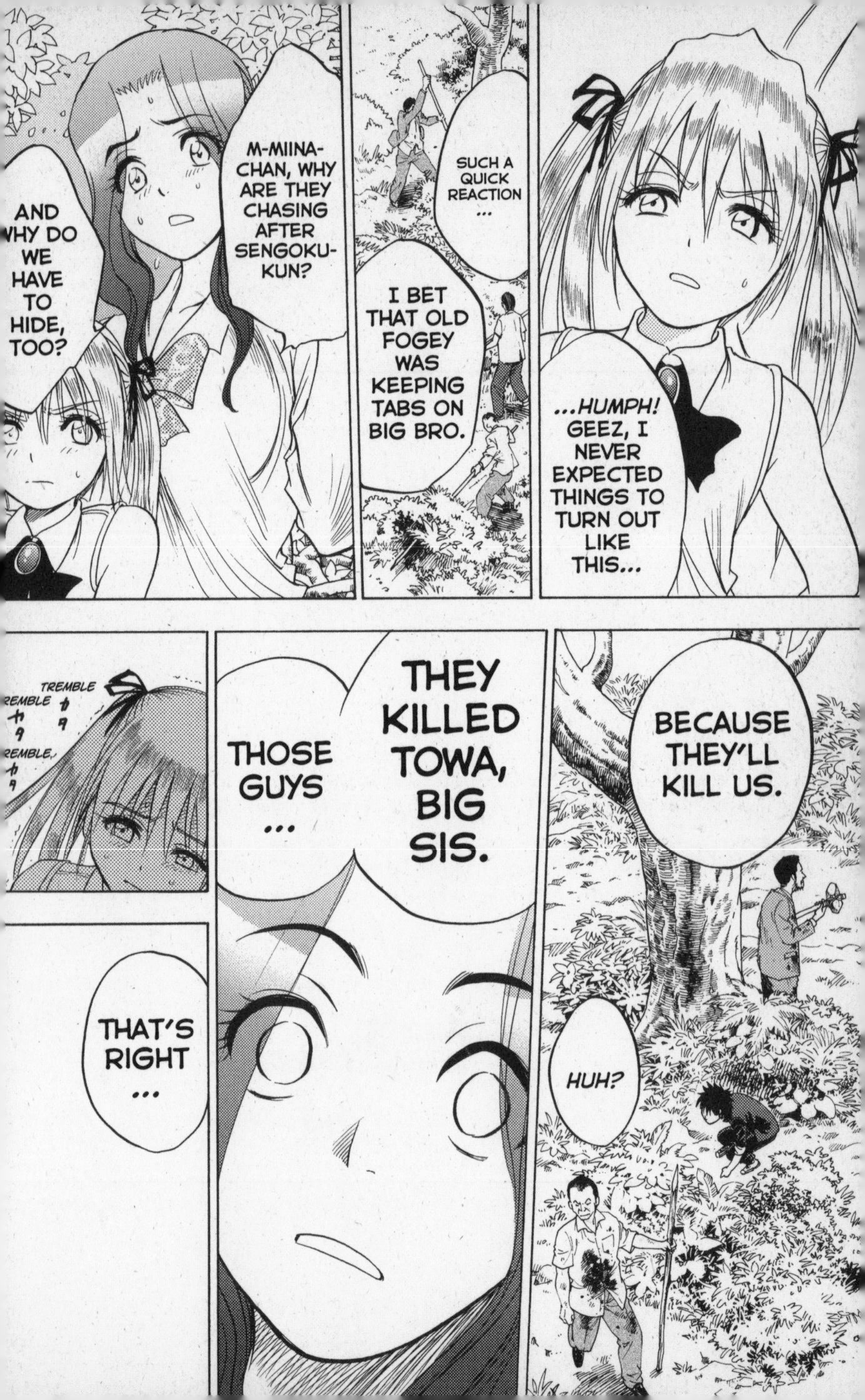
...HUMPH! GEEZ, I NEVER EXPECTED THINGS TO TURN OUT LIKE THIS...
SUCH A QUICK REACTION...
I BET THAT OLD FOGEY WAS KEEPING TABS ON BIG BRO.
M-MIINA-CHAN, WHY ARE THEY CHASING AFTER SENGOKU-KUN?
AND WHY DO WE HAVE TO HIDE, TOO?
BECAUSE THEY'LL KILL US.
HUH?
THEY KILLED TOWA, BIG SIS.
THOSE GUYS...
TREMBLE カタ
REMBLE カタ
REMBLE, カタ
THAT'S RIGHT...

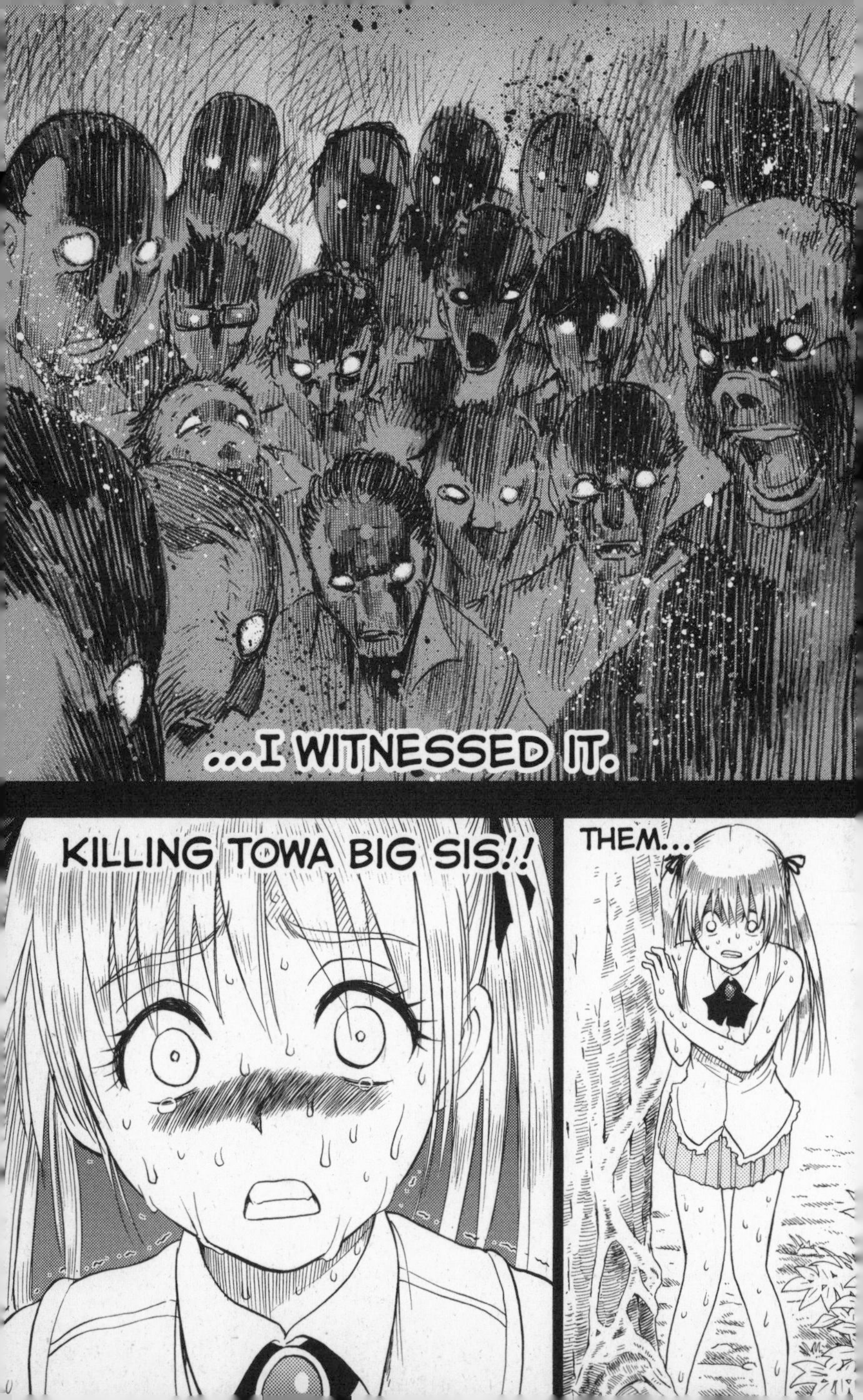
...I WITNESSED IT.
THEM...
KILLING TOWA BIG SIS!!

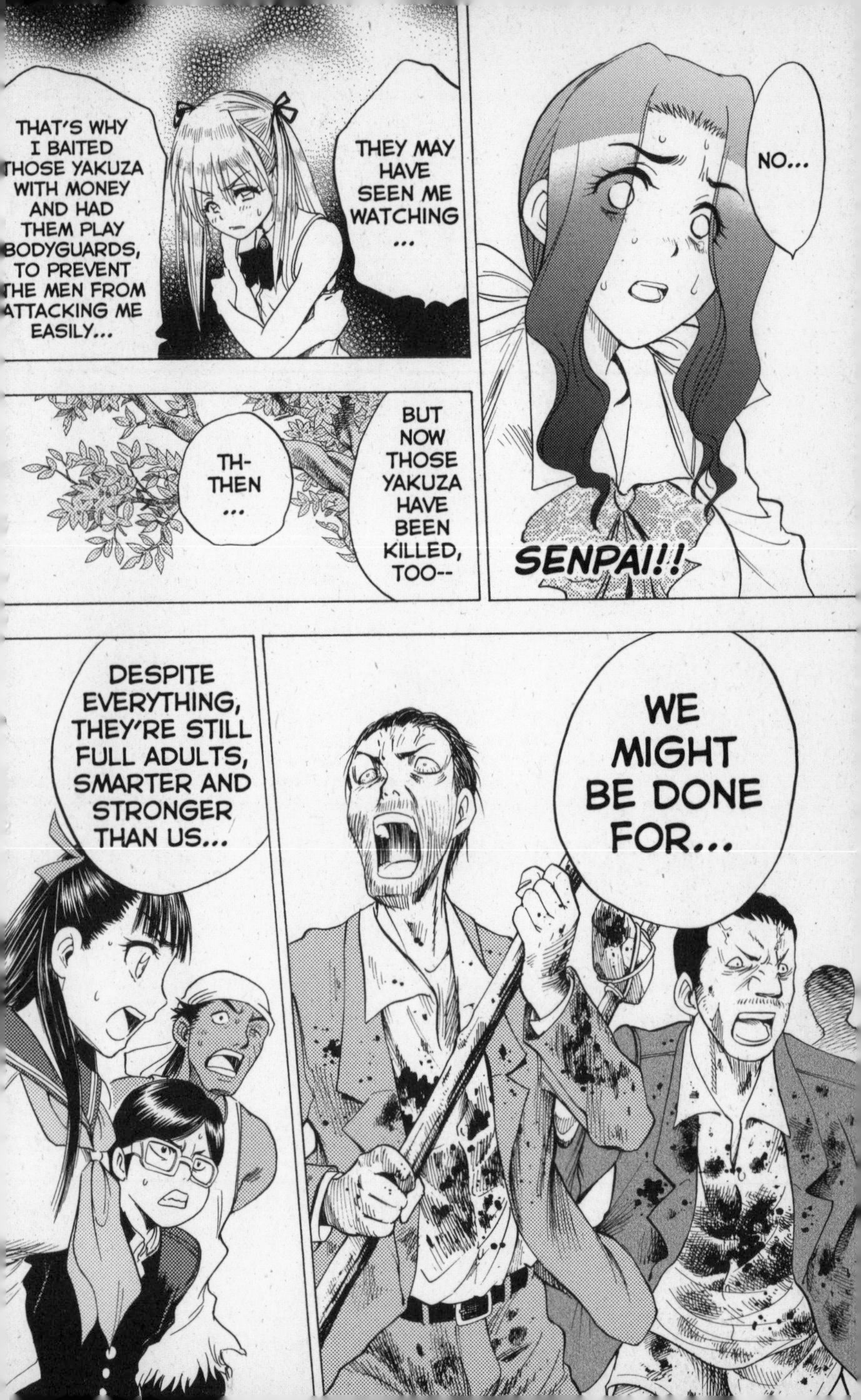
NO...
SENPAI!!
THEY MAY HAVE SEEN ME WATCHING...
THAT'S WHY I BAITED THOSE YAKUZA WITH MONEY AND HAD THEM PLAY BODYGUARDS, TO PREVENT THE MEN FROM ATTACKING ME EASILY...
BUT NOW THOSE YAKUZA HAVE BEEN KILLED, TOO--
TH-THEN...
WE MIGHT BE DONE FOR...
DESPITE EVERYTHING, THEY'RE STILL FULL ADULTS, SMARTER AND STRONGER THAN US...

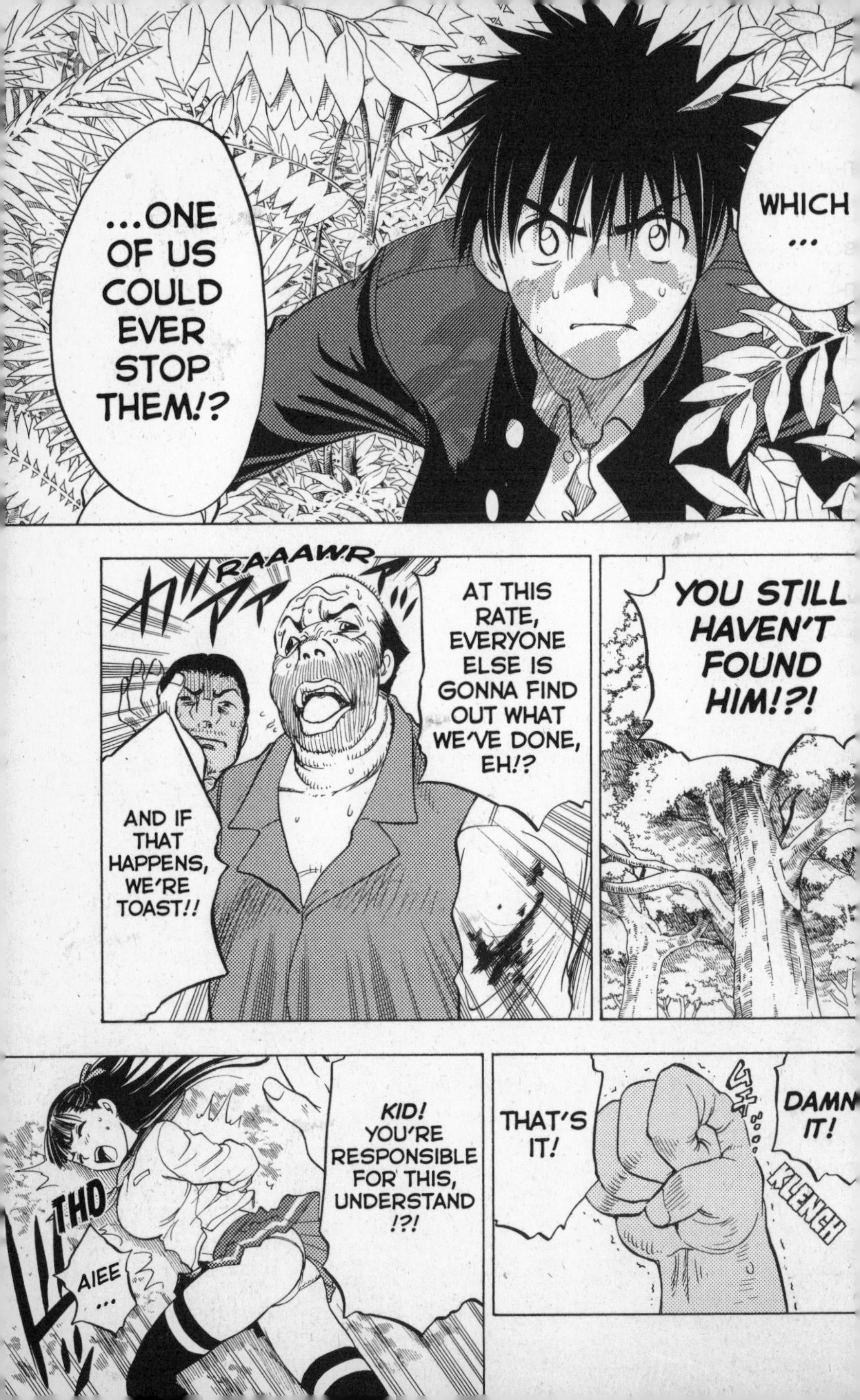
WHICH ...
...ONE OF US COULD EVER STOP THEM!?
YOU STILL HAVEN'T FOUND HIM!?!
RAAAWR
AT THIS RATE, EVERYONE ELSE IS GONNA FIND OUT WHAT WE'VE DONE, EH!?
AND IF THAT HAPPENS, WE'RE TOAST!!
DAMN IT!
KLENCH
THAT'S IT!
KID! YOU'RE RESPONSIBLE FOR THIS, UNDERSTAND !?!
THD
AIEE ...

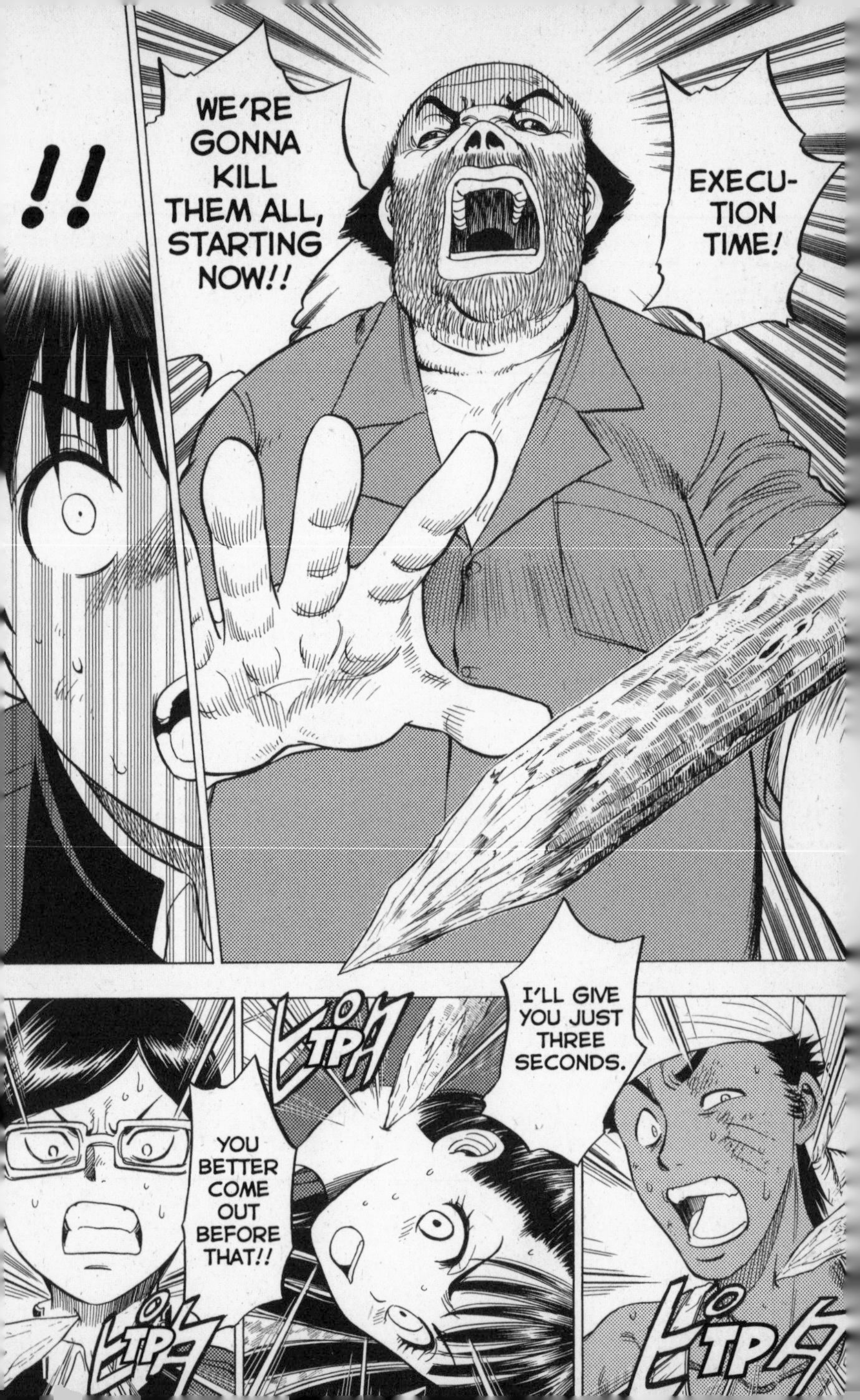
EXECUTION TIME!
WE'RE GONNA KILL THEM ALL, STARTING NOW!!
!!
I'LL GIVE YOU JUST THREE SECONDS.
TP
TP
YOU BETTER COME OUT BEFORE THAT!!
TP

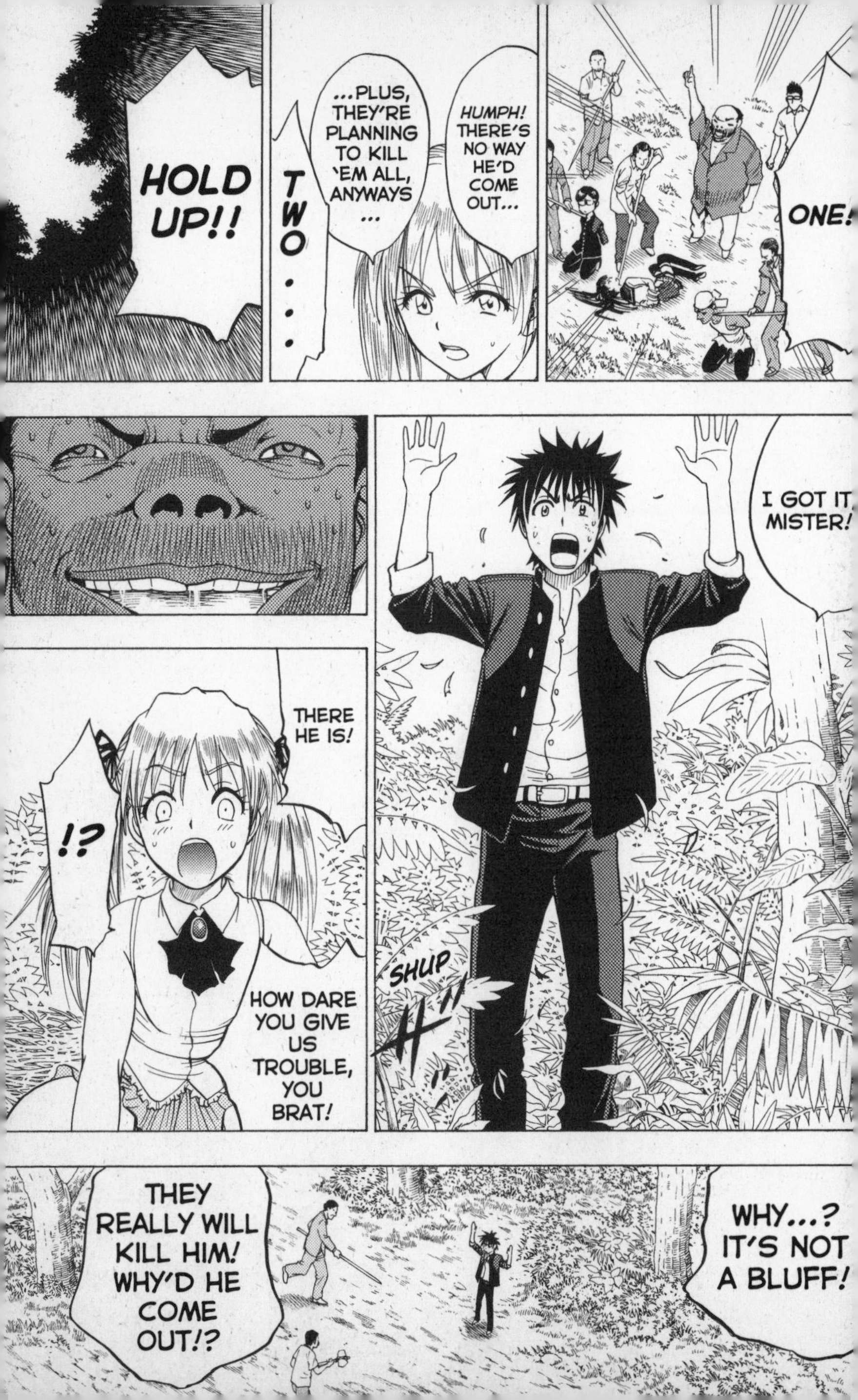
ONE!
HUMPH! THERE'S NO WAY HE'D COME OUT...
...PLUS, THEY'RE PLANNING TO KILL 'EM ALL, ANYWAYS ...
TWO...
HOLD UP!!
I GOT IT, MISTER!
SHUP
THERE HE IS!
!?
HOW DARE YOU GIVE US TROUBLE, YOU BRAT!
WHY...? IT'S NOT A BLUFF!
THEY REALLY WILL KILL HIM! WHY'D HE COME OUT!?

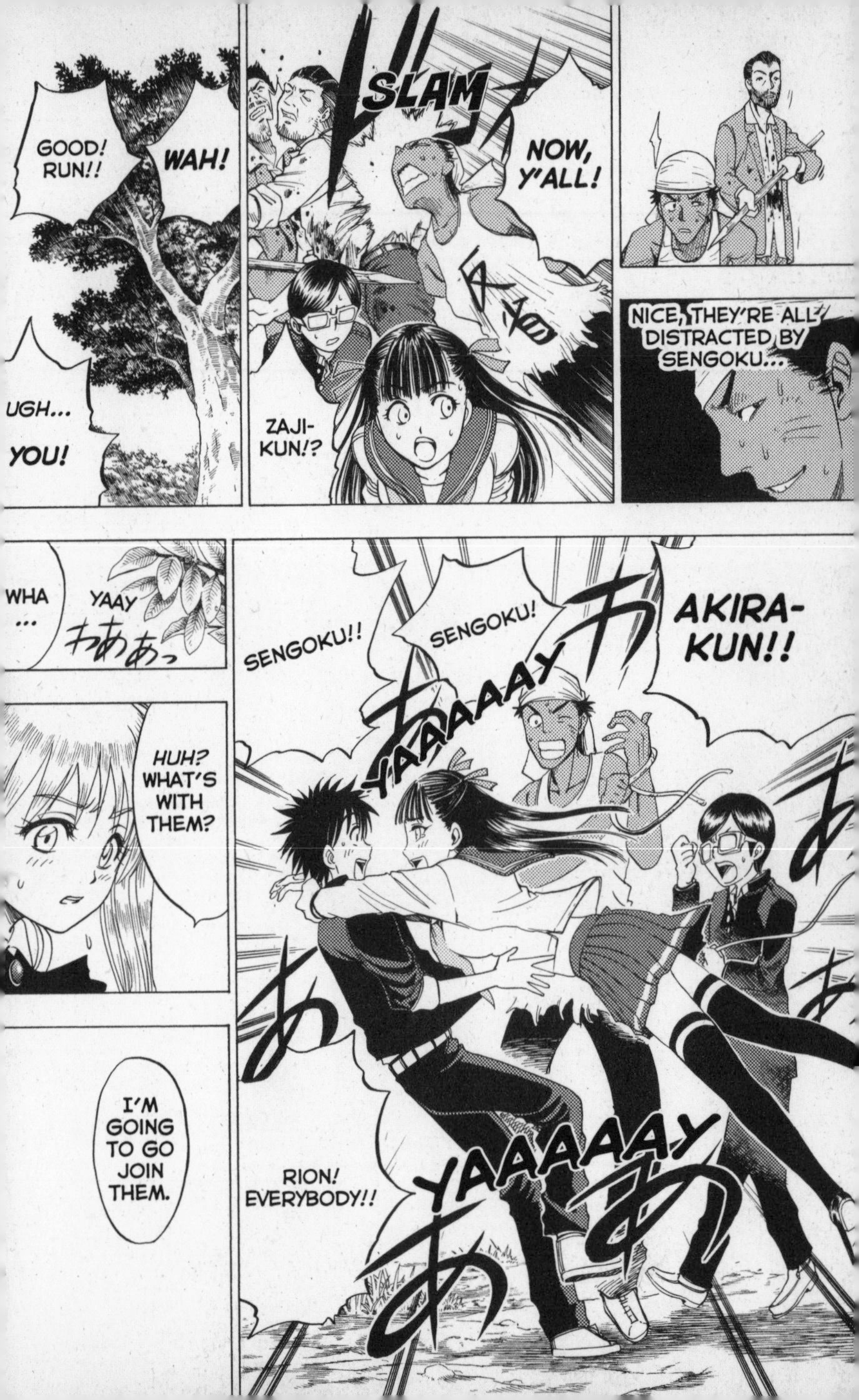
NICE, THEY'RE ALL DISTRACTED BY SENGOKU...
SLAM
NOW, Y'ALL!
ZAJI-KUN!?
GOOD! RUN!!
WAH!
UGH...
YOU!
AKIRA-KUN!!
SENGOKU!
SENGOKU!!
YAAAAAAY
YAAAAAAY
RION! EVERYBODY!!
WHA...
YAAY
わあああっ
HUH? WHAT'S WITH THEM?
I'M GOING TO GO JOIN THEM.

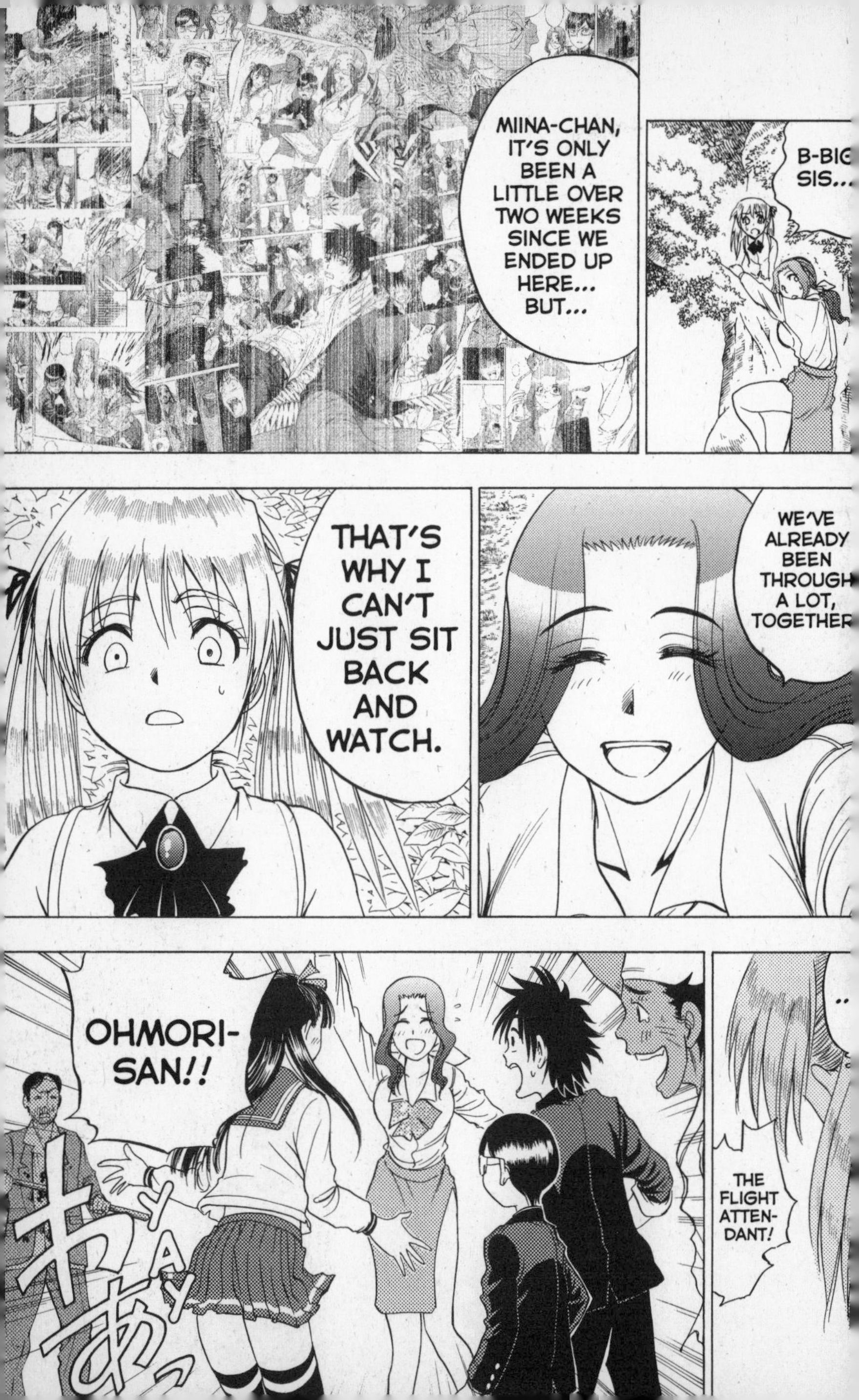
B-BIG SIS...
MIINA-CHAN, IT'S ONLY BEEN A LITTLE OVER TWO WEEKS SINCE WE ENDED UP HERE... BUT...
WE'VE ALREADY BEEN THROUGH A LOT, TOGETHER
THAT'S WHY I CAN'T JUST SIT BACK AND WATCH.
...
THE FLIGHT ATTEN-DANT!
OHMORI-SAN!!
YAY

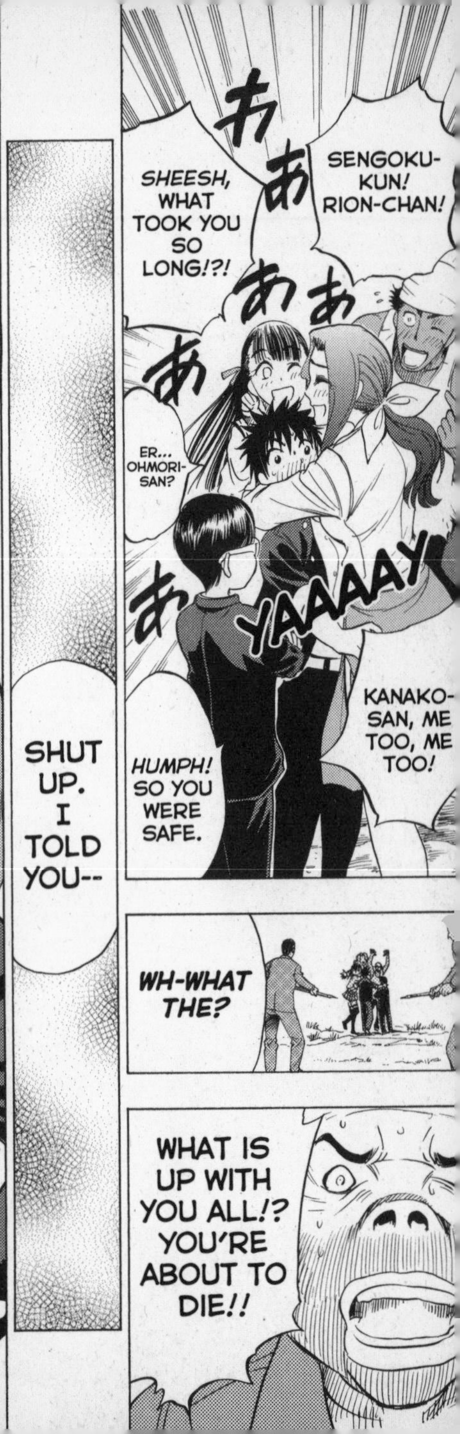
SENGOKU-KUN! RION-CHAN!
SHEESH, WHAT TOOK YOU SO LONG!?!
ああ
ああ
あ
ER... OHMORI-SAN?
あ
YAAAAY
KANAKO-SAN, ME TOO, ME TOO!
HUMPH! SO YOU WERE SAFE.
WH-WHAT THE?
WHAT IS UP WITH YOU ALL!? YOU'RE ABOUT TO DIE!!
SHUT UP. I TOLD YOU--
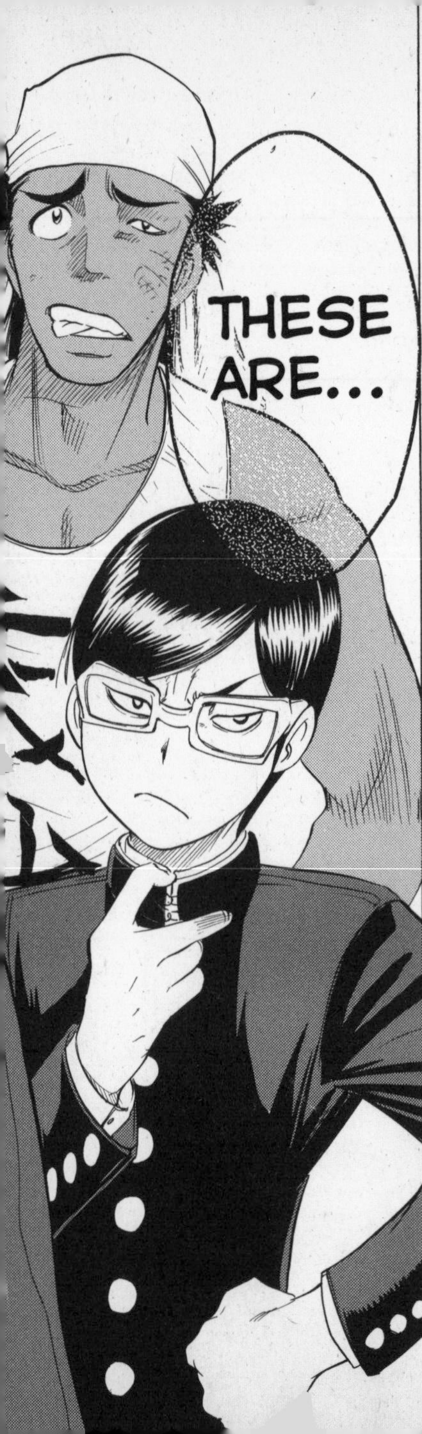
THESE ARE...

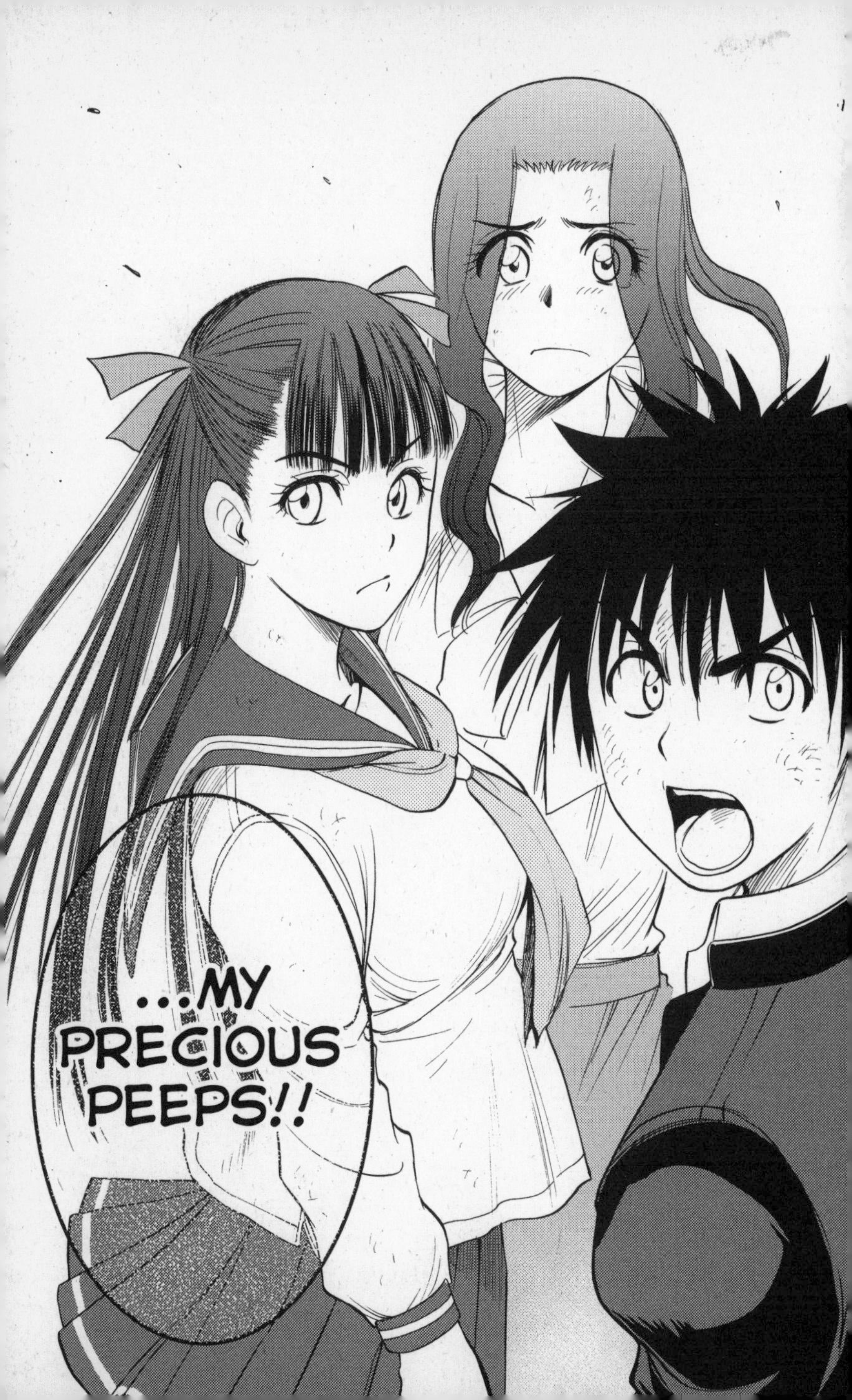
...MY PRECIOUS PEEPS!!

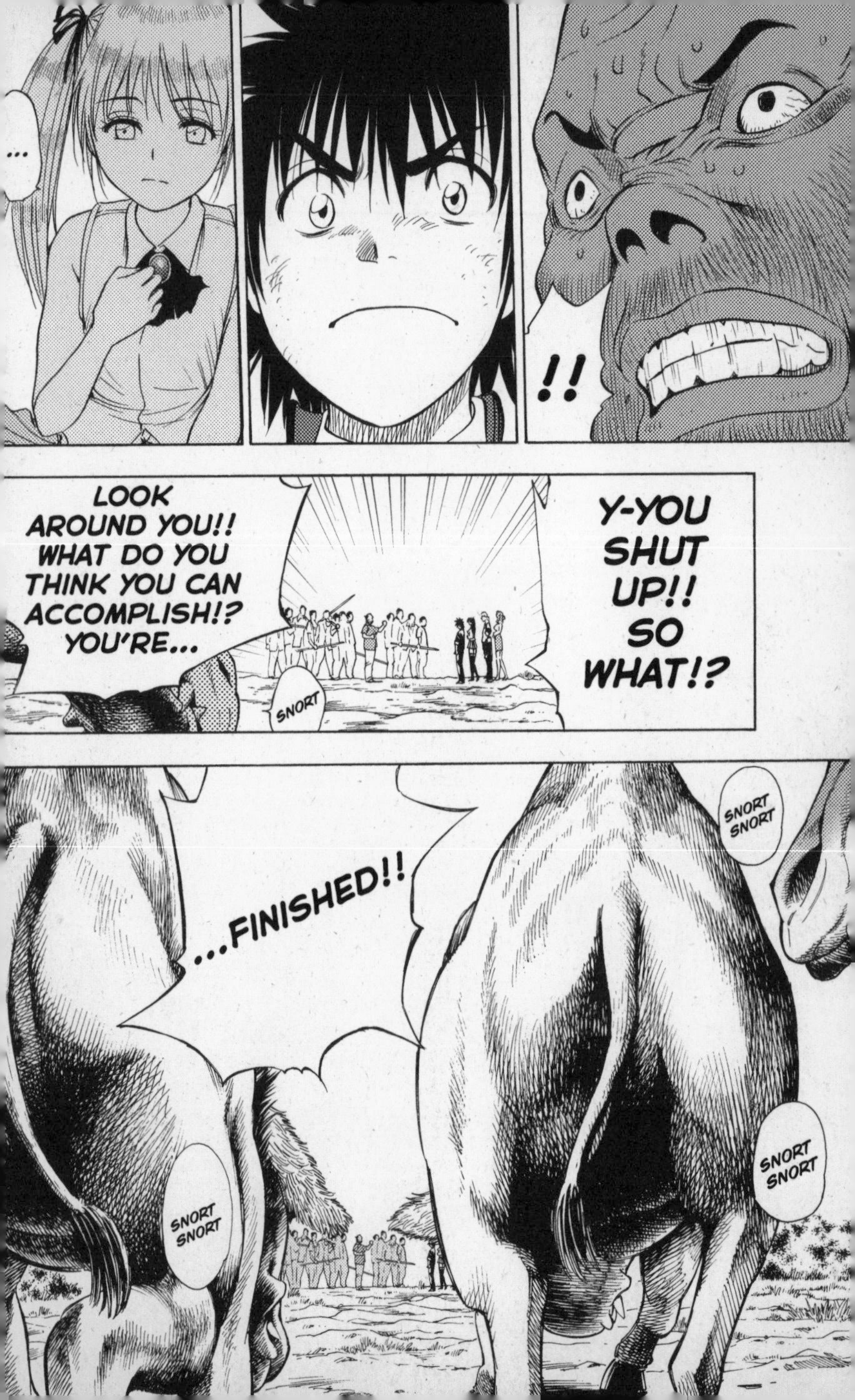
!!
...
Y-YOU SHUT UP!! SO WHAT!?
LOOK AROUND YOU!! WHAT DO YOU THINK YOU CAN ACCOMPLISH!? YOU'RE...
SNORT
SNORT SNORT
...FINISHED!!
SNORT SNORT
SNORT SNORT

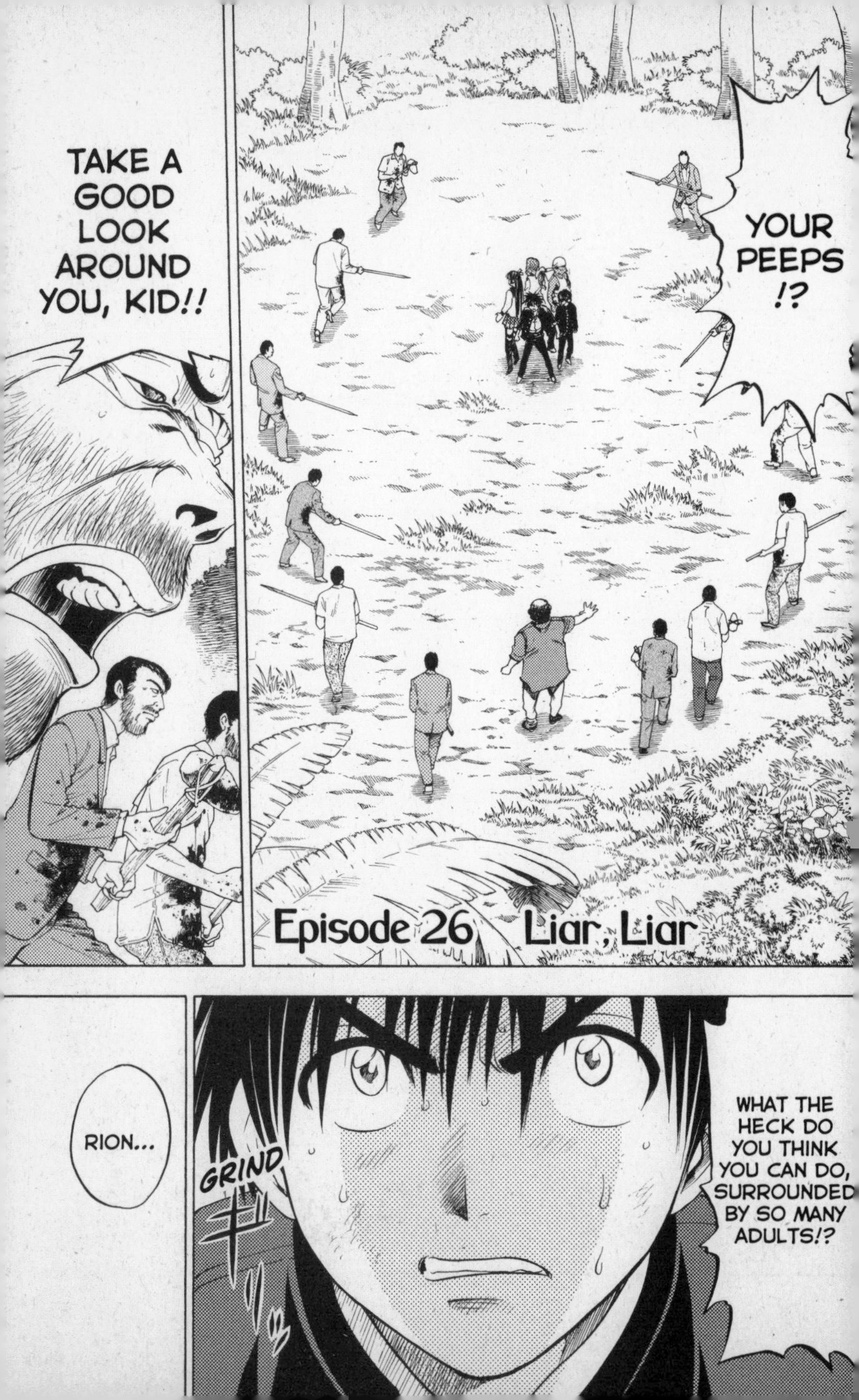
YOUR PEEPS!?
Episode 26 Liar, Liar
TAKE A GOOD LOOK AROUND YOU, KID!!
WHAT THE HECK DO YOU THINK YOU CAN DO, SURROUNDED BY SO MANY ADULTS!?
GRIND
RION...

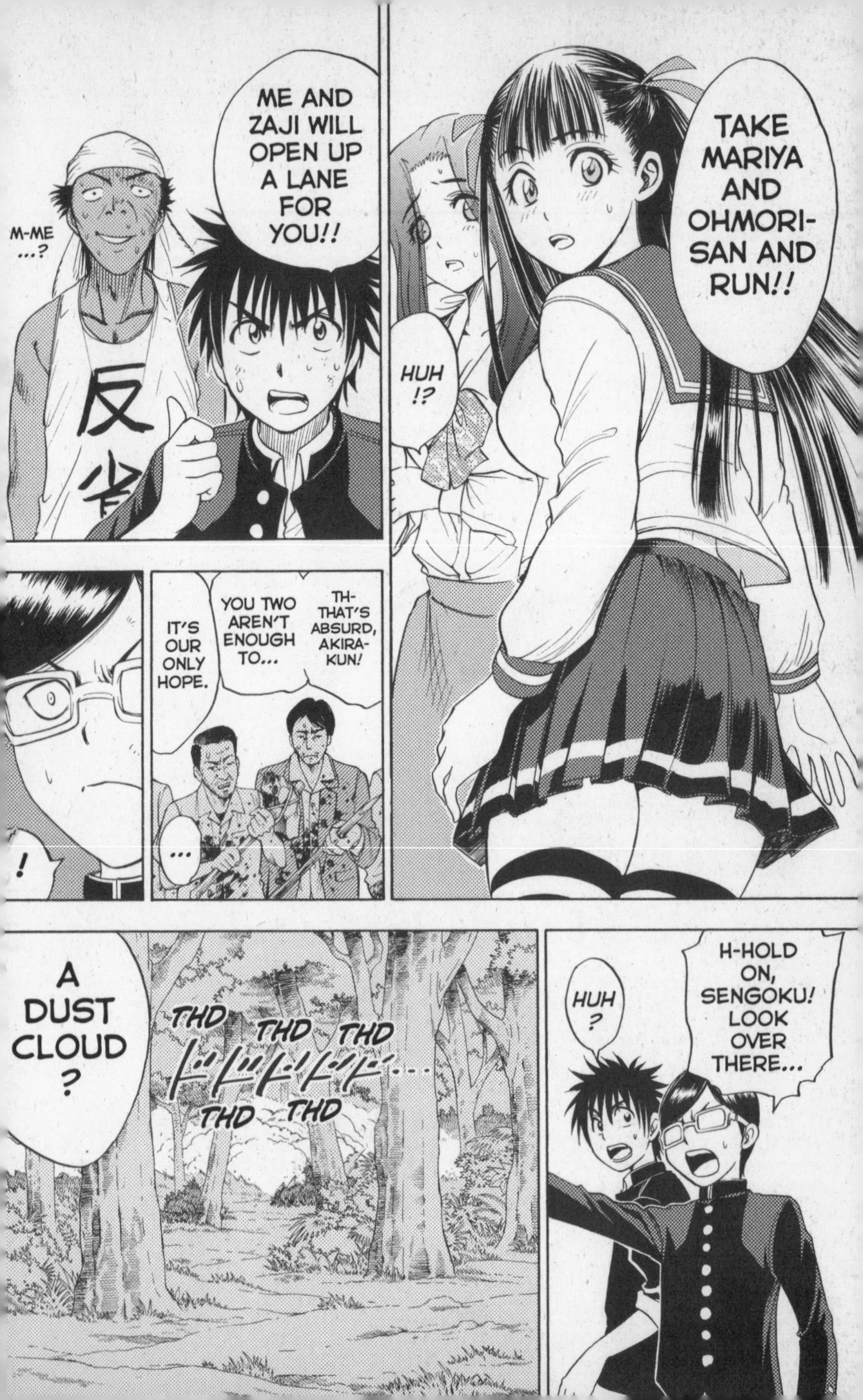
TAKE MARIYA AND OHMORI-SAN AND RUN!!
HUH!?
ME AND ZAJI WILL OPEN UP A LANE FOR YOU!!
M-ME...?
TH-THAT'S ABSURD, AKIRA-KUN!
YOU TWO AREN'T ENOUGH TO...
IT'S OUR ONLY HOPE.
...
!
H-HOLD ON, SENGOKU! LOOK OVER THERE...
HUH?
THD THD THD
ドドドドド...
THD THD
A DUST CLOUD?

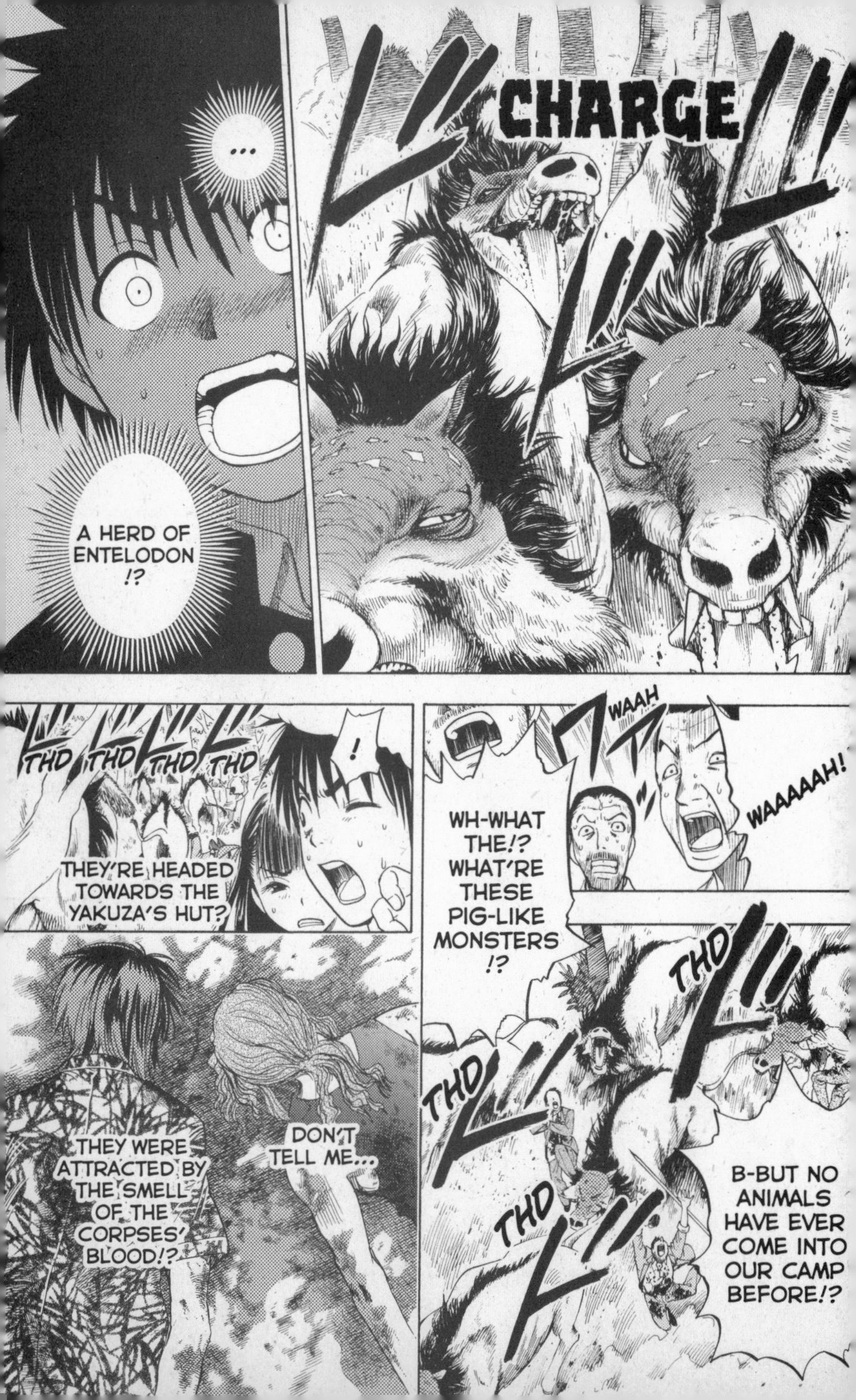
CHARGE
...
A HERD OF ENTELODON !?
WAAH
WAAAAAH!
WH-WHAT THE!? WHAT'RE THESE PIG-LIKE MONSTERS !?
THD THD THD THD
!
THEY'RE HEADED TOWARDS THE YAKUZA'S HUT?
THD
THD
THD
B-BUT NO ANIMALS HAVE EVER COME INTO OUR CAMP BEFORE!?
DON'T TELL ME...
THEY WERE ATTRACTED BY THE SMELL OF THE CORPSES' BLOOD!?

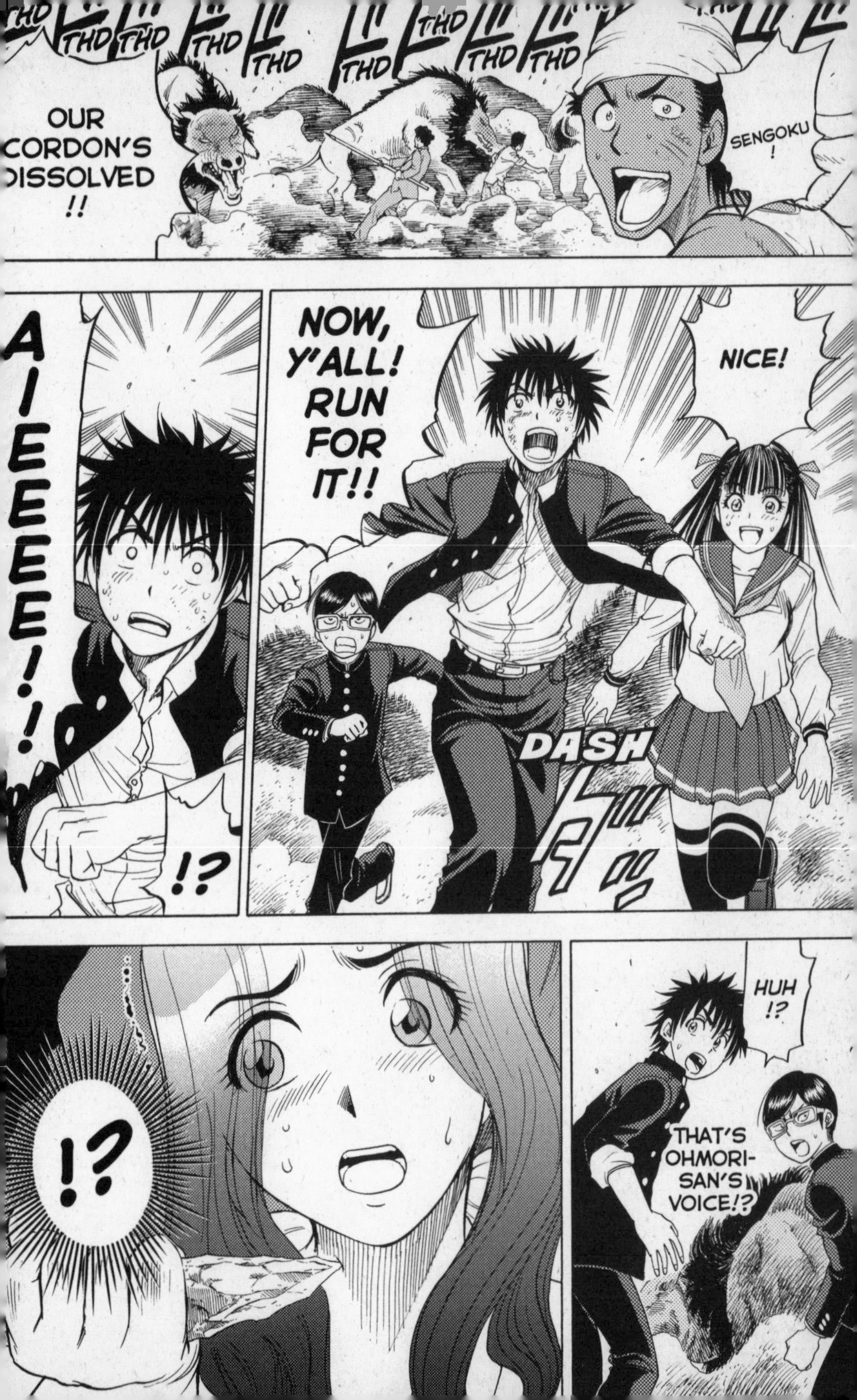
THD THD THD THD THD THD THD THD THD
SENGOKU!
OUR CORDON'S DISSOLVED!!
NICE!
NOW, Y'ALL! RUN FOR IT!!
DASH
AIEEEEE!!!
!?
HUH!?
THAT'S OHMORI-SAN'S VOICE!?
!?

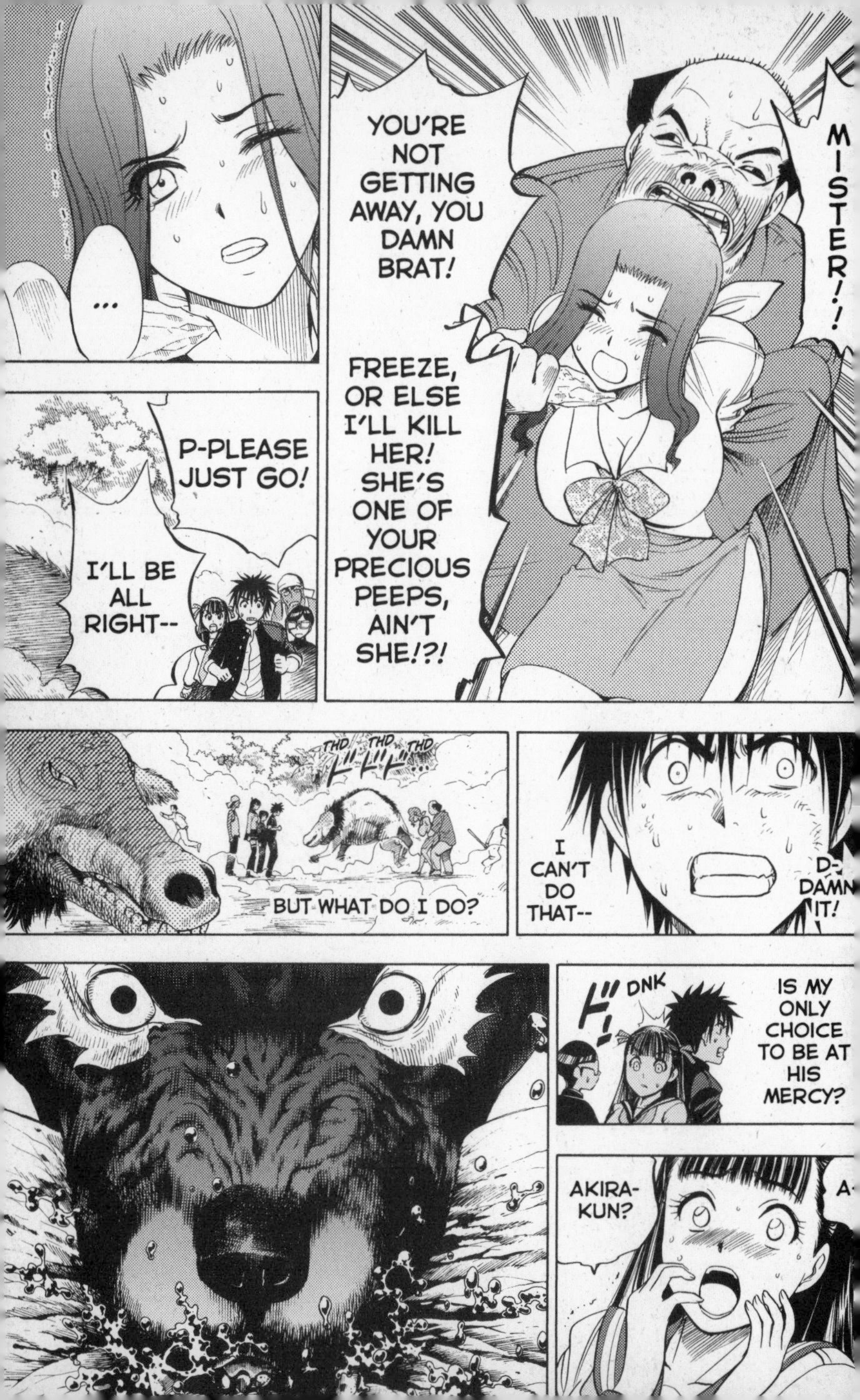
MISTER!!
YOU'RE NOT GETTING AWAY, YOU DAMN BRAT!
FREEZE, OR ELSE I'LL KILL HER! SHE'S ONE OF YOUR PRECIOUS PEEPS, AIN'T SHE!?!
...
P-PLEASE JUST GO!
I'LL BE ALL RIGHT--
D-DAMN IT!
I CAN'T DO THAT--
THD THD THD
BUT WHAT DO I DO?
IS MY ONLY CHOICE TO BE AT HIS MERCY?
DNK
A-
AKIRA-KUN?

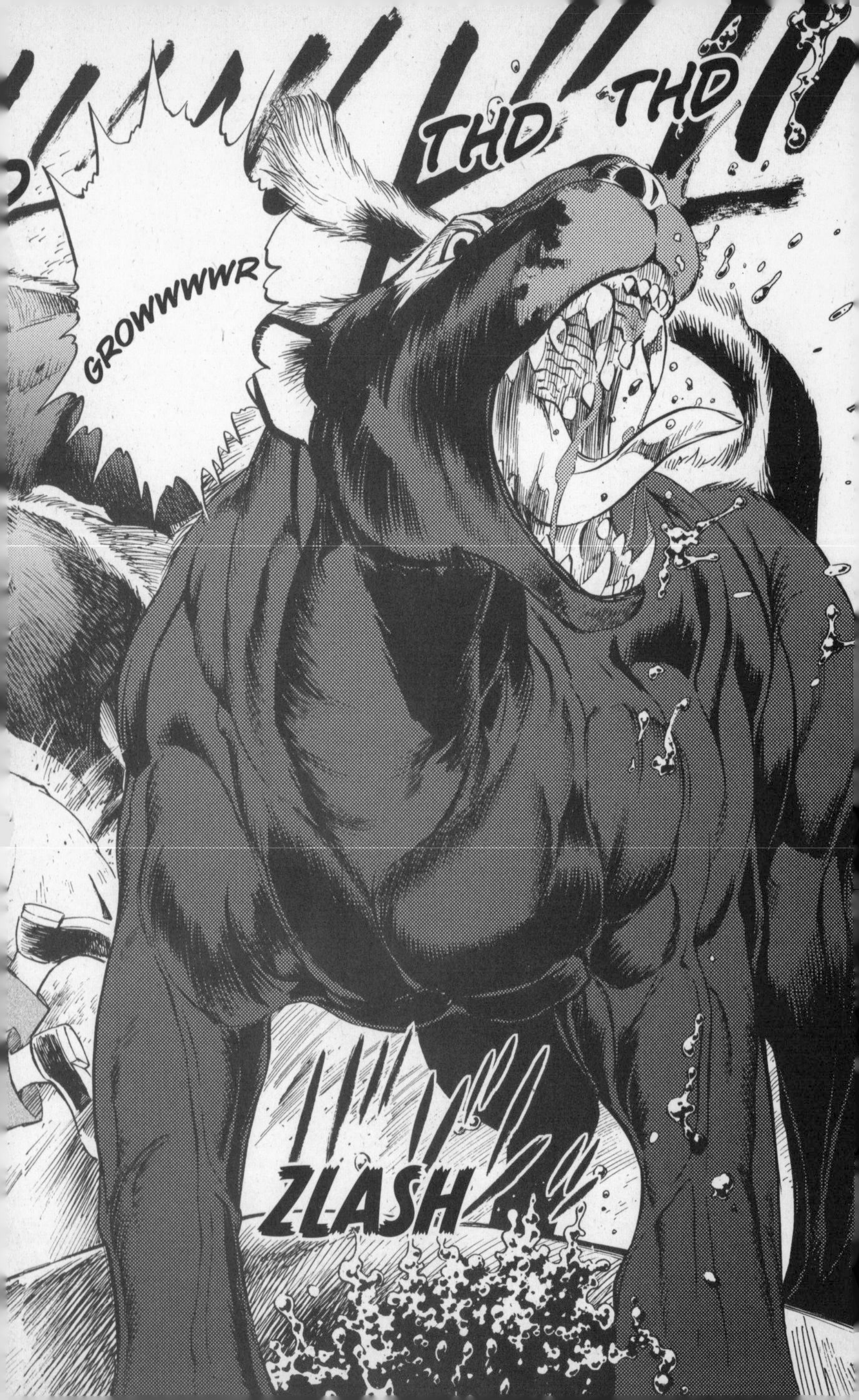
THD
THD
GROWWWWR
ZLASH

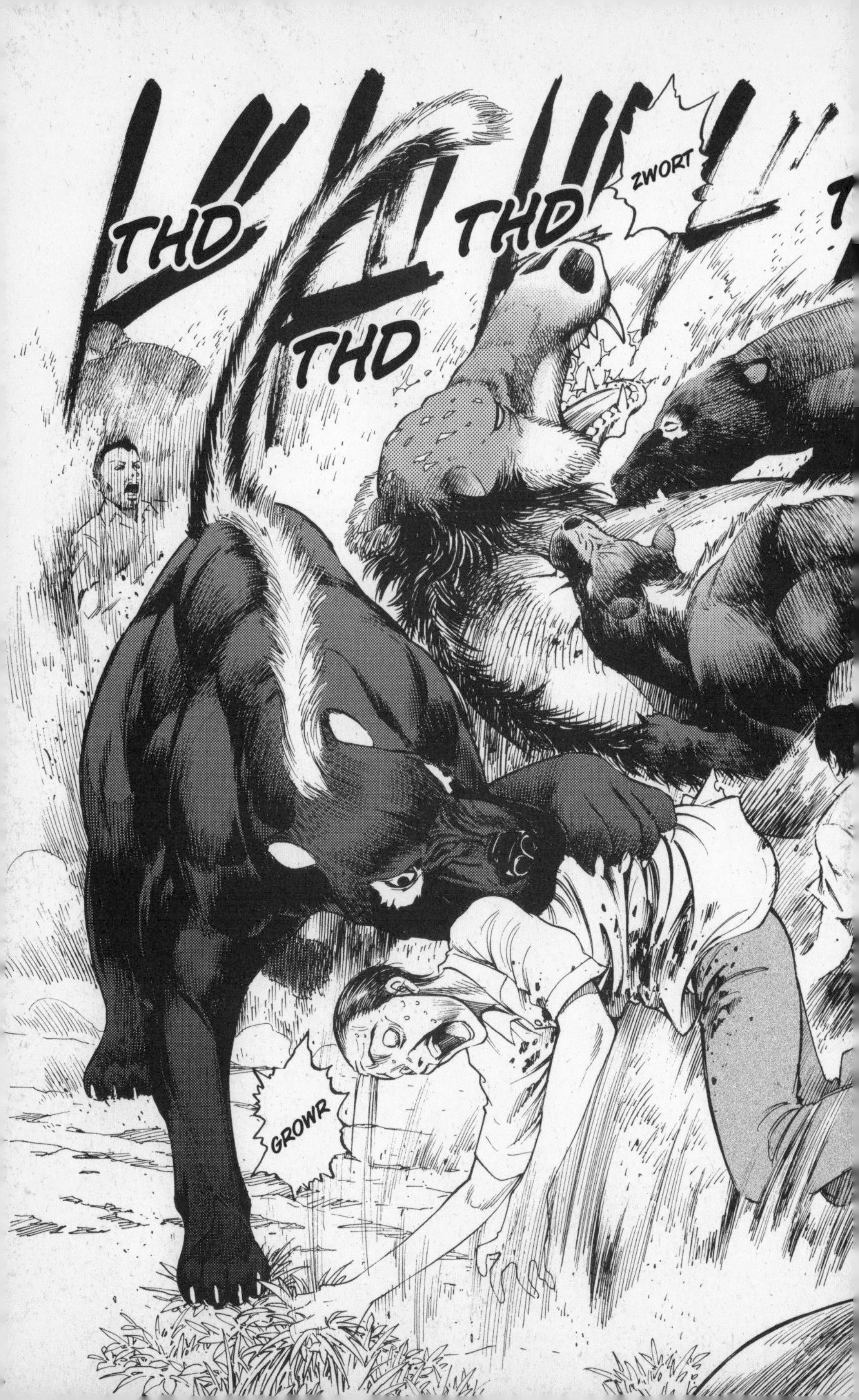
ZWORT
THD
THD
THD
GROWR

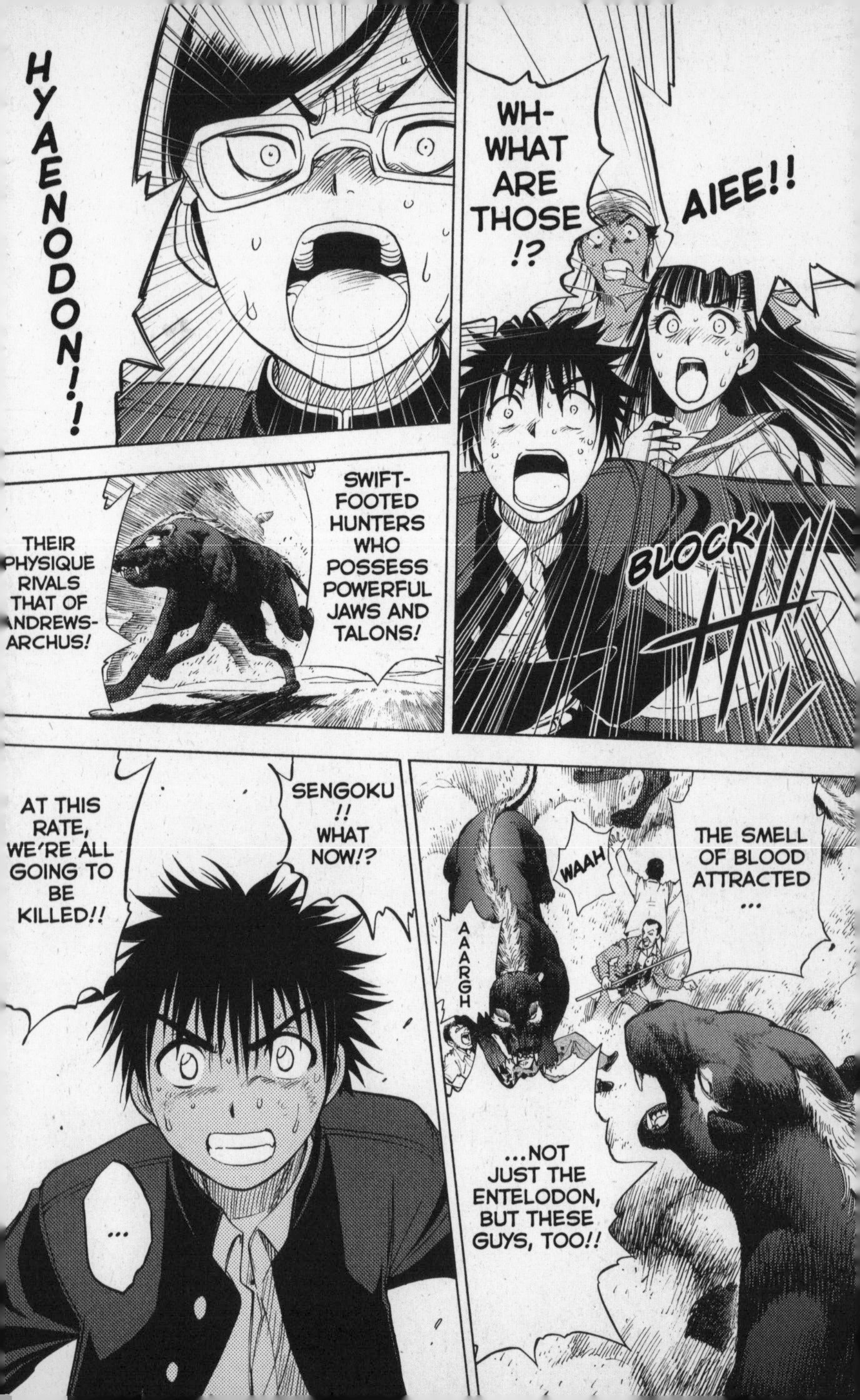
AIEE!!
WH- WHAT ARE THOSE !?
BLOCK
HYAENODON!!
SWIFT-FOOTED HUNTERS WHO POSSESS POWERFUL JAWS AND TALONS!
THEIR PHYSIQUE RIVALS THAT OF ANDREWS-ARCHUS!
THE SMELL OF BLOOD ATTRACTED ...
WAAH
AAARGH
...NOT JUST THE ENTELODON, BUT THESE GUYS, TOO!!
SENGOKU !! WHAT NOW!?
AT THIS RATE, WE'RE ALL GOING TO BE KILLED!!
...

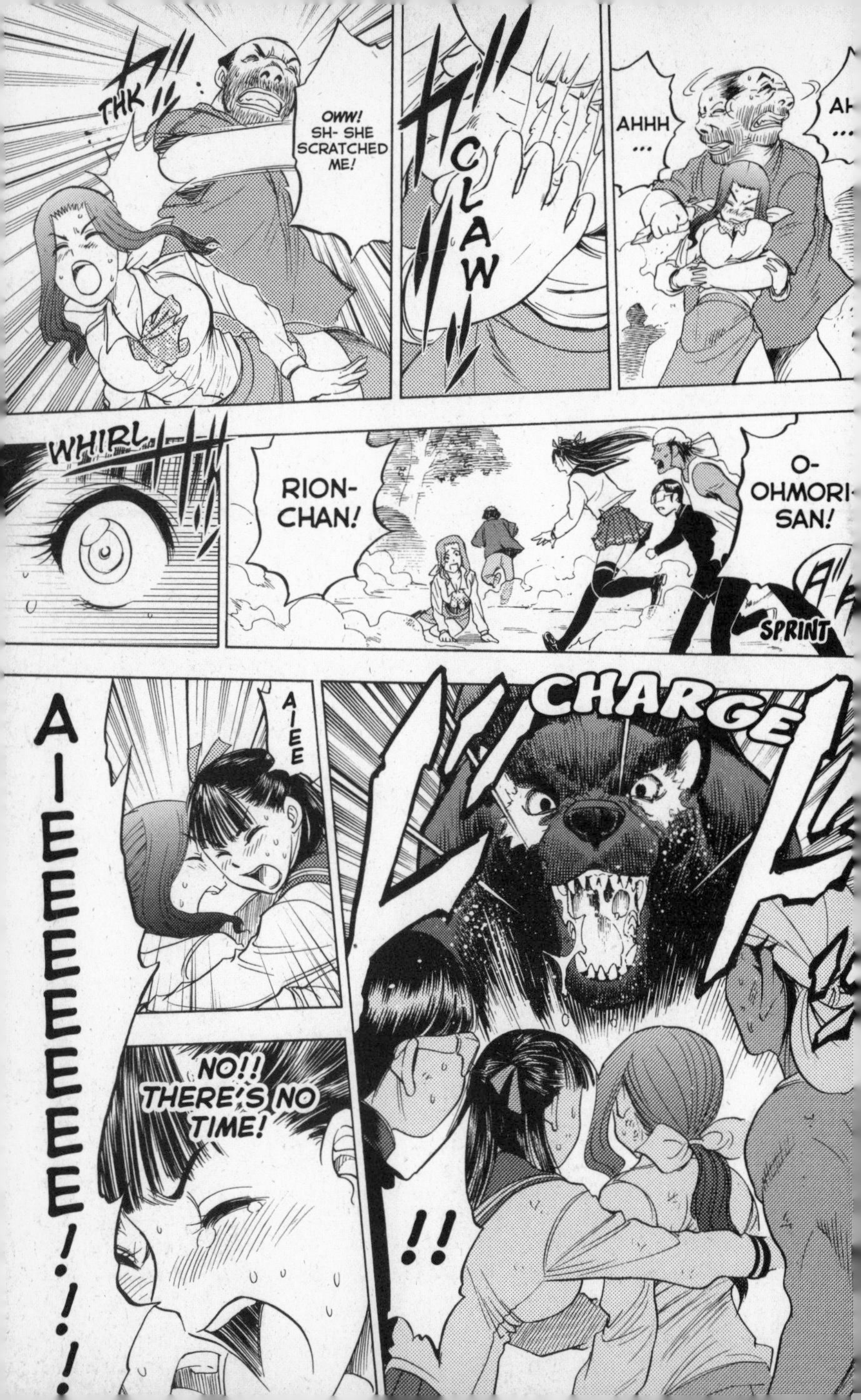
AH ...
AHHH ...
CLAW
THK
OWW! SH- SHE SCRATCHED ME!
O- OHMORI-SAN!
SPRINT
RION-CHAN!
WHIRL
CHARGE
!!
AIEE
NO!! THERE'S NO TIME!
AIEEEEEEE!!!

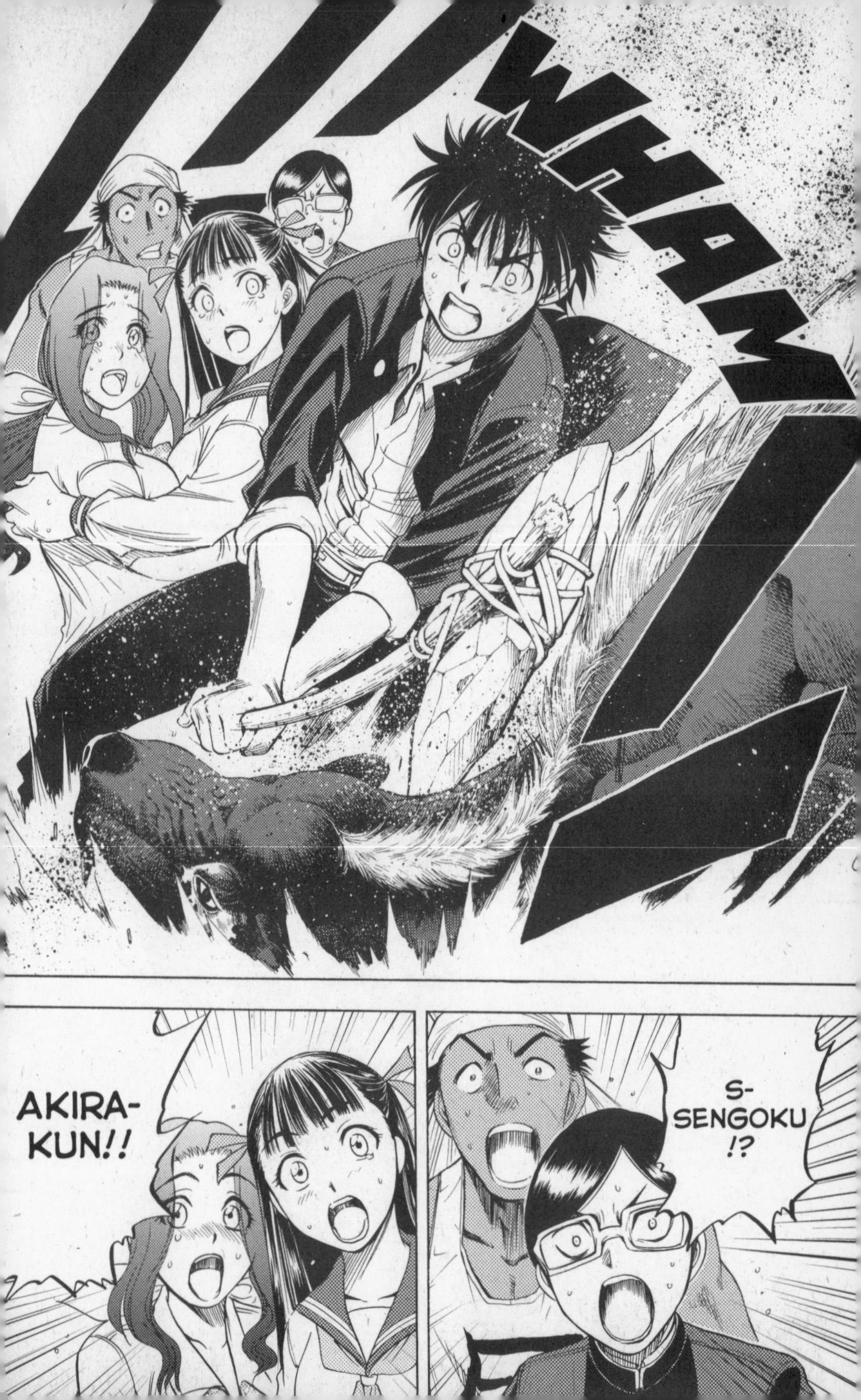
WHAM!
S-SENGOKU!?
AKIRA-KUN!!

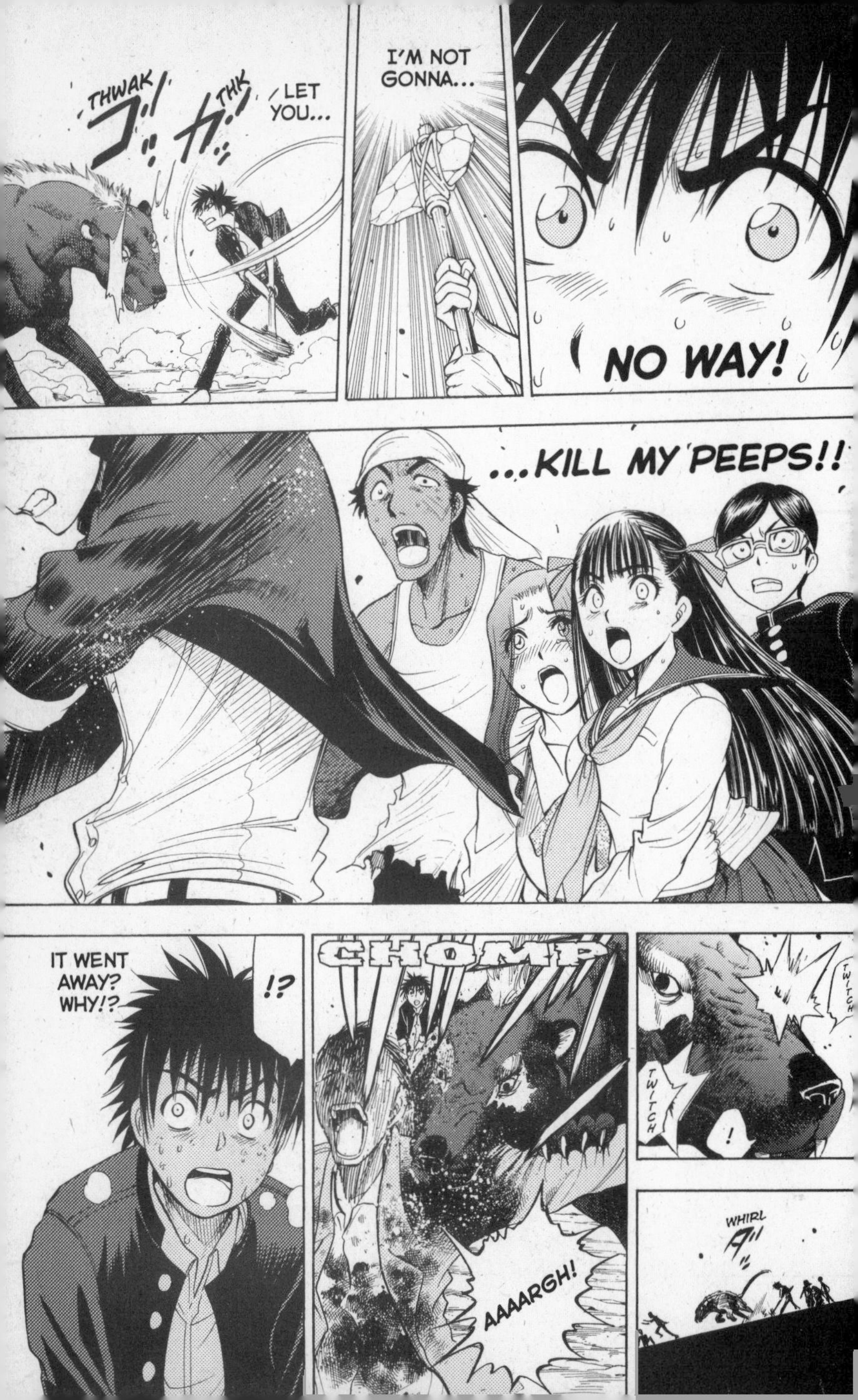
NO WAY!
I'M NOT GONNA...
LET YOU...
THK
THWAK
...KILL MY PEEPS!!
TWITCH
TWITCH
!
WHIRL
CHOMP
AAAARGH!
!?
IT WENT AWAY? WHY!?

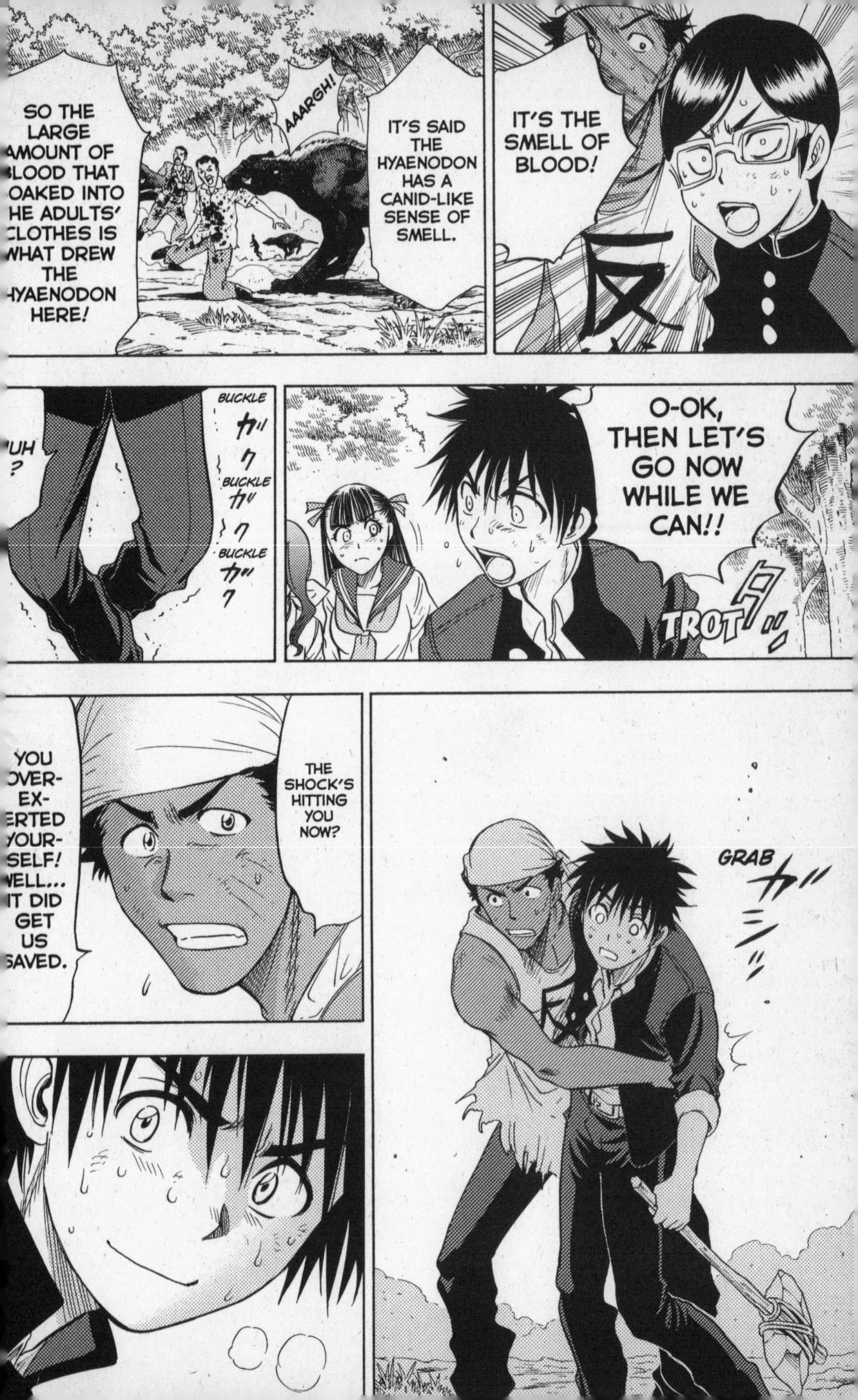
IT'S THE SMELL OF BLOOD!
IT'S SAID THE HYAENODON HAS A CANID-LIKE SENSE OF SMELL.
AAARGH!
SO THE LARGE AMOUNT OF BLOOD THAT SOAKED INTO THE ADULTS' CLOTHES IS WHAT DREW THE HYAENODON HERE!
O-OK, THEN LET'S GO NOW WHILE WE CAN!!
TROT タッ
BUCKLE ガク
BUCKLE ガク
BUCKLE ガク
HUH?
GRAB ガッ
THE SHOCK'S HITTING YOU NOW?
YOU OVER-EXERTED YOURSELF! WELL... IT DID GET US SAVED.

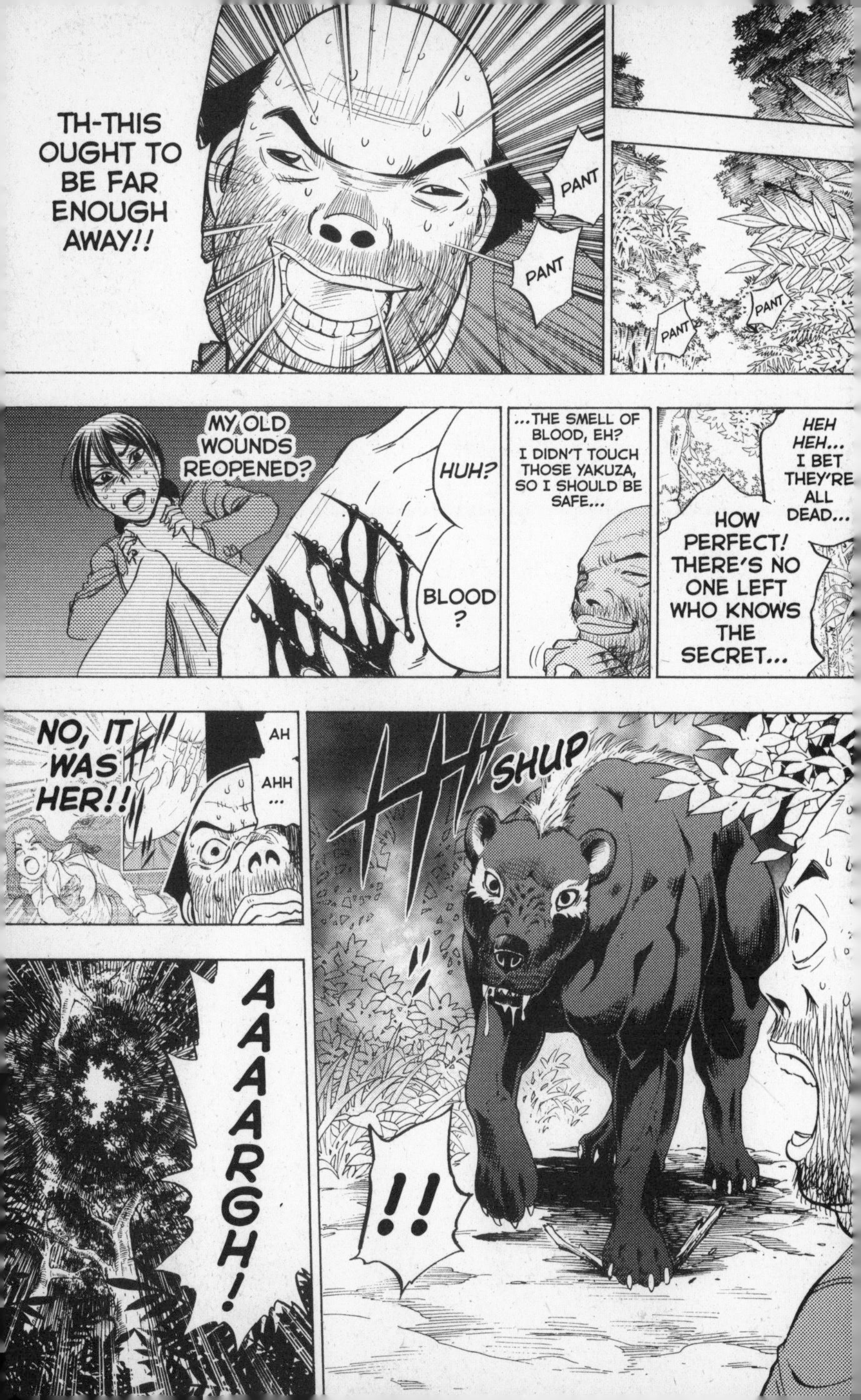
PANT
PANT
PANT
PANT
TH-THIS OUGHT TO BE FAR ENOUGH AWAY!!
HEH HEH... I BET THEY'RE ALL DEAD...
HOW PERFECT! THERE'S NO ONE LEFT WHO KNOWS THE SECRET...
...THE SMELL OF BLOOD, EH? I DIDN'T TOUCH THOSE YAKUZA, SO I SHOULD BE SAFE...
HUH?
BLOOD ?
MY OLD WOUNDS REOPENED?
SHUP
!!
AH
AHH ...
NO, IT WAS HER!!
AAAARGH!

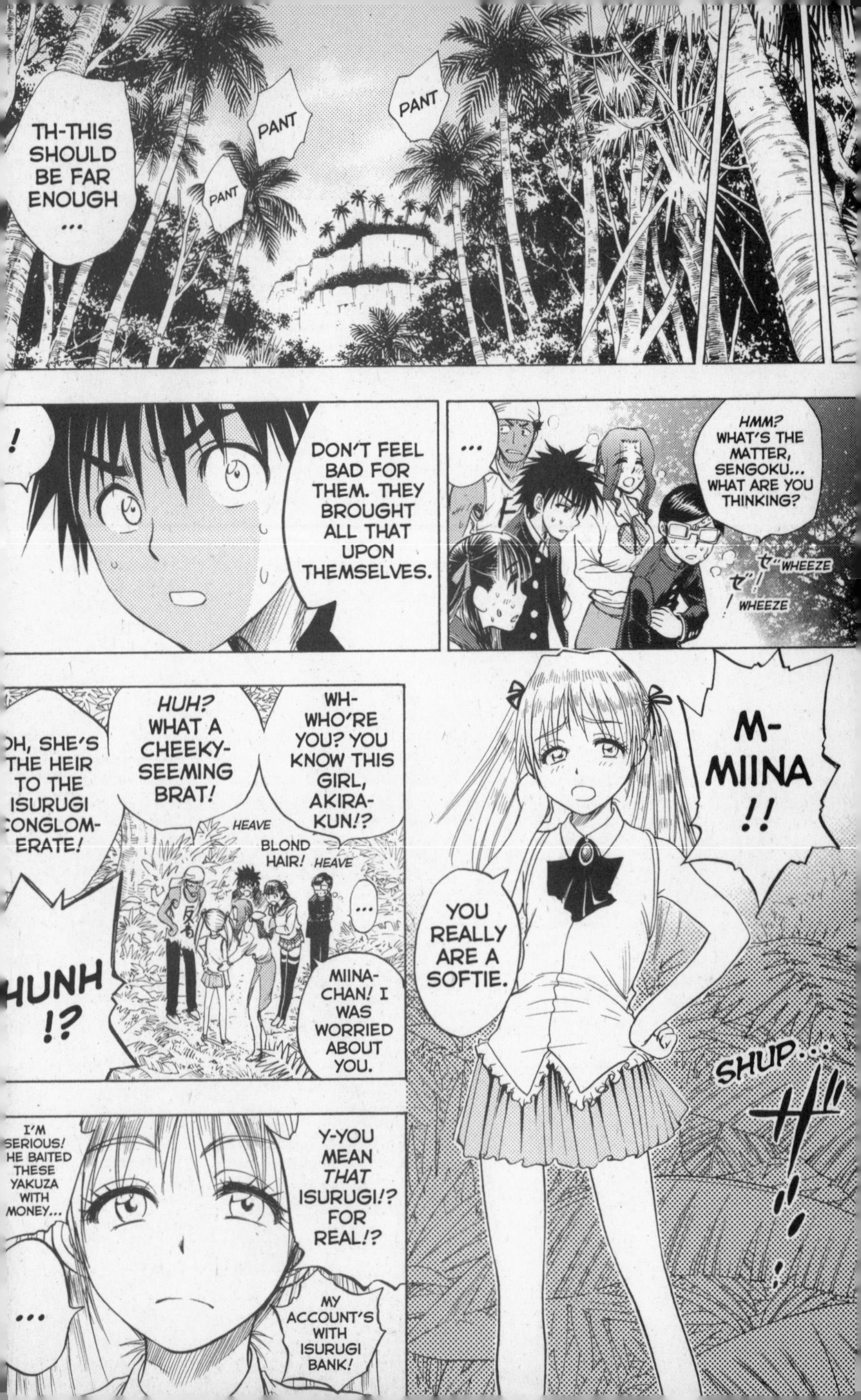
PANT
PANT
PANT
TH-THIS SHOULD BE FAR ENOUGH...
HMM? WHAT'S THE MATTER, SENGOKU... WHAT ARE YOU THINKING?
...
WHEEZE
WHEEZE
DON'T FEEL BAD FOR THEM. THEY BROUGHT ALL THAT UPON THEMSELVES.
!
M-MIINA!!
YOU REALLY ARE A SOFTIE.
SHUP...
WH-WHO'RE YOU? YOU KNOW THIS GIRL, AKIRA-KUN!?
HUH? WHAT A CHEEKY-SEEMING BRAT!
OH, SHE'S THE HEIR TO THE ISURUGI CONGLOMERATE!
HEAVE
BLOND HAIR!
HEAVE
...
MIINA-CHAN! I WAS WORRIED ABOUT YOU.
HUNH!?
Y-YOU MEAN THAT ISURUGI!? FOR REAL!?
I'M SERIOUS! HE BAITED THESE YAKUZA WITH MONEY...
MY ACCOUNT'S WITH ISURUGI BANK!
...

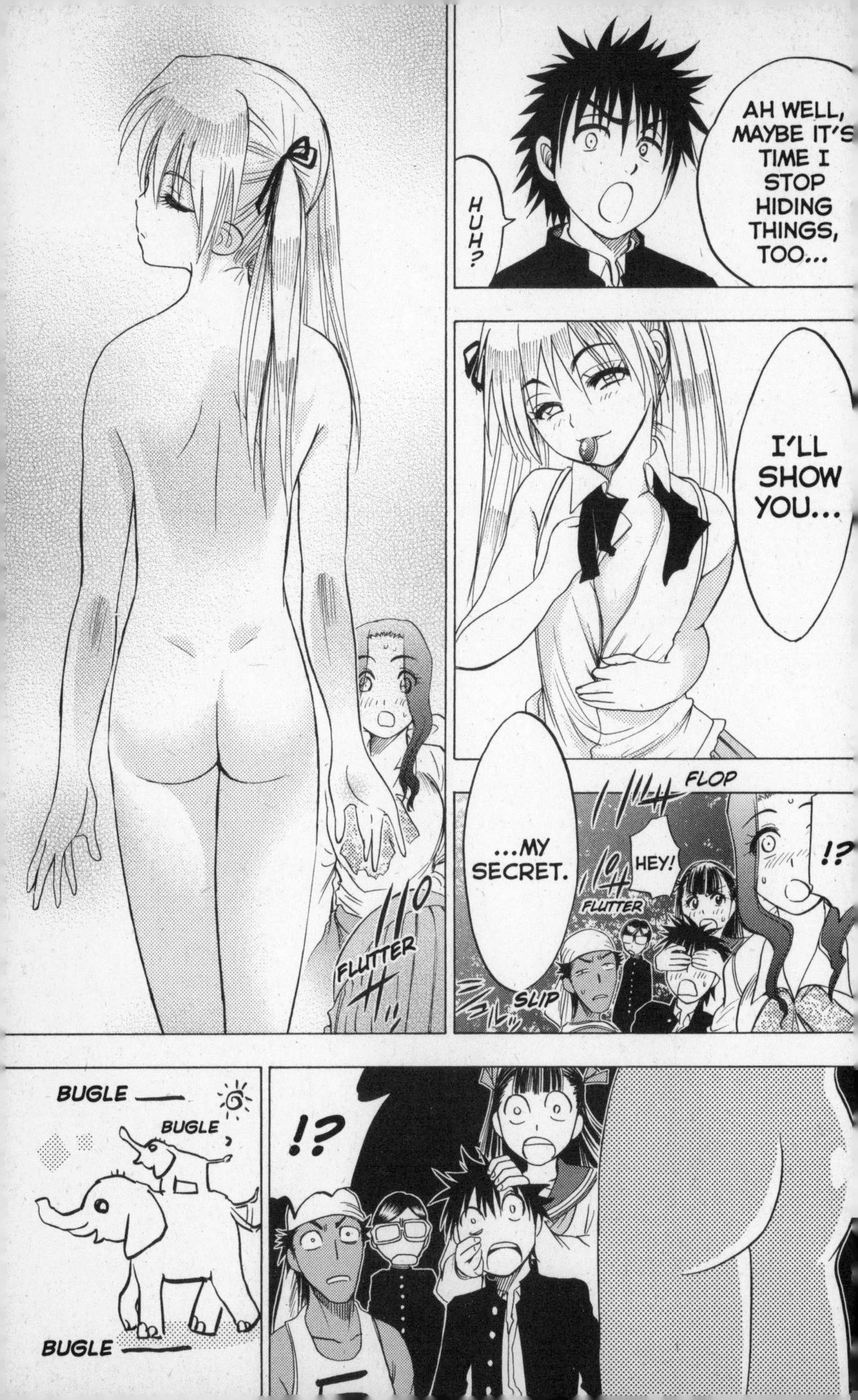
AH WELL, MAYBE IT'S TIME I STOP HIDING THINGS, TOO...
HUH?
I'LL SHOW YOU...
...MY SECRET.
FLOP
!?
HEY!
FLUTTER
SLIP
FLUTTER
!?
BUGLE
BUGLE
BUGLE

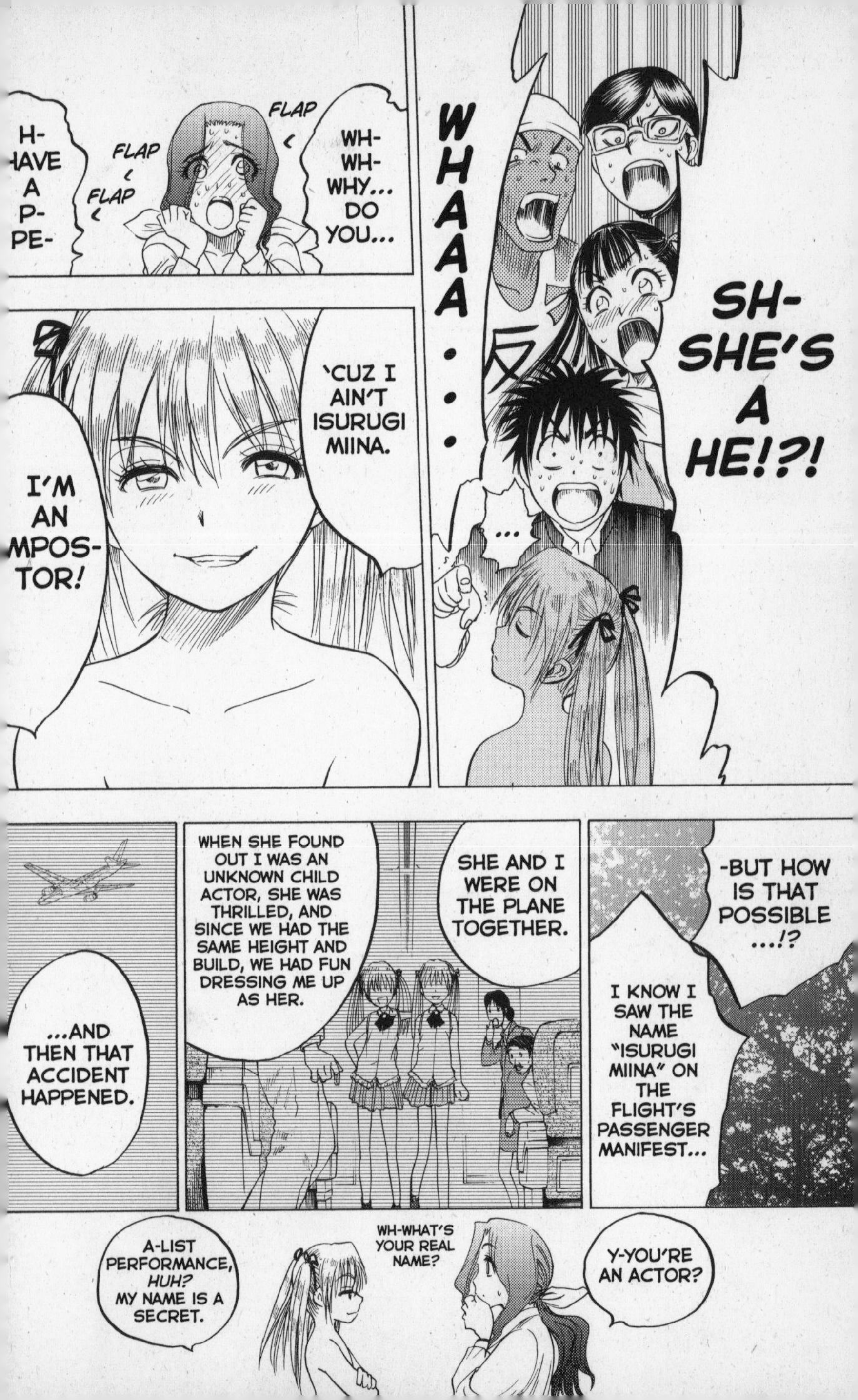

WHAAAA...
SH-SHE'S A HE!?!
...
WH-WH-WHY... DO YOU...
FLAP FLAP FLAP
H-HAVE A P-PE-
'CUZ I AIN'T ISURUGI MIINA.
I'M AN MPOS-TOR!
-BUT HOW IS THAT POSSIBLE...!?
I KNOW I SAW THE NAME "ISURUGI MIINA" ON THE FLIGHT'S PASSENGER MANIFEST...
SHE AND I WERE ON THE PLANE TOGETHER.
WHEN SHE FOUND OUT I WAS AN UNKNOWN CHILD ACTOR, SHE WAS THRILLED, AND SINCE WE HAD THE SAME HEIGHT AND BUILD, WE HAD FUN DRESSING ME UP AS HER.
...AND THEN THAT ACCIDENT HAPPENED.
Y-YOU'RE AN ACTOR?
WH-WHAT'S YOUR REAL NAME?
A-LIST PERFORMANCE, HUH? MY NAME IS A SECRET.

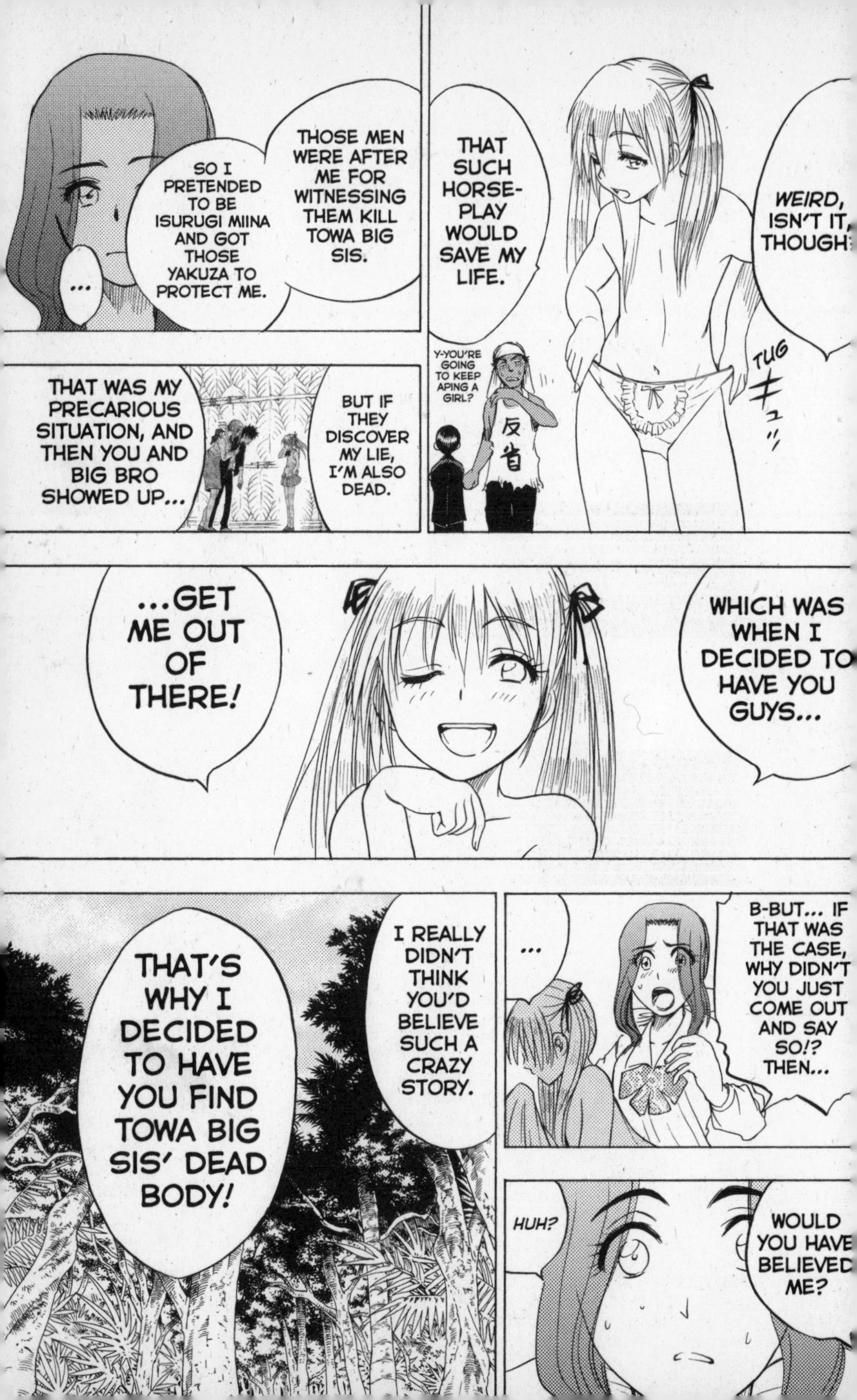
WEIRD, ISN'T IT, THOUGH?
THAT SUCH HORSE-PLAY WOULD SAVE MY LIFE.
TUG
Y-YOU'RE GOING TO KEEP APING A GIRL?
反省
THOSE MEN WERE AFTER ME FOR WITNESSING THEM KILL TOWA BIG SIS.
SO I PRETENDED TO BE ISURUGI MIINA AND GOT THOSE YAKUZA TO PROTECT ME.
...
BUT IF THEY DISCOVER MY LIE, I'M ALSO DEAD.
THAT WAS MY PRECARIOUS SITUATION, AND THEN YOU AND BIG BRO SHOWED UP...
WHICH WAS WHEN I DECIDED TO HAVE YOU GUYS...
...GET ME OUT OF THERE!
B-BUT... IF THAT WAS THE CASE, WHY DIDN'T YOU JUST COME OUT AND SAY SO!? THEN...
...
WOULD YOU HAVE BELIEVED ME?
HUH?
I REALLY DIDN'T THINK YOU'D BELIEVE SUCH A CRAZY STORY.
THAT'S WHY I DECIDED TO HAVE YOU FIND TOWA BIG SIS' DEAD BODY!

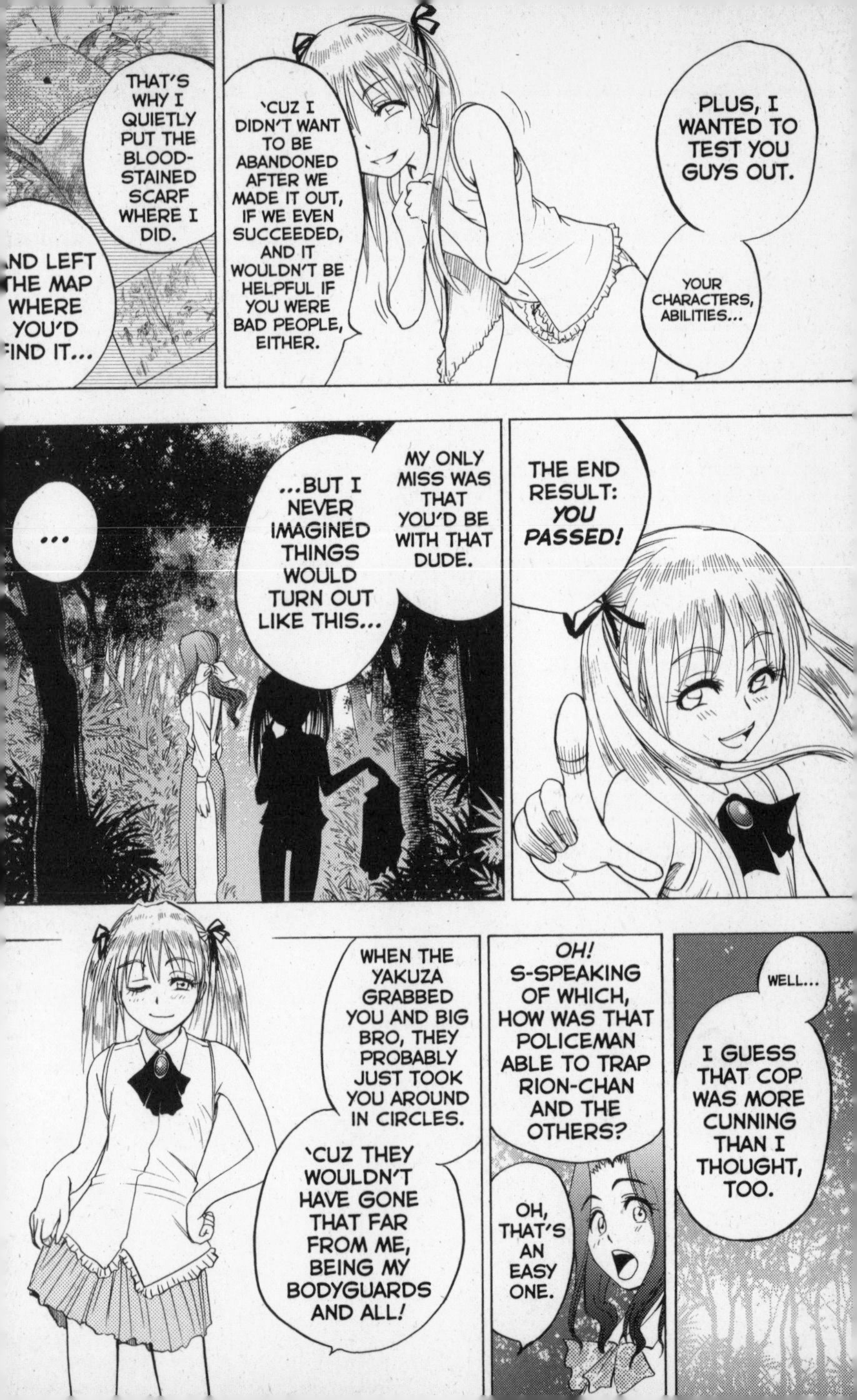
PLUS, I WANTED TO TEST YOU GUYS OUT.
YOUR CHARACTERS, ABILITIES...
'CUZ I DIDN'T WANT TO BE ABANDONED AFTER WE MADE IT OUT, IF WE EVEN SUCCEEDED, AND IT WOULDN'T BE HELPFUL IF YOU WERE BAD PEOPLE, EITHER.
THAT'S WHY I QUIETLY PUT THE BLOOD-STAINED SCARF WHERE I DID.
AND LEFT THE MAP WHERE YOU'D FIND IT...
THE END RESULT: *YOU PASSED!*
MY ONLY MISS WAS THAT YOU'D BE WITH THAT DUDE.
...BUT I NEVER IMAGINED THINGS WOULD TURN OUT LIKE THIS...
...
WELL...
I GUESS THAT COP WAS MORE CUNNING THAN I THOUGHT, TOO.
OH! S-SPEAKING OF WHICH, HOW WAS THAT POLICEMAN ABLE TO TRAP RION-CHAN AND THE OTHERS?
OH, THAT'S AN EASY ONE.
WHEN THE YAKUZA GRABBED YOU AND BIG BRO, THEY PROBABLY JUST TOOK YOU AROUND IN CIRCLES.
'CUZ THEY WOULDN'T HAVE GONE THAT FAR FROM ME, BEING MY BODYGUARDS AND ALL!

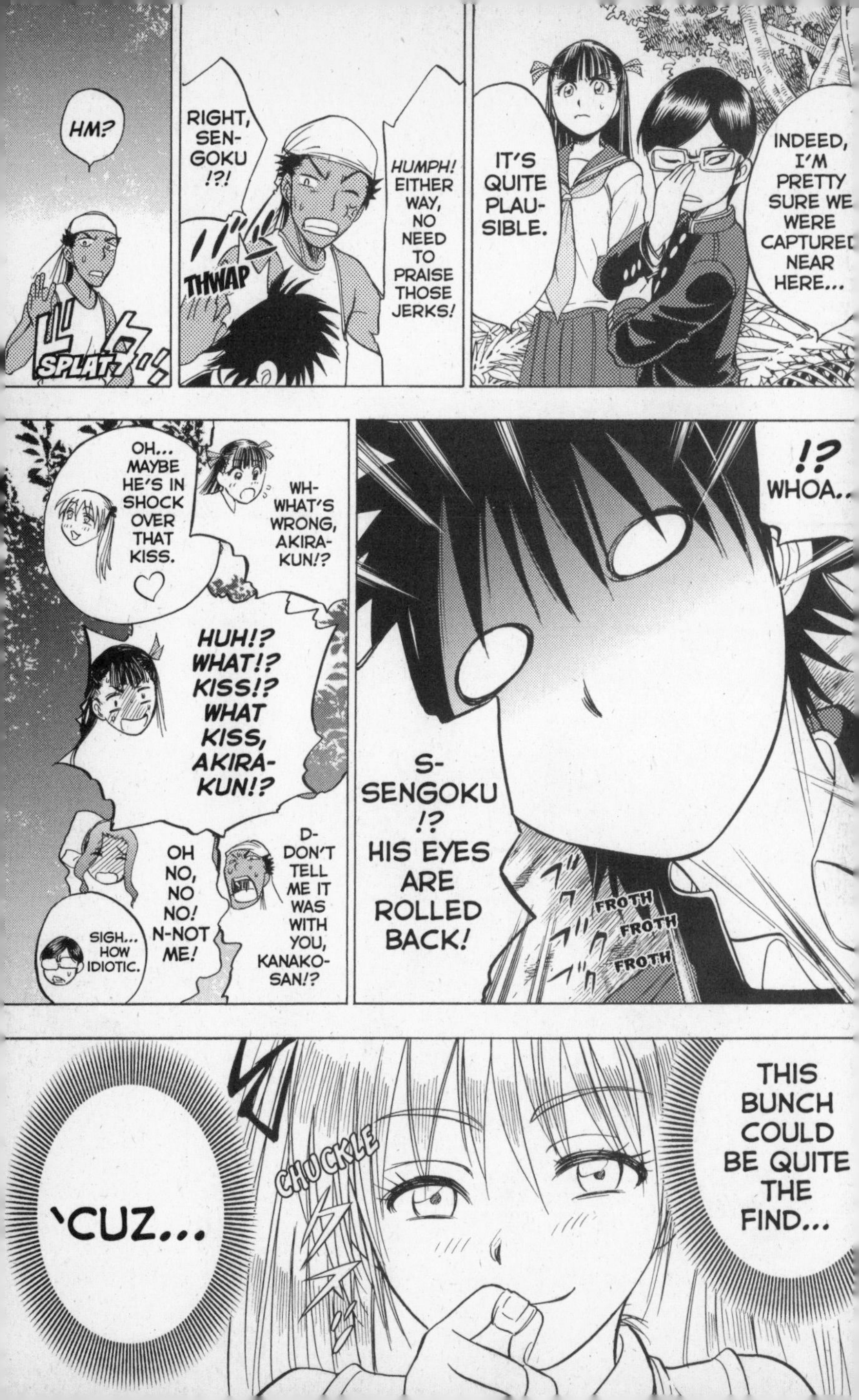
INDEED, I'M PRETTY SURE WE WERE CAPTURED NEAR HERE...
IT'S QUITE PLAUSIBLE.
HUMPH! EITHER WAY, NO NEED TO PRAISE THOSE JERKS!
RIGHT, SENGOKU !?!
THWAP
HM?
SPLAT
!? WHOA...
S-SENGOKU !? HIS EYES ARE ROLLED BACK!
FROTH FROTH FROTH
WH-WHAT'S WRONG, AKIRA-KUN!?
OH... MAYBE HE'S IN SHOCK OVER THAT KISS. ♡
HUH!? WHAT!? KISS!? WHAT KISS, AKIRA-KUN!?
D-DON'T TELL ME IT WAS WITH YOU, KANAKO-SAN!?
OH NO, NO NO! N-NOT ME!
SIGH... HOW IDIOTIC.
THIS BUNCH COULD BE QUITE THE FIND...
CHUCKLE
'CUZ...

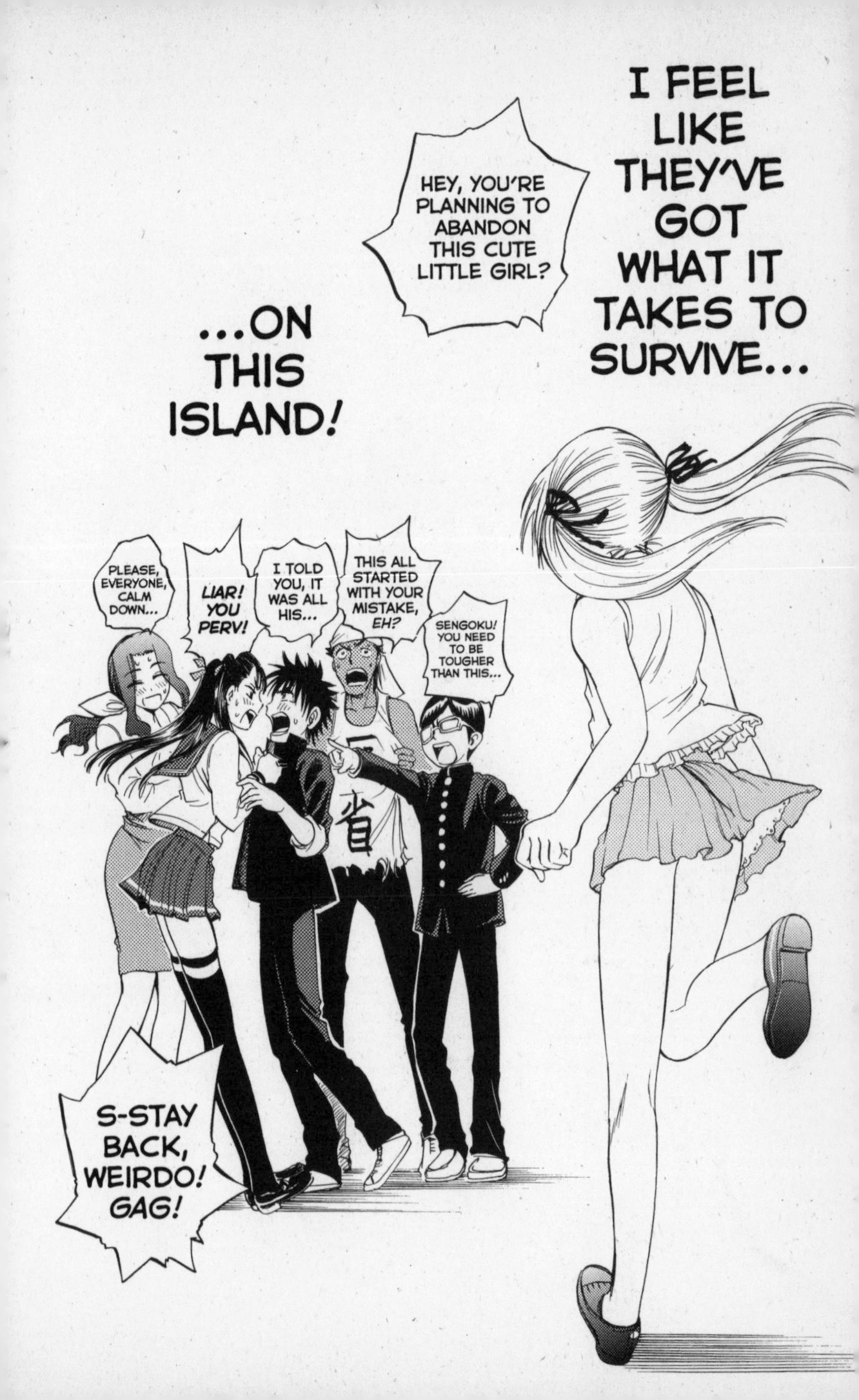
I FEEL LIKE THEY'VE GOT WHAT IT TAKES TO SURVIVE...
HEY, YOU'RE PLANNING TO ABANDON THIS CUTE LITTLE GIRL?
...ON THIS ISLAND!
SENGOKU! YOU NEED TO BE TOUGHER THAN THIS...
THIS ALL STARTED WITH YOUR MISTAKE, EH?
I TOLD YOU, IT WAS ALL HIS...
LIAR! YOU PERV!
PLEASE, EVERYONE, CALM DOWN...
S-STAY BACK, WEIRDO! GAG!

S-SO MIINA-CHAN, THAT STORY ABOUT YOU MARRYING THAT OLDER MAN...
ALL LIES. ♡
WHAT!? WHY WOULD YOU TELL SUCH A LIE!?
LEAVE ME ALONE.
IT WAS PAINFUL FOR ME, TOO! THE BLOOD ON THAT SCARF WAS MINE!
AND WHY DID YOU KISS SENGOKU-KUN... *UNNH?*
Smooch

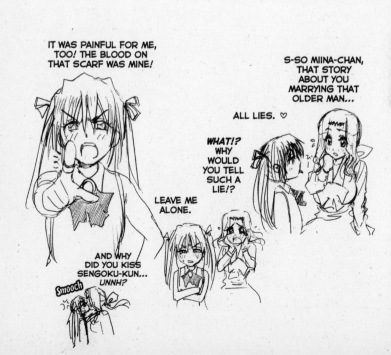

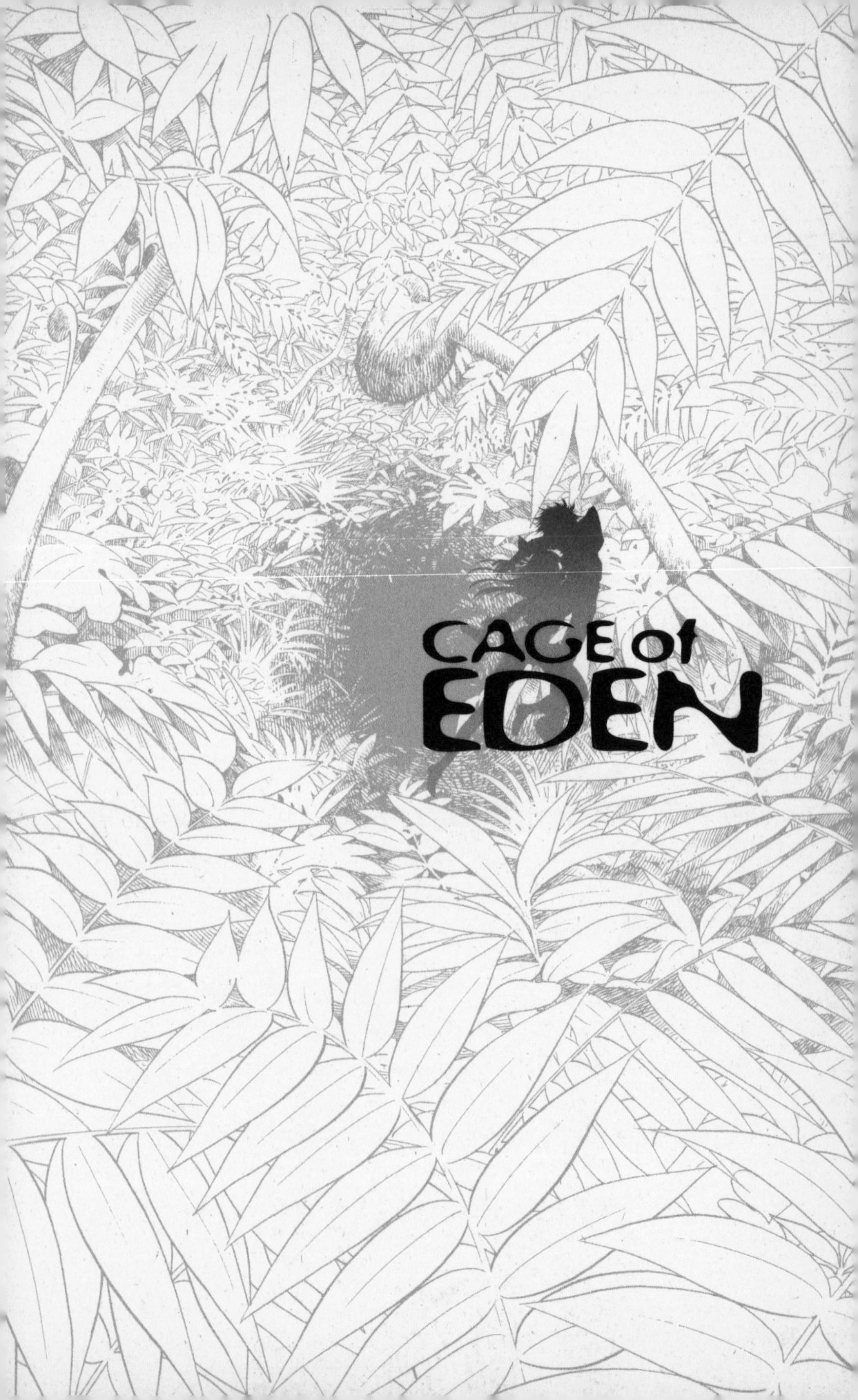
CAGE of
EDEN

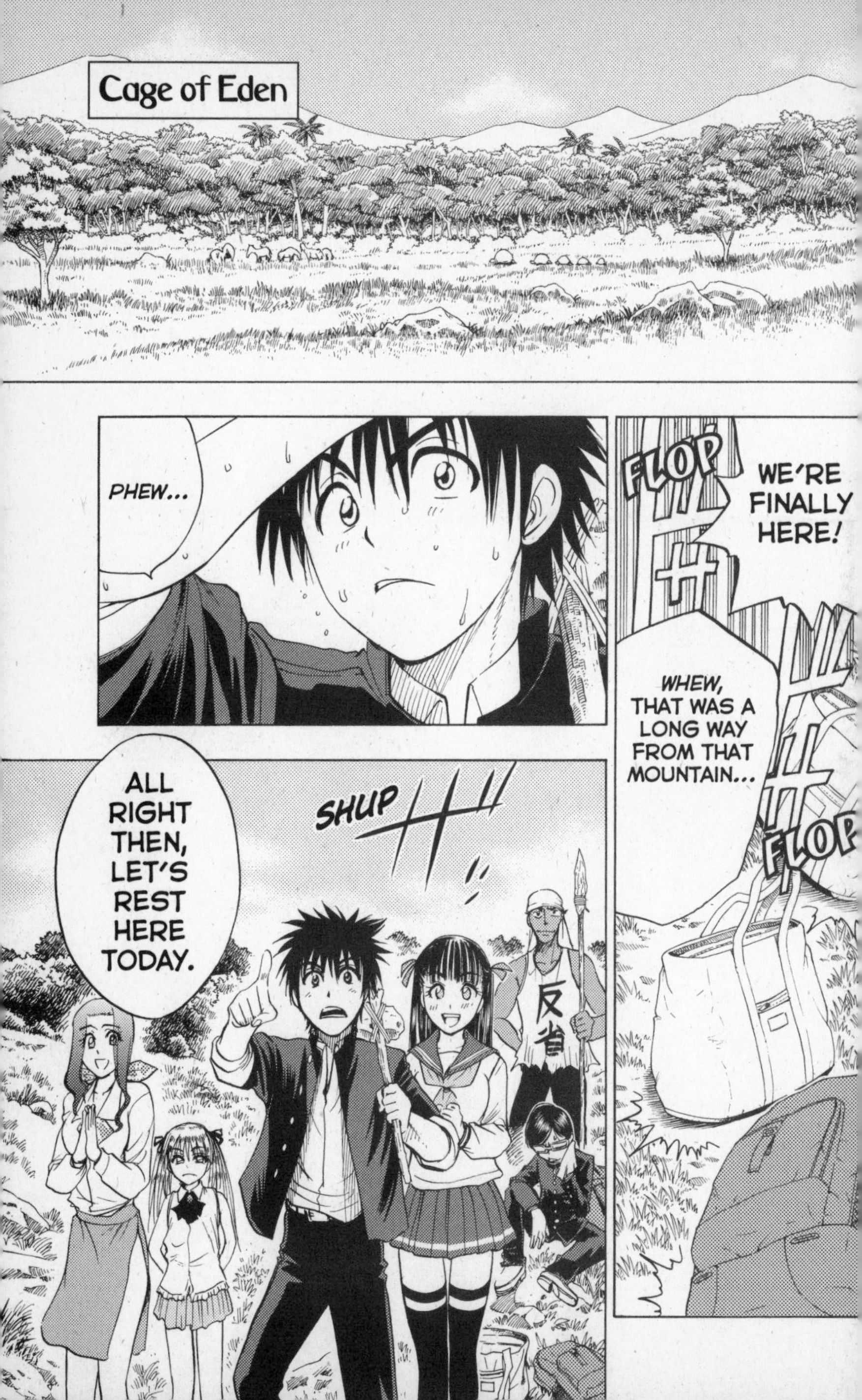
Cage of Eden
FLOP
WE'RE FINALLY HERE!
WHEW, THAT WAS A LONG WAY FROM THAT MOUNTAIN...
FLOP
PHEW...
ALL RIGHT THEN, LET'S REST HERE TODAY.
SHUP

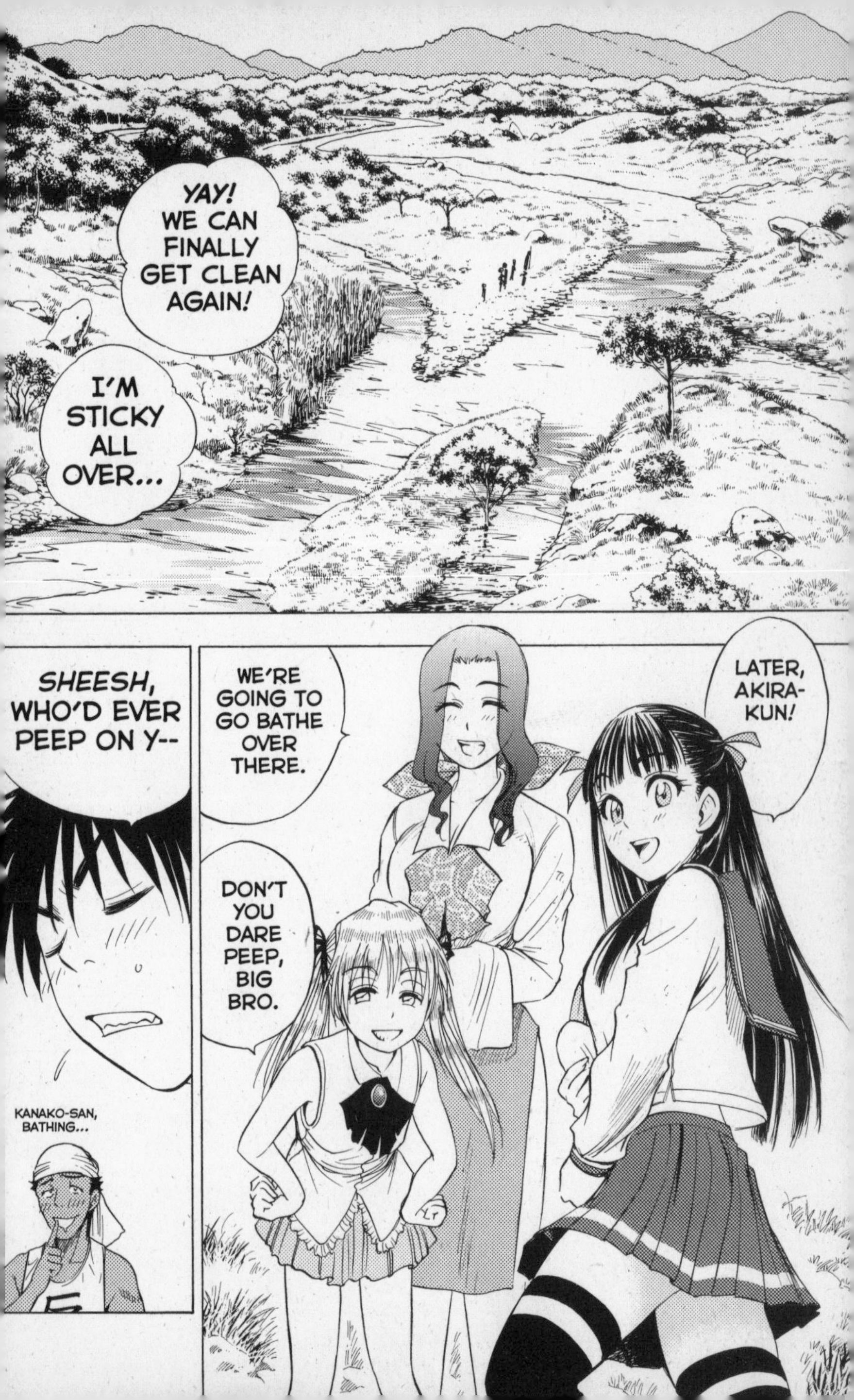
YAY! WE CAN FINALLY GET CLEAN AGAIN!
I'M STICKY ALL OVER...
LATER, AKIRA-KUN!
WE'RE GOING TO GO BATHE OVER THERE.
DON'T YOU DARE PEEP, BIG BRO.
SHEESH, WHO'D EVER PEEP ON Y--
KANAKO-SAN, BATHING...

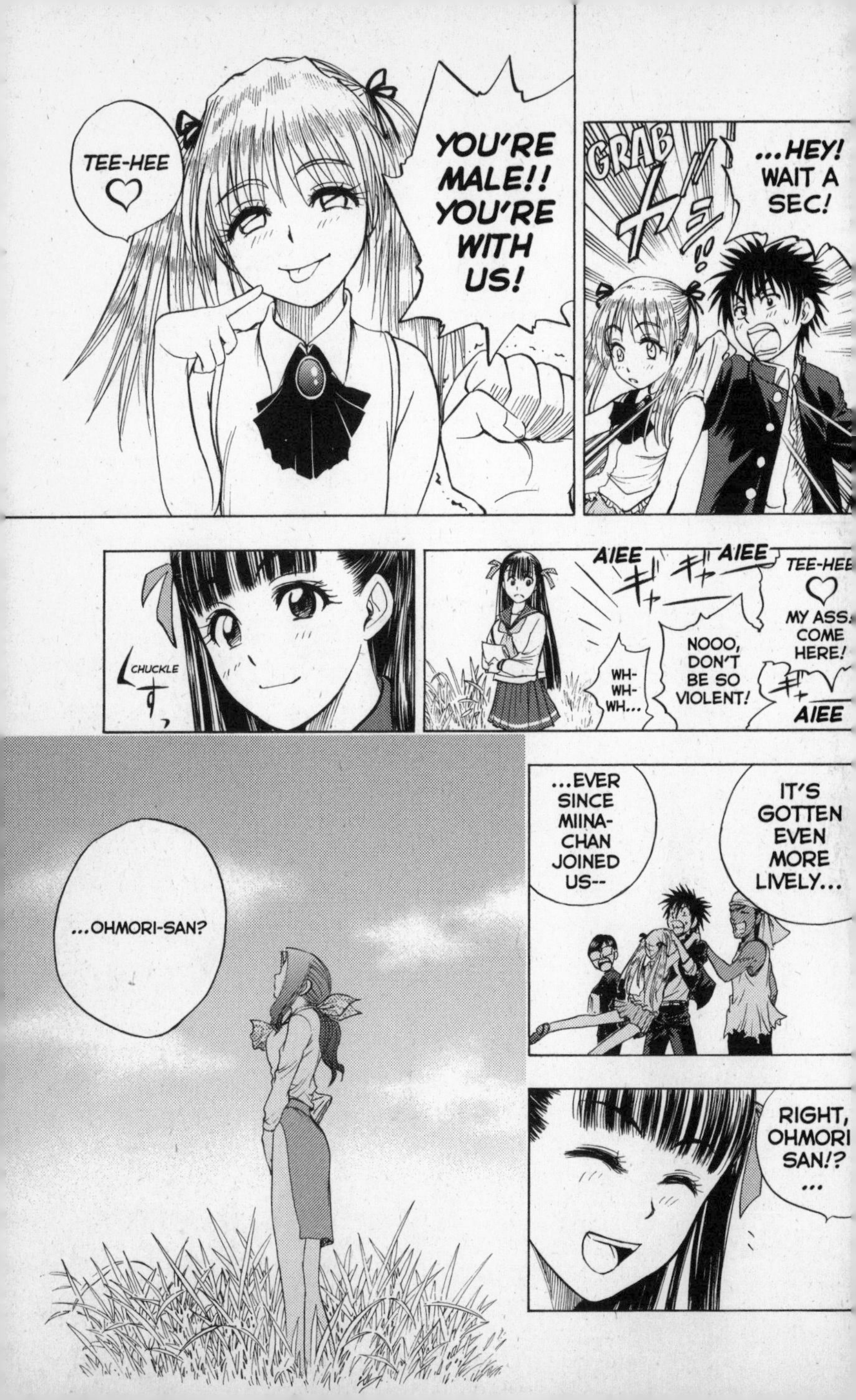
...HEY! WAIT A SEC!
GRAB
YOU'RE MALE!! YOU'RE WITH US!
TEE-HEE ♡
AIEE
AIEE
TEE-HEE ♡ MY ASS. COME HERE!
NOOO, DON'T BE SO VIOLENT!
WH-WH-WH...
AIEE
CHUCKLE
IT'S GOTTEN EVEN MORE LIVELY...
...EVER SINCE MIINA-CHAN JOINED US--
RIGHT, OHMORI SAN!? ...
...OHMORI-SAN?

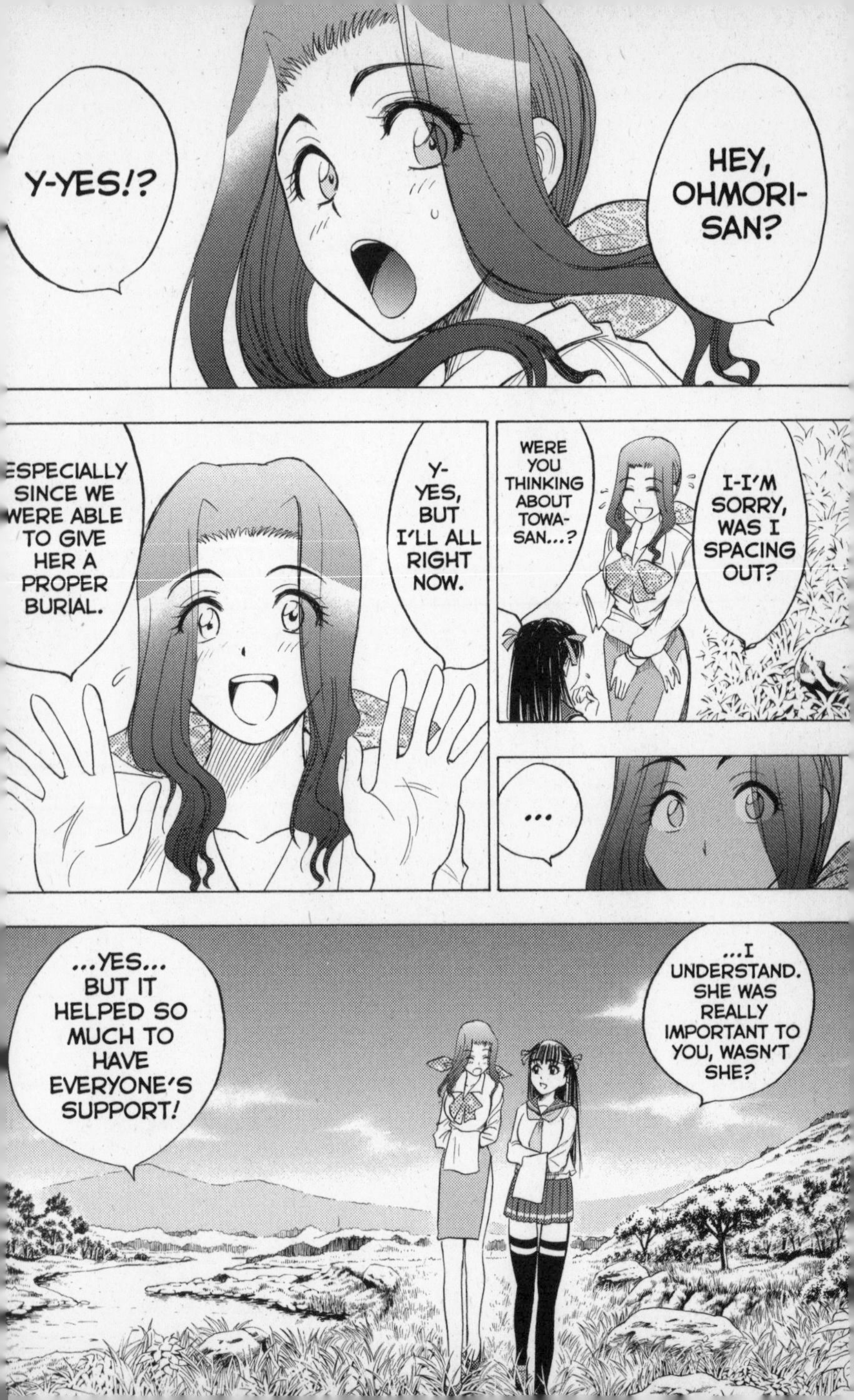
HEY, OHMORI-SAN?
Y-YES!?
I-I'M SORRY, WAS I SPACING OUT?
WERE YOU THINKING ABOUT TOWA-SAN...?
...
Y-YES, BUT I'LL ALL RIGHT NOW.
ESPECIALLY SINCE WE WERE ABLE TO GIVE HER A PROPER BURIAL.
...I UNDERSTAND. SHE WAS REALLY IMPORTANT TO YOU, WASN'T SHE?
...YES... BUT IT HELPED SO MUCH TO HAVE EVERYONE'S SUPPORT!

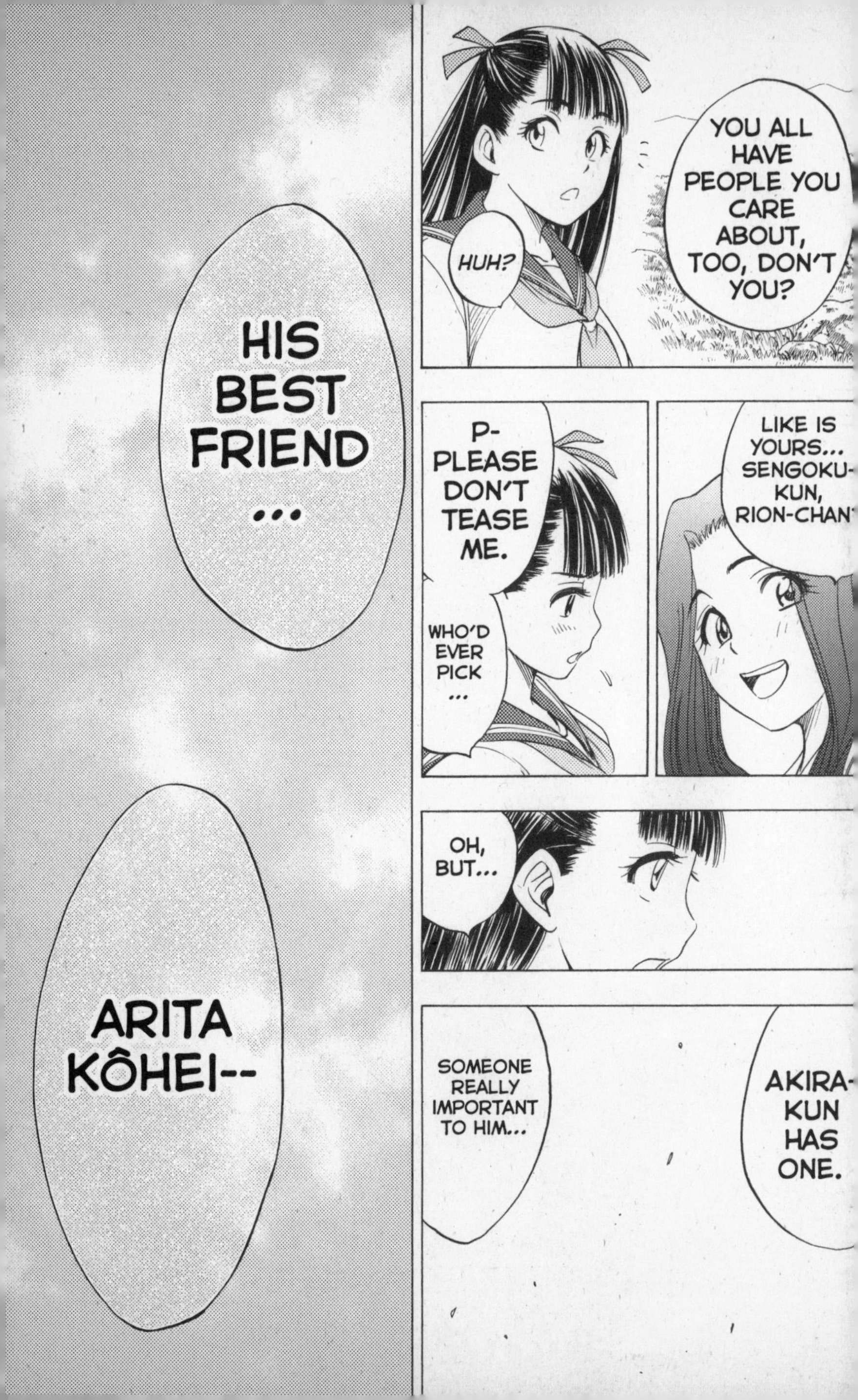
YOU ALL HAVE PEOPLE YOU CARE ABOUT, TOO, DON'T YOU?
HUH?
LIKE IS YOURS... SENGOKU-KUN, RION-CHAN
P-PLEASE DON'T TEASE ME.
WHO'D EVER PICK ...
OH, BUT...
AKIRA-KUN HAS ONE.
SOMEONE REALLY IMPORTANT TO HIM...
HIS BEST FRIEND ...
ARITA KÔHEI--

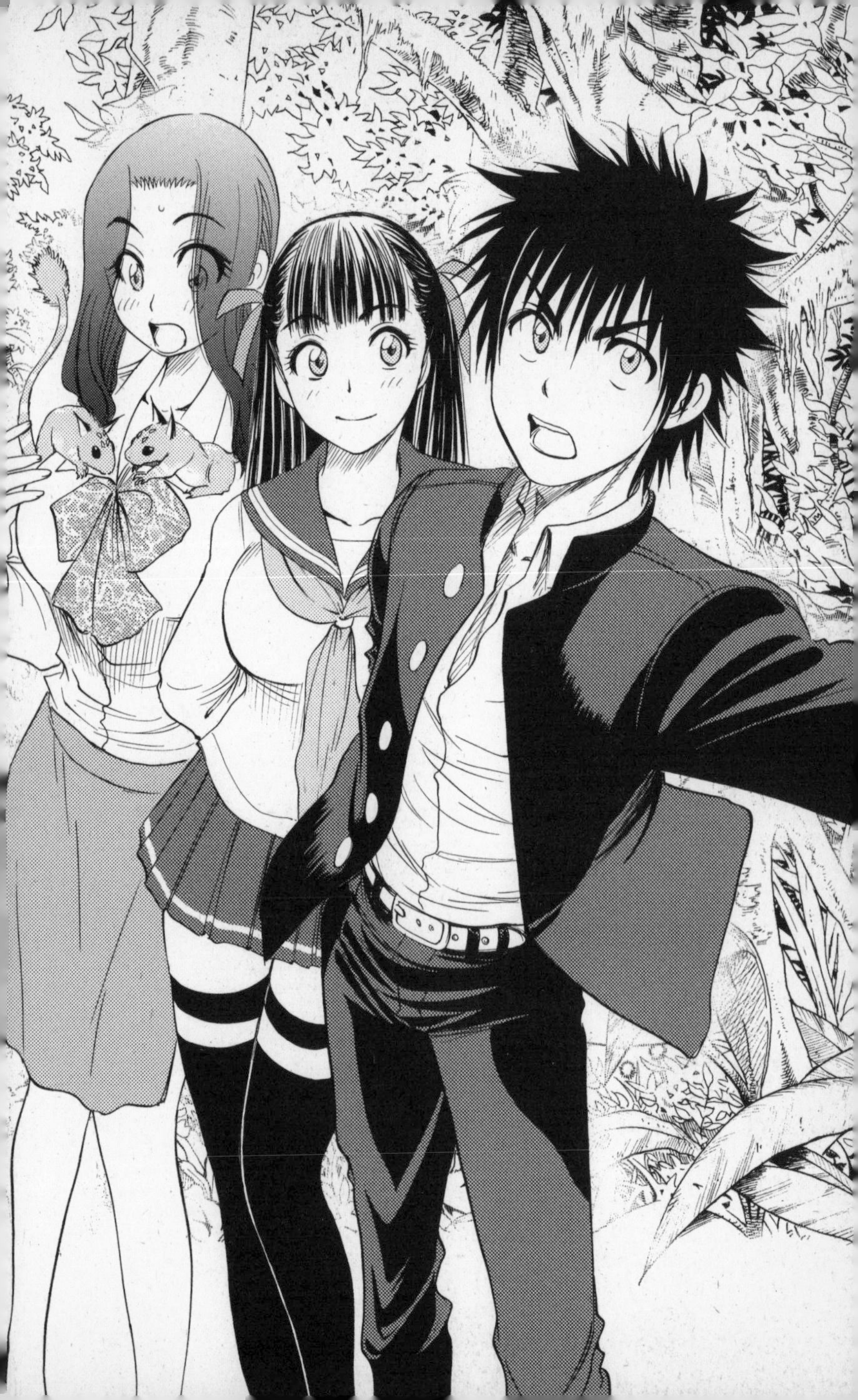

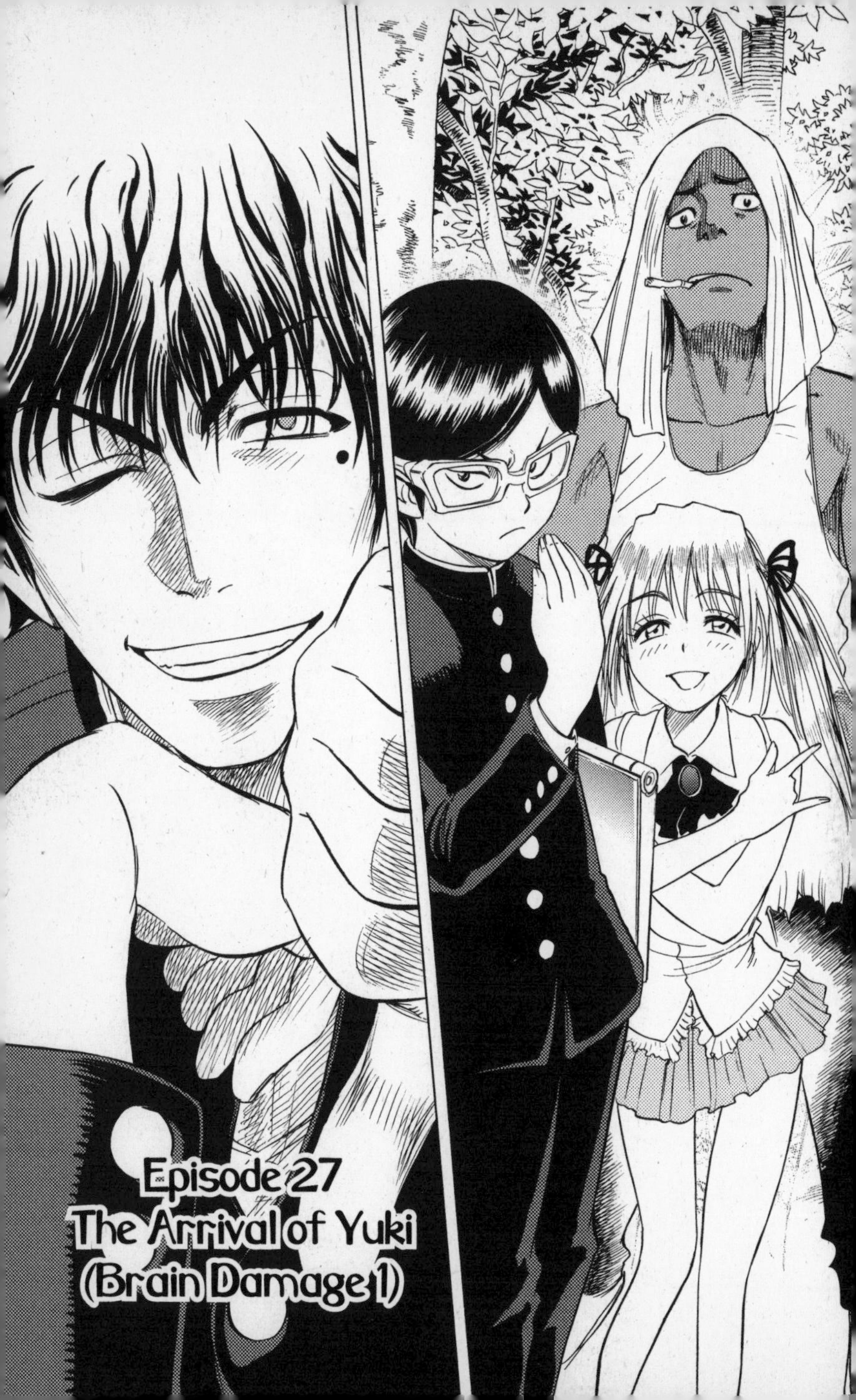
Episode 27
The Arrival of Yuki
(Brain Damage 1)

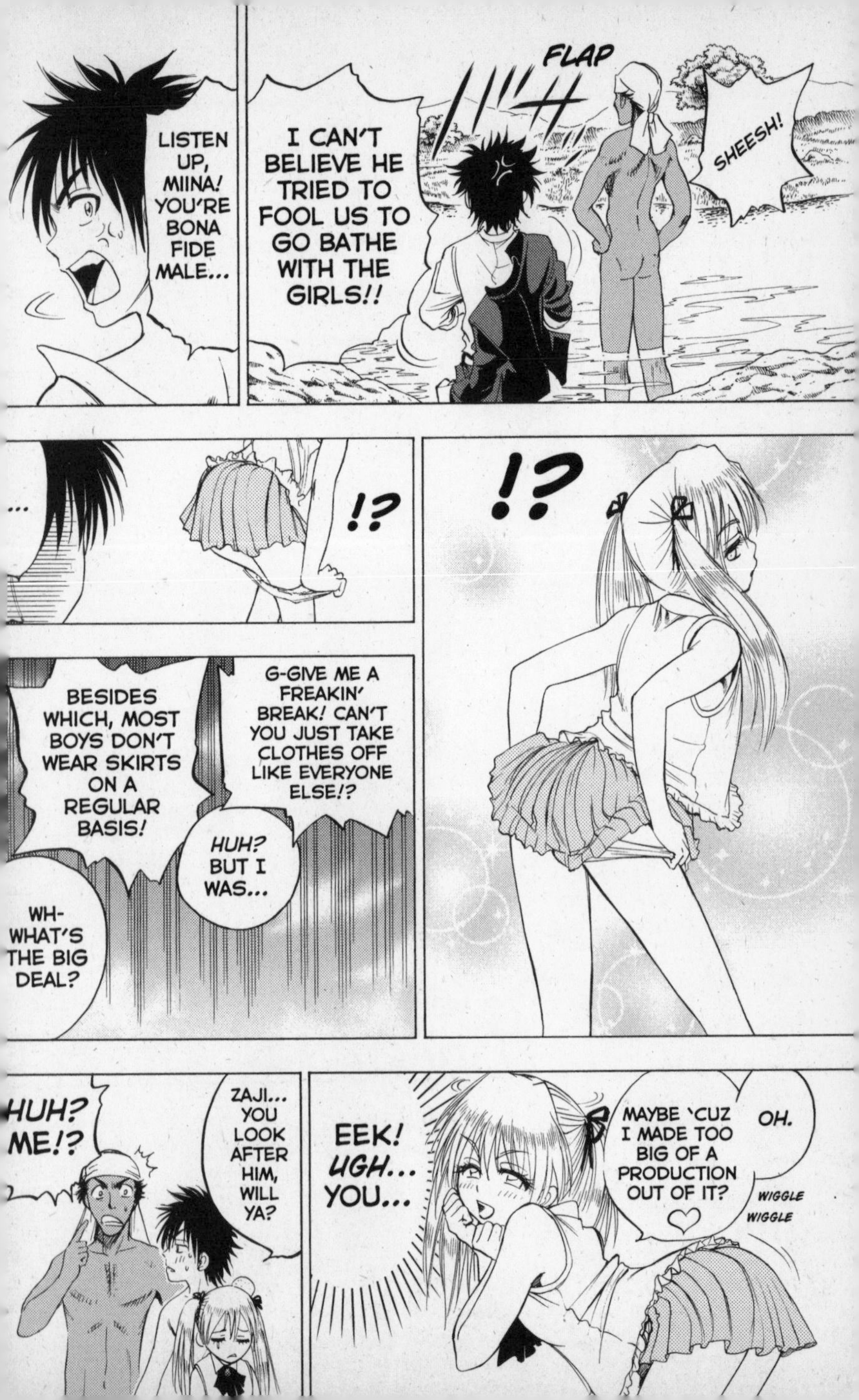
SHEESH!
FLAP
I CAN'T BELIEVE HE TRIED TO FOOL US TO GO BATHE WITH THE GIRLS!!
LISTEN UP, MIINA! YOU'RE BONA FIDE MALE...
!?
!?
...
G-GIVE ME A FREAKIN' BREAK! CAN'T YOU JUST TAKE CLOTHES OFF LIKE EVERYONE ELSE!?
BESIDES WHICH, MOST BOYS DON'T WEAR SKIRTS ON A REGULAR BASIS!
HUH? BUT I WAS...
WH-WHAT'S THE BIG DEAL?
OH.
MAYBE 'CUZ I MADE TOO BIG OF A PRODUCTION OUT OF IT? ♡
WIGGLE WIGGLE
EEK! UGH... YOU...
ZAJI... YOU LOOK AFTER HIM, WILL YA?
HUH? ME!?

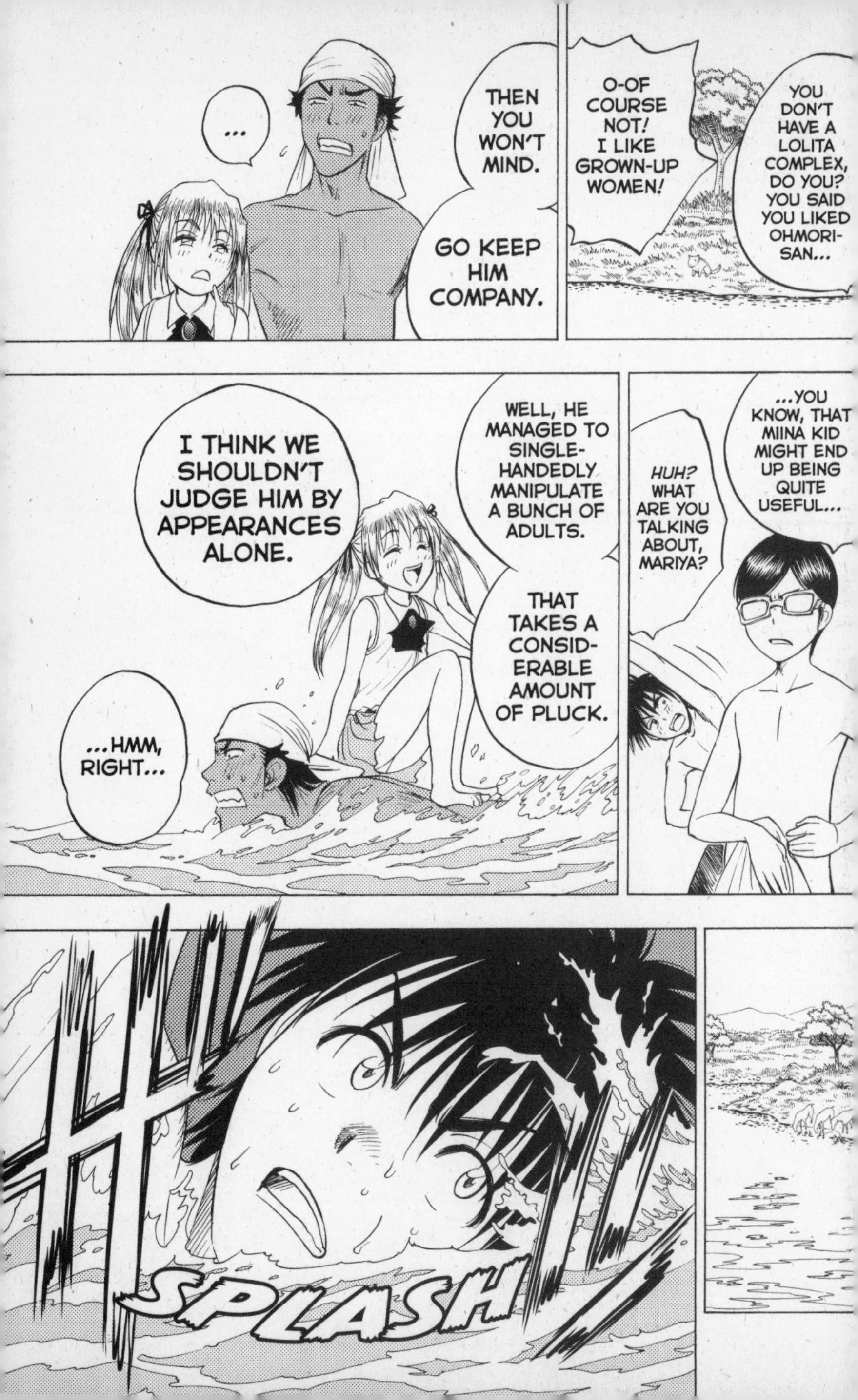
YOU DON'T HAVE A LOLITA COMPLEX, DO YOU? YOU SAID YOU LIKED OHMORI-SAN...
O-OF COURSE NOT! I LIKE GROWN-UP WOMEN!
THEN YOU WON'T MIND.
GO KEEP HIM COMPANY.
...
...YOU KNOW, THAT MIINA KID MIGHT END UP BEING QUITE USEFUL...
HUH? WHAT ARE YOU TALKING ABOUT, MARIYA?
WELL, HE MANAGED TO SINGLE-HANDEDLY MANIPULATE A BUNCH OF ADULTS.
THAT TAKES A CONSID-ERABLE AMOUNT OF PLUCK.
I THINK WE SHOULDN'T JUDGE HIM BY APPEARANCES ALONE.
...HMM, RIGHT...
SPLASH

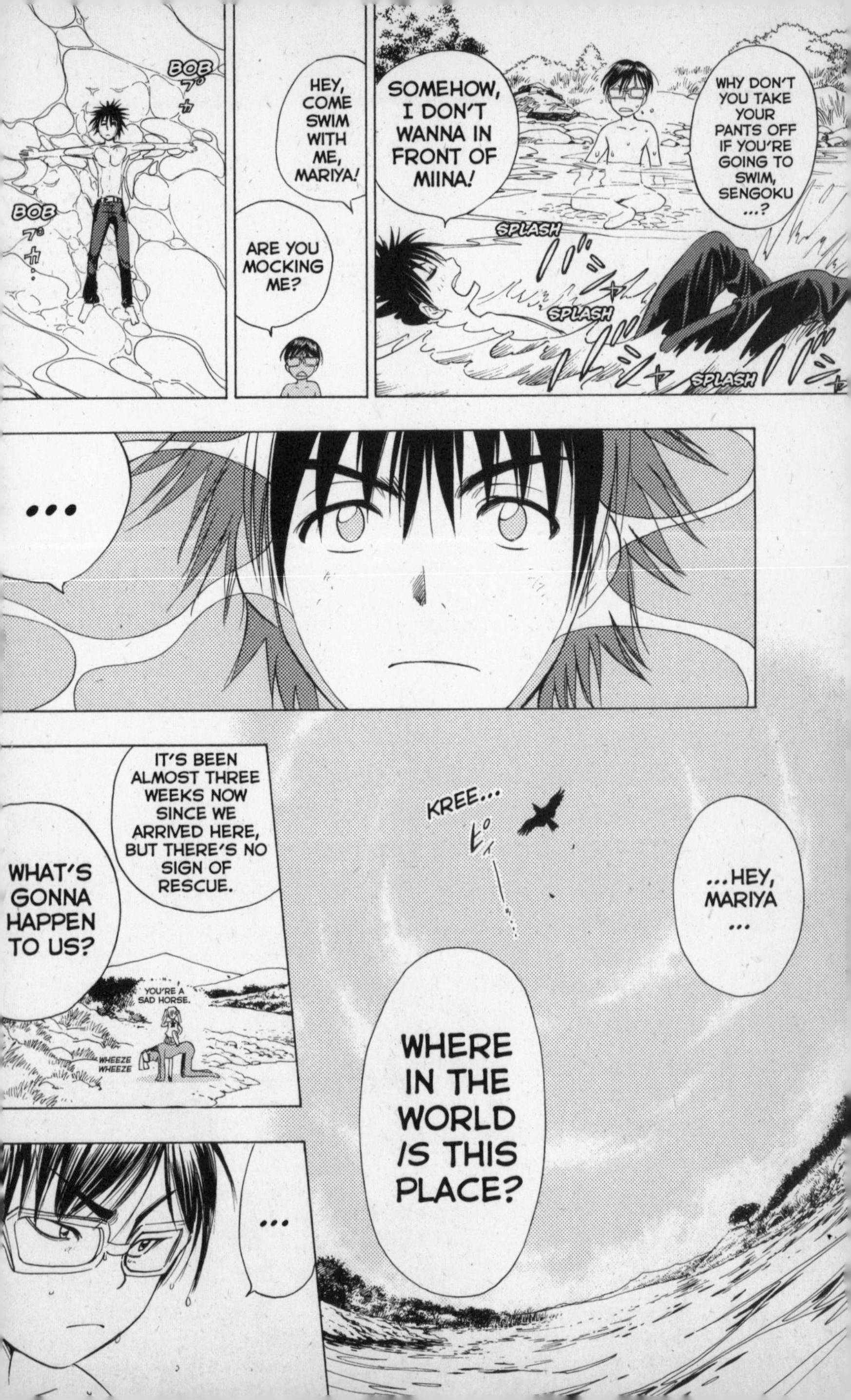
WHY DON'T YOU TAKE YOUR PANTS OFF IF YOU'RE GOING TO SWIM, SENGOKU ...?
SOMEHOW, I DON'T WANNA IN FRONT OF MIINA!
SPLASH
SPLASH
SPLASH
HEY, COME SWIM WITH ME, MARIYA!
ARE YOU MOCKING ME?
BOB
BOB
...
...HEY, MARIYA ...
KREE...
WHERE IN THE WORLD IS THIS PLACE?
IT'S BEEN ALMOST THREE WEEKS NOW SINCE WE ARRIVED HERE, BUT THERE'S NO SIGN OF RESCUE.
WHAT'S GONNA HAPPEN TO US?
YOU'RE A SAD HORSE.
WHEEZE WHEEZE
...

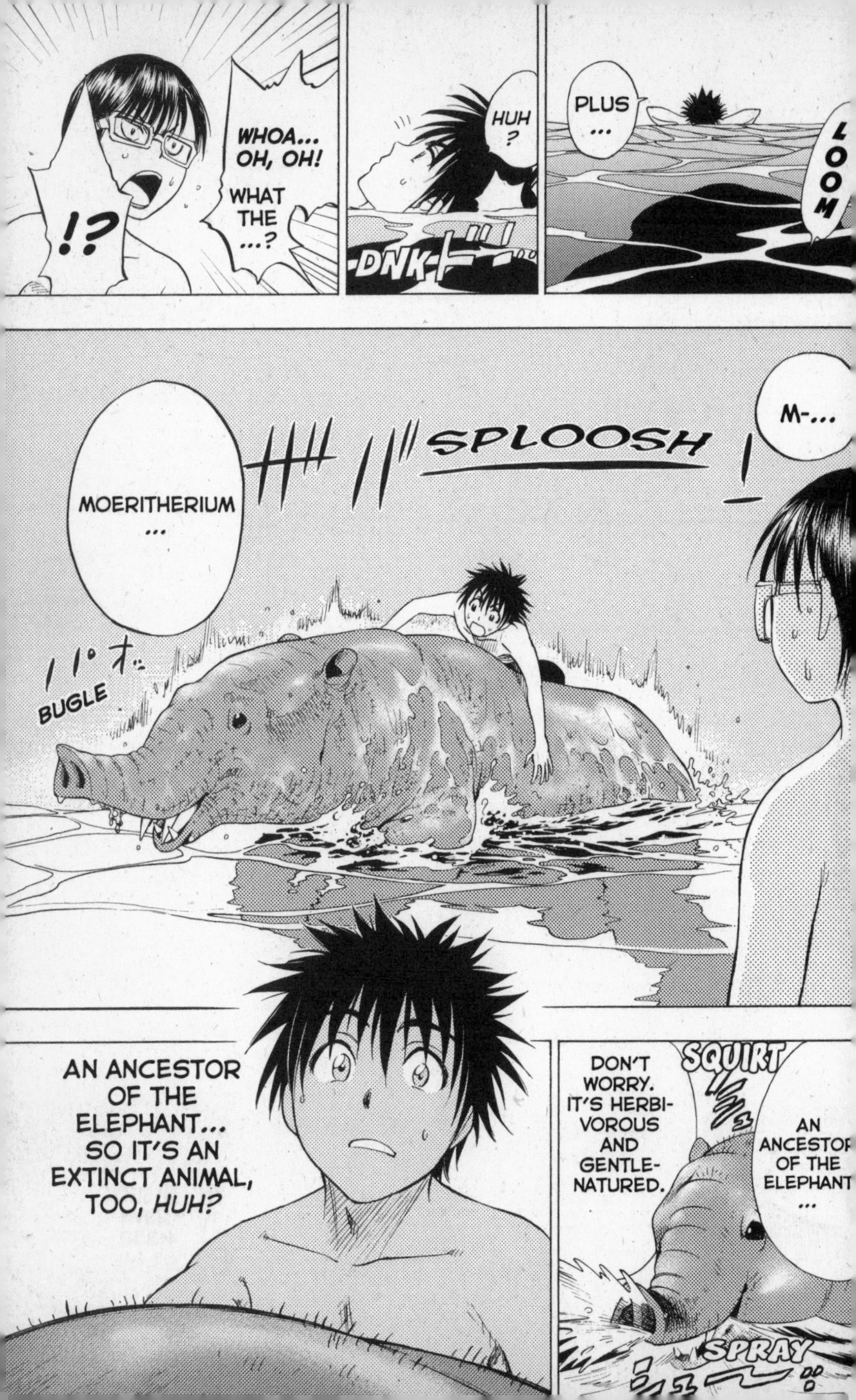
PLUS ...
LOOM
HUH ?
DNK
WHOA... OH, OH!
WHAT THE ...?
!?
M-...
SPLOOSH
MOERITHERIUM ...
BUGLE
AN ANCESTOR OF THE ELEPHANT ...
SQUIRT
DON'T WORRY. IT'S HERBI-VOROUS AND GENTLE-NATURED.
SPRAY
AN ANCESTOR OF THE ELEPHANT... SO IT'S AN EXTINCT ANIMAL, TOO, *HUH?*

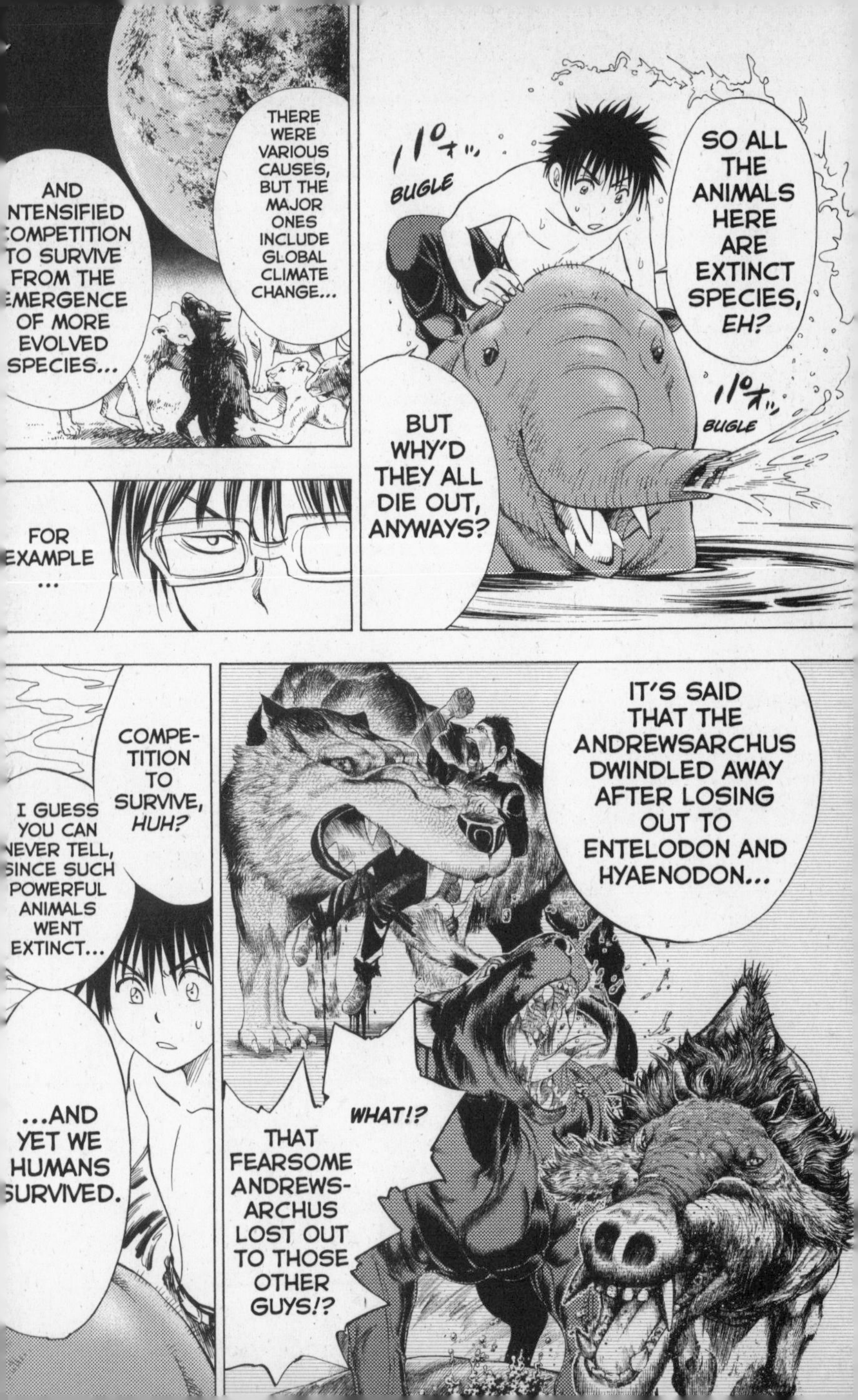
SO ALL THE ANIMALS HERE ARE EXTINCT SPECIES, EH?
BUGLE
BUGLE
BUT WHY'D THEY ALL DIE OUT, ANYWAYS?
THERE WERE VARIOUS CAUSES, BUT THE MAJOR ONES INCLUDE GLOBAL CLIMATE CHANGE...
AND NTENSIFIED OMPETITION TO SURVIVE FROM THE MERGENCE OF MORE EVOLVED SPECIES...
FOR XAMPLE ...
IT'S SAID THAT THE ANDREWSARCHUS DWINDLED AWAY AFTER LOSING OUT TO ENTELODON AND HYAENODON...
WHAT!?
THAT FEARSOME ANDREWS-ARCHUS LOST OUT TO THOSE OTHER GUYS!?
COMPE-TITION TO SURVIVE, HUH?
I GUESS YOU CAN EVER TELL, INCE SUCH POWERFUL ANIMALS WENT EXTINCT...
...AND YET WE HUMANS URVIVED.

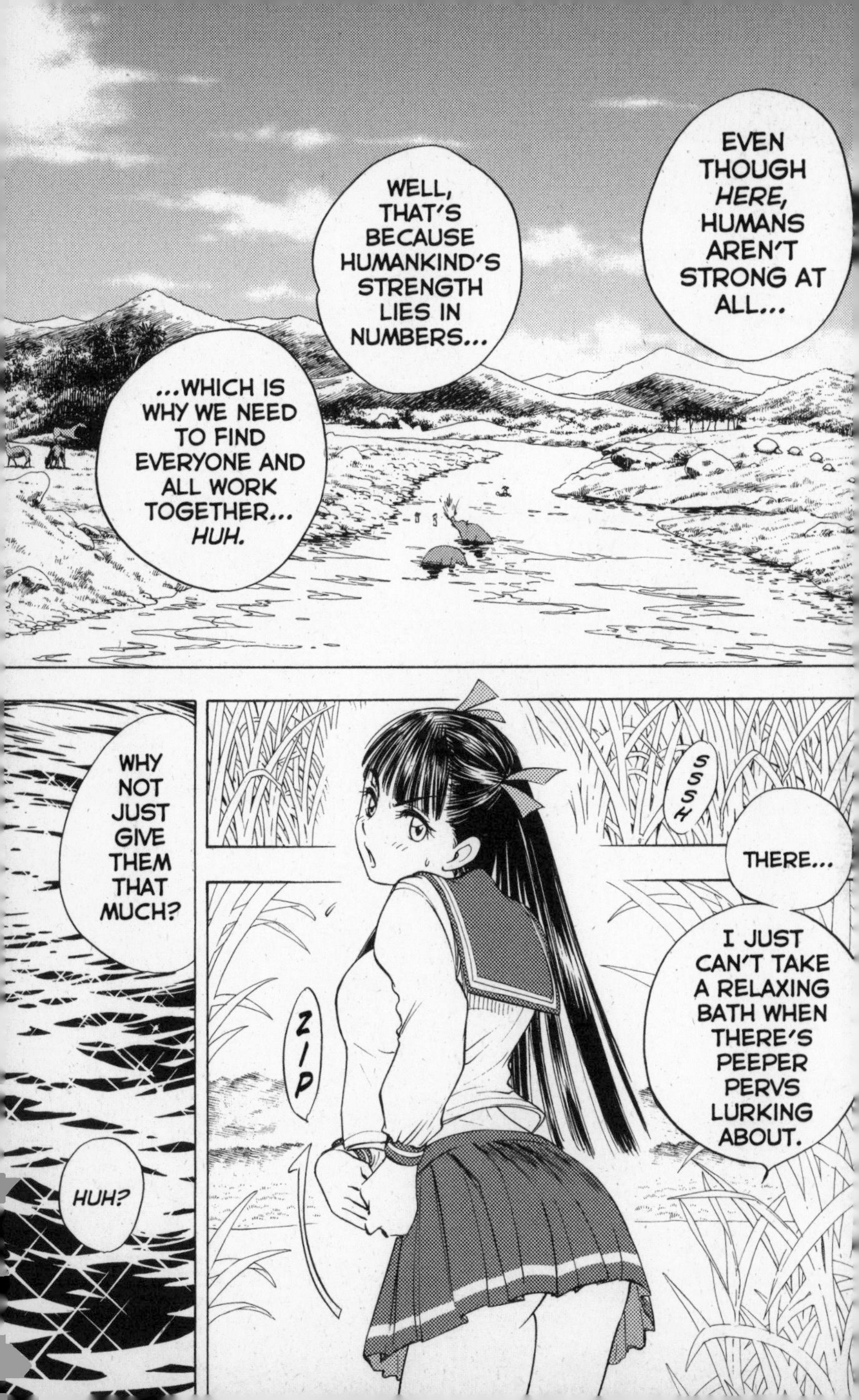
EVEN THOUGH *HERE,* HUMANS AREN'T STRONG AT ALL...
WELL, THAT'S BECAUSE HUMANKIND'S STRENGTH LIES IN NUMBERS...
...WHICH IS WHY WE NEED TO FIND EVERYONE AND ALL WORK TOGETHER... *HUH.*
SSSH
THERE...
I JUST CAN'T TAKE A RELAXING BATH WHEN THERE'S PEEPER PERVS LURKING ABOUT.
ZIP
WHY NOT JUST GIVE THEM THAT MUCH?
HUH?

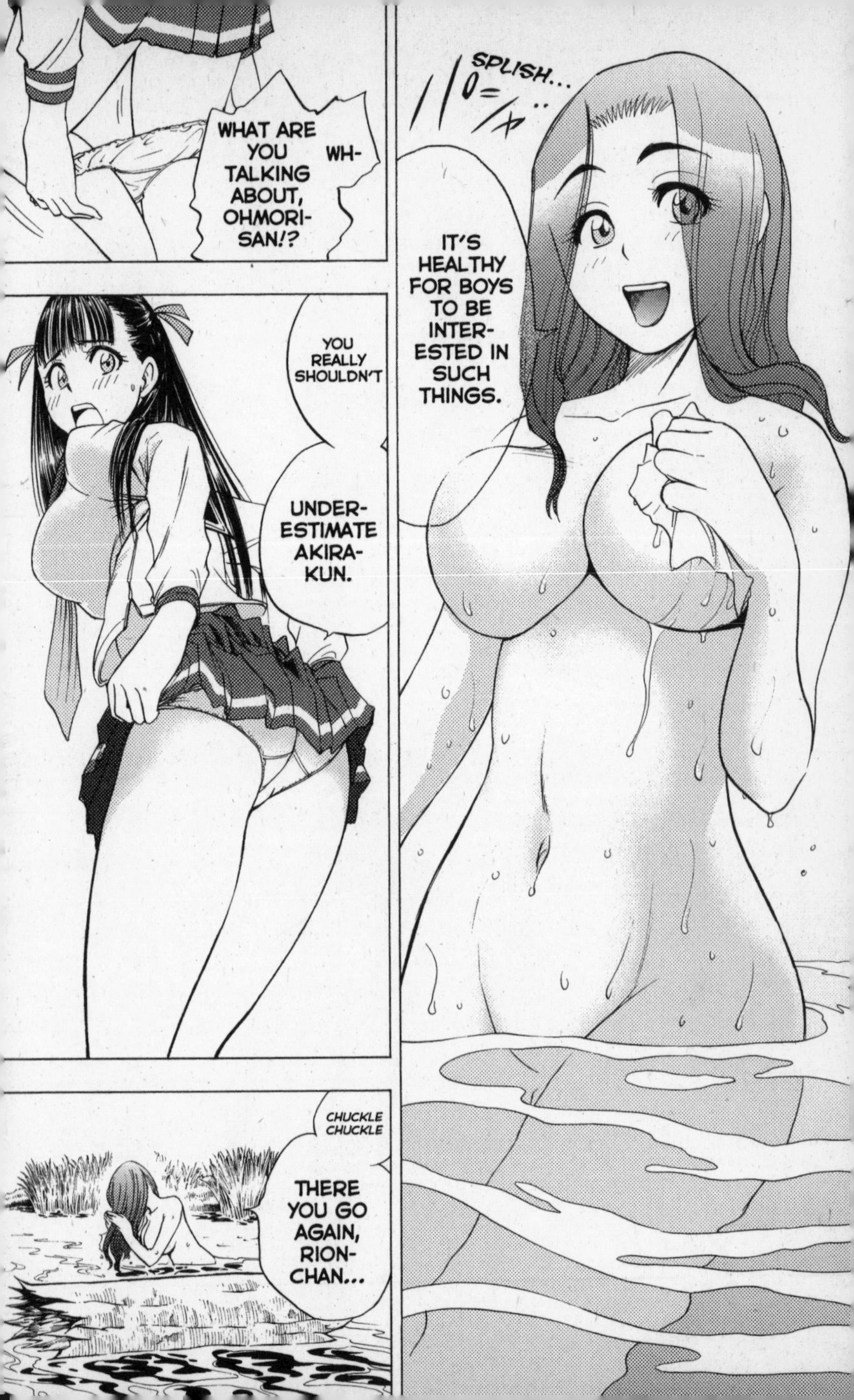
SPLISH...
IT'S HEALTHY FOR BOYS TO BE INTER-ESTED IN SUCH THINGS.
WH-
WHAT ARE YOU TALKING ABOUT, OHMORI-SAN!?
YOU REALLY SHOULDN'T
UNDER-ESTIMATE AKIRA-KUN.
CHUCKLE CHUCKLE
THERE YOU GO AGAIN, RION-CHAN...

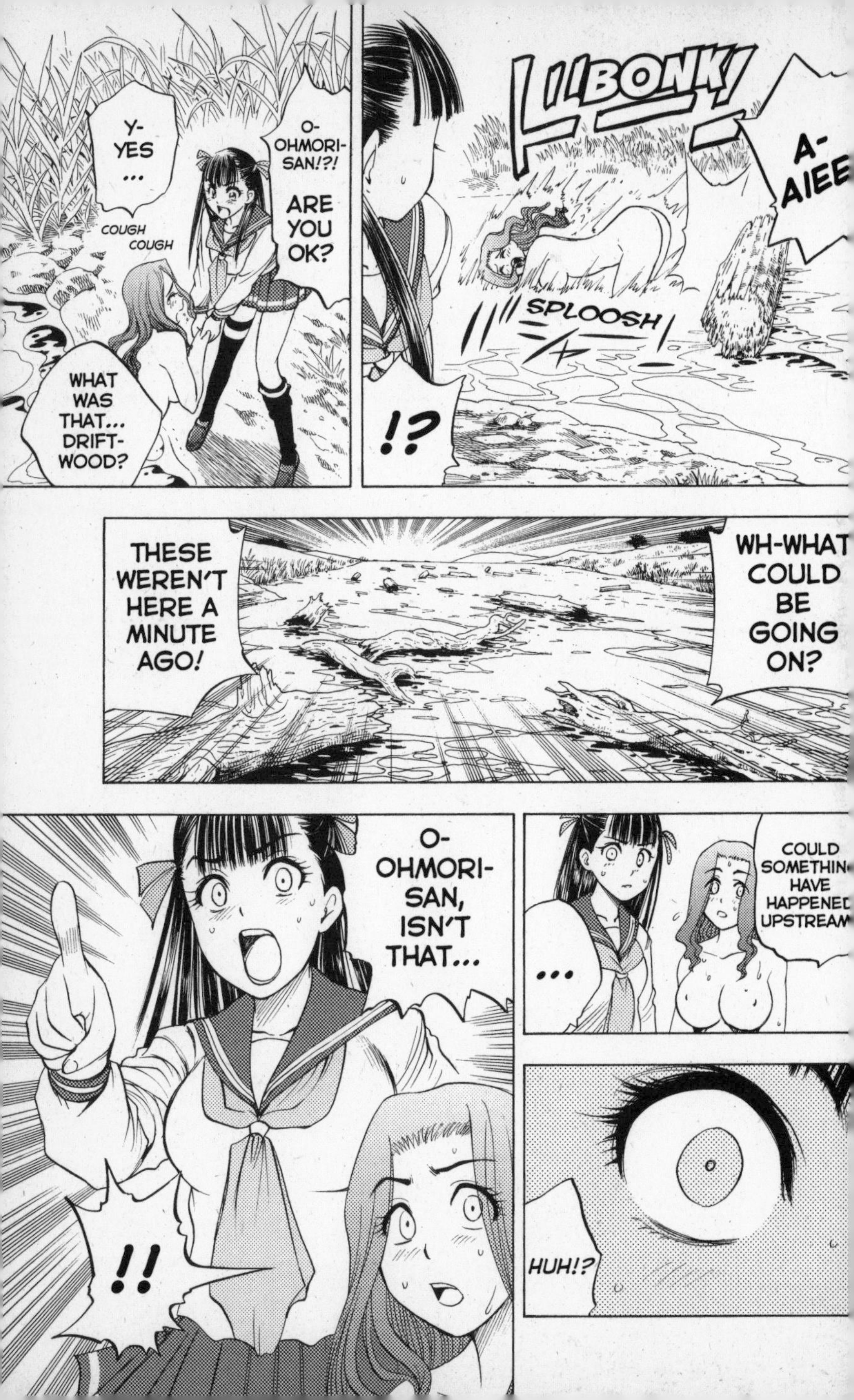
BONK!
A- AIEE
SPLOOSH
!?
O- OHMORI-SAN!?! ARE YOU OK?
Y- YES ...
COUGH COUGH
WHAT WAS THAT... DRIFT- WOOD?
WH-WHAT COULD BE GOING ON?
THESE WEREN'T HERE A MINUTE AGO!
COULD SOMETHIN HAVE HAPPENED UPSTREAM
...
HUH!?
O- OHMORI- SAN, ISN'T THAT...
!!

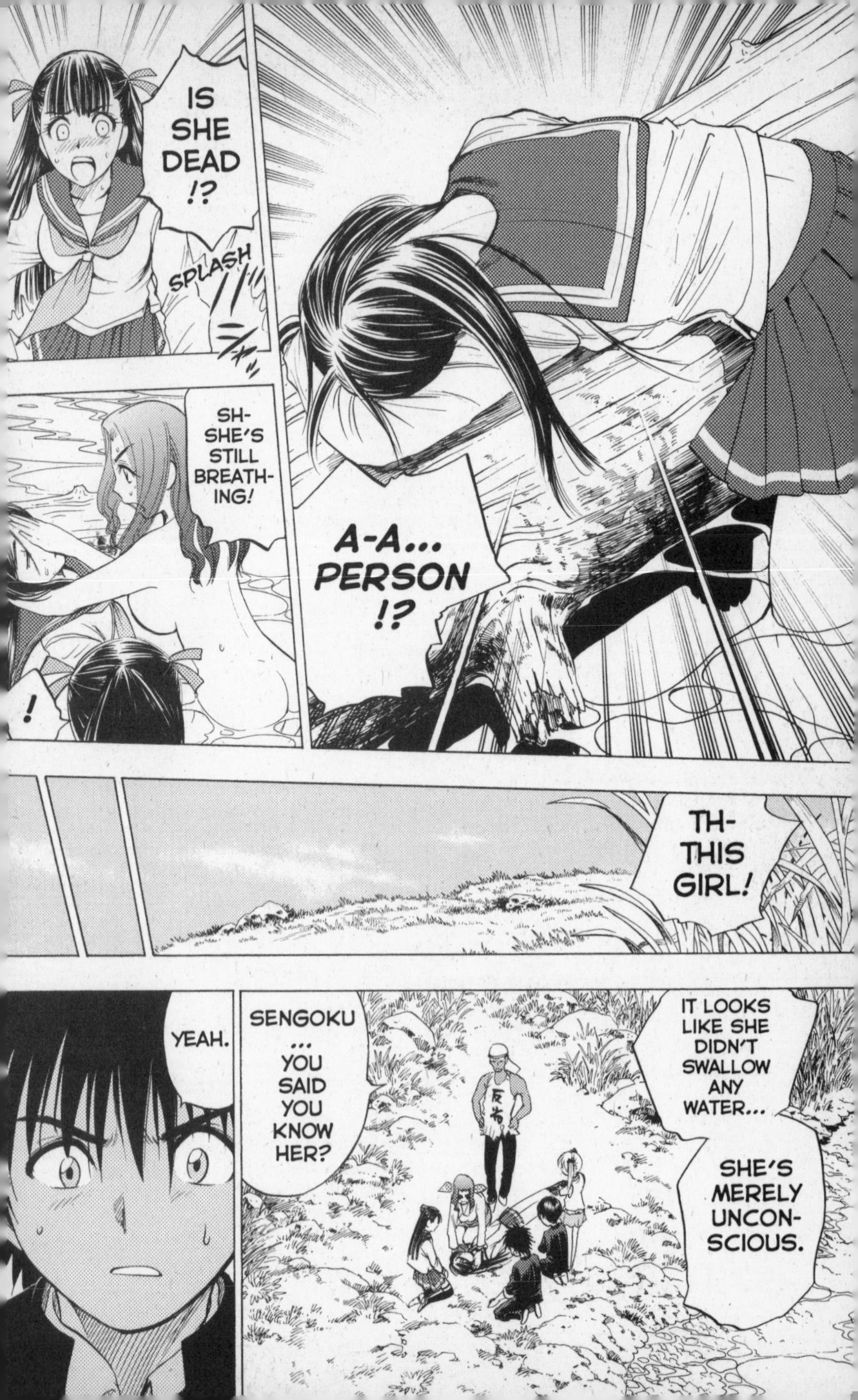
A-A... PERSON!?
IS SHE DEAD!?
SPLASH
SH-SHE'S STILL BREATHING!
!
TH-THIS GIRL!
IT LOOKS LIKE SHE DIDN'T SWALLOW ANY WATER...
SHE'S MERELY UNCONSCIOUS.
SENGOKU... YOU SAID YOU KNOW HER?
YEAH.

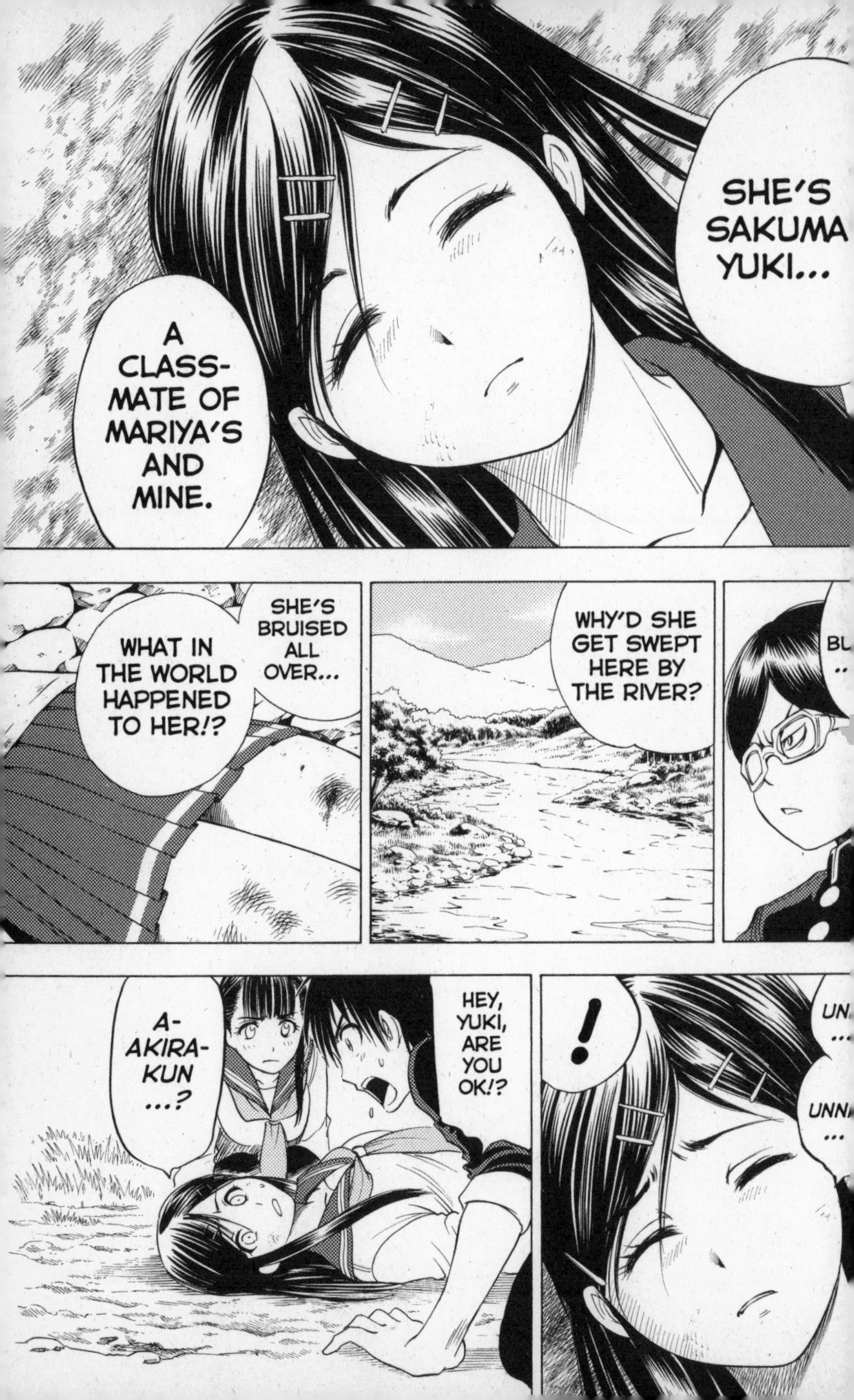
SHE'S SAKUMA YUKI...
A CLASSMATE OF MARIYA'S AND MINE.
WHY'D SHE GET SWEPT HERE BY THE RIVER?
SHE'S BRUISED ALL OVER...
WHAT IN THE WORLD HAPPENED TO HER!?
!
HEY, YUKI, ARE YOU OK!?
A-AKIRA-KUN ...?

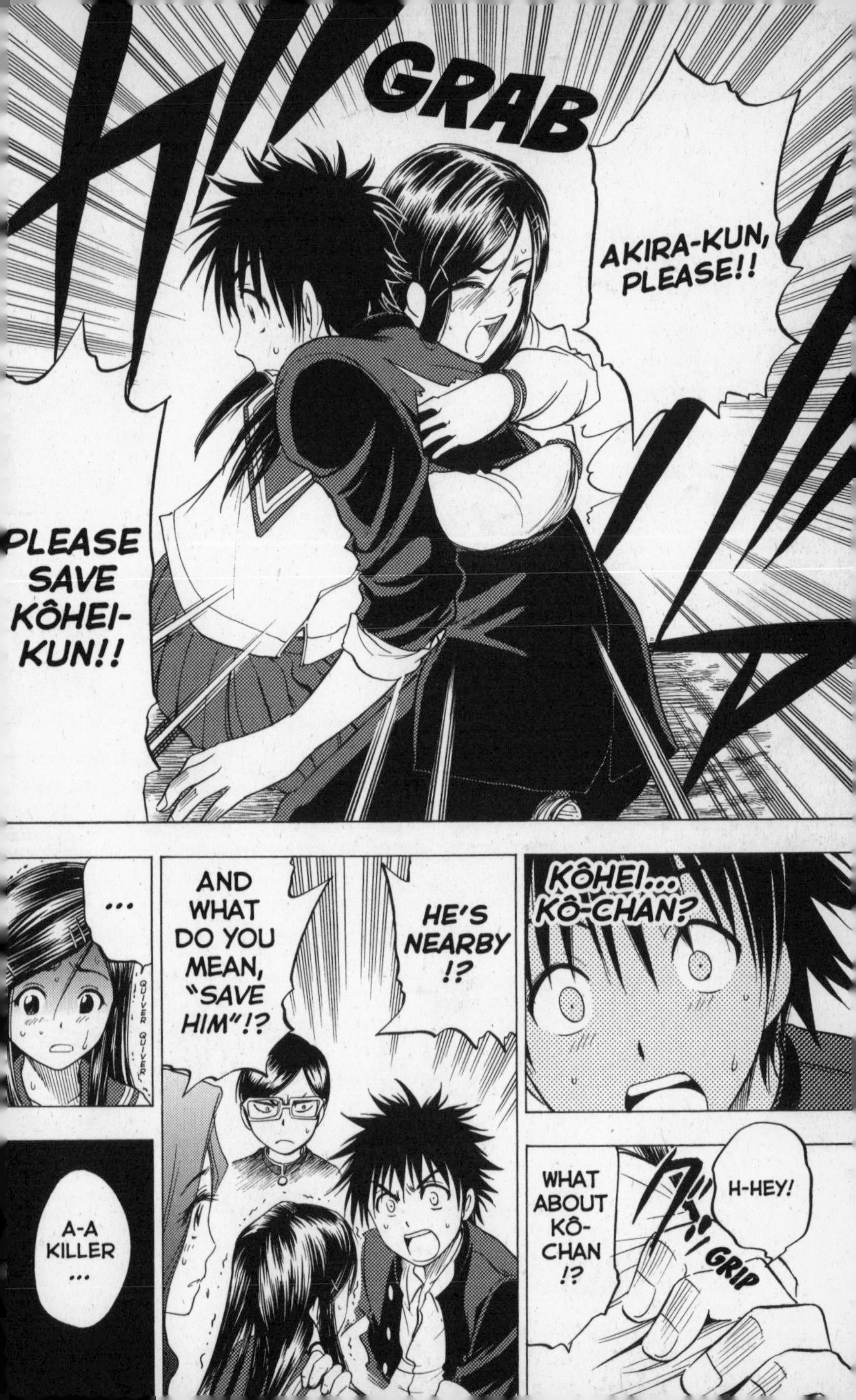
GRAB
AKIRA-KUN, PLEASE!!
PLEASE SAVE KÔHEI-KUN!!
KÔHEI... KÔ-CHAN?
H-HEY!
GRIP
WHAT ABOUT KÔ-CHAN!?
HE'S NEARBY!?
AND WHAT DO YOU MEAN, "SAVE HIM"!?
...
QUIVER QUIVER
A-A KILLER...

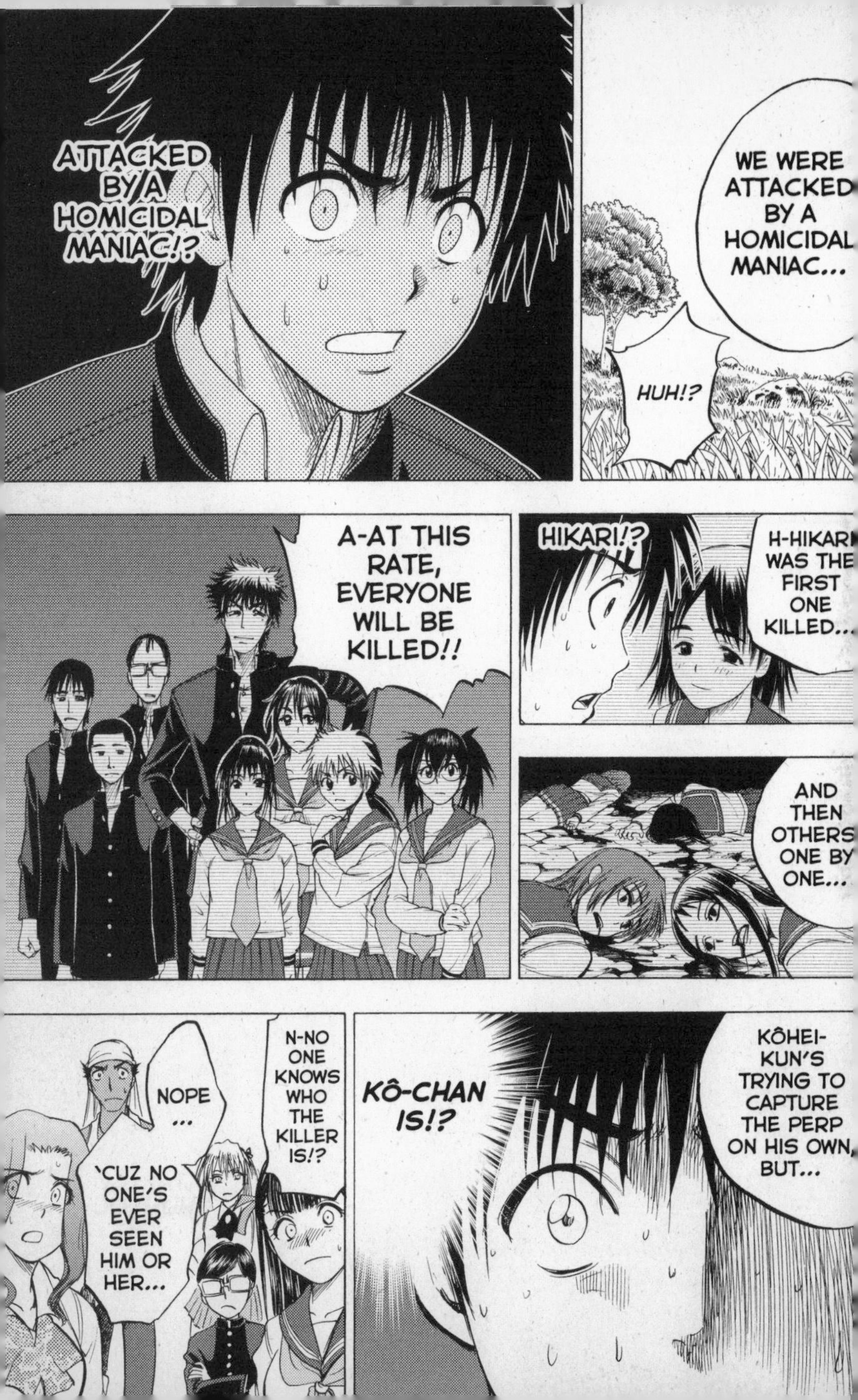

WE WERE ATTACKED BY A HOMICIDAL MANIAC...
HUH!?
ATTACKED BY A HOMICIDAL MANIAC!?
H-HIKARI WAS THE FIRST ONE KILLED...
HIKARI!?
AND THEN OTHERS ONE BY ONE...
A-AT THIS RATE, EVERYONE WILL BE KILLED!!
KÔHEI-KUN'S TRYING TO CAPTURE THE PERP ON HIS OWN, BUT...
KÔ-CHAN IS!?
N-NO ONE KNOWS WHO THE KILLER IS!?
NOPE ...
`CUZ NO ONE'S EVER SEEN HIM OR HER...

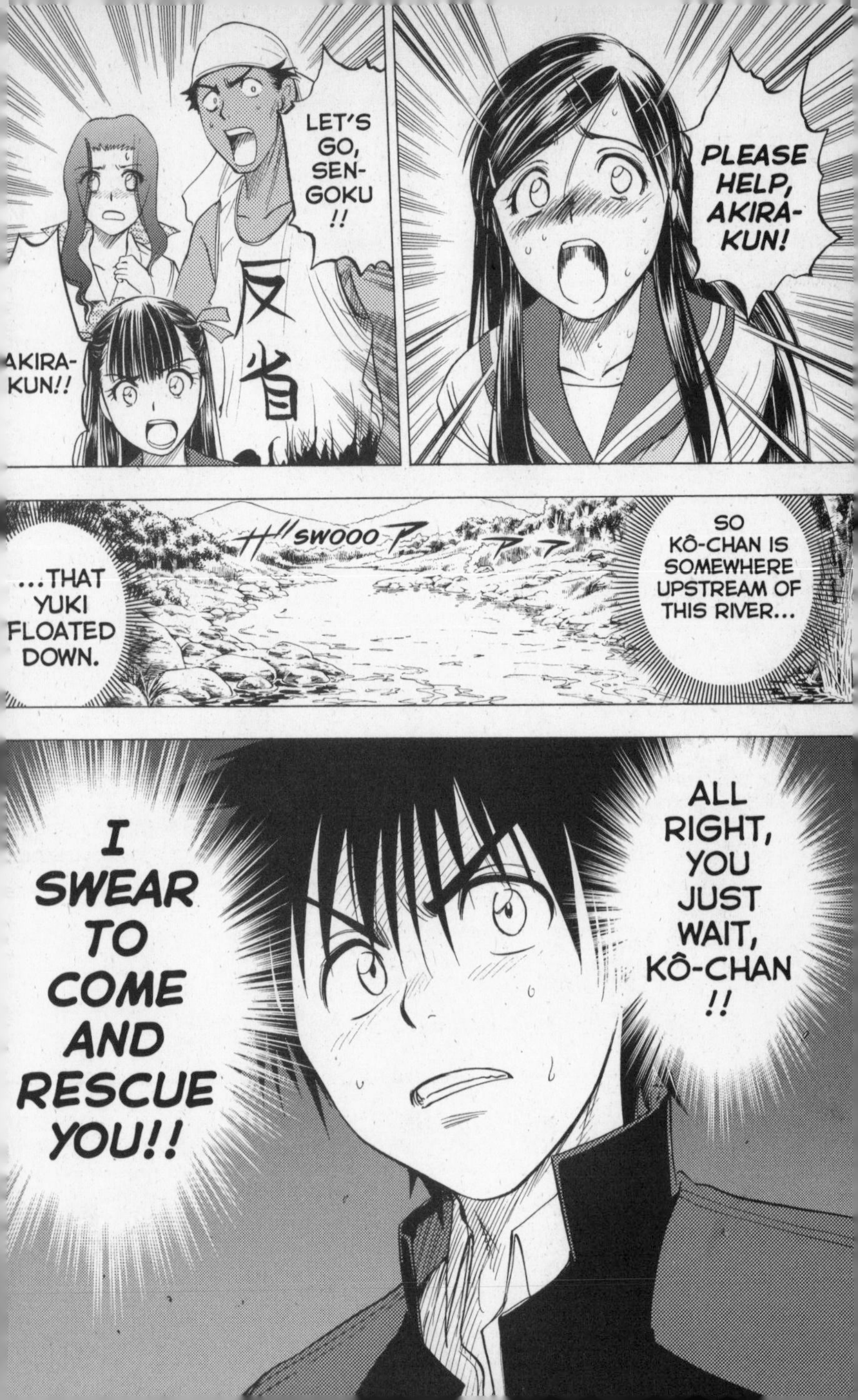
PLEASE HELP, AKIRA-KUN!
LET'S GO, SEN-GOKU!!
AKIRA-KUN!!
SO KÔ-CHAN IS SOMEWHERE UPSTREAM OF THIS RIVER...
SWOOO
...THAT YUKI FLOATED DOWN.
ALL RIGHT, YOU JUST WAIT, KÔ-CHAN!!
I SWEAR TO COME AND RESCUE YOU!!

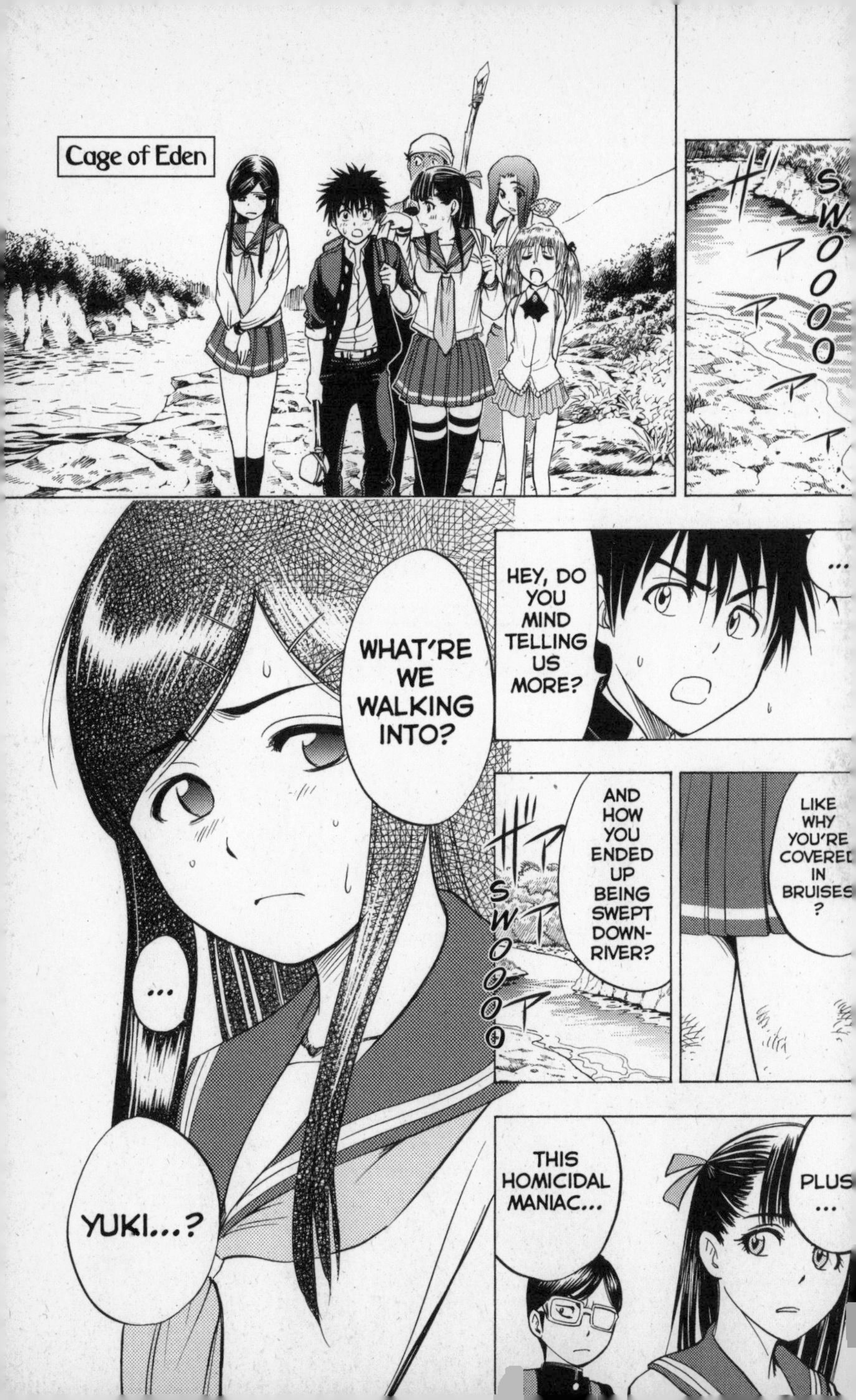
SWOOOOOO
Cage of Eden
...
HEY, DO YOU MIND TELLING US MORE?
LIKE WHY YOU'RE COVERED IN BRUISES?
AND HOW YOU ENDED UP BEING SWEPT DOWN-RIVER?
SWOOOOOO
PLUS...
THIS HOMICIDAL MANIAC...
WHAT'RE WE WALKING INTO?
...
YUKI...?

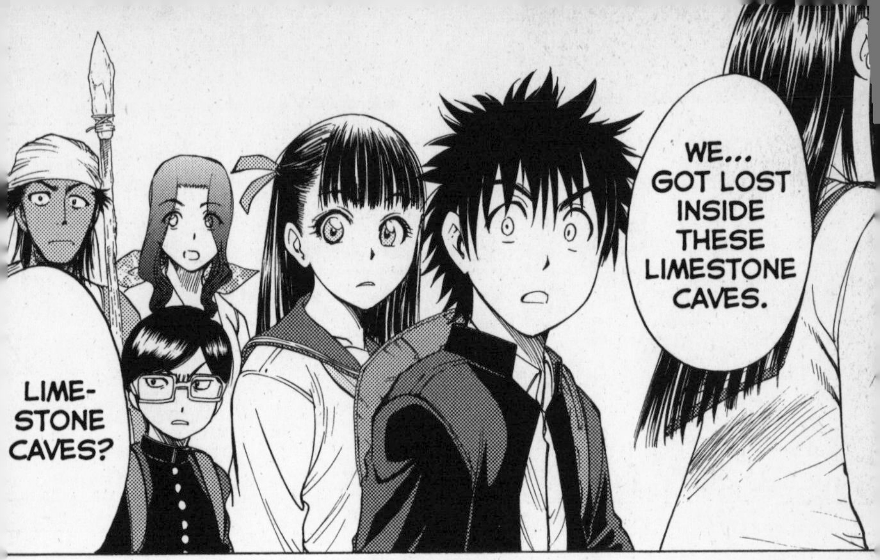
WE... GOT LOST INSIDE THESE LIMESTONE CAVES.
LIME-STONE CAVES?

Episode 28
Underground World (Brain Damage 2)

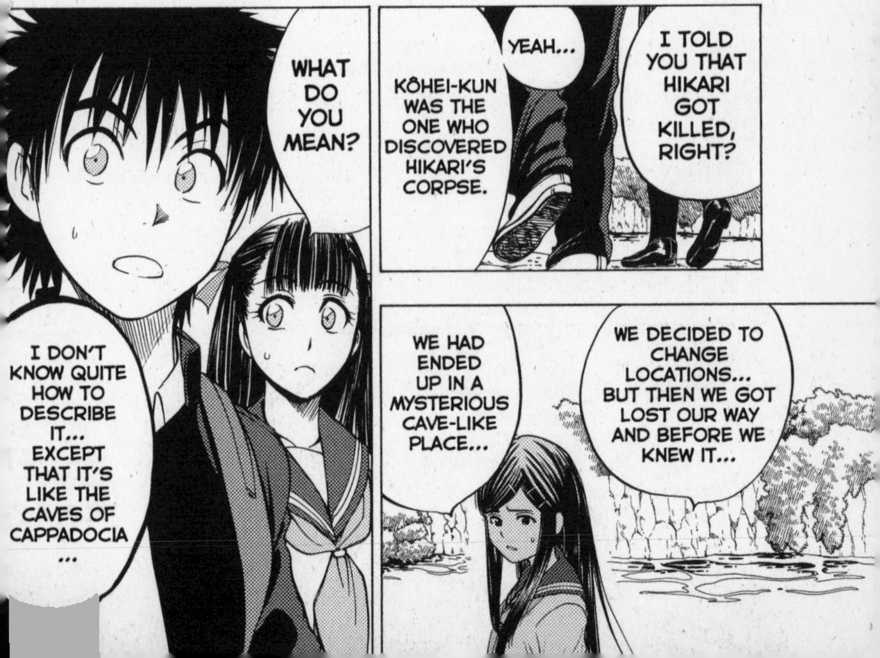
I TOLD YOU THAT HIKARI GOT KILLED, RIGHT?
YEAH...
KÔHEI-KUN WAS THE ONE WHO DISCOVERED HIKARI'S CORPSE.
WE DECIDED TO CHANGE LOCATIONS... BUT THEN WE GOT LOST OUR WAY AND BEFORE WE KNEW IT...
WE HAD ENDED UP IN A MYSTERIOUS CAVE-LIKE PLACE...
WHAT DO YOU MEAN?
I DON'T KNOW QUITE HOW TO DESCRIBE IT... EXCEPT THAT IT'S LIKE THE CAVES OF CAPPADOCIA ...

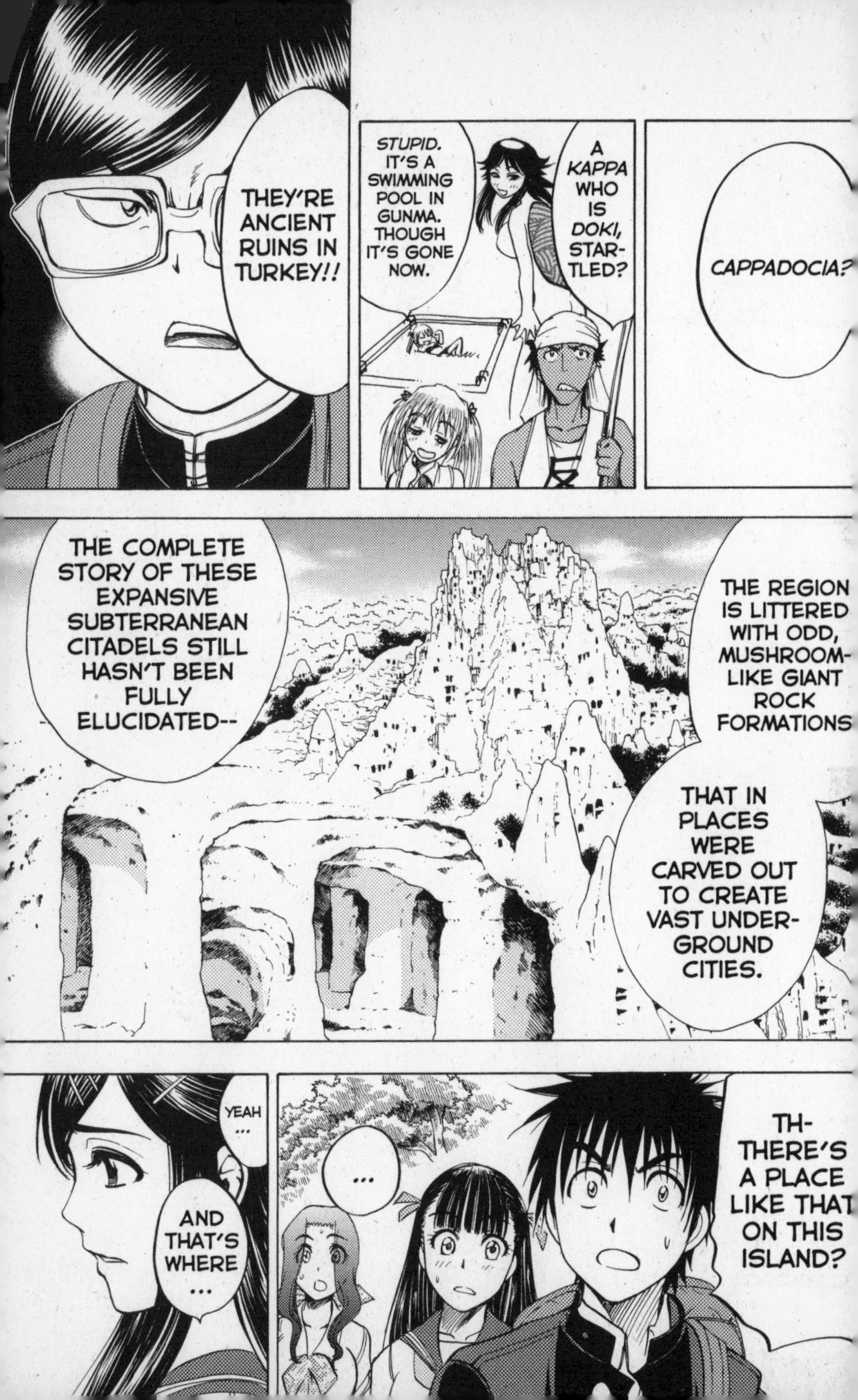
CAPPADOCIA?
A KAPPA WHO IS DOKI, STAR-TLED?
STUPID. IT'S A SWIMMING POOL IN GUNMA. THOUGH IT'S GONE NOW.
THEY'RE ANCIENT RUINS IN TURKEY!!
THE REGION IS LITTERED WITH ODD, MUSHROOM-LIKE GIANT ROCK FORMATIONS
THAT IN PLACES WERE CARVED OUT TO CREATE VAST UNDER-GROUND CITIES.
THE COMPLETE STORY OF THESE EXPANSIVE SUBTERRANEAN CITADELS STILL HASN'T BEEN FULLY ELUCIDATED--
TH- THERE'S A PLACE LIKE THAT ON THIS ISLAND?
...
YEAH ...
AND THAT'S WHERE ...

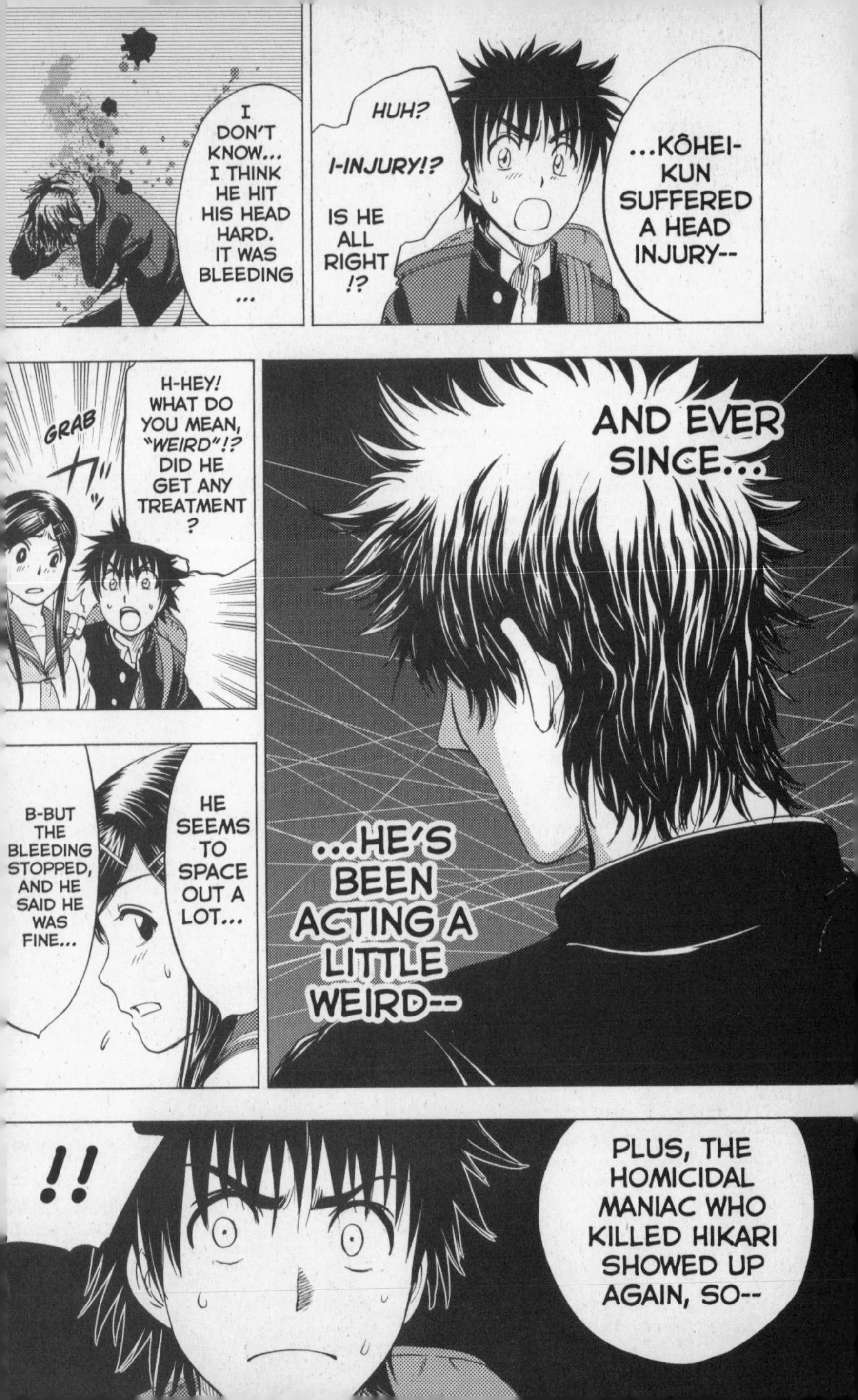
...KÔHEI-KUN SUFFERED A HEAD INJURY--
HUH?
I-INJURY!?
IS HE ALL RIGHT !?
I DON'T KNOW... I THINK HE HIT HIS HEAD HARD. IT WAS BLEEDING ...
AND EVER SINCE...
...HE'S BEEN ACTING A LITTLE WEIRD--
GRAB
H-HEY! WHAT DO YOU MEAN, "WEIRD"!? DID HE GET ANY TREATMENT ?
HE SEEMS TO SPACE OUT A LOT...
B-BUT THE BLEEDING STOPPED, AND HE SAID HE WAS FINE...
PLUS, THE HOMICIDAL MANIAC WHO KILLED HIKARI SHOWED UP AGAIN, SO--
!!

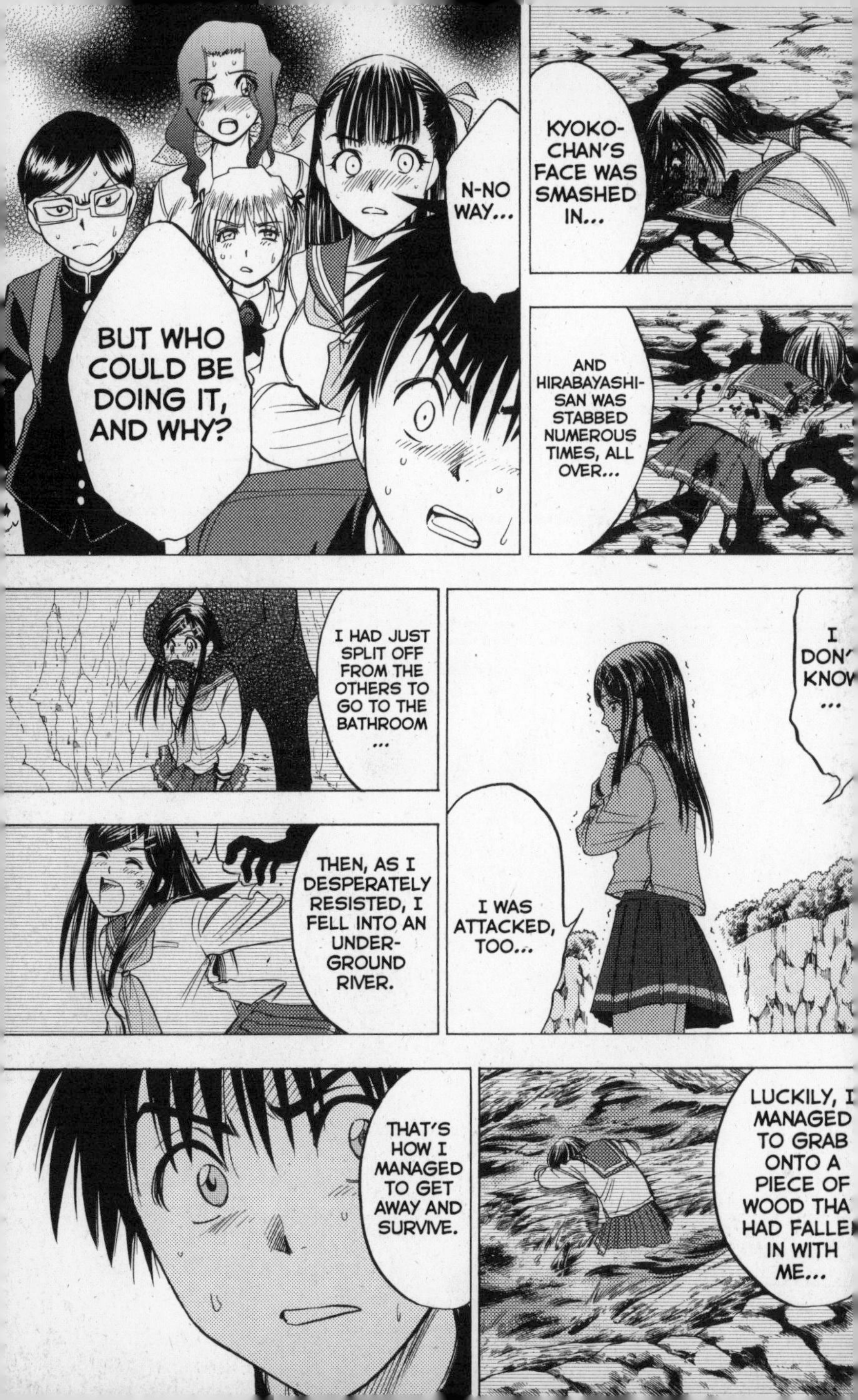
KYOKO-CHAN'S FACE WAS SMASHED IN...
AND HIRABAYASHI-SAN WAS STABBED NUMEROUS TIMES, ALL OVER...
N-NO WAY...
BUT WHO COULD BE DOING IT, AND WHY?
I DON' KNOW ...
I WAS ATTACKED, TOO...
I HAD JUST SPLIT OFF FROM THE OTHERS TO GO TO THE BATHROOM ...
THEN, AS I DESPERATELY RESISTED, I FELL INTO AN UNDER-GROUND RIVER.
LUCKILY, I MANAGED TO GRAB ONTO A PIECE OF WOOD THA HAD FALLE IN WITH ME...
THAT'S HOW I MANAGED TO GET AWAY AND SURVIVE.

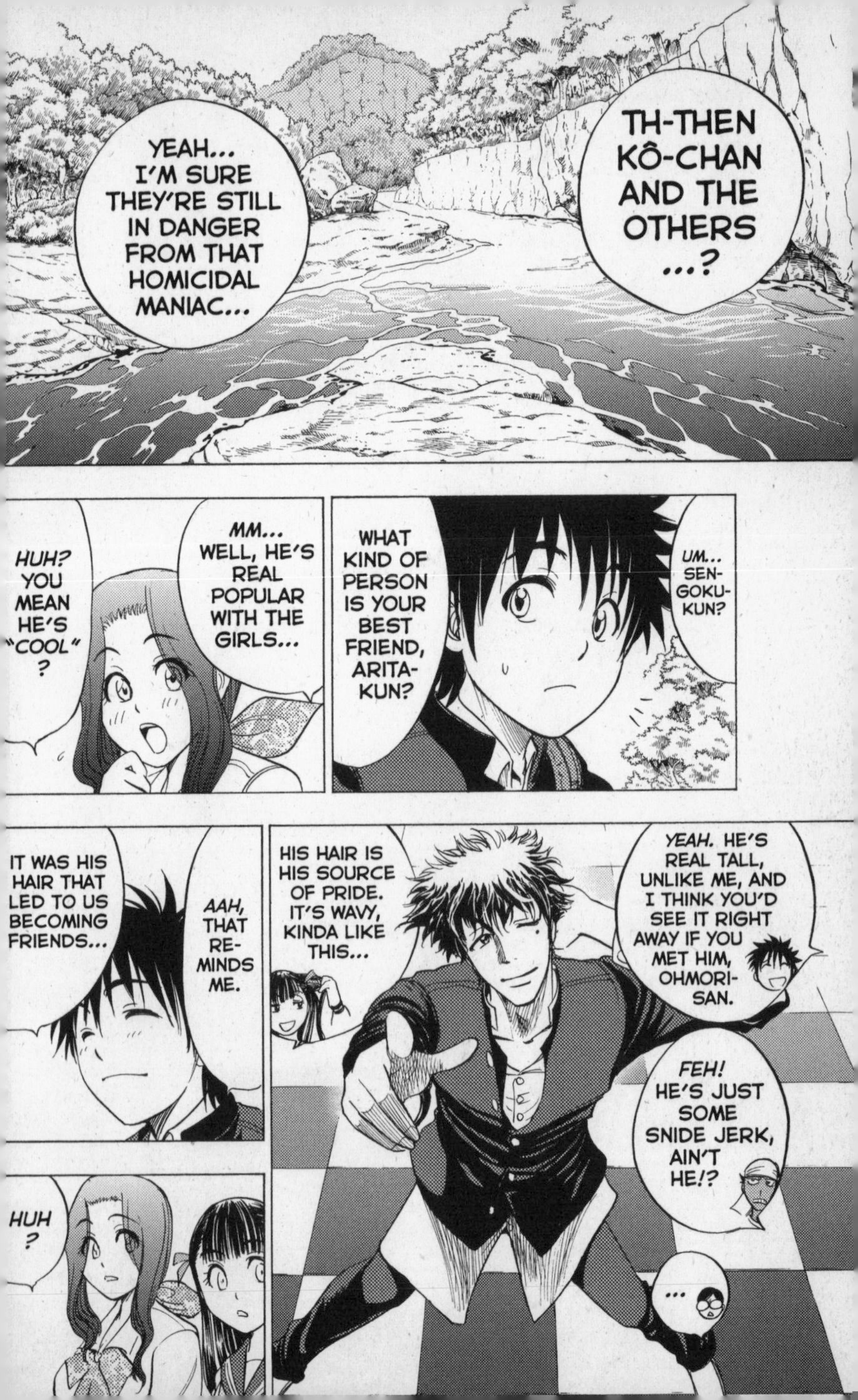
TH-THEN KÔ-CHAN AND THE OTHERS ...?
YEAH... I'M SURE THEY'RE STILL IN DANGER FROM THAT HOMICIDAL MANIAC...
UM... SEN-GOKU-KUN?
WHAT KIND OF PERSON IS YOUR BEST FRIEND, ARITA-KUN?
MM... WELL, HE'S REAL POPULAR WITH THE GIRLS...
HUH? YOU MEAN HE'S "COOL"?
YEAH. HE'S REAL TALL, UNLIKE ME, AND I THINK YOU'D SEE IT RIGHT AWAY IF YOU MET HIM, OHMORI-SAN.
HIS HAIR IS HIS SOURCE OF PRIDE. IT'S WAVY, KINDA LIKE THIS...
FEH! HE'S JUST SOME SNIDE JERK, AIN'T HE!?
...
AAH, THAT RE-MINDS ME.
IT WAS HIS HAIR THAT LED TO US BECOMING FRIENDS...
HUH?

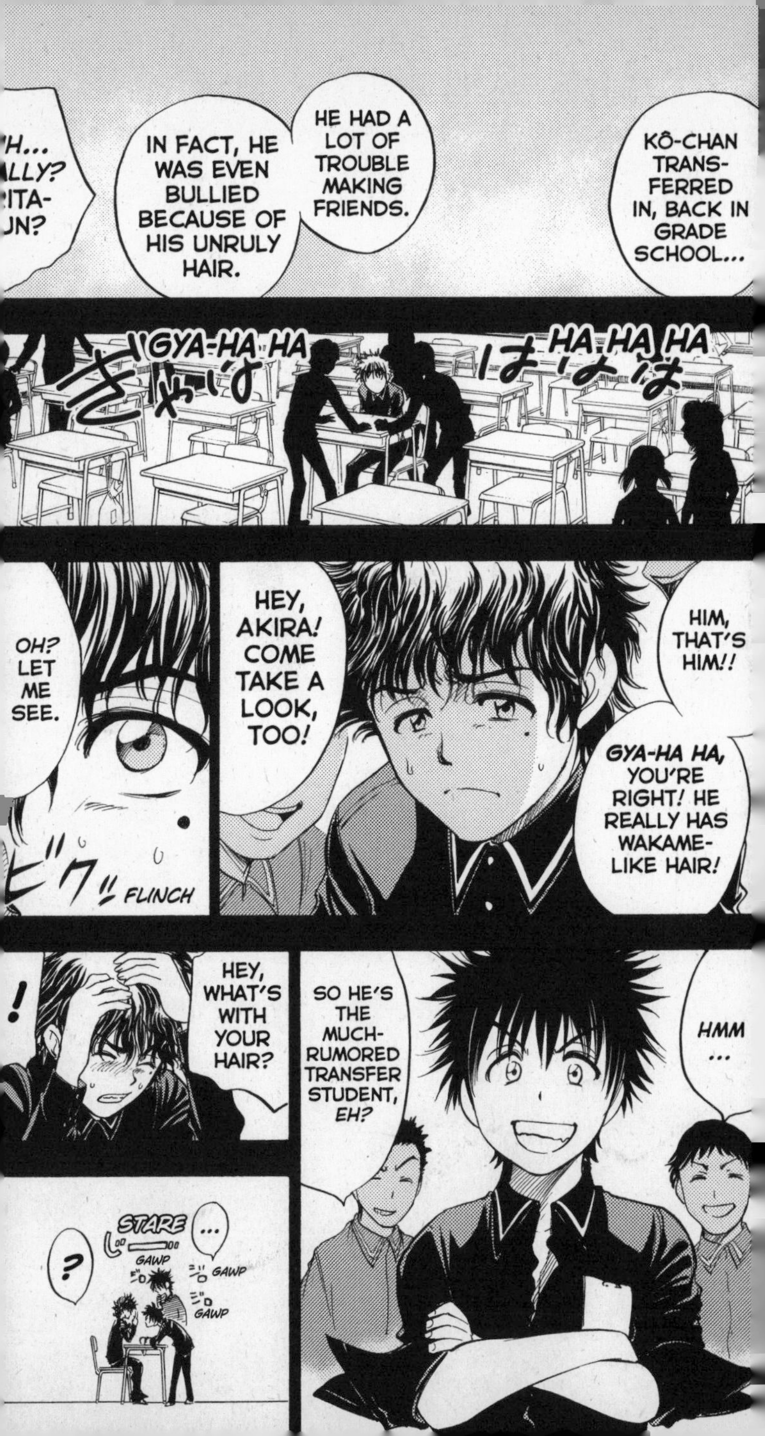
KÔ-CHAN TRANSFERRED IN, BACK IN GRADE SCHOOL...
HE HAD A LOT OF TROUBLE MAKING FRIENDS.
IN FACT, HE WAS EVEN BULLIED BECAUSE OF HIS UNRULY HAIR.
H... ALLY? RITA- UN?
HA HA HA
GYA-HA HA
HIM, THAT'S HIM!!
GYA-HA HA, YOU'RE RIGHT! HE REALLY HAS WAKAME-LIKE HAIR!
HEY, AKIRA! COME TAKE A LOOK, TOO!
OH? LET ME SEE.
FLINCH
HMM...
SO HE'S THE MUCH-RUMORED TRANSFER STUDENT, EH?
HEY, WHAT'S WITH YOUR HAIR?
!
...
STARE
GAWP
GAWP
GAWP
?

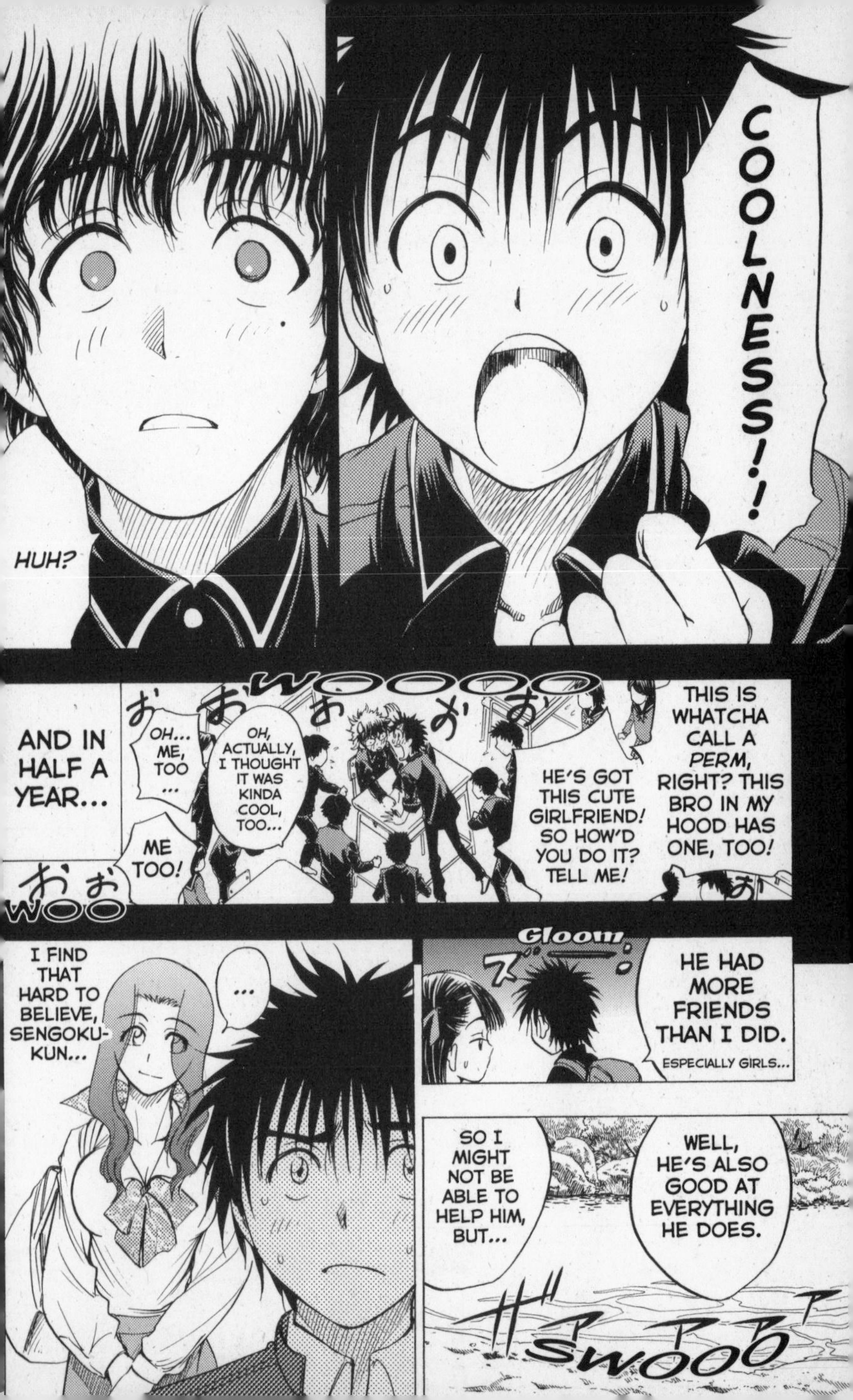
COOLNESS!!
HUH?
WOOOOO
THIS IS WHATCHA CALL A *PERM*, RIGHT? THIS BRO IN MY HOOD HAS ONE, TOO!
HE'S GOT THIS CUTE GIRLFRIEND! SO HOW'D YOU DO IT? TELL ME!
OH, ACTUALLY, I THOUGHT IT WAS KINDA COOL, TOO...
OH... ME, TOO ...
ME TOO!
AND IN HALF A YEAR...
WOO
Gloom
HE HAD MORE FRIENDS THAN I DID.
ESPECIALLY GIRLS...
WELL, HE'S ALSO GOOD AT EVERYTHING HE DOES.
SO I MIGHT NOT BE ABLE TO HELP HIM, BUT...
SWOOO
I FIND THAT HARD TO BELIEVE, SENGOKU-KUN...
...

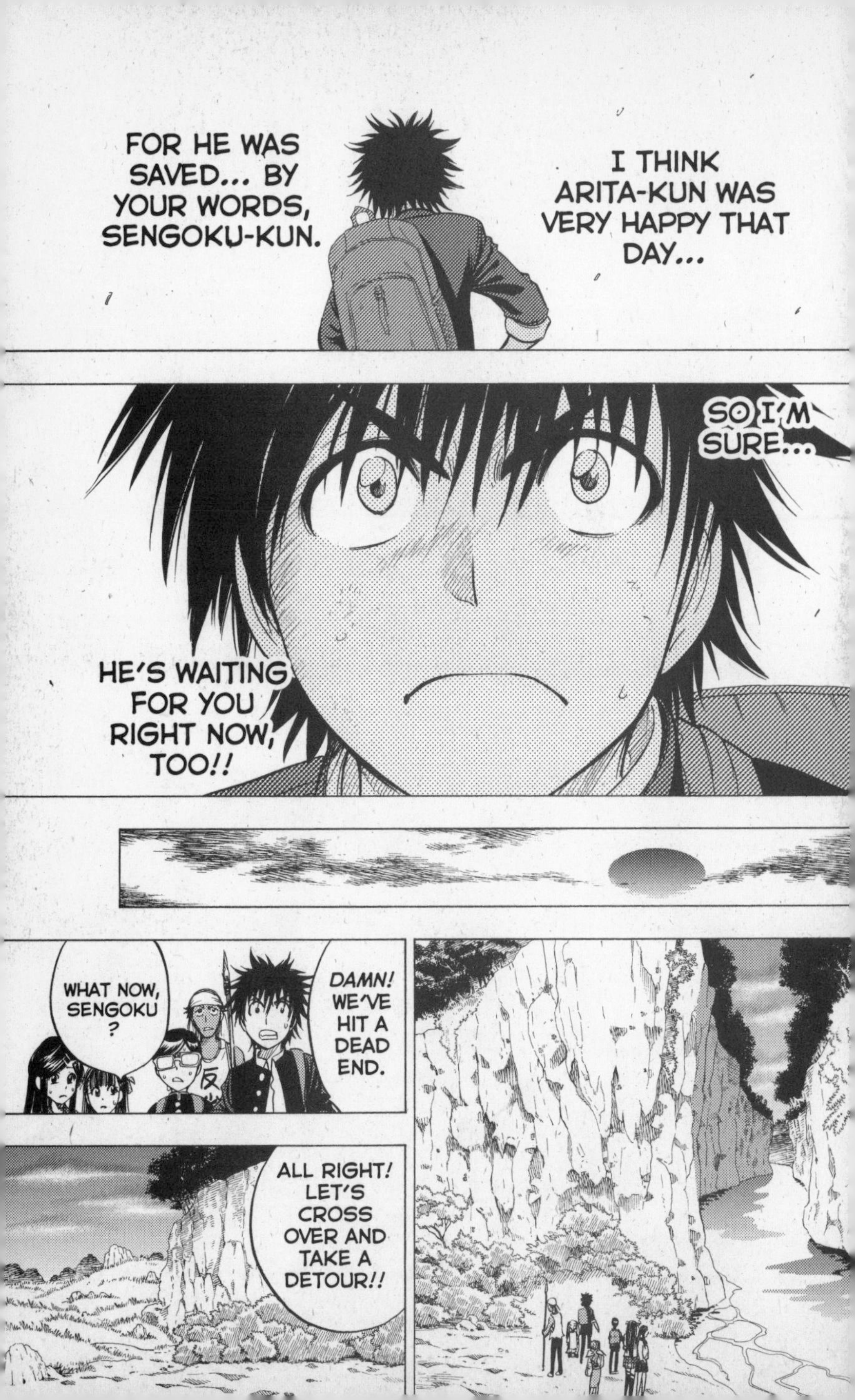
I THINK ARITA-KUN WAS VERY HAPPY THAT DAY...
FOR HE WAS SAVED... BY YOUR WORDS, SENGOKU-KUN.
SO I'M SURE...
HE'S WAITING FOR YOU RIGHT NOW, TOO!!
DAMN! WE'VE HIT A DEAD END.
WHAT NOW, SENGOKU?
ALL RIGHT! LET'S CROSS OVER AND TAKE A DETOUR!!

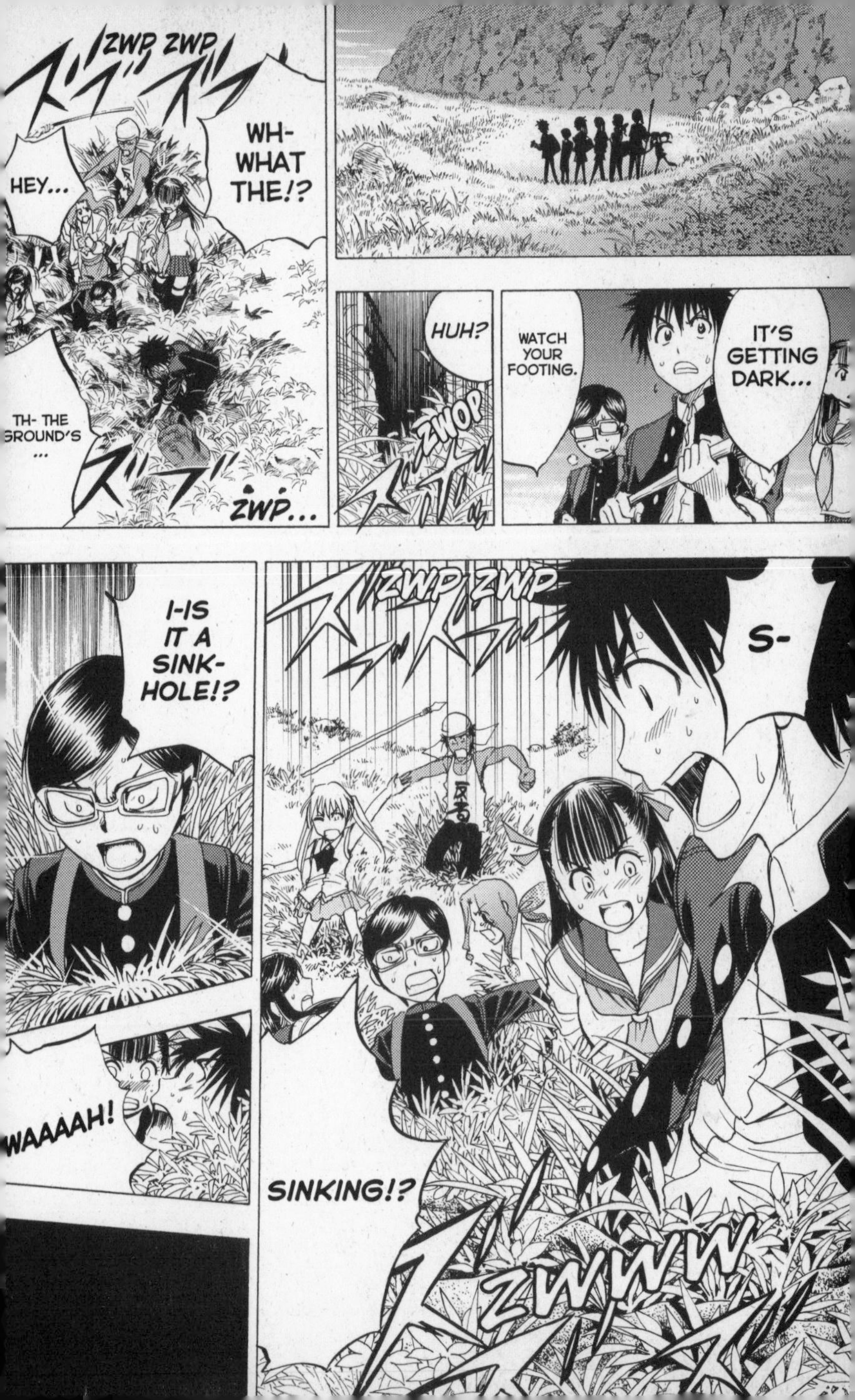
IT'S GETTING DARK...
WATCH YOUR FOOTING.
HUH?
ZWOP
ZWP ZWP
WH- WHAT THE!?
HEY...
TH- THE GROUND'S ...
ZWP...
ZWP ZWP
S-
SINKING!?
ZWWW
I-IS IT A SINK-HOLE!?
WAAAAH!

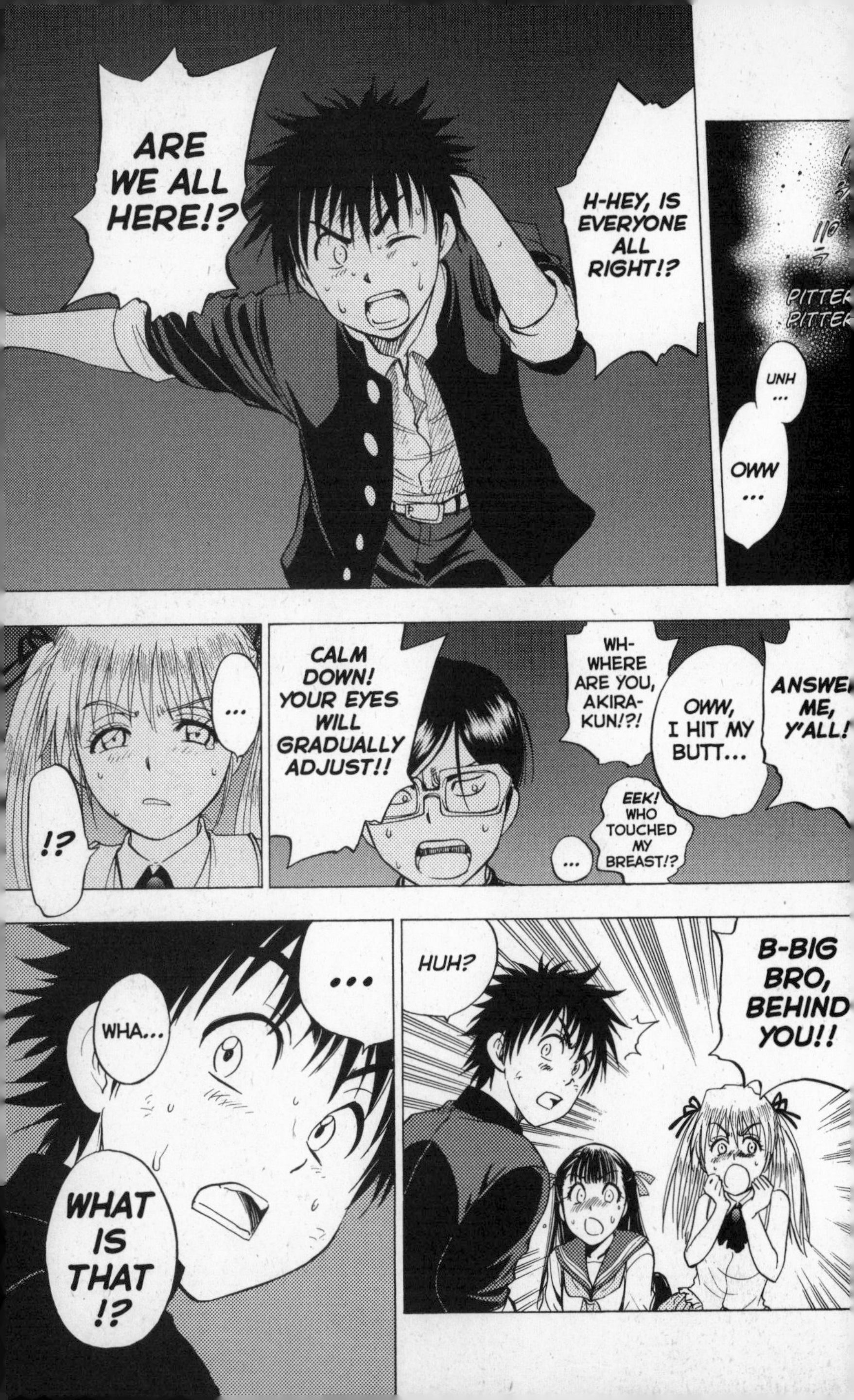
PITTER
PITTER
UNH ...
OWW ...
H-HEY, IS EVERYONE ALL RIGHT!?
ARE WE ALL HERE!?
ANSWE ME, Y'ALL!
WH- WHERE ARE YOU, AKIRA-KUN!?!
OWW, I HIT MY BUTT...
EEK! WHO TOUCHED MY BREAST!?
...
CALM DOWN! YOUR EYES WILL GRADUALLY ADJUST!!
...
!?
B-BIG BRO, BEHIND YOU!!
HUH?
...
WHA...
WHAT IS THAT!?

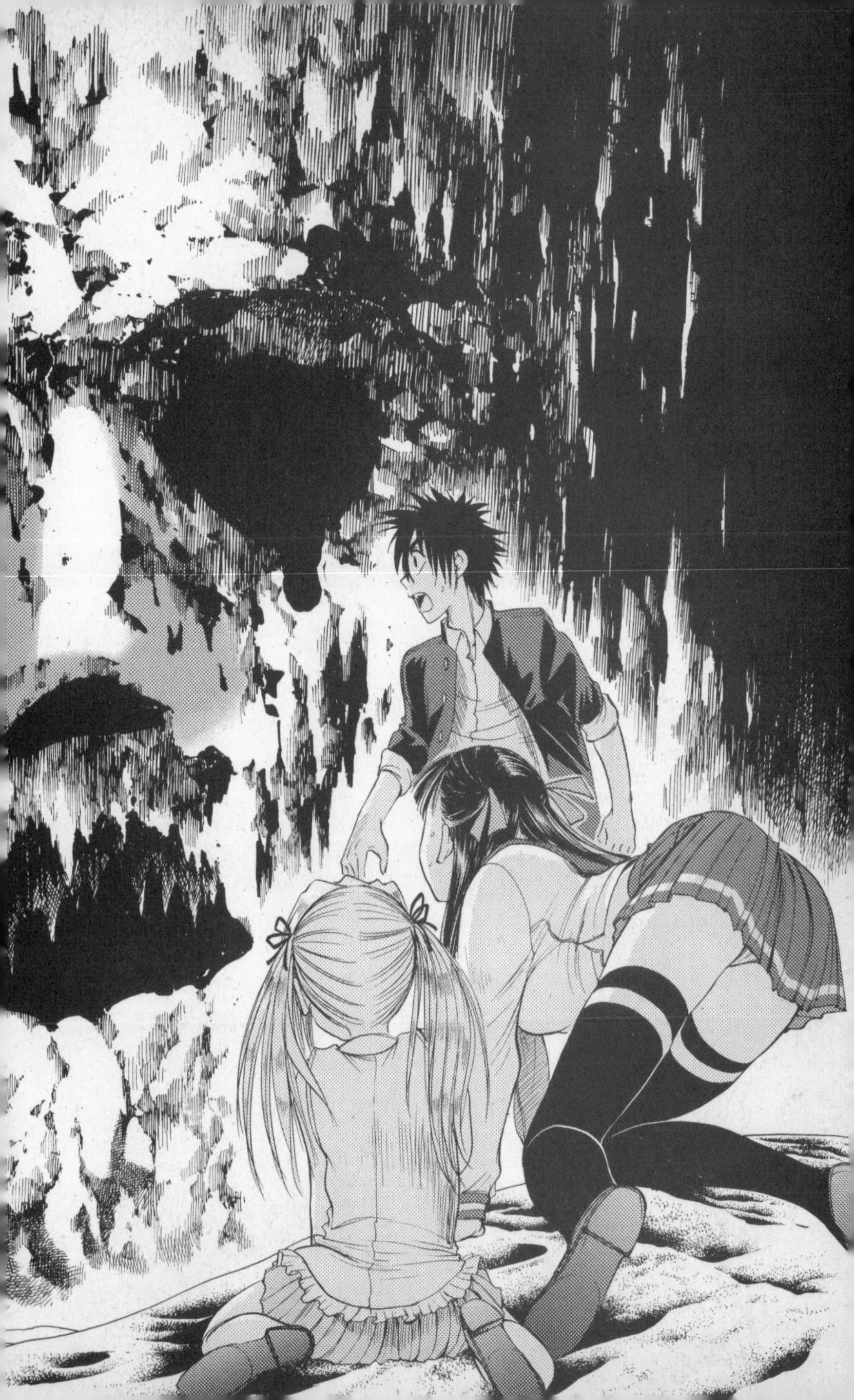

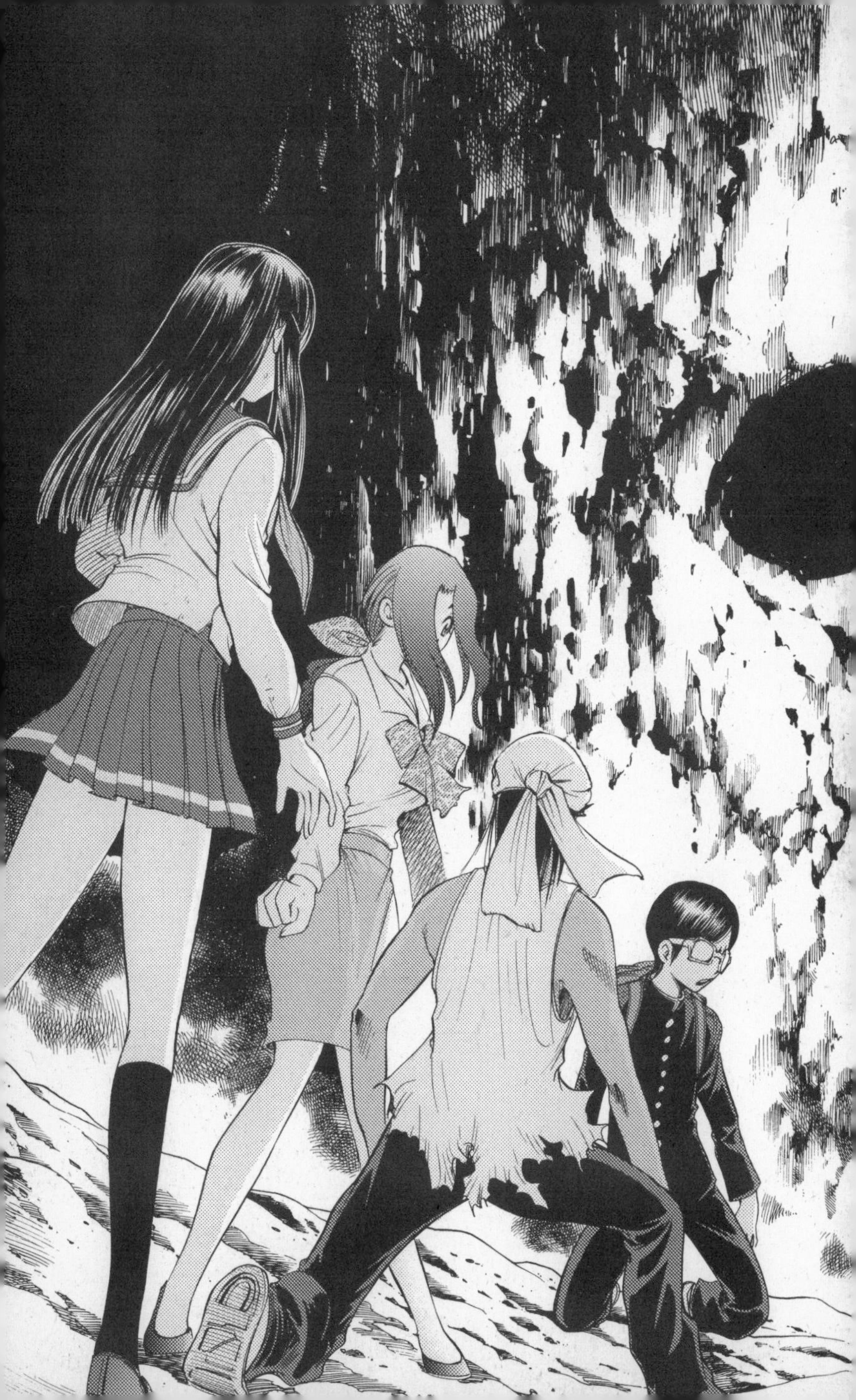

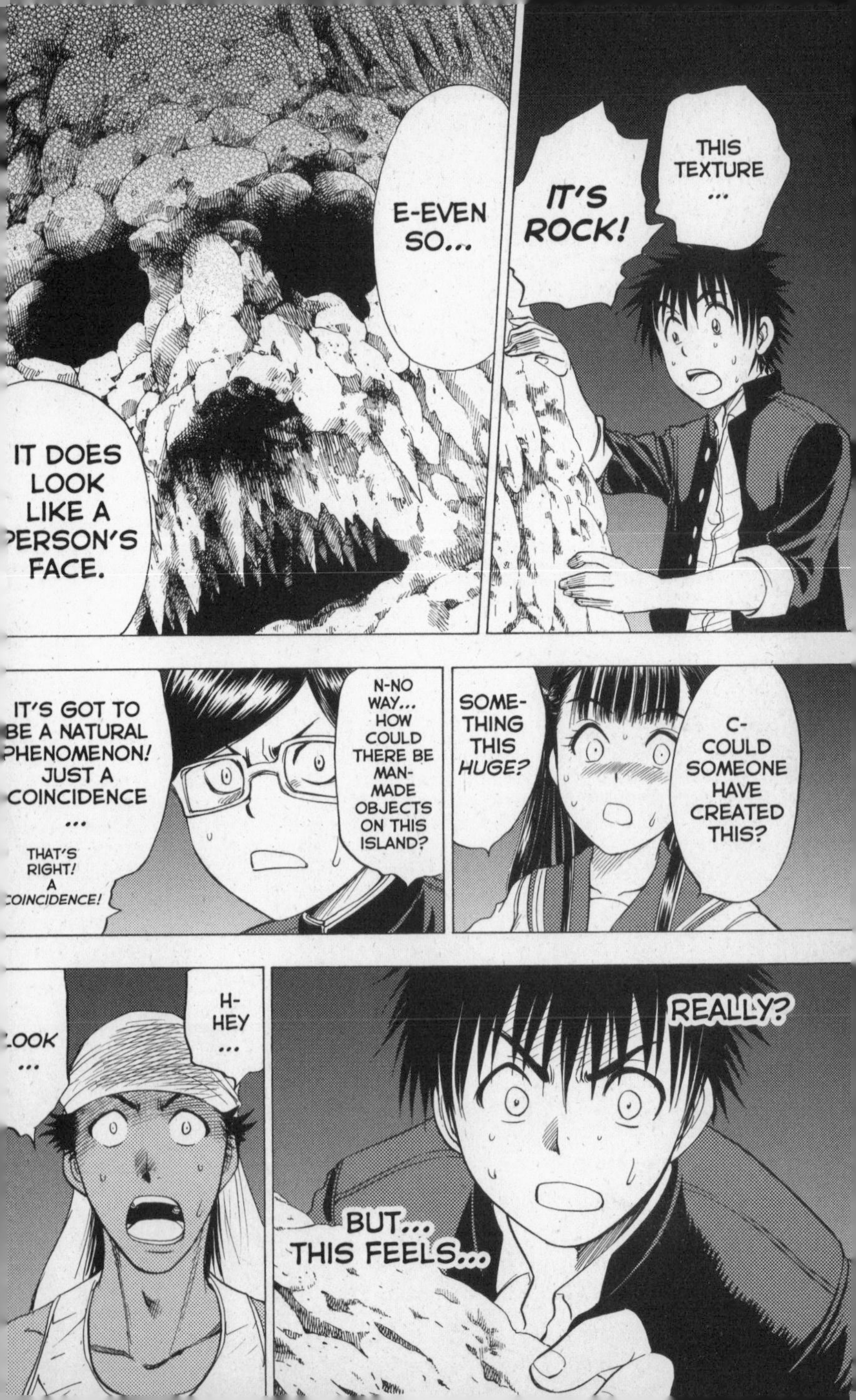
THIS TEXTURE ...
IT'S ROCK!
E-EVEN SO...
IT DOES LOOK LIKE A PERSON'S FACE.
C-COULD SOMEONE HAVE CREATED THIS?
SOMETHING THIS *HUGE?*
N-NO WAY... HOW COULD THERE BE MAN-MADE OBJECTS ON THIS ISLAND?
IT'S GOT TO BE A NATURAL PHENOMENON! JUST A COINCIDENCE ...
THAT'S RIGHT! A COINCIDENCE!
REALLY?
BUT... THIS FEELS...
H-HEY ...
LOOK ...

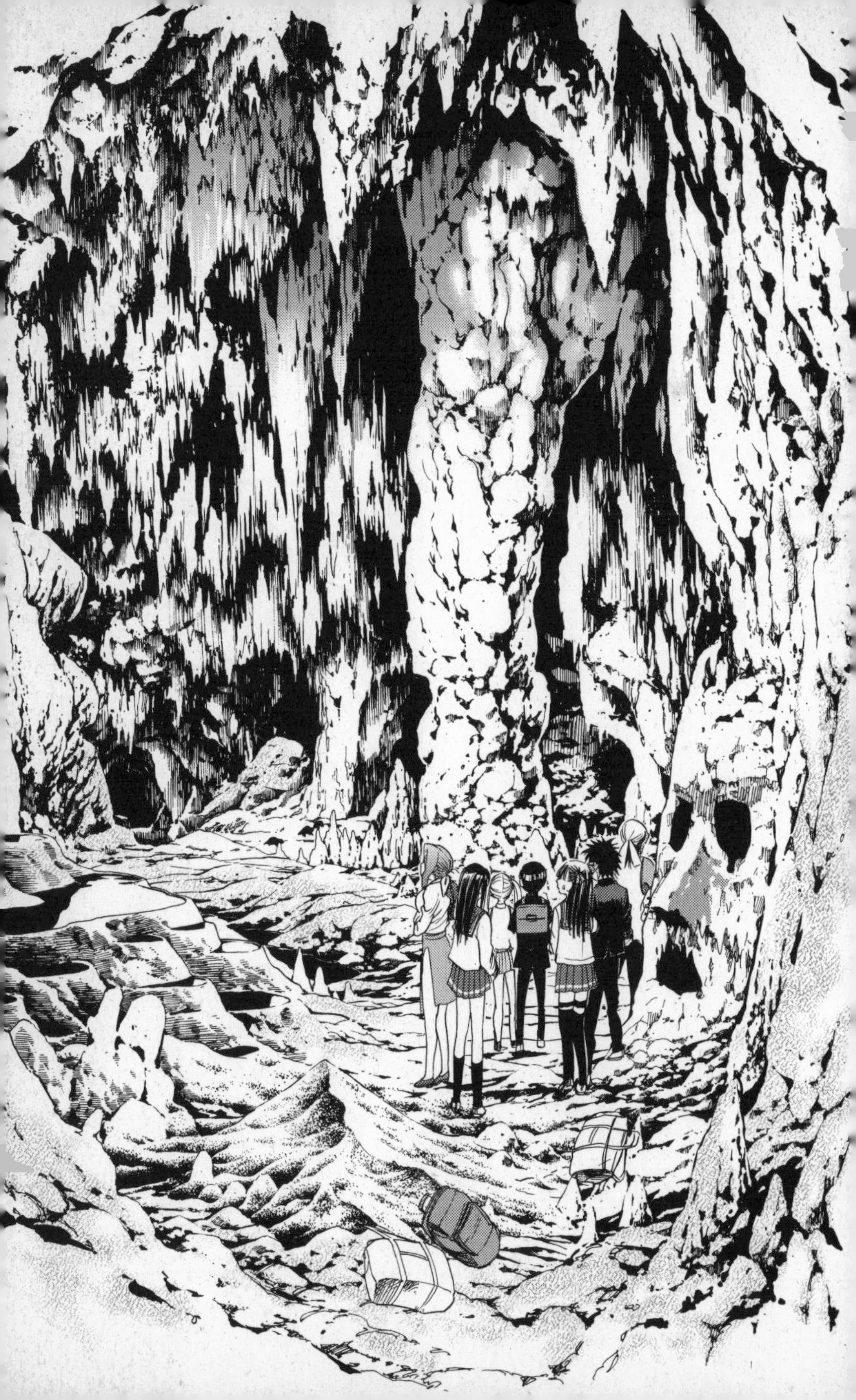

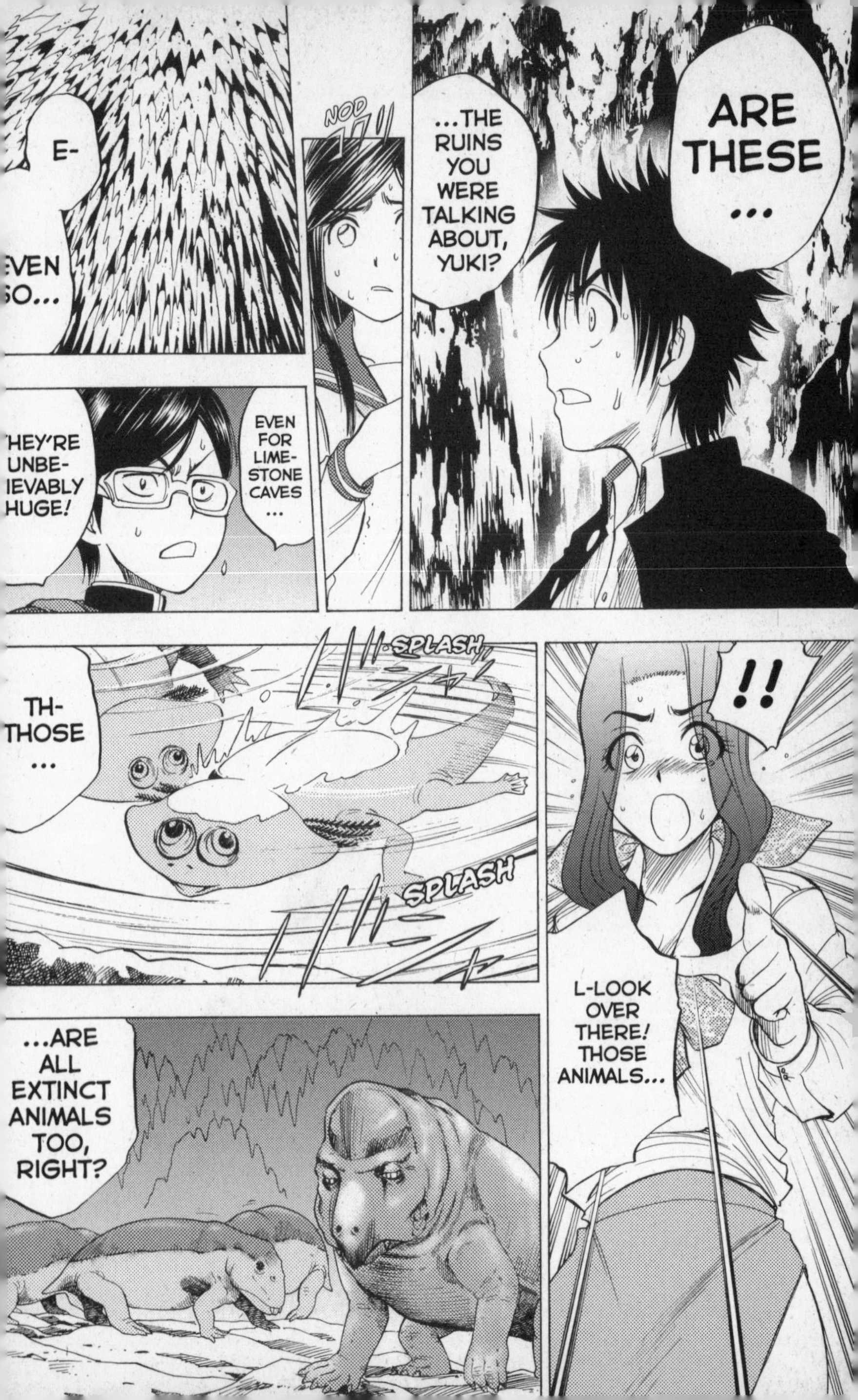
ARE THESE...
...THE RUINS YOU WERE TALKING ABOUT, YUKI?
NOD
EVEN FOR LIME-STONE CAVES...
E-
EVEN SO...
THEY'RE UNBE-LIEVABLY HUGE!
!!
L-LOOK OVER THERE! THOSE ANIMALS...
SPLASH
TH-THOSE...
SPLASH
...ARE ALL EXTINCT ANIMALS TOO, RIGHT?

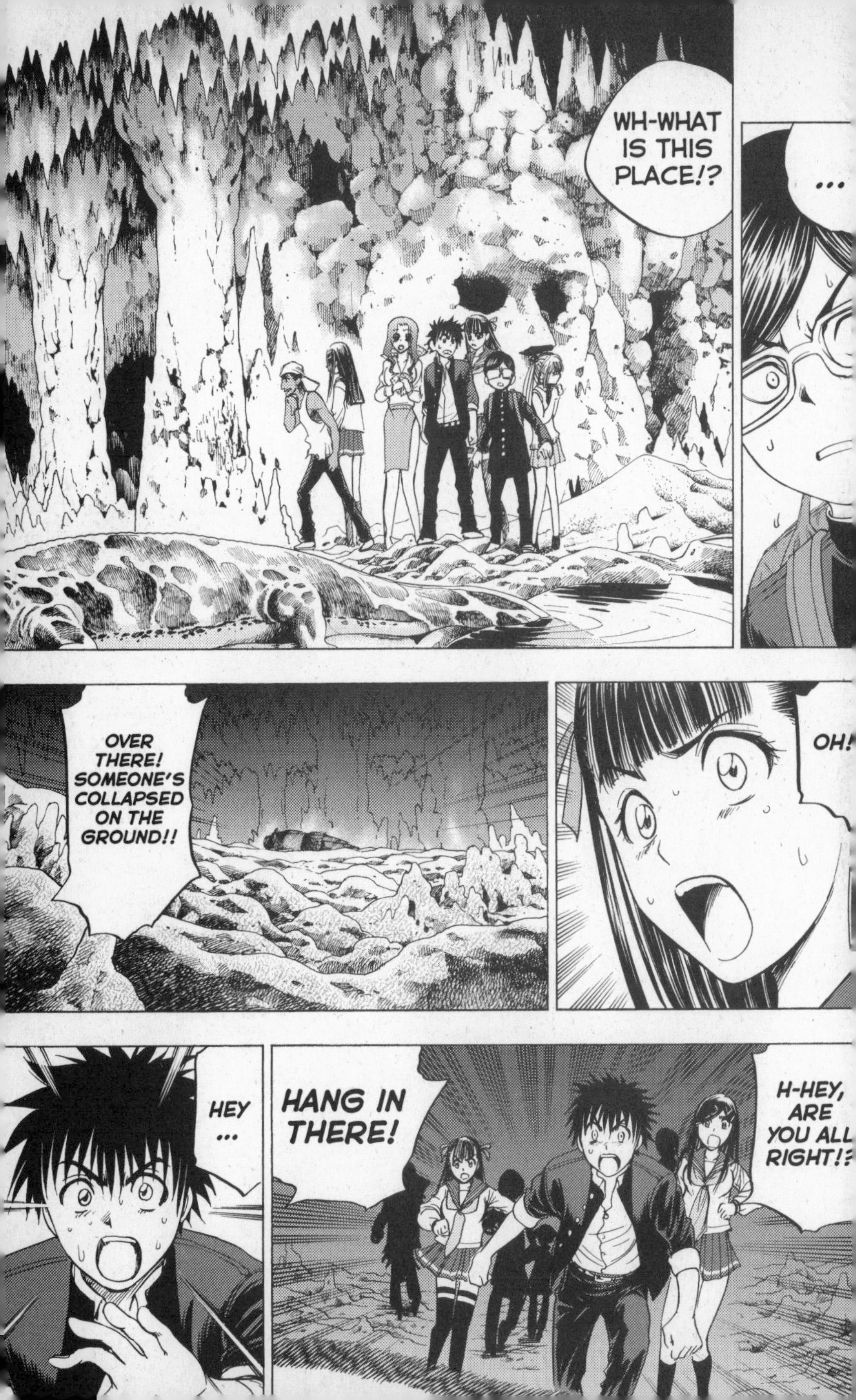
...
WH-WHAT IS THIS PLACE!?
OH!
OVER THERE! SOMEONE'S COLLAPSED ON THE GROUND!!
H-HEY, ARE YOU ALL RIGHT!?
HANG IN THERE!
HEY ...

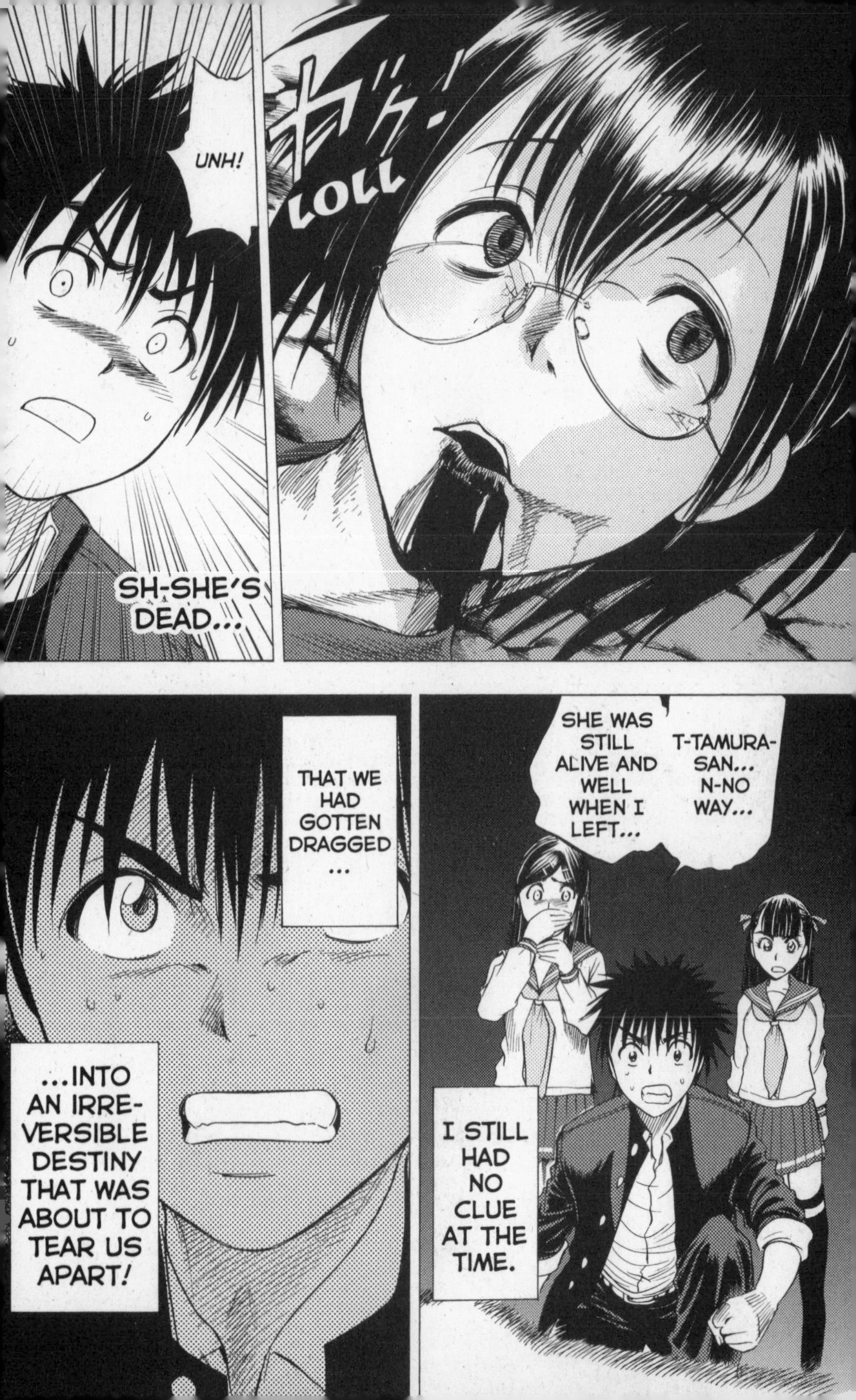
LOLL
UNH!
SH-SHE'S DEAD...
T-TAMURA-SAN... N-NO WAY...
SHE WAS STILL ALIVE AND WELL WHEN I LEFT...
I STILL HAD NO CLUE AT THE TIME.
THAT WE HAD GOTTEN DRAGGED...
...INTO AN IRRE-VERSIBLE DESTINY THAT WAS ABOUT TO TEAR US APART!

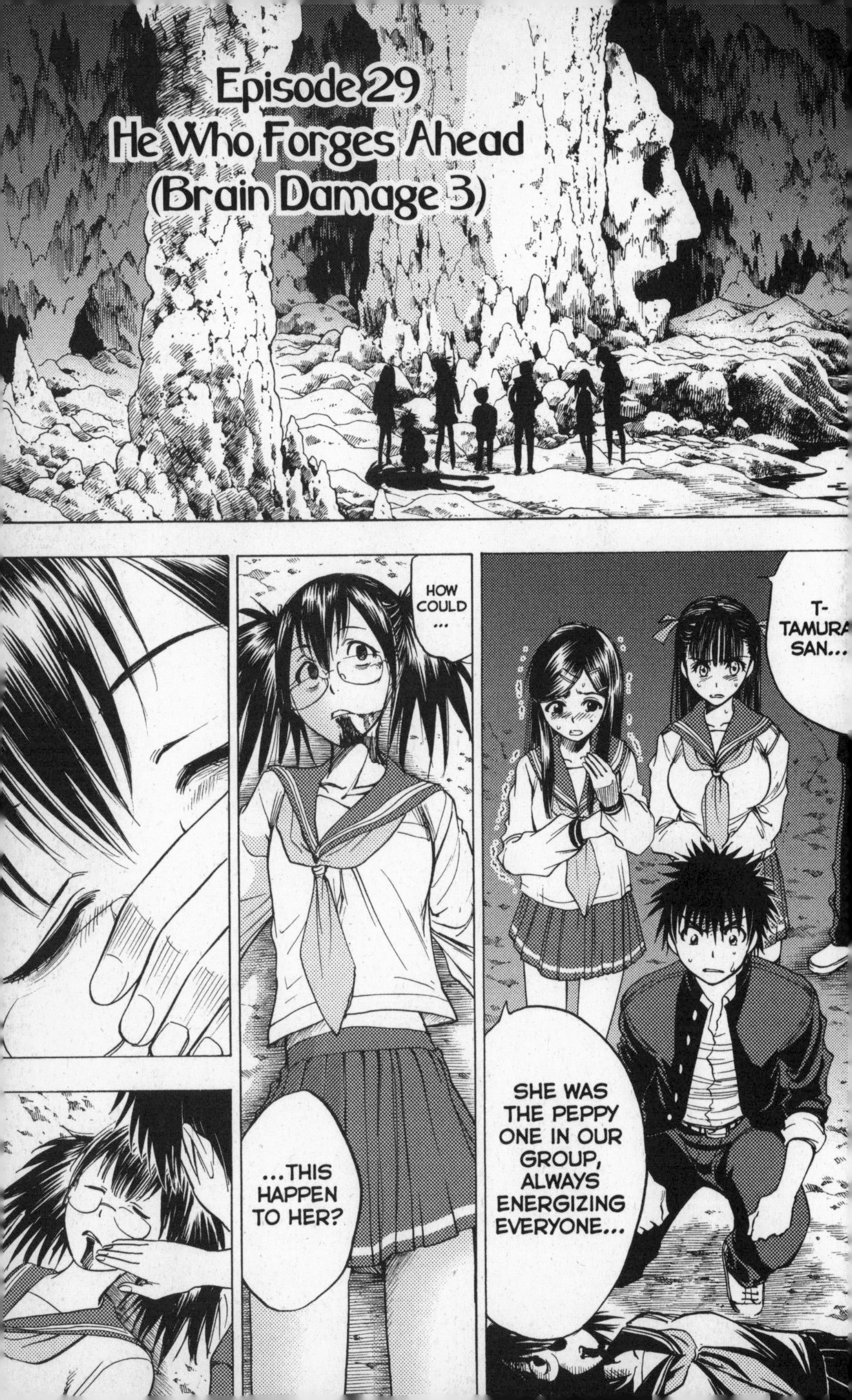
Episode 29
He Who Forges Ahead
(Brain Damage 3)
T-TAMURA SAN...
SHE WAS THE PEPPY ONE IN OUR GROUP, ALWAYS ENERGIZING EVERYONE...
HOW COULD ...
...THIS HAPPEN TO HER?

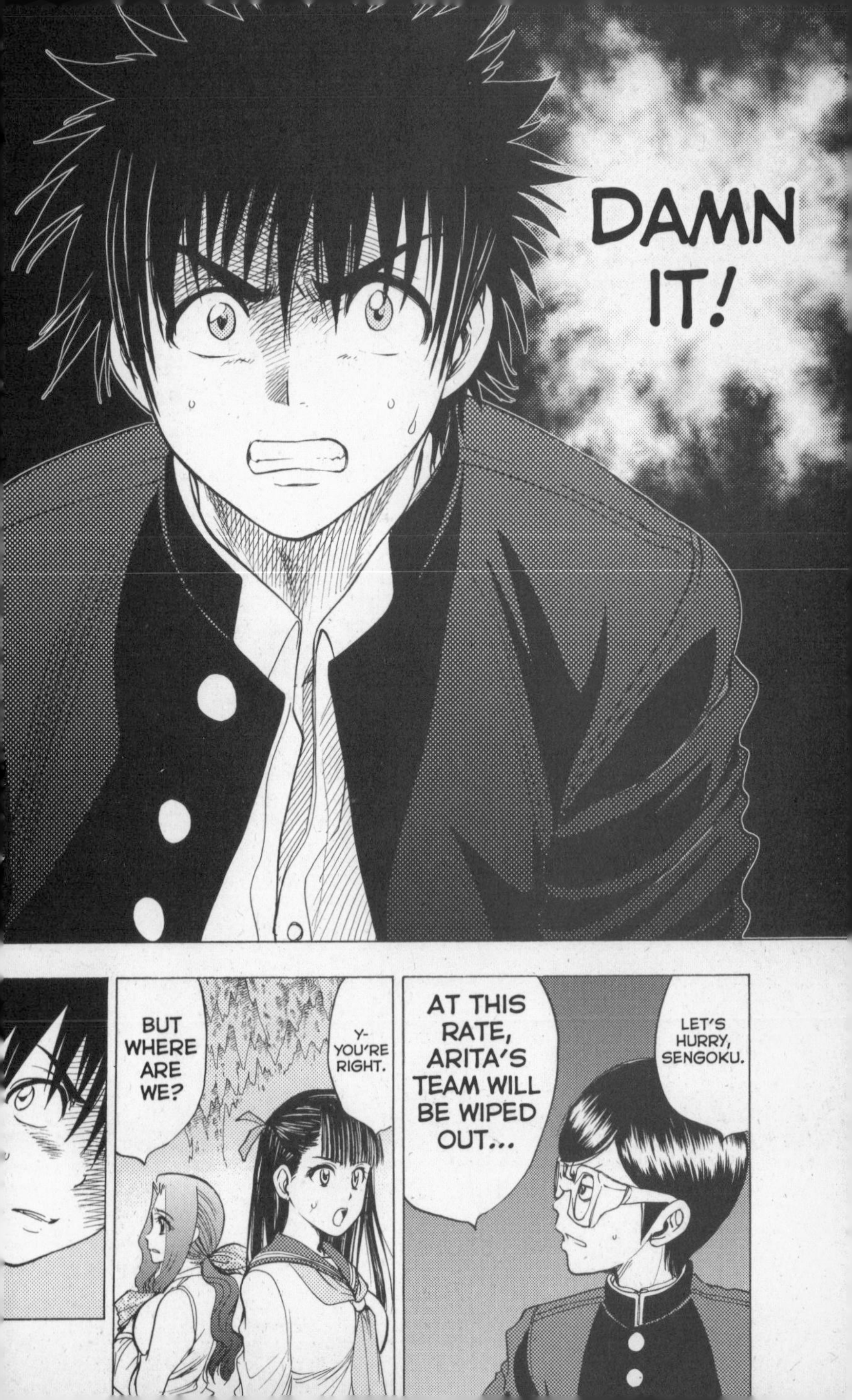
DAMN IT!
LET'S HURRY, SENGOKU.
AT THIS RATE, ARITA'S TEAM WILL BE WIPED OUT...
Y-YOU'RE RIGHT.
BUT WHERE ARE WE?

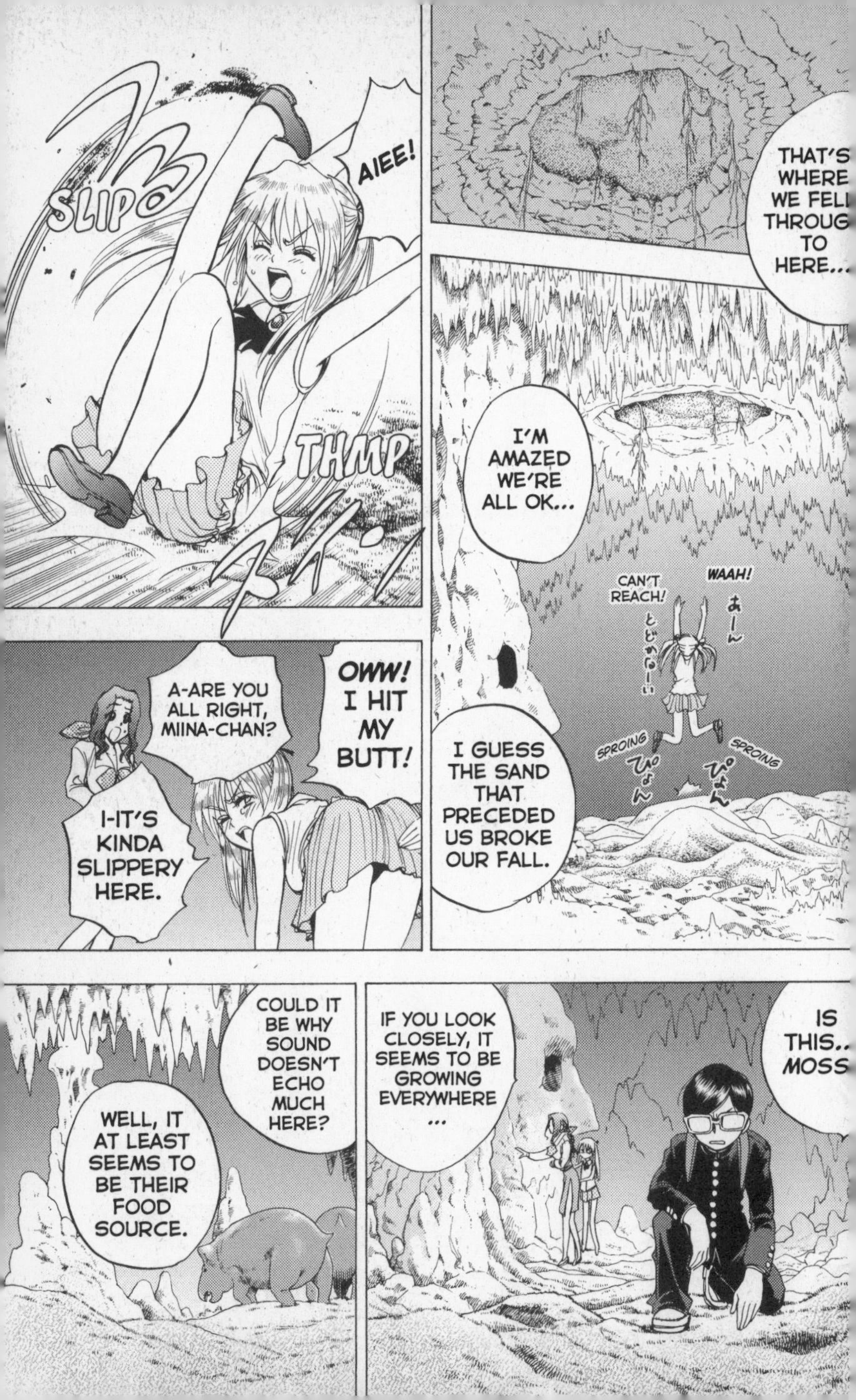
THAT'S WHERE WE FELL THROUG TO HERE...
I'M AMAZED WE'RE ALL OK...
CAN'T REACH!
とどかねーい
WAAH!
あーん
SPROING
ぴょん
SPROING
ぴょん
I GUESS THE SAND THAT PRECEDED US BROKE OUR FALL.
AIEE!
SLIP
THMP
OWW! I HIT MY BUTT!
A-ARE YOU ALL RIGHT, MIINA-CHAN?
I-IT'S KINDA SLIPPERY HERE.
IS THIS.. MOSS
IF YOU LOOK CLOSELY, IT SEEMS TO BE GROWING EVERYWHERE ...
COULD IT BE WHY SOUND DOESN'T ECHO MUCH HERE?
WELL, IT AT LEAST SEEMS TO BE THEIR FOOD SOURCE.

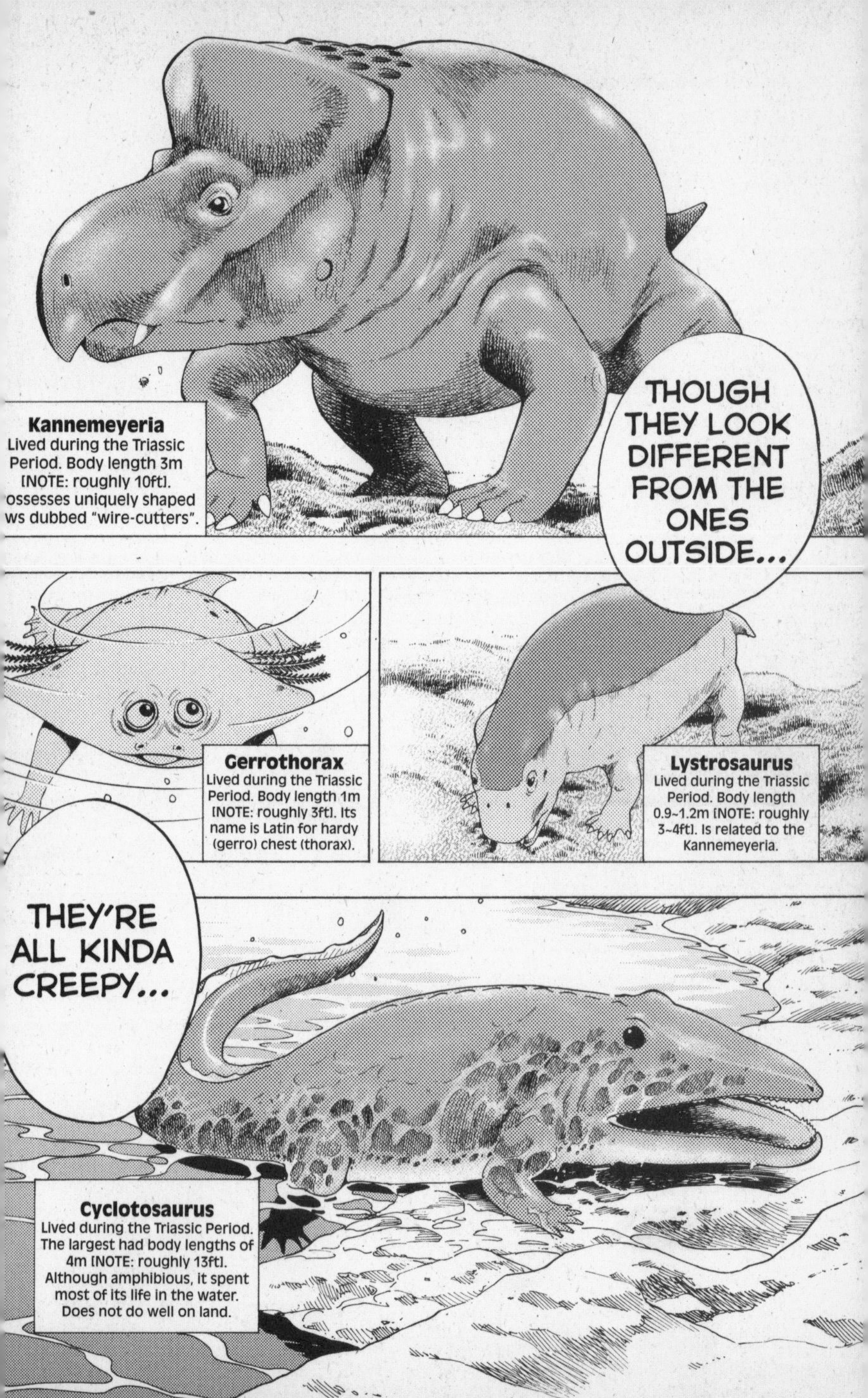
THOUGH THEY LOOK DIFFERENT FROM THE ONES OUTSIDE...
Kannemeyeria
Lived during the Triassic Period. Body length 3m [NOTE: roughly 10ft]. ossesses uniquely shaped ws dubbed "wire-cutters".
Lystrosaurus
Lived during the Triassic Period. Body length 0.9~1.2m [NOTE: roughly 3~4ft]. Is related to the Kannemeyeria.
Gerrothorax
Lived during the Triassic Period. Body length 1m [NOTE: roughly 3ft]. Its name is Latin for hardy (gerro) chest (thorax).
THEY'RE ALL KINDA CREEPY...
Cyclotosaurus
Lived during the Triassic Period. The largest had body lengths of 4m [NOTE: roughly 13ft]. Although amphibious, it spent most of its life in the water. Does not do well on land.

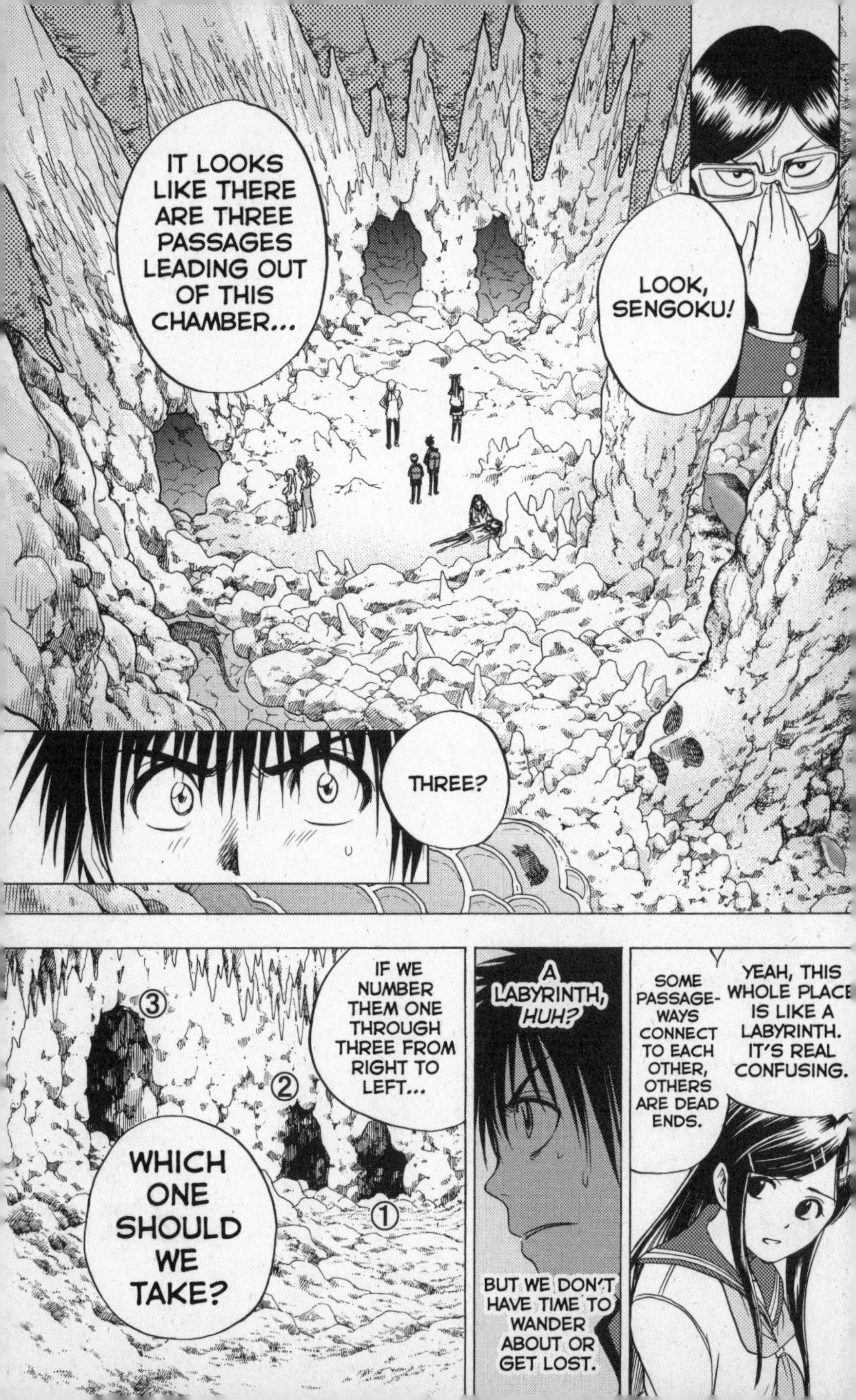
LOOK, SENGOKU!
IT LOOKS LIKE THERE ARE THREE PASSAGES LEADING OUT OF THIS CHAMBER...
THREE?
YEAH, THIS WHOLE PLACE IS LIKE A LABYRINTH. IT'S REAL CONFUSING.
SOME PASSAGEWAYS CONNECT TO EACH OTHER, OTHERS ARE DEAD ENDS.
A LABYRINTH, HUH?
BUT WE DON'T HAVE TIME TO WANDER ABOUT OR GET LOST.
IF WE NUMBER THEM ONE THROUGH THREE FROM RIGHT TO LEFT...
③
②
①
WHICH ONE SHOULD WE TAKE?

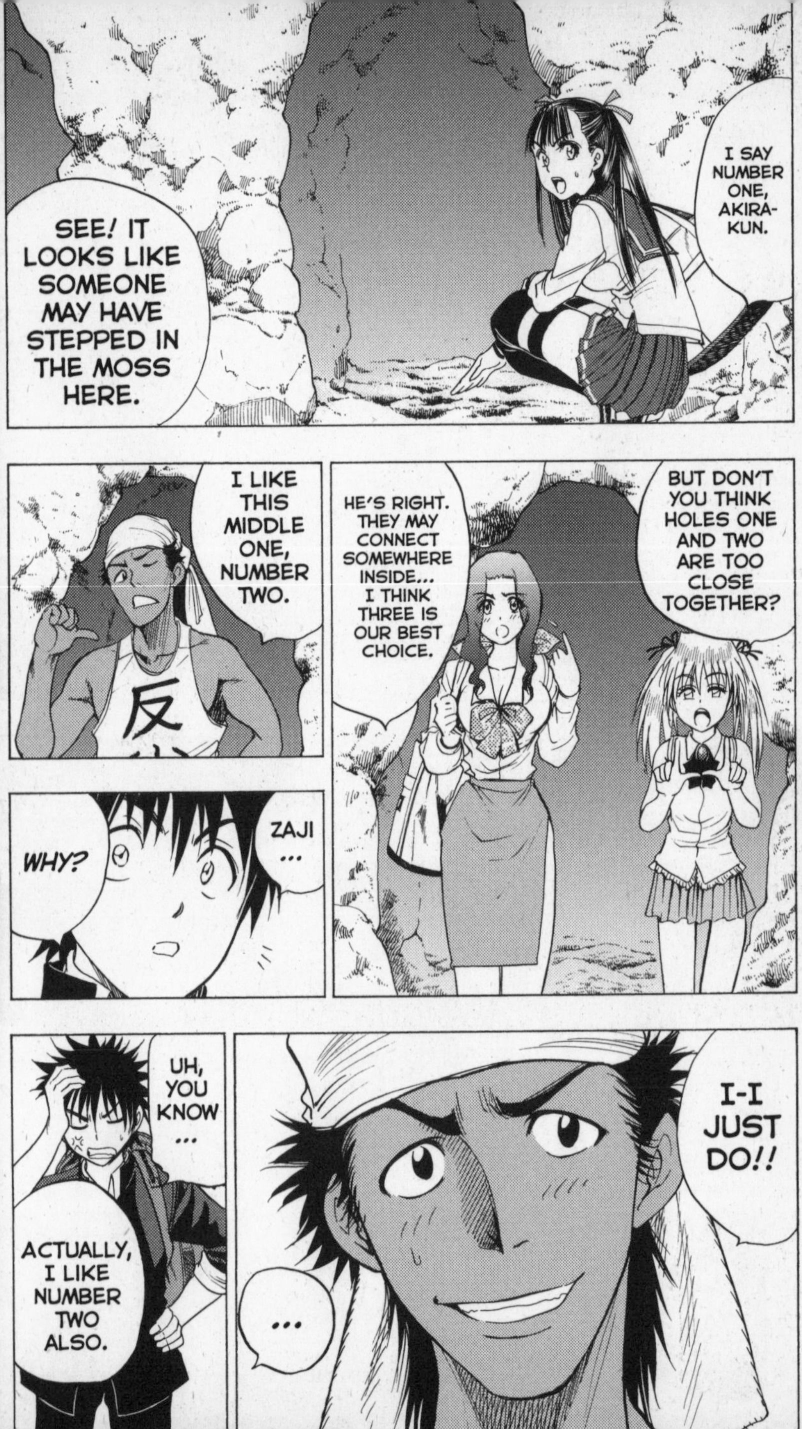
I SAY NUMBER ONE, AKIRA-KUN.
SEE! IT LOOKS LIKE SOMEONE MAY HAVE STEPPED IN THE MOSS HERE.
BUT DON'T YOU THINK HOLES ONE AND TWO ARE TOO CLOSE TOGETHER?
HE'S RIGHT. THEY MAY CONNECT SOMEWHERE INSIDE... I THINK THREE IS OUR BEST CHOICE.
I LIKE THIS MIDDLE ONE, NUMBER TWO.
ZAJI ...
WHY?
I-I JUST DO!!
...
UH, YOU KNOW ...
ACTUALLY, I LIKE NUMBER TWO ALSO.

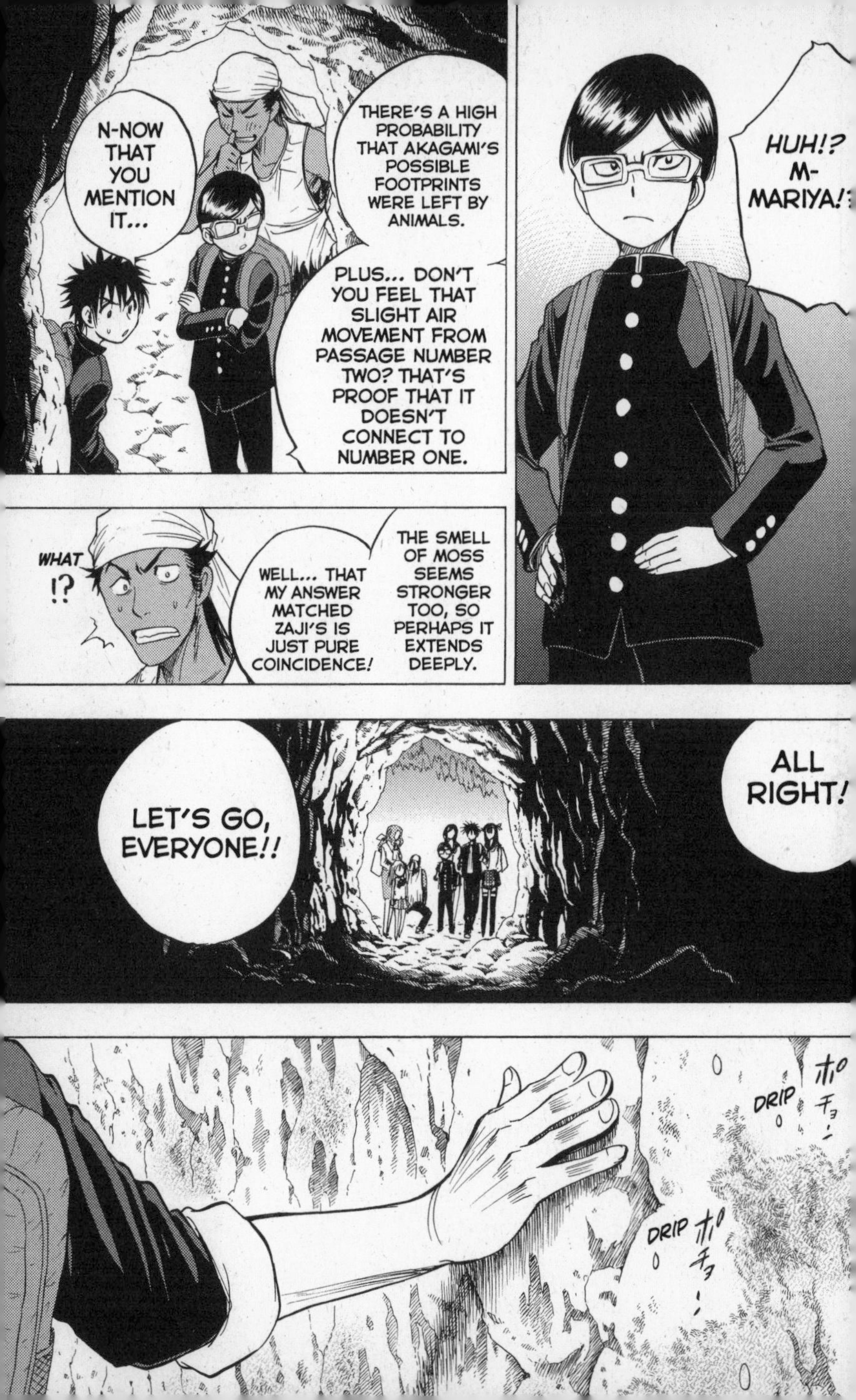
HUH!? M-MARIYA!?
THERE'S A HIGH PROBABILITY THAT AKAGAMI'S POSSIBLE FOOTPRINTS WERE LEFT BY ANIMALS.
PLUS... DON'T YOU FEEL THAT SLIGHT AIR MOVEMENT FROM PASSAGE NUMBER TWO? THAT'S PROOF THAT IT DOESN'T CONNECT TO NUMBER ONE.
N-NOW THAT YOU MENTION IT...
THE SMELL OF MOSS SEEMS STRONGER TOO, SO PERHAPS IT EXTENDS DEEPLY.
WELL... THAT MY ANSWER MATCHED ZAJI'S IS JUST PURE COINCIDENCE!
WHAT !?
ALL RIGHT!
LET'S GO, EVERYONE!!
ポチョ!
DRIP
ポチョ!
DRIP

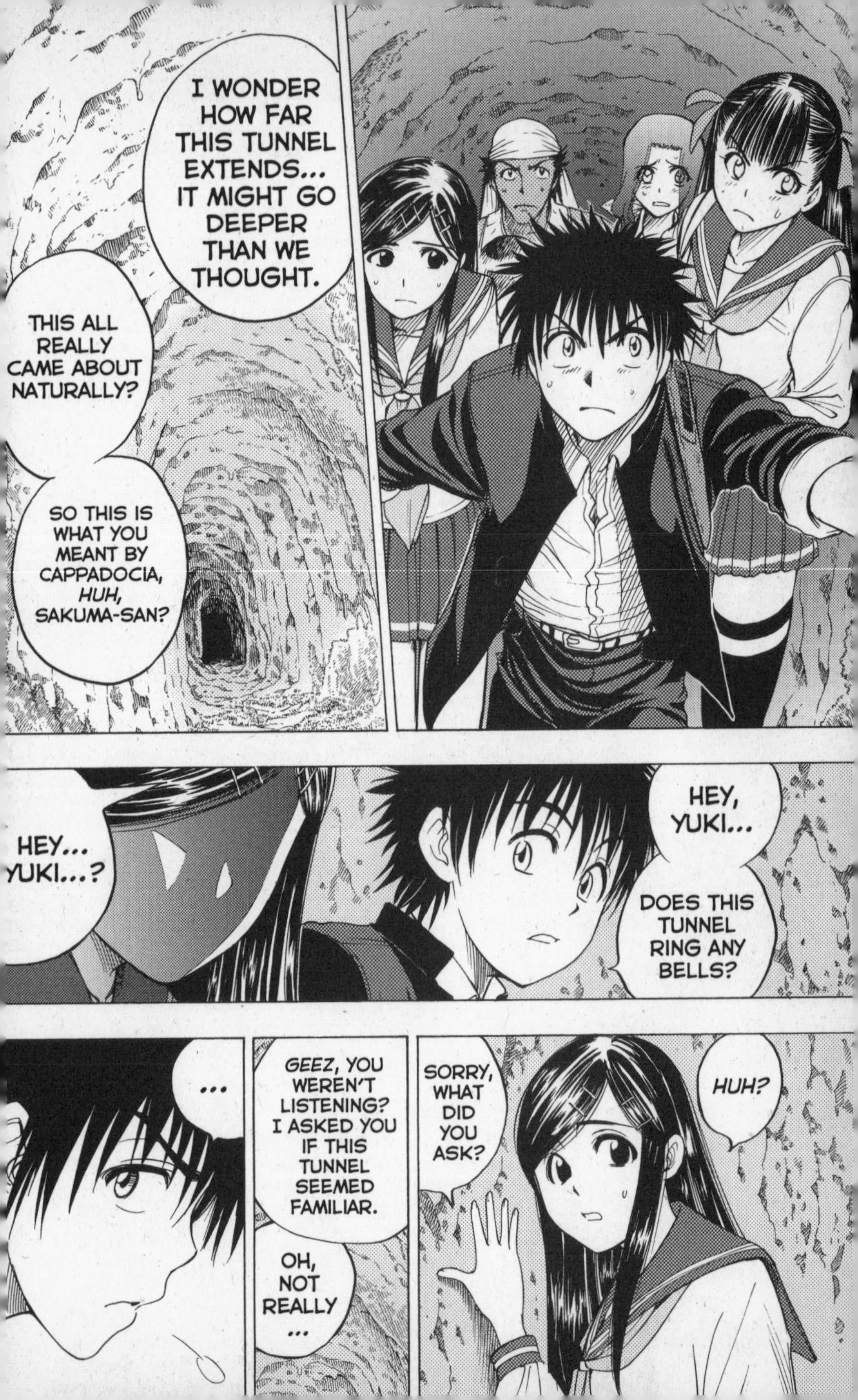
I WONDER HOW FAR THIS TUNNEL EXTENDS... IT MIGHT GO DEEPER THAN WE THOUGHT.
THIS ALL REALLY CAME ABOUT NATURALLY?
SO THIS IS WHAT YOU MEANT BY CAPPADOCIA, *HUH,* SAKUMA-SAN?
HEY, YUKI...
DOES THIS TUNNEL RING ANY BELLS?
HEY... YUKI...?
HUH?
SORRY, WHAT DID YOU ASK?
GEEZ, YOU WEREN'T LISTENING? I ASKED YOU IF THIS TUNNEL SEEMED FAMILIAR.
OH, NOT REALLY ...
...

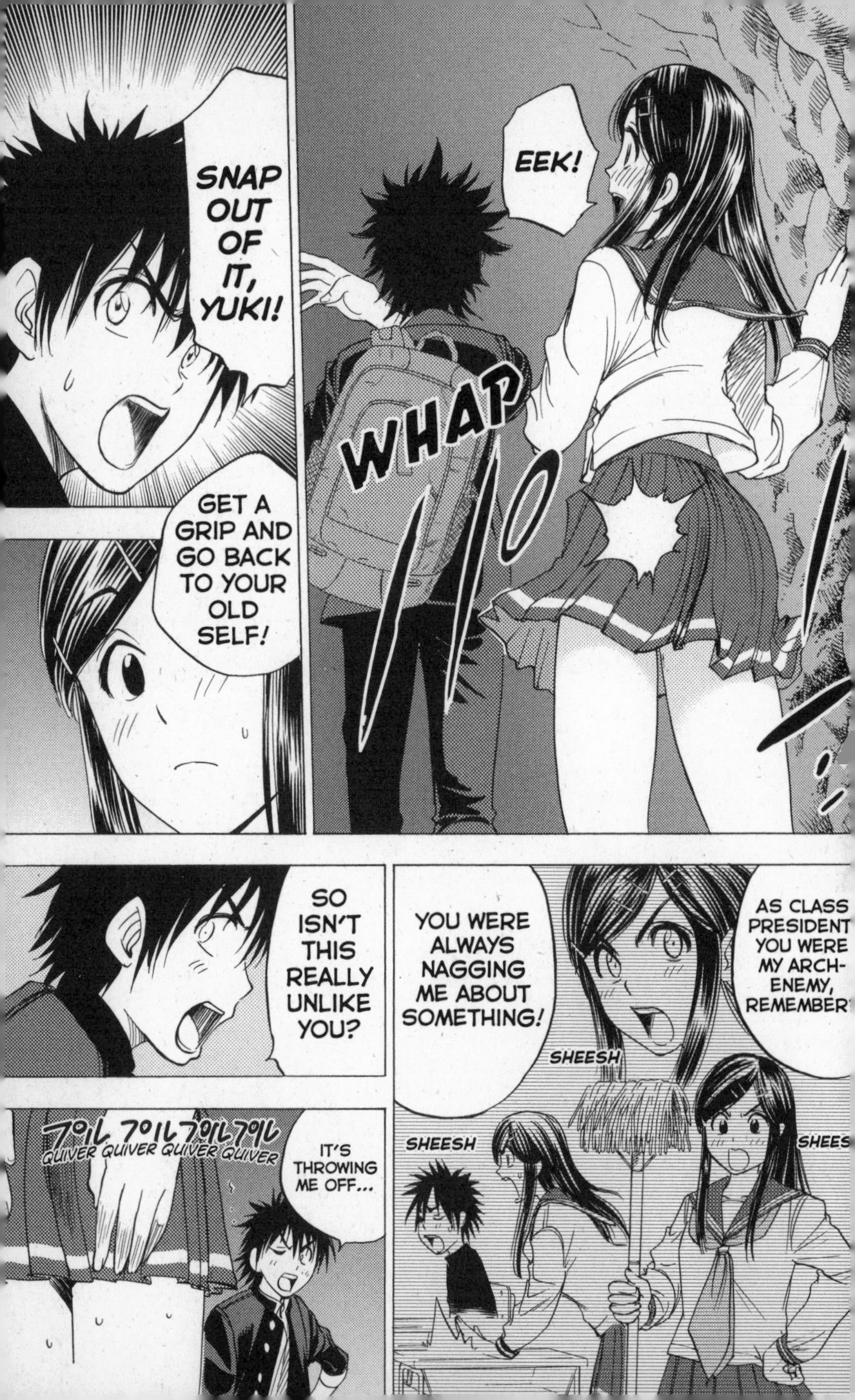
EEK!
WHAP
SNAP OUT OF IT, YUKI!
GET A GRIP AND GO BACK TO YOUR OLD SELF!
AS CLASS PRESIDENT YOU WERE MY ARCH-ENEMY, REMEMBER
YOU WERE ALWAYS NAGGING ME ABOUT SOMETHING!
SHEES
SHEESH
SHEESH
SO ISN'T THIS REALLY UNLIKE YOU?
プルプルプルプル
QUIVER QUIVER QUIVER QUIVER
IT'S THROWING ME OFF...

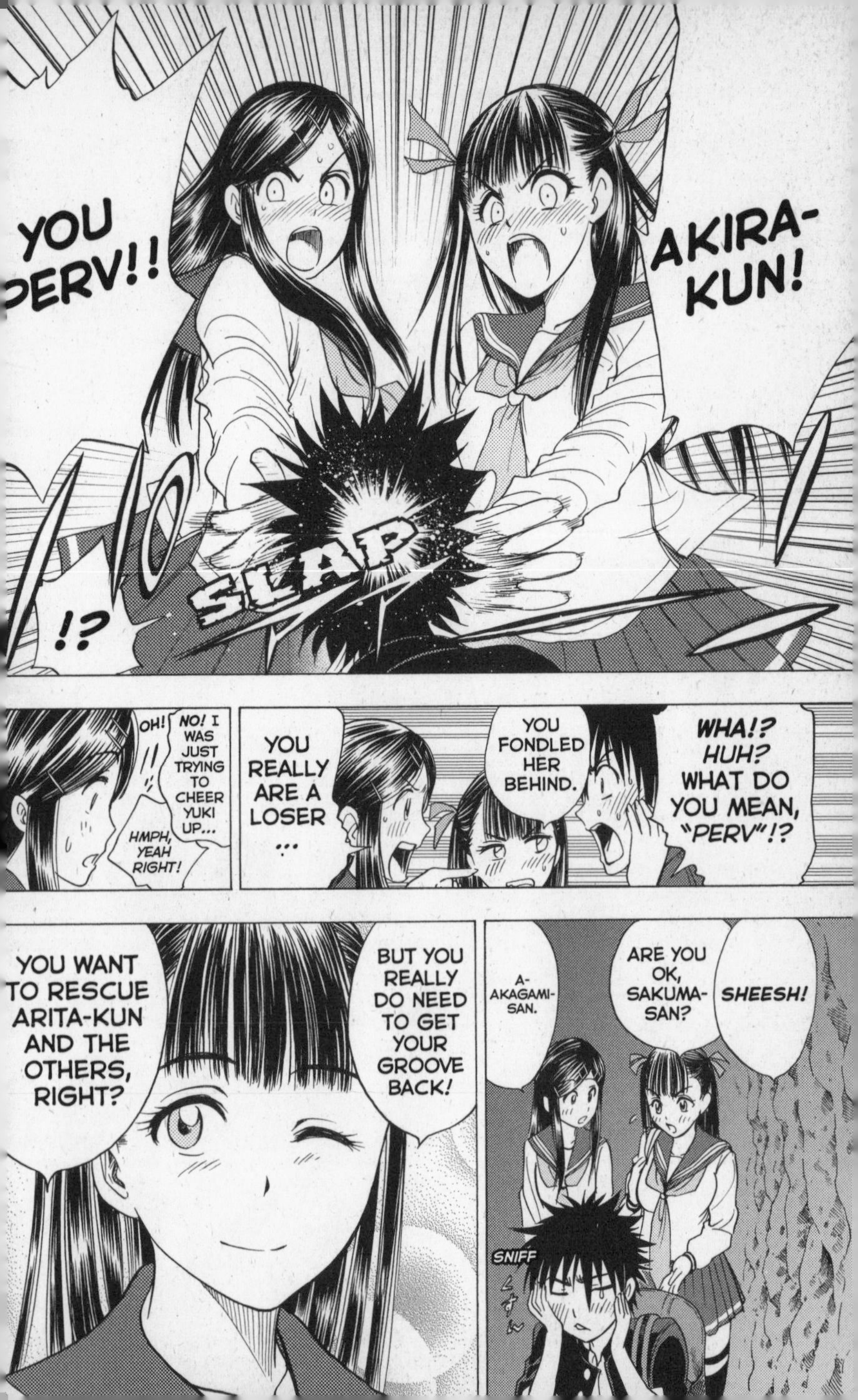
AKIRA-KUN!
YOU PERV!!
SLAP
!?
WHA!? HUH? WHAT DO YOU MEAN, "PERV"!?
YOU FONDLED HER BEHIND.
YOU REALLY ARE A LOSER ...
NO! I WAS JUST TRYING TO CHEER YUKI UP...
OH!
HMPH, YEAH RIGHT!
SHEESH!
ARE YOU OK, SAKUMA-SAN?
A-AKAGAMI-SAN.
SNIFF
BUT YOU REALLY DO NEED TO GET YOUR GROOVE BACK!
YOU WANT TO RESCUE ARITA-KUN AND THE OTHERS, RIGHT?

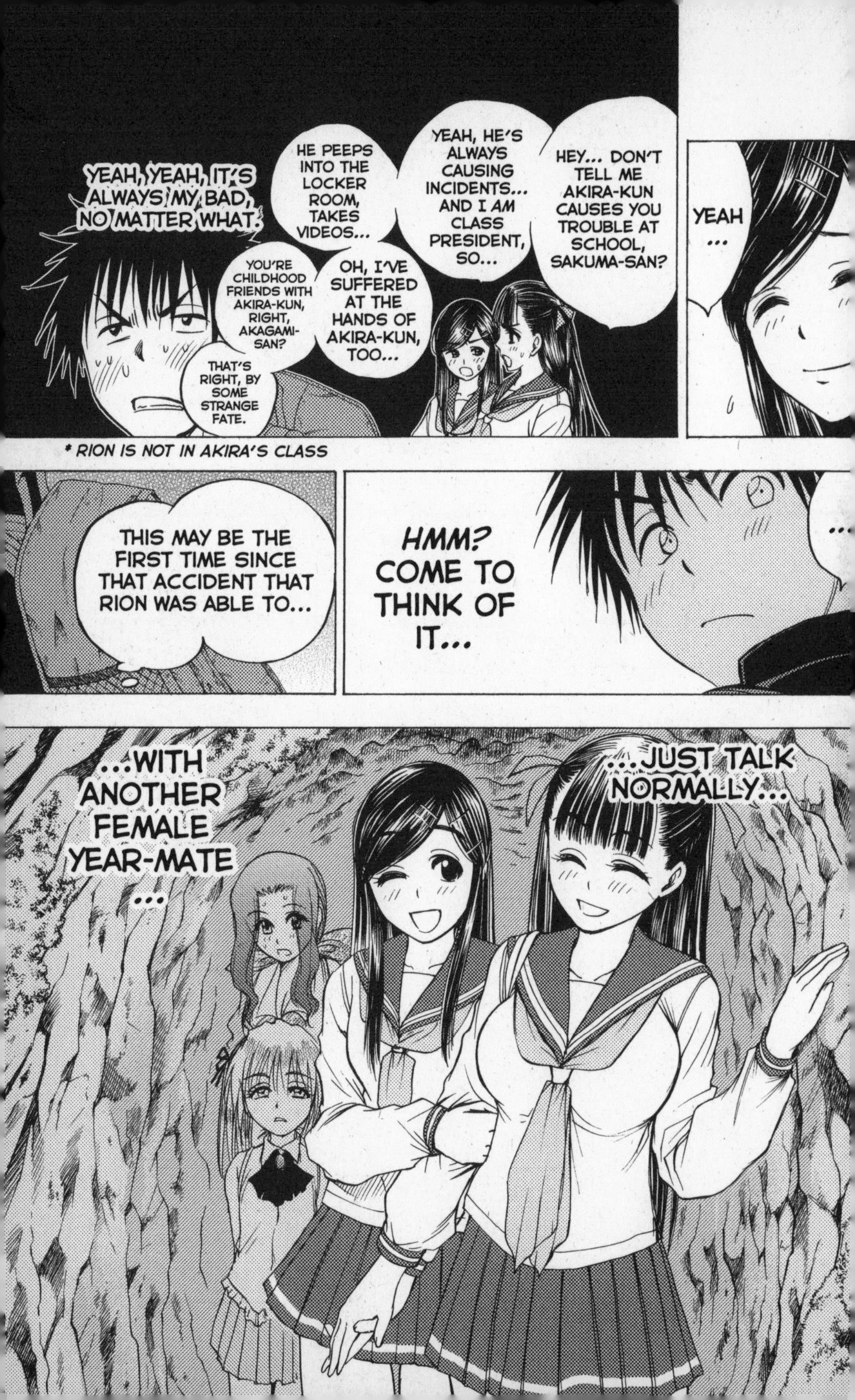
YEAH ...
HEY... DON'T TELL ME AKIRA-KUN CAUSES YOU TROUBLE AT SCHOOL, SAKUMA-SAN?
YEAH, HE'S ALWAYS CAUSING INCIDENTS... AND I *AM* CLASS PRESIDENT, SO...
HE PEEPS INTO THE LOCKER ROOM, TAKES VIDEOS...
OH, I'VE SUFFERED AT THE HANDS OF AKIRA-KUN, TOO...
YOU'RE CHILDHOOD FRIENDS WITH AKIRA-KUN, RIGHT, AKAGAMI-SAN?
YEAH, YEAH, IT'S ALWAYS MY BAD, NO MATTER WHAT.
THAT'S RIGHT, BY SOME STRANGE FATE.
* RION IS NOT IN AKIRA'S CLASS
...
HMM? COME TO THINK OF IT...
THIS MAY BE THE FIRST TIME SINCE THAT ACCIDENT THAT RION WAS ABLE TO...
...JUST TALK NORMALLY...
...WITH ANOTHER FEMALE YEAR-MATE ...

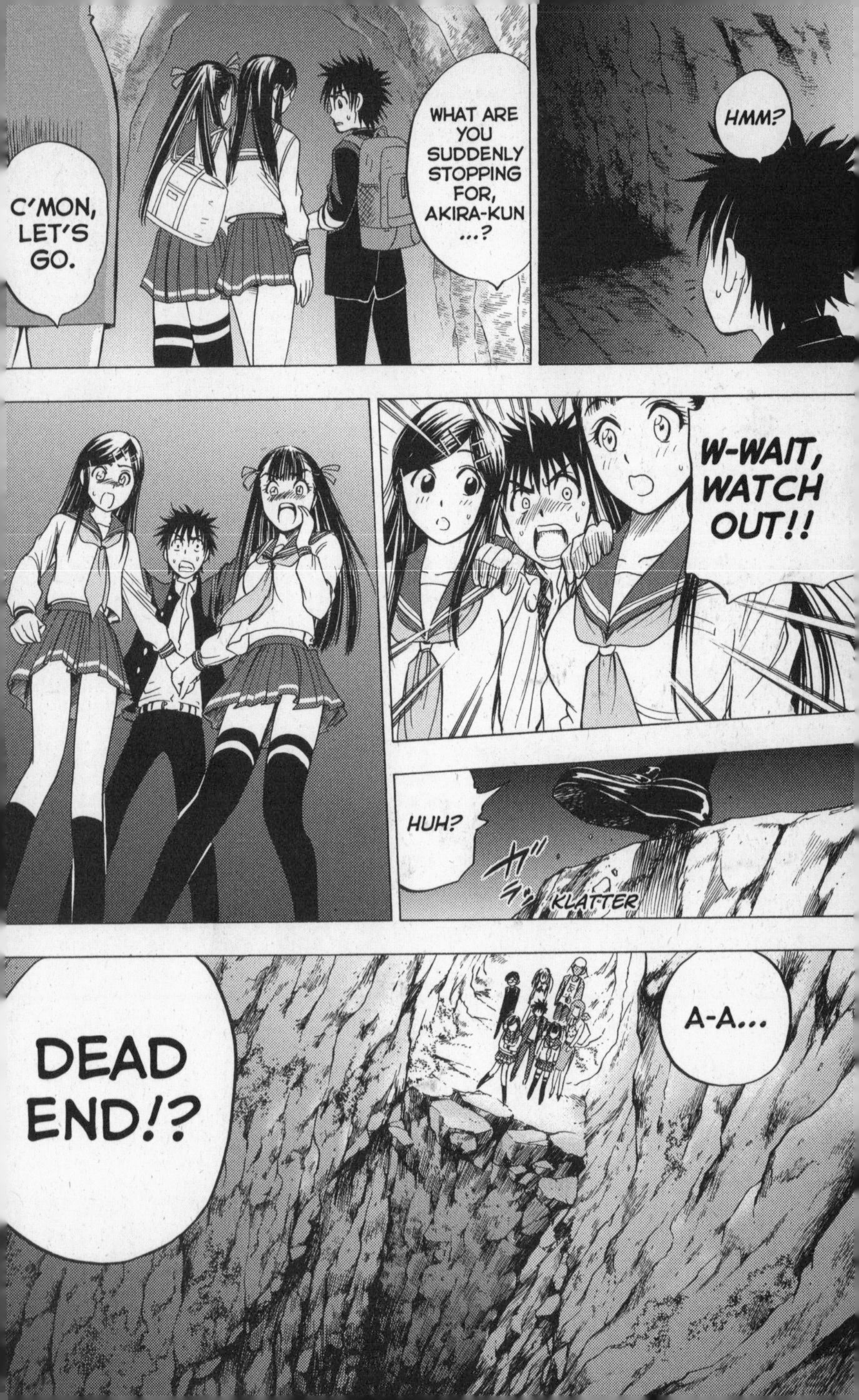
HMM?
WHAT ARE YOU SUDDENLY STOPPING FOR, AKIRA-KUN ...?
C'MON, LET'S GO.
W-WAIT, WATCH OUT!!
HUH?
KLATTER
A-A...
DEAD END!?

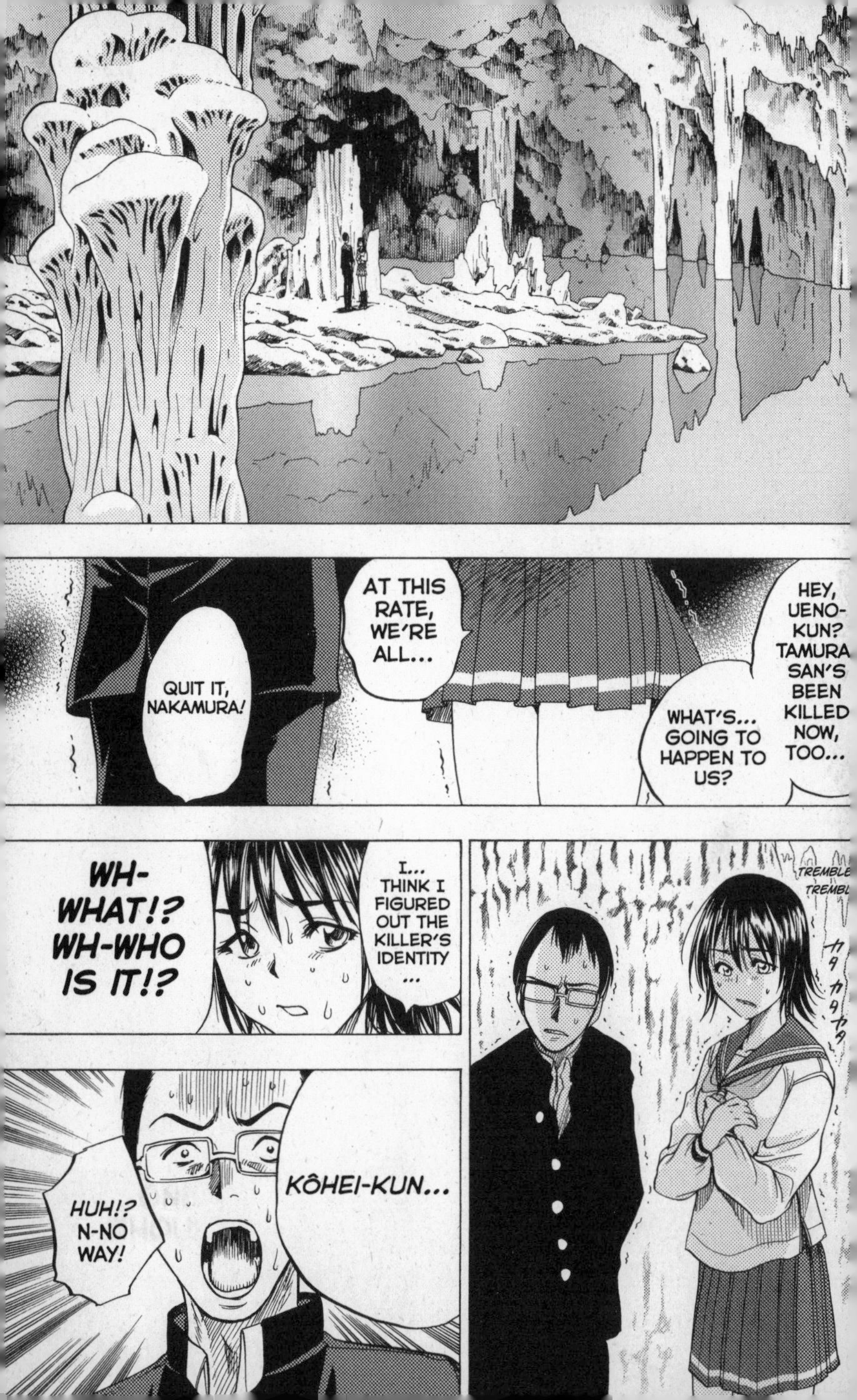
HEY, UENO-KUN? TAMURA-SAN'S BEEN KILLED NOW, TOO...
WHAT'S... GOING TO HAPPEN TO US?
AT THIS RATE, WE'RE ALL...
QUIT IT, NAKAMURA!
TREMBLE
TREMBL
カタカタカタ
I... THINK I FIGURED OUT THE KILLER'S IDENTITY...
WH-WHAT!? WH-WHO IS IT!?
KÔHEI-KUN...
HUH!? N-NO WAY!

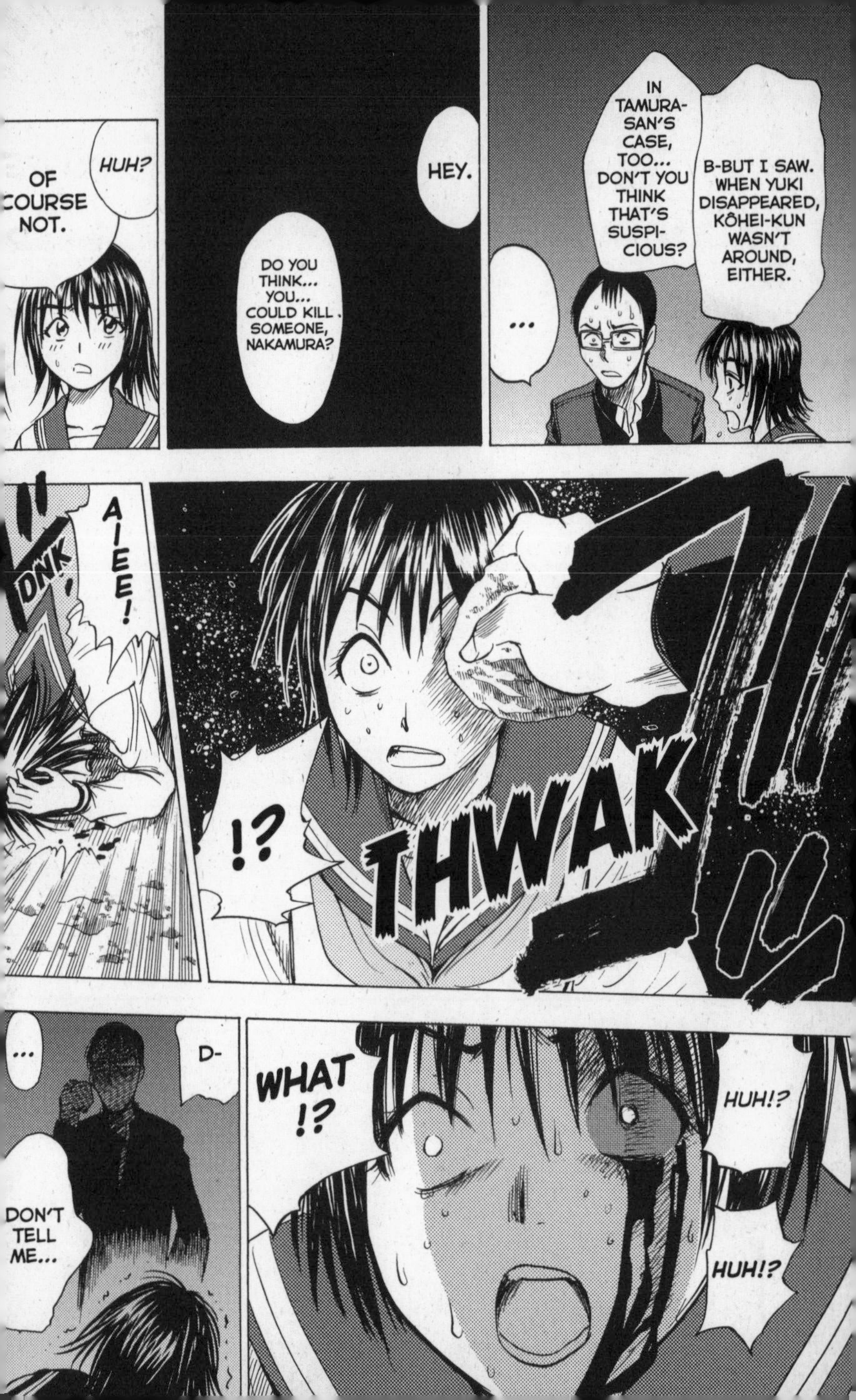
B-BUT I SAW. WHEN YUKI DISAPPEARED, KÔHEI-KUN WASN'T AROUND, EITHER.
IN TAMURA-SAN'S CASE, TOO... DON'T YOU THINK THAT'S SUSPICIOUS?
...
HEY.
DO YOU THINK... YOU... COULD KILL SOMEONE, NAKAMURA?
HUH?
OF COURSE NOT.
THWAK
!?
AIEEE!
DNK
HUH!?
HUH!?
WHAT!?
D-
...
DON'T TELL ME...

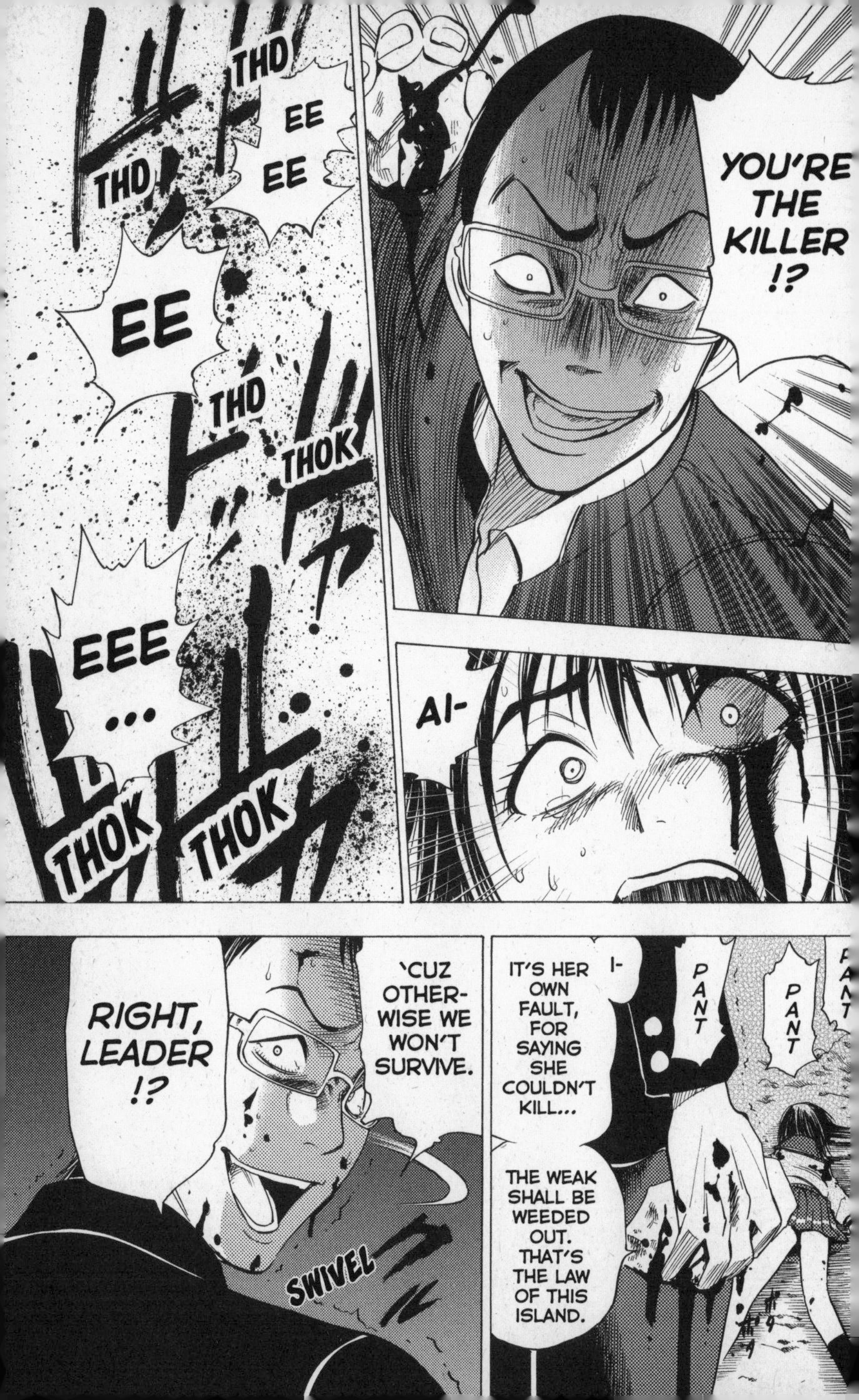
YOU'RE THE KILLER !?
AI-
THD
EE EE
THD
EE
THD
THOK
EEE ...
THOK
THOK
PANT
PANT
PANT
I-
IT'S HER OWN FAULT, FOR SAYING SHE COULDN'T KILL...
THE WEAK SHALL BE WEEDED OUT. THAT'S THE LAW OF THIS ISLAND.
'CUZ OTHER-WISE WE WON'T SURVIVE.
RIGHT, LEADER !?
SWIVEL

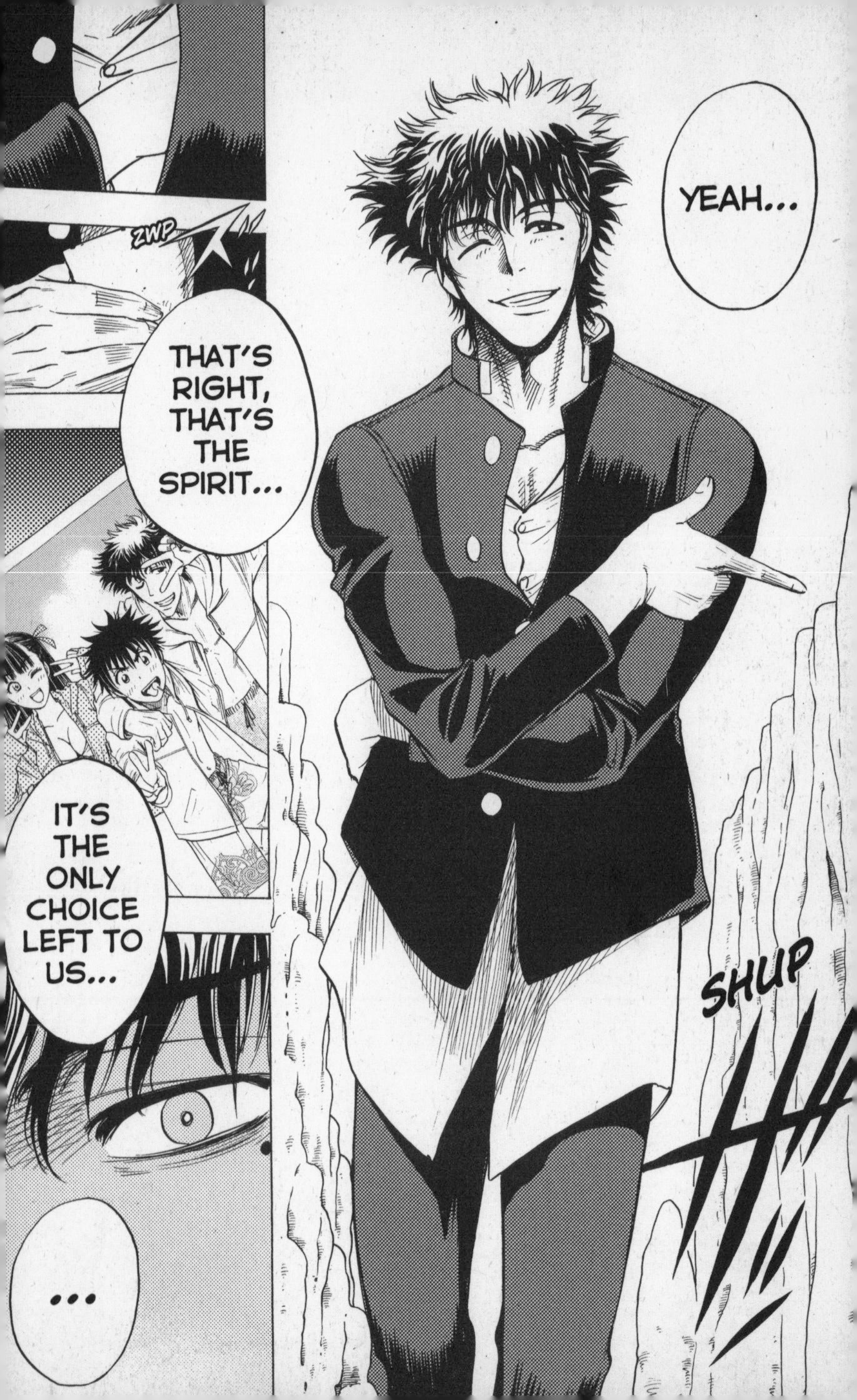
YEAH...
SHUP
ZWP
THAT'S RIGHT, THAT'S THE SPIRIT...
IT'S THE ONLY CHOICE LEFT TO US...
...

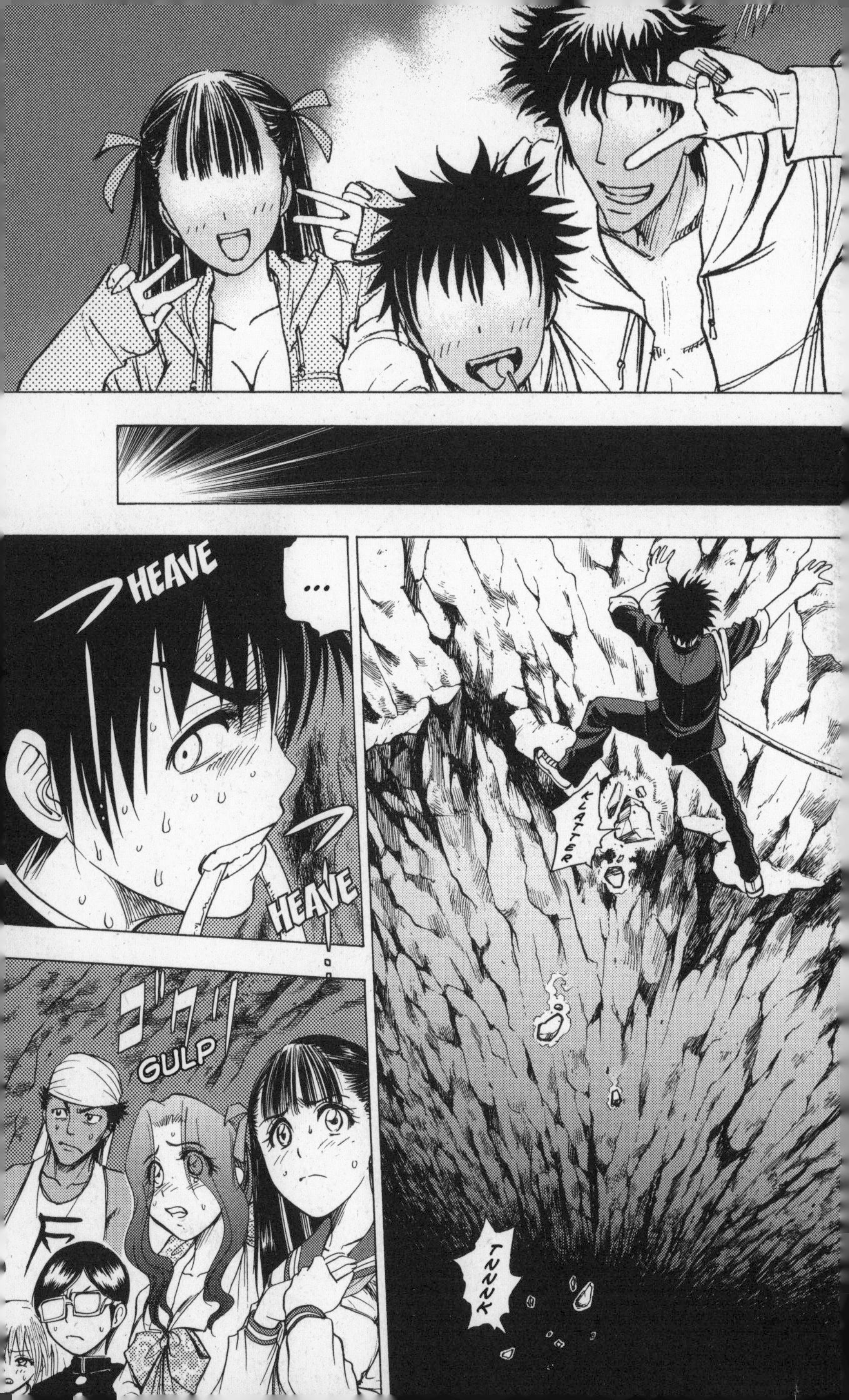
KLATTER
TNNNK
HEAVE
...
HEAVE
ゴクリ
GULP

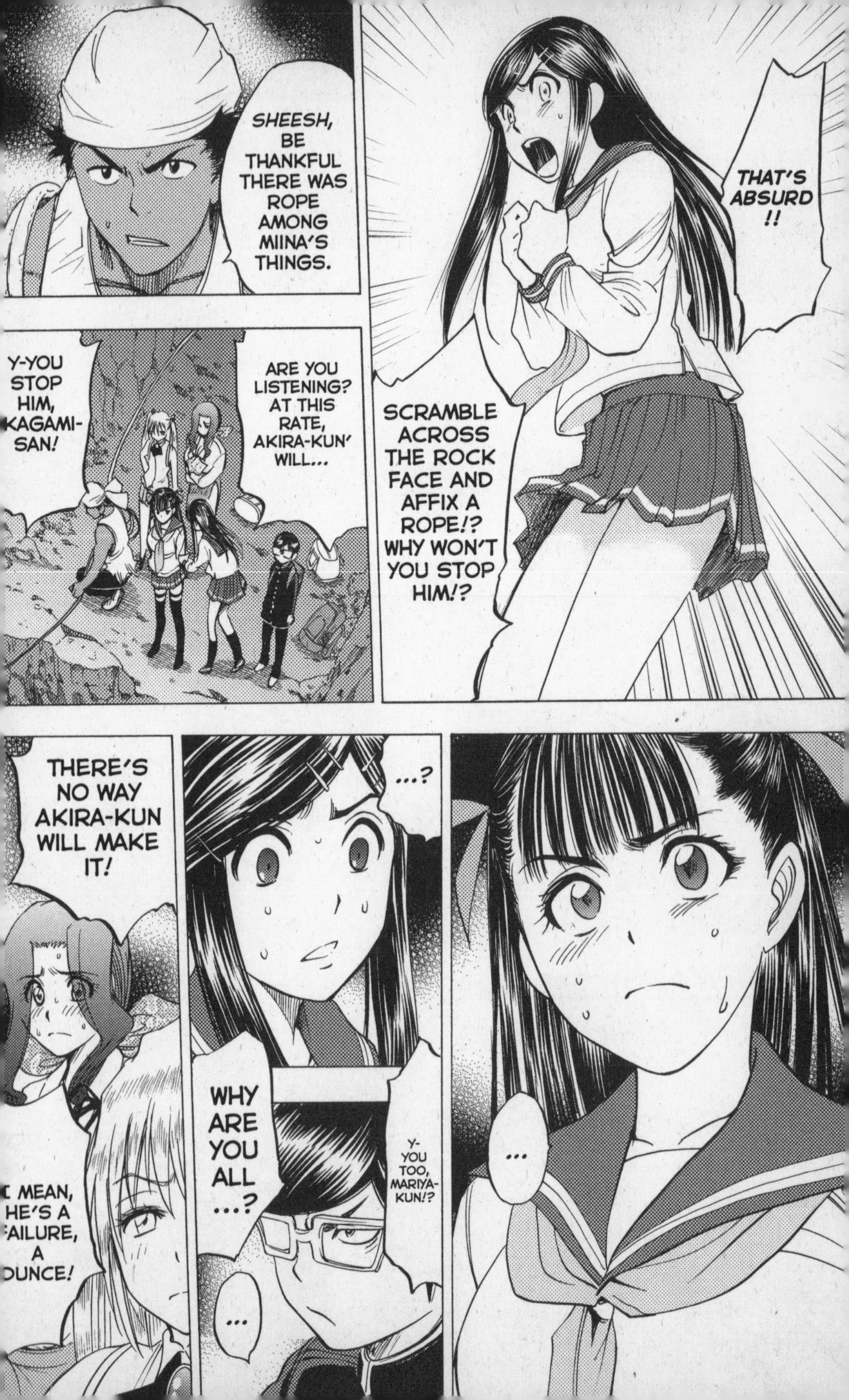
THAT'S ABSURD!!
SCRAMBLE ACROSS THE ROCK FACE AND AFFIX A ROPE!? WHY WON'T YOU STOP HIM!?
SHEESH, BE THANKFUL THERE WAS ROPE AMONG MIINA'S THINGS.
ARE YOU LISTENING? AT THIS RATE, AKIRA-KUN WILL...
Y-YOU STOP HIM, KAGAMI-SAN!
...
...?
WHY ARE YOU ALL...?
Y-YOU TOO, MARIYA-KUN!?
...
THERE'S NO WAY AKIRA-KUN WILL MAKE IT!
I MEAN, HE'S A FAILURE, A DUNCE!

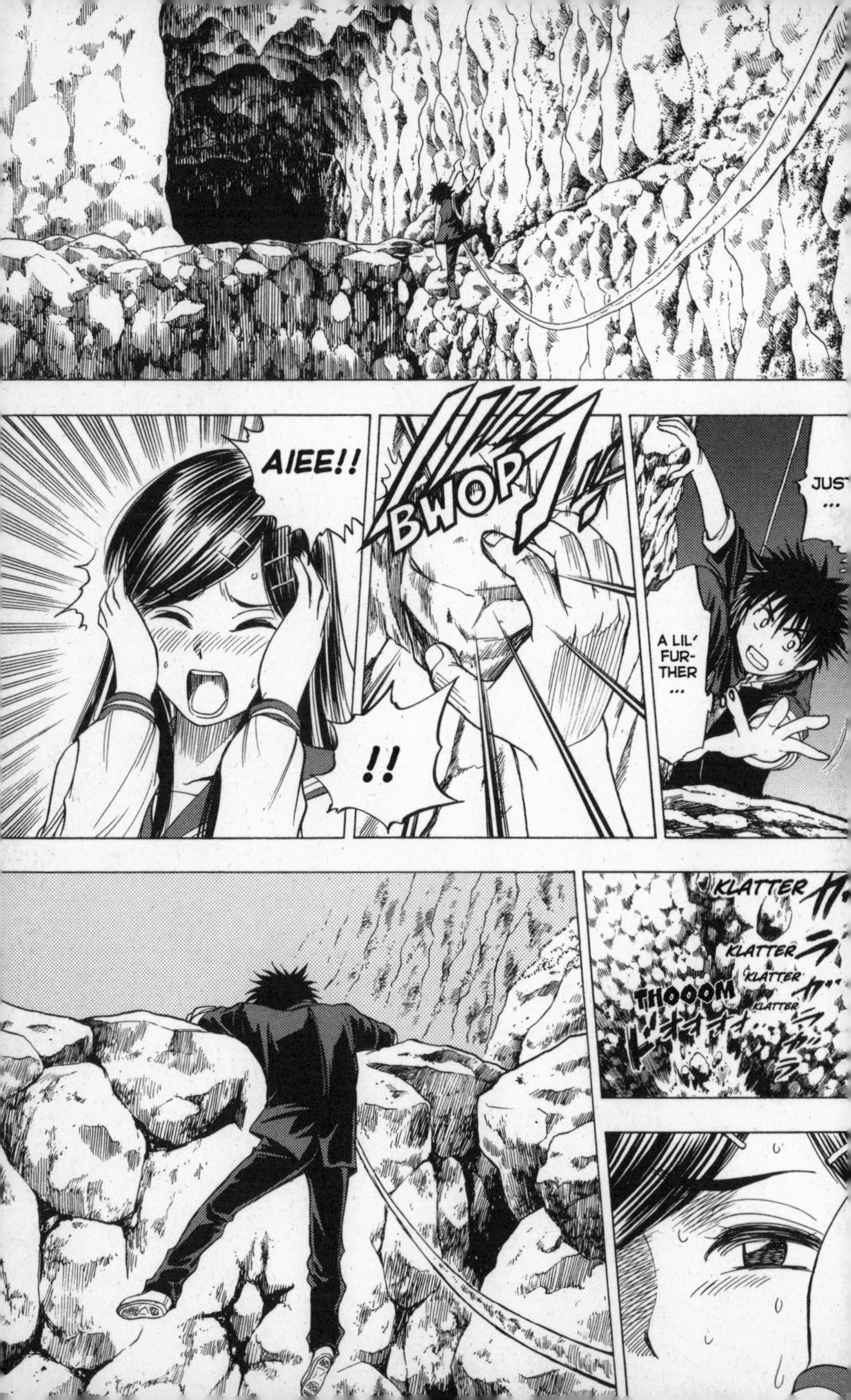
JUST ...
A LIL' FUR-THER ...
BWOP
!!
AIEE!!
KLATTER
KLATTER
KLATTER
THOOOM
KLATTER

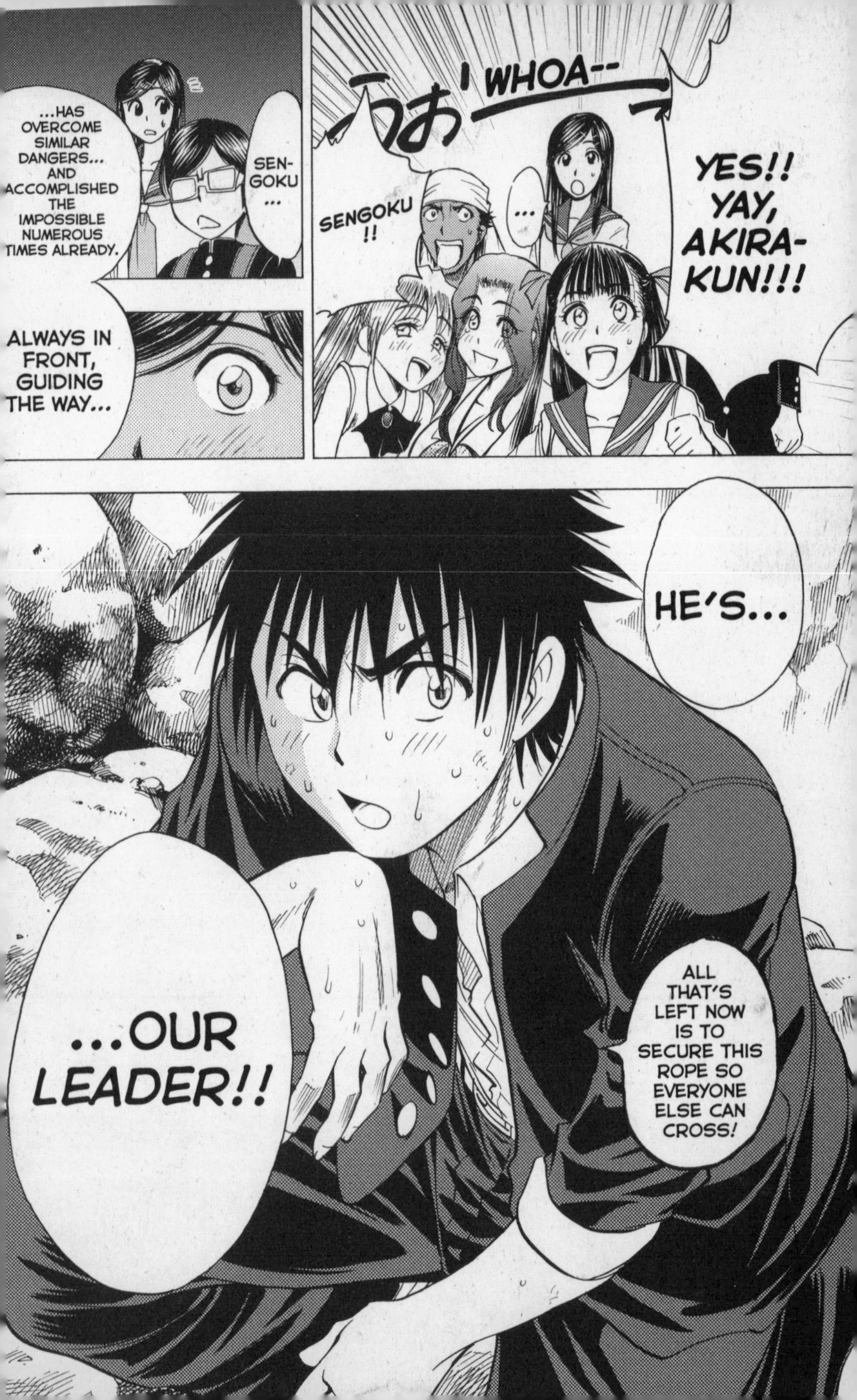
うお WHOA--
YES!! YAY, AKIRA-KUN!!!
...
SENGOKU !!
SEN-GOKU ...
...HAS OVERCOME SIMILAR DANGERS... AND ACCOMPLISHED THE IMPOSSIBLE NUMEROUS TIMES ALREADY.
ALWAYS IN FRONT, GUIDING THE WAY...
HE'S...
...OUR LEADER!!
ALL THAT'S LEFT NOW IS TO SECURE THIS ROPE SO EVERYONE ELSE CAN CROSS!

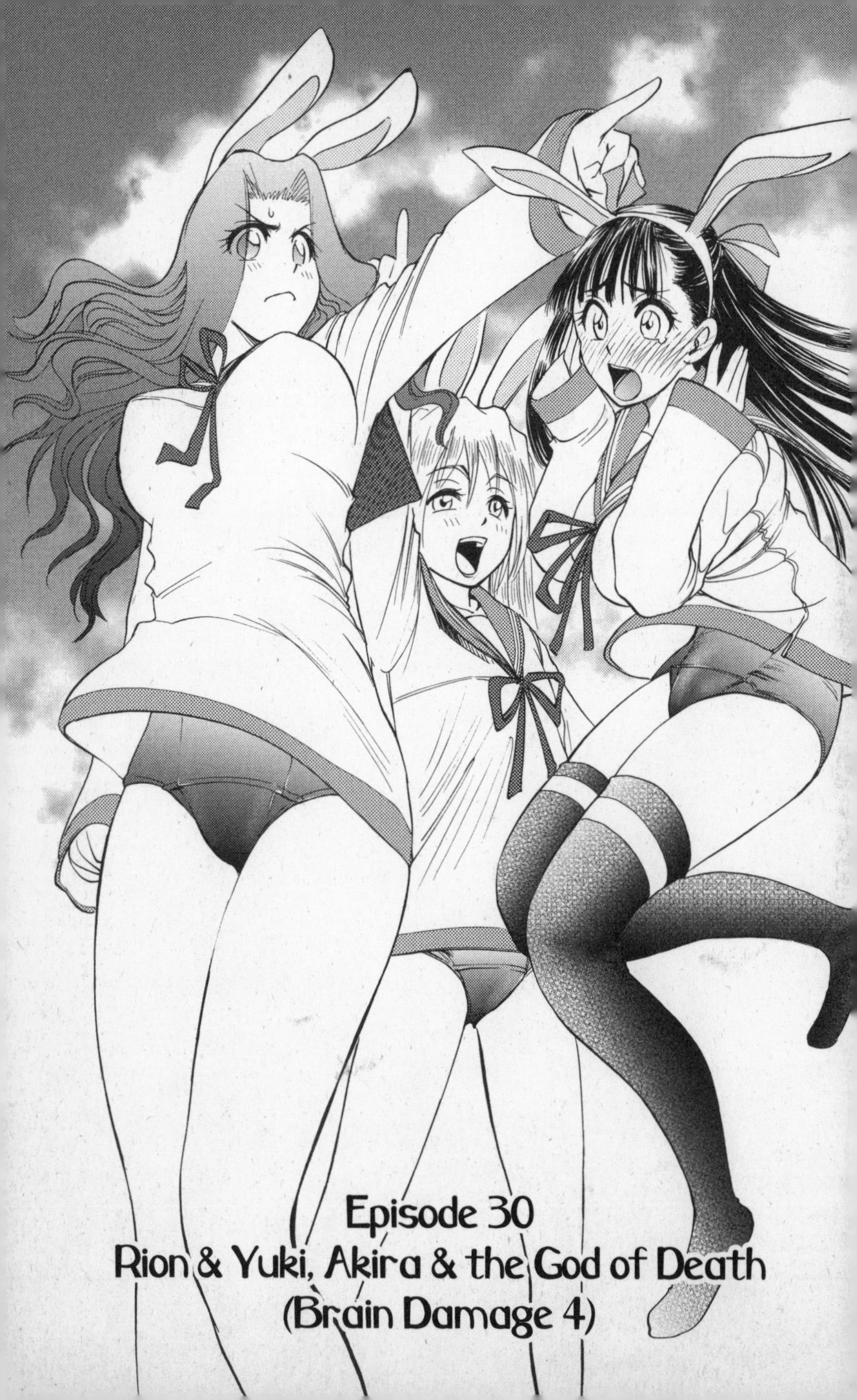

Episode 30
Rion & Yuki, Akira & the God of Death (Brain Damage 4)

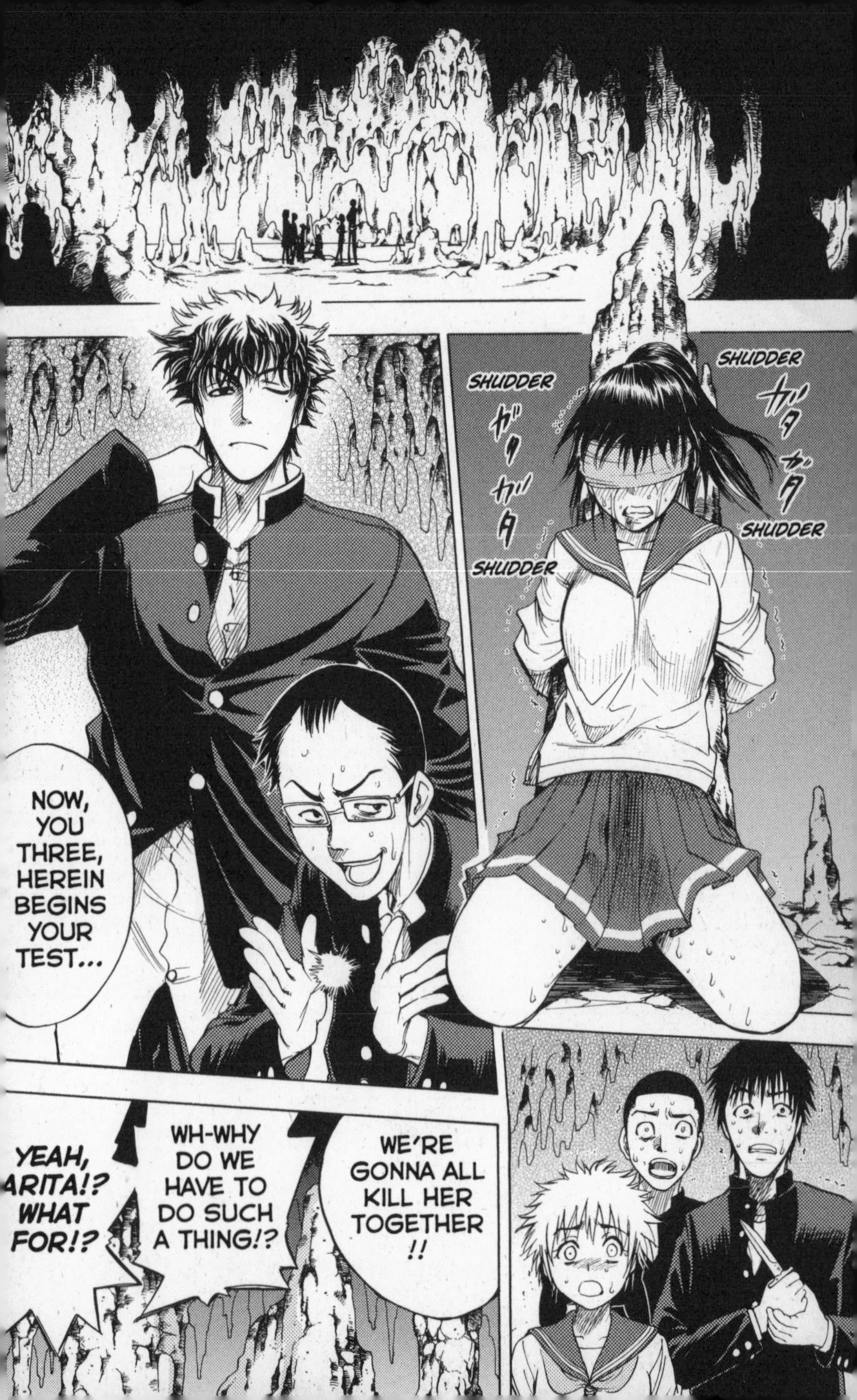
SHUDDER
ガタガタ
SHUDDER
SHUDDER
ガタガタ
SHUDDER
NOW, YOU THREE, HEREIN BEGINS YOUR TEST...
WE'RE GONNA ALL KILL HER TOGETHER!!
WH-WHY DO WE HAVE TO DO SUCH A THING!?
YEAH, ARITA!? WHAT FOR!?

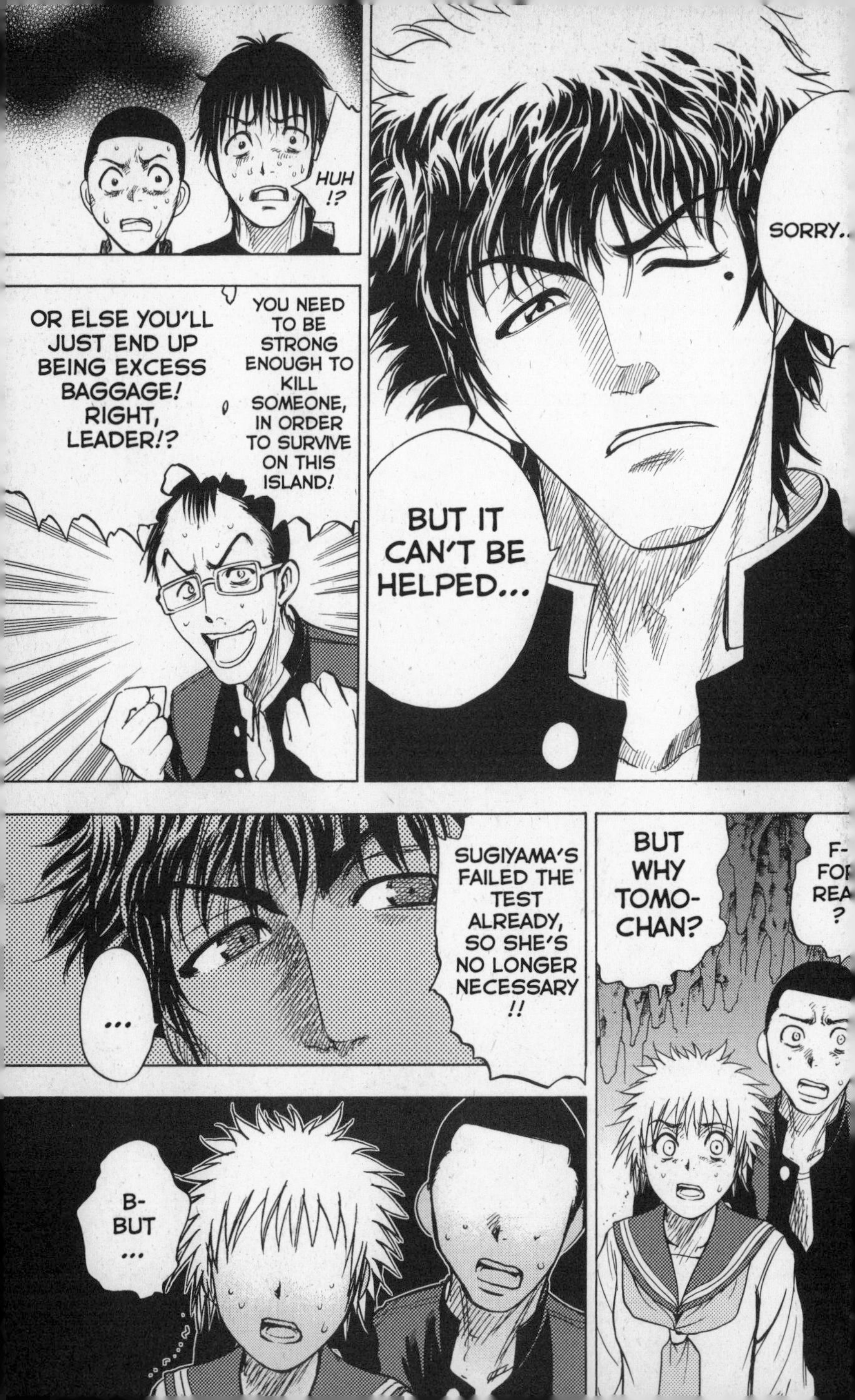
SORRY...
BUT IT CAN'T BE HELPED...
HUH !?
YOU NEED TO BE STRONG ENOUGH TO KILL SOMEONE, IN ORDER TO SURVIVE ON THIS ISLAND!
OR ELSE YOU'LL JUST END UP BEING EXCESS BAGGAGE! RIGHT, LEADER!?
F- FO REA ?
BUT WHY TOMO-CHAN?
SUGIYAMA'S FAILED THE TEST ALREADY, SO SHE'S NO LONGER NECESSARY !!
...
B- BUT ...

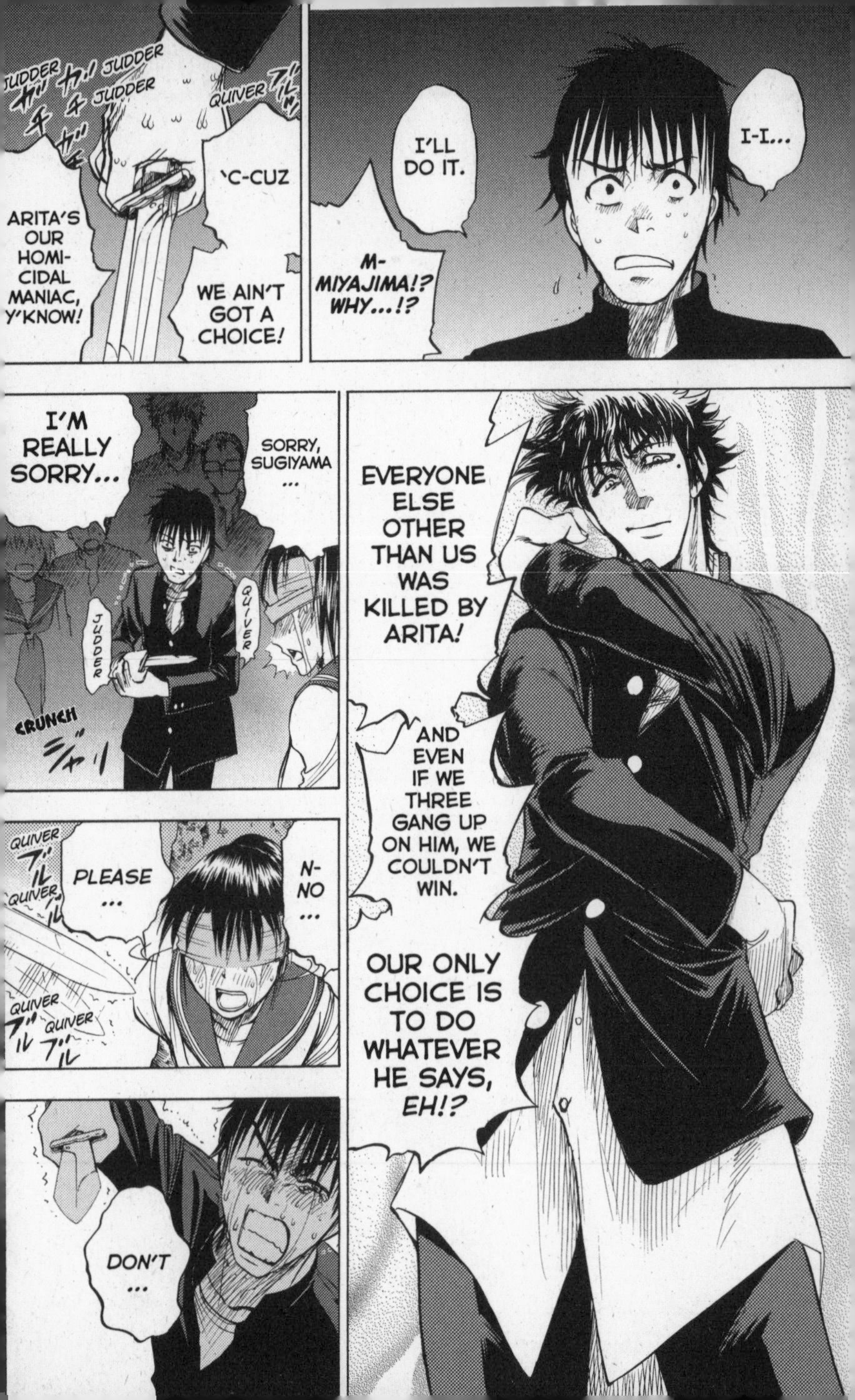
I-I...
I'LL DO IT.
M- MIYAJIMA!? WHY...!?
JUDDER
JUDDER
JUDDER
QUIVER
'C-CUZ
WE AIN'T GOT A CHOICE!
ARITA'S OUR HOMICIDAL MANIAC, Y'KNOW!
EVERYONE ELSE OTHER THAN US WAS KILLED BY ARITA!
AND EVEN IF WE THREE GANG UP ON HIM, WE COULDN'T WIN.
OUR ONLY CHOICE IS TO DO WHATEVER HE SAYS, EH!?
SORRY, SUGIYAMA ...
I'M REALLY SORRY...
QUIVER
JUDDER
CRUNCH
N-NO ...
PLEASE ...
QUIVER
QUIVER
QUIVER
QUIVER
DON'T ...

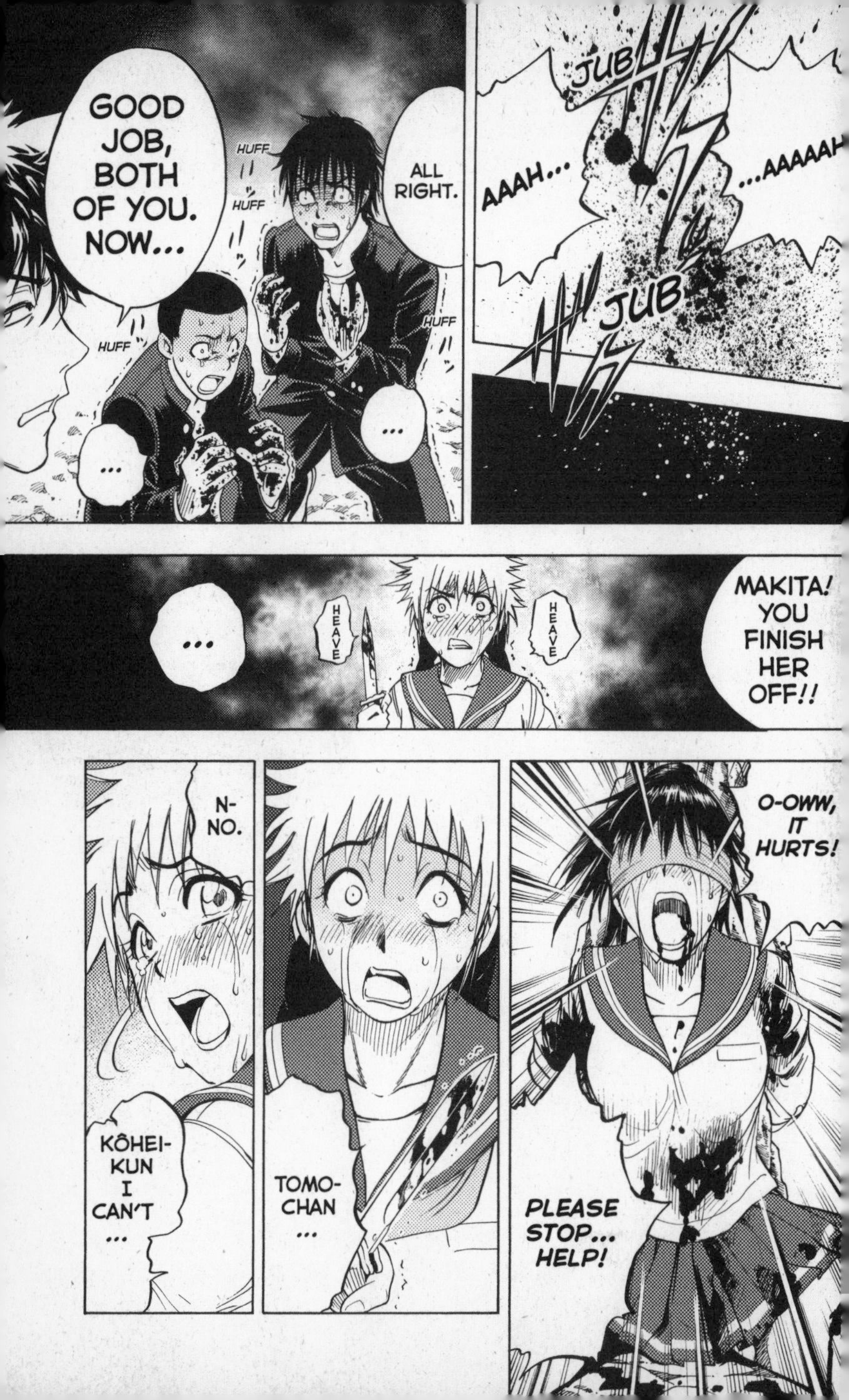
JUB
...AAAAAH
AAAH...
JUB
ALL RIGHT.
GOOD JOB, BOTH OF YOU. NOW...
HUFF
HUFF
HUFF
...
HUFF
...
MAKITA! YOU FINISH HER OFF!!
HEAVE
HEAVE
...
O-OWW, IT HURTS!
PLEASE STOP... HELP!
TOMO-CHAN ...
N-NO.
KÔHEI-KUN I CAN'T ...

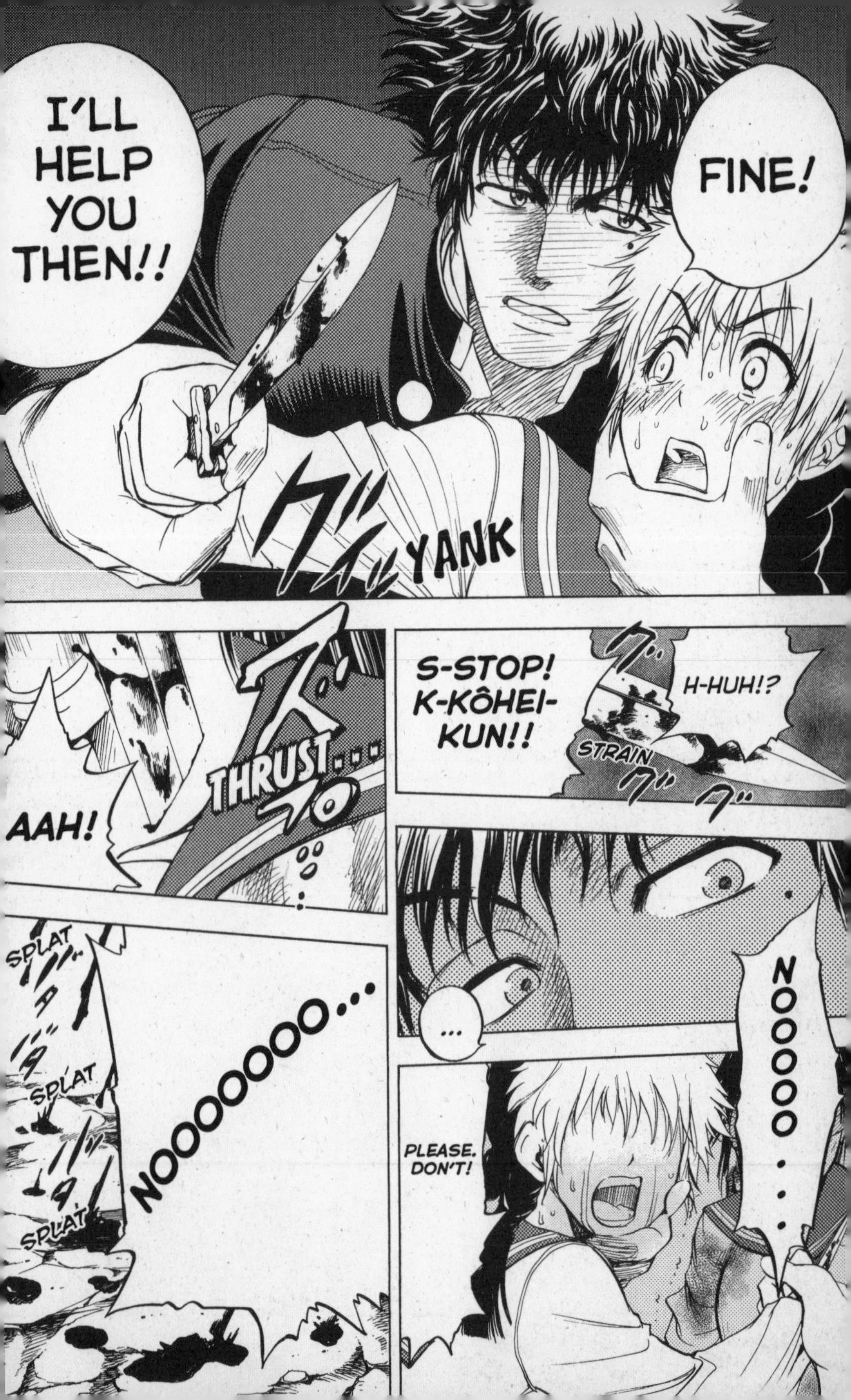
FINE!
I'LL HELP YOU THEN!!
YANK
S-STOP! K-KÔHEI-KUN!!
H-HUH!?
STRAIN
THRUST...
AAH!
...
NOOOOOO...
PLEASE. DON'T!
NOOOOOOO...
SPLAT
SPLAT
SPLAT

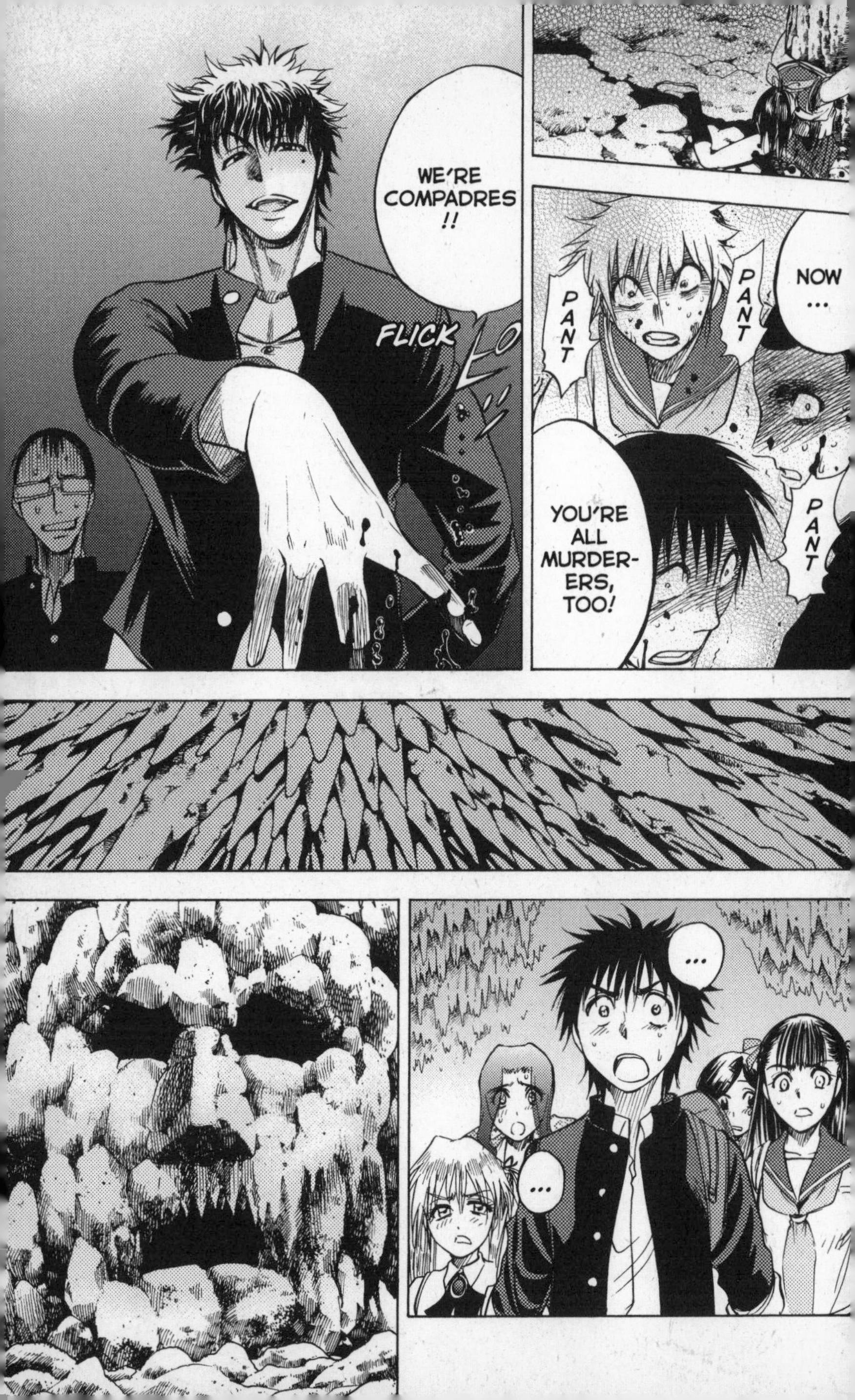
NOW ...
PANT
PANT
YOU'RE ALL MURDERERS, TOO!
PANT
WE'RE COMPADRES !!
FLICK
...
...

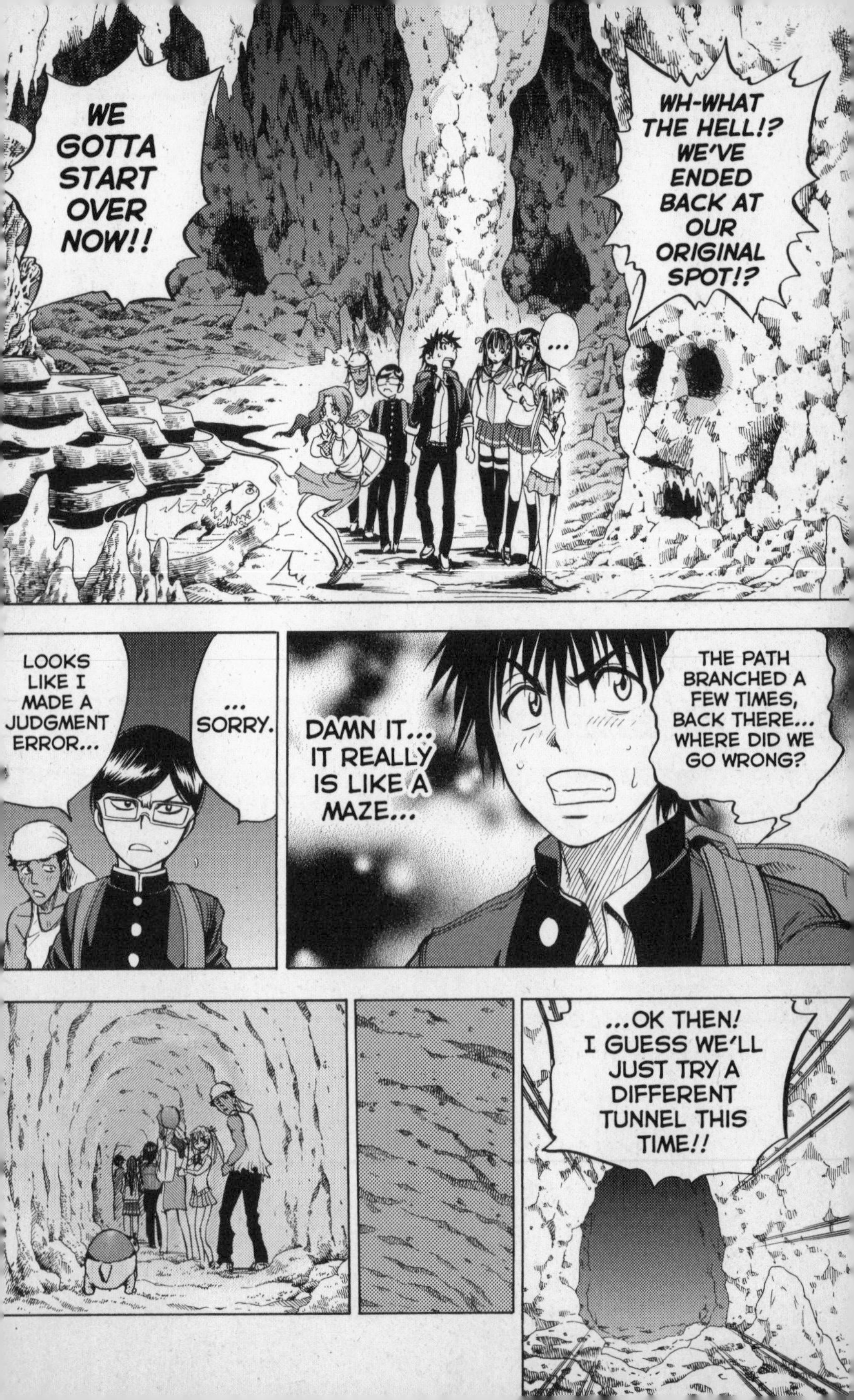
WH-WHAT THE HELL!? WE'VE ENDED BACK AT OUR ORIGINAL SPOT!?
...
WE GOTTA START OVER NOW!!
THE PATH BRANCHED A FEW TIMES, BACK THERE... WHERE DID WE GO WRONG?
DAMN IT... IT REALLY IS LIKE A MAZE...
... SORRY.
LOOKS LIKE I MADE A JUDGMENT ERROR...
...OK THEN! I GUESS WE'LL JUST TRY A DIFFERENT TUNNEL THIS TIME!!

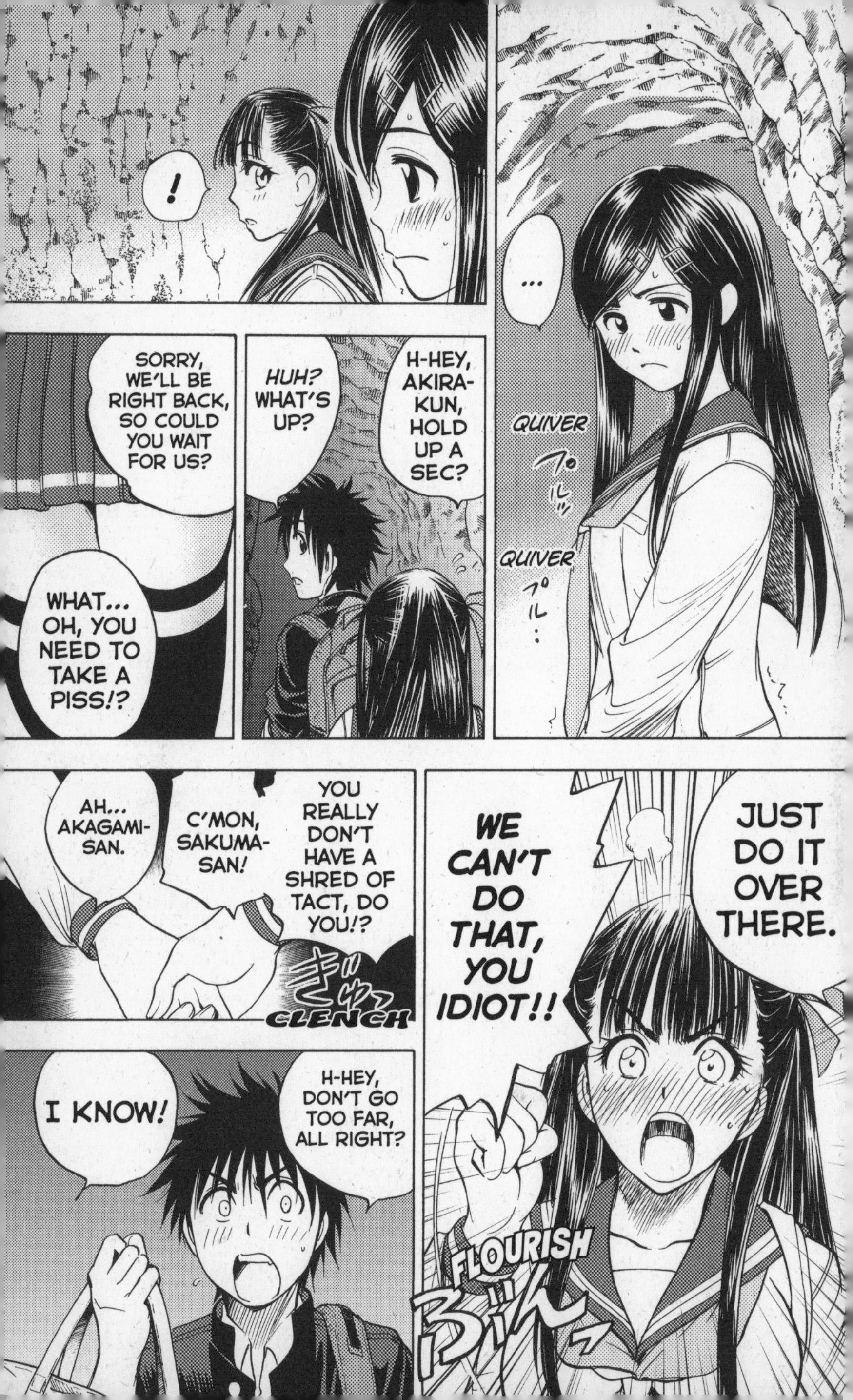
...
QUIVER
プルッ
QUIVER
プル…
!
H-HEY, AKIRA-KUN, HOLD UP A SEC?
HUH? WHAT'S UP?
SORRY, WE'LL BE RIGHT BACK, SO COULD YOU WAIT FOR US?
WHAT... OH, YOU NEED TO TAKE A PISS!?
JUST DO IT OVER THERE.
WE CAN'T DO THAT, YOU IDIOT!!
FLOURISH
ぶんっ
YOU REALLY DON'T HAVE A SHRED OF TACT, DO YOU!?
C'MON, SAKUMA-SAN!
AH... AKAGAMI-SAN.
ぎゅっ
CLENCH
H-HEY, DON'T GO TOO FAR, ALL RIGHT?
I KNOW!

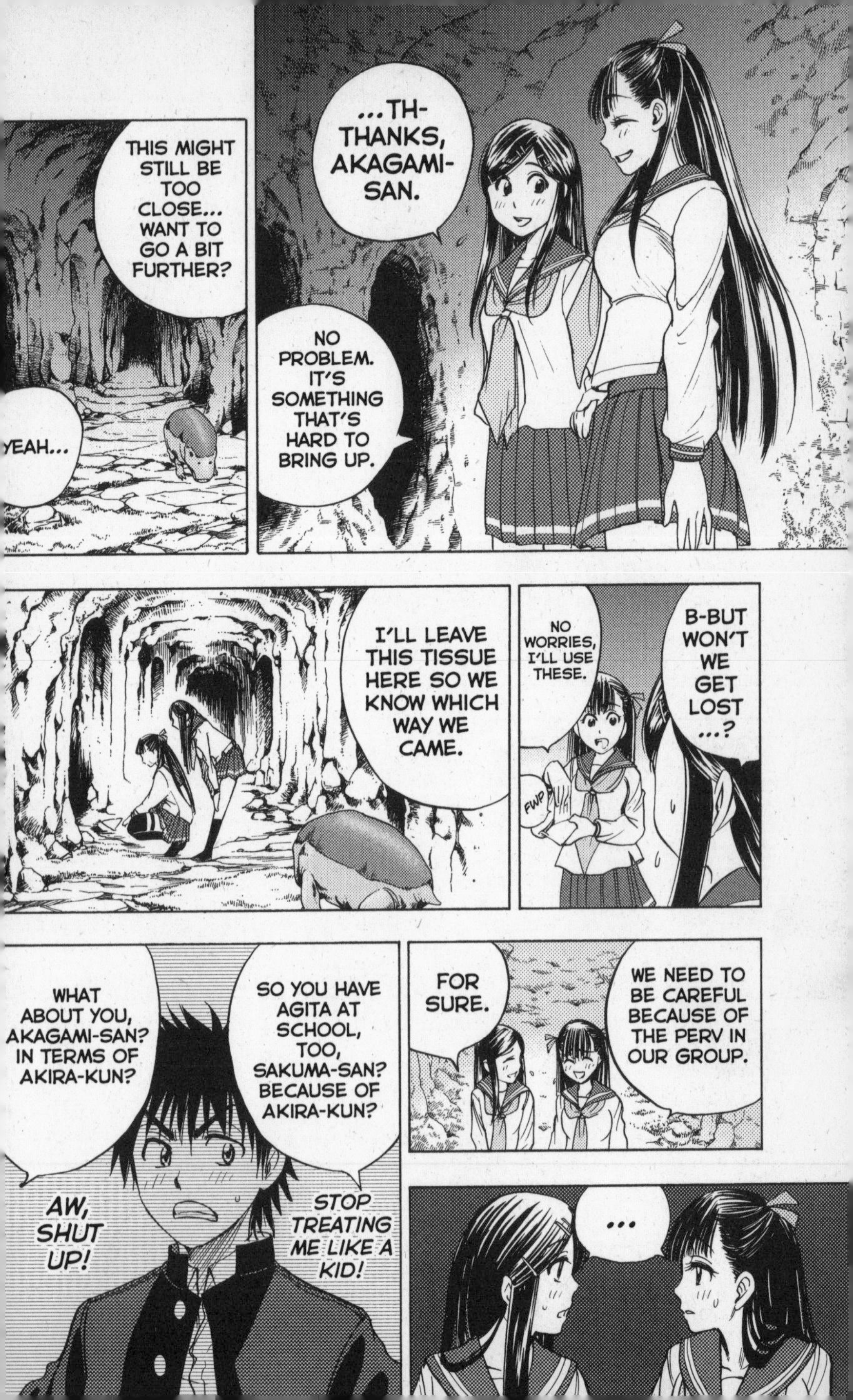
...TH-THANKS, AKAGAMI-SAN.
NO PROBLEM. IT'S SOMETHING THAT'S HARD TO BRING UP.
THIS MIGHT STILL BE TOO CLOSE... WANT TO GO A BIT FURTHER?
YEAH...
B-BUT WON'T WE GET LOST ...?
NO WORRIES, I'LL USE THESE.
FWP
I'LL LEAVE THIS TISSUE HERE SO WE KNOW WHICH WAY WE CAME.
WE NEED TO BE CAREFUL BECAUSE OF THE PERV IN OUR GROUP.
FOR SURE.
...
SO YOU HAVE AGITA AT SCHOOL, TOO, SAKUMA-SAN? BECAUSE OF AKIRA-KUN?
WHAT ABOUT YOU, AKAGAMI-SAN? IN TERMS OF AKIRA-KUN?
STOP TREATING ME LIKE A KID!
AW, SHUT UP!

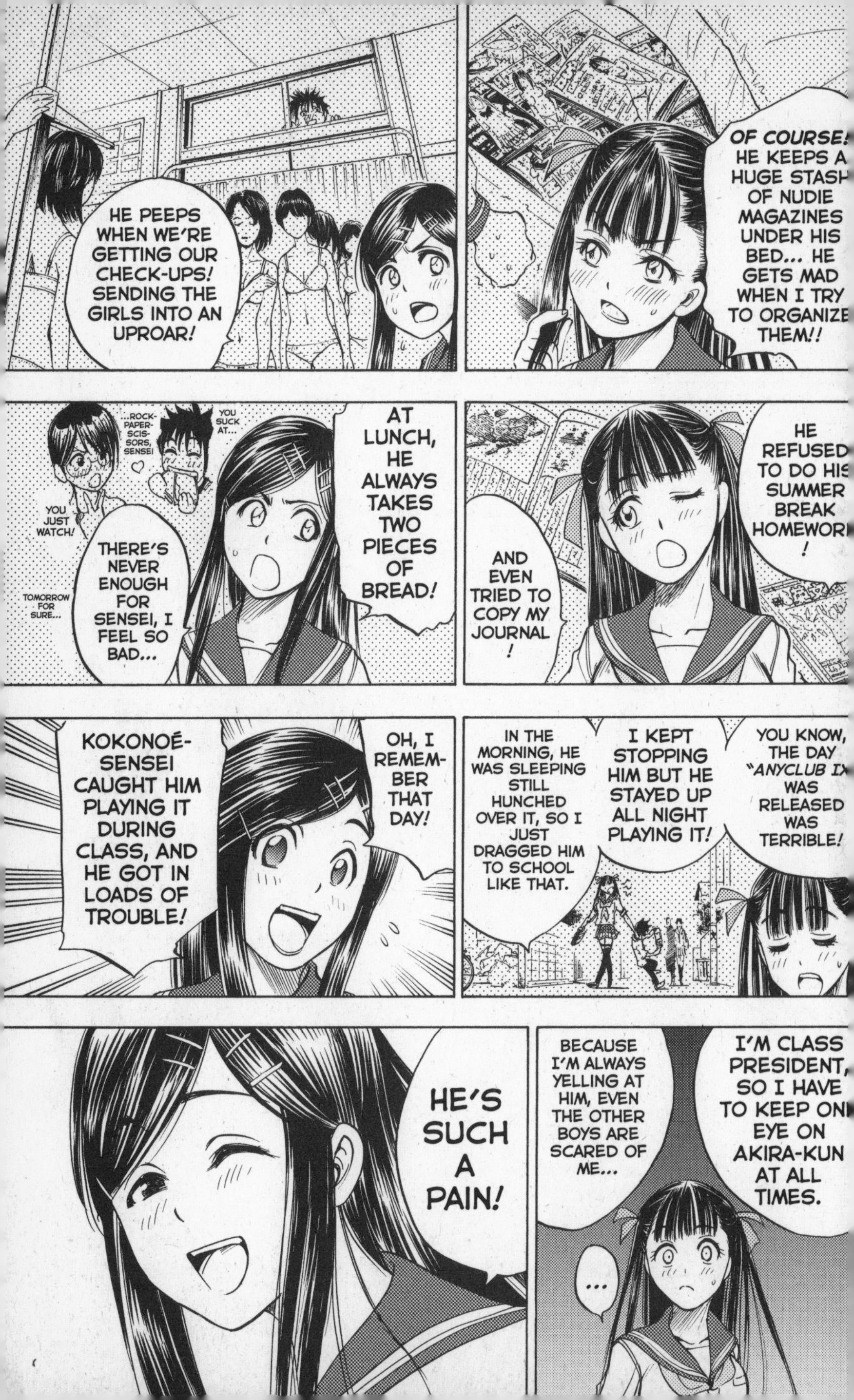
OF COURSE! HE KEEPS A HUGE STASH OF NUDIE MAGAZINES UNDER HIS BED... HE GETS MAD WHEN I TRY TO ORGANIZE THEM!!
HE PEEPS WHEN WE'RE GETTING OUR CHECK-UPS! SENDING THE GIRLS INTO AN UPROAR!
HE REFUSED TO DO HIS SUMMER BREAK HOMEWORK!
AND EVEN TRIED TO COPY MY JOURNAL!
AT LUNCH, HE ALWAYS TAKES TWO PIECES OF BREAD!
YOU SUCK AT...
...ROCK-PAPER-SCISSORS, SENSEI
YOU JUST WATCH!
THERE'S NEVER ENOUGH FOR SENSEI, I FEEL SO BAD...
TOMORROW FOR SURE...
YOU KNOW, THE DAY "ANYCLUB IX" WAS RELEASED WAS TERRIBLE!
I KEPT STOPPING HIM BUT HE STAYED UP ALL NIGHT PLAYING IT!
IN THE MORNING, HE WAS SLEEPING STILL HUNCHED OVER IT, SO I JUST DRAGGED HIM TO SCHOOL LIKE THAT.
OH, I REMEMBER THAT DAY!
KOKONOÉ-SENSEI CAUGHT HIM PLAYING IT DURING CLASS, AND HE GOT IN LOADS OF TROUBLE!
I'M CLASS PRESIDENT, SO I HAVE TO KEEP ONE EYE ON AKIRA-KUN AT ALL TIMES.
BECAUSE I'M ALWAYS YELLING AT HIM, EVEN THE OTHER BOYS ARE SCARED OF ME...
...
HE'S SUCH A PAIN!

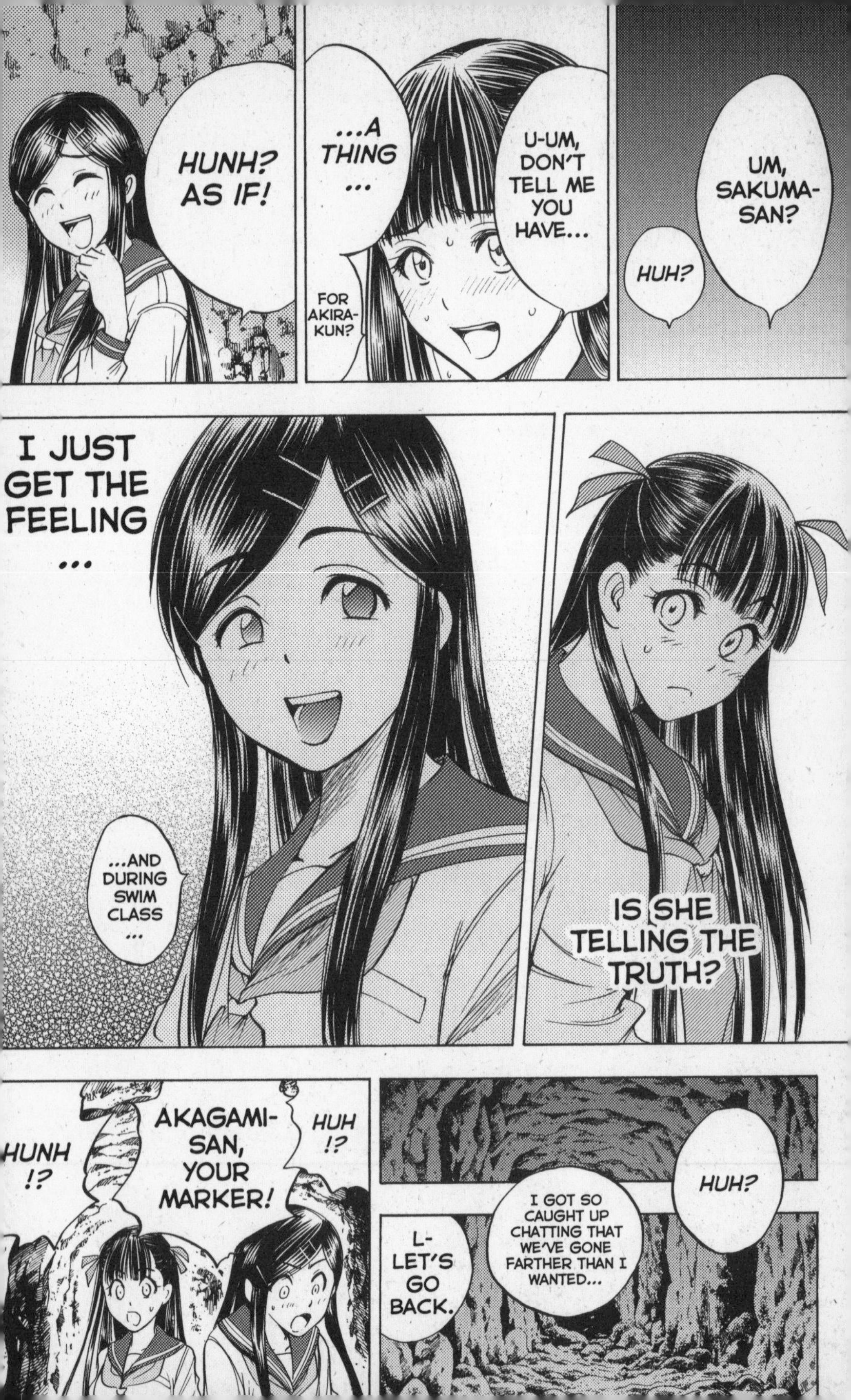
UM, SAKUMA-SAN?
HUH?
U-UM, DON'T TELL ME YOU HAVE...
...A THING ...
FOR AKIRA-KUN?
HUNH? AS IF!
IS SHE TELLING THE TRUTH?
I JUST GET THE FEELING ...
...AND DURING SWIM CLASS ...
HUH?
I GOT SO CAUGHT UP CHATTING THAT WE'VE GONE FARTHER THAN I WANTED...
L-LET'S GO BACK.
HUH !?
AKAGAMI-SAN, YOUR MARKER!
HUNH !?

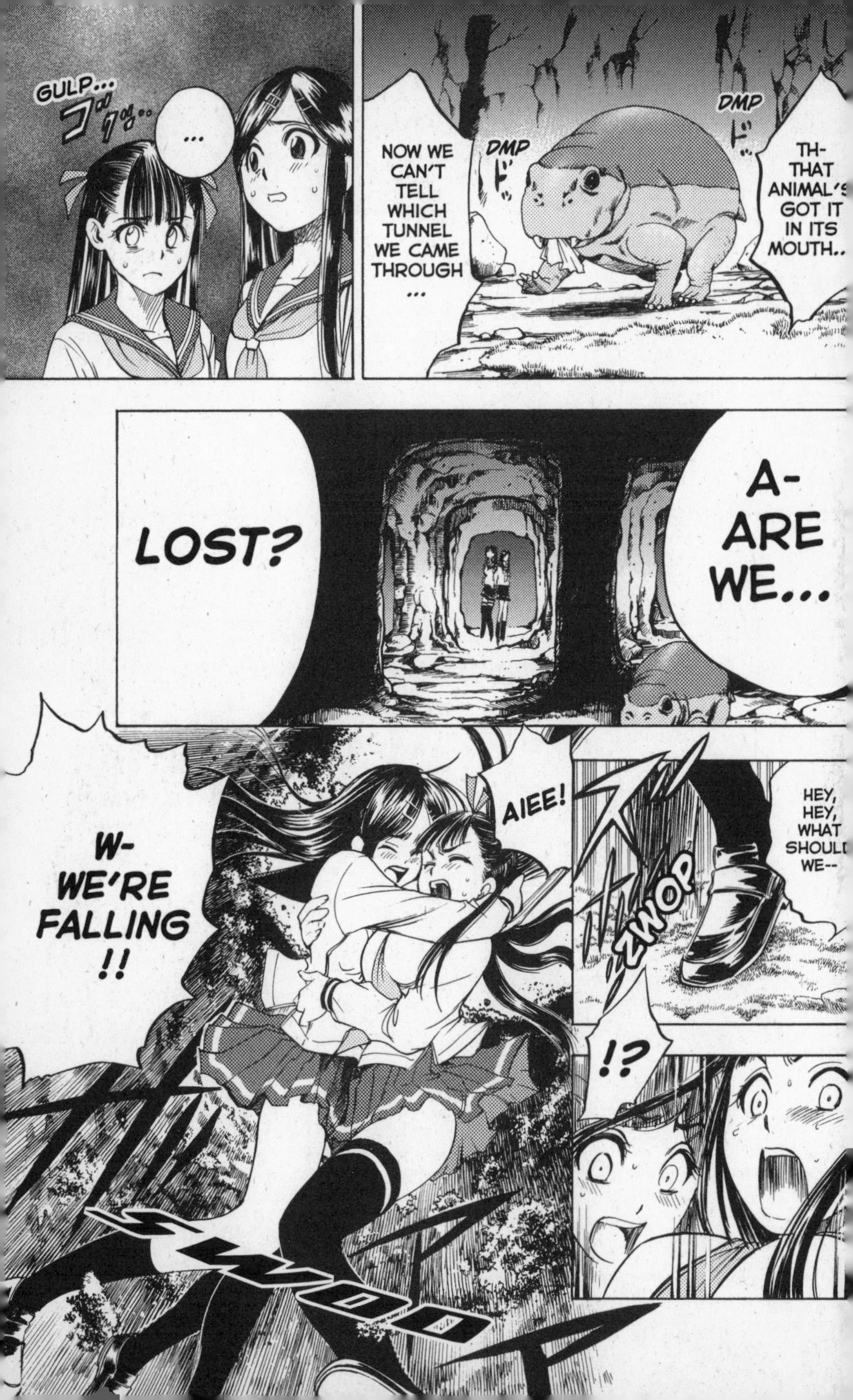
DMP
ド…
TH- THAT ANIMAL'S GOT IT IN ITS MOUTH..
DMP
ドッ
NOW WE CAN'T TELL WHICH TUNNEL WE CAME THROUGH ...
GULP...
...
A- ARE WE...
LOST?
HEY, HEY, WHAT SHOULD WE--
ZWOP
!?
AIEE!
W- WE'RE FALLING !!

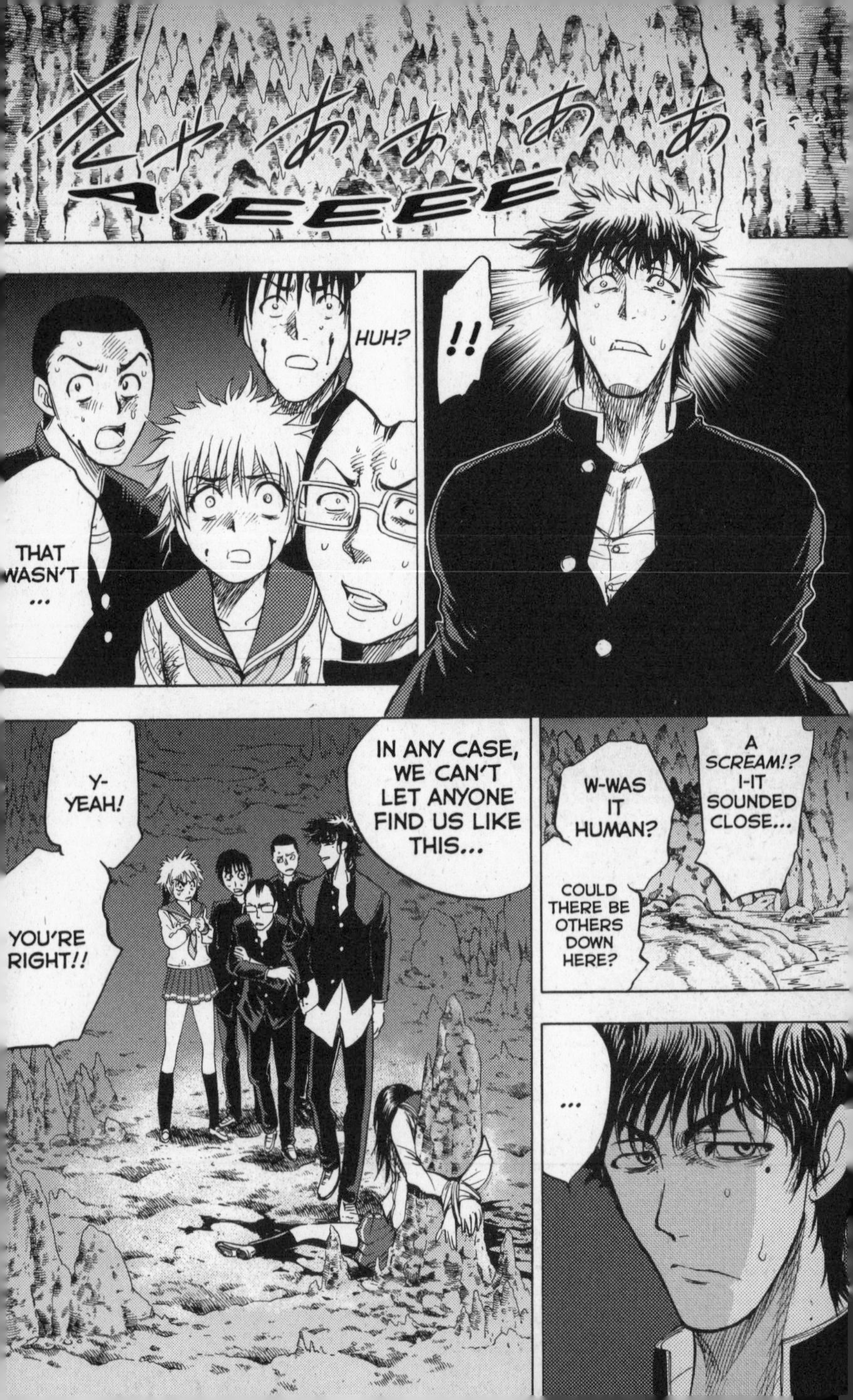

きゃああああ
AIEEEE
!!
HUH?
THAT WASN'T ...
A SCREAM!? I-IT SOUNDED CLOSE...
W-WAS IT HUMAN?
COULD THERE BE OTHERS DOWN HERE?
...
IN ANY CASE, WE CAN'T LET ANYONE FIND US LIKE THIS...
Y-YEAH!
YOU'RE RIGHT!!

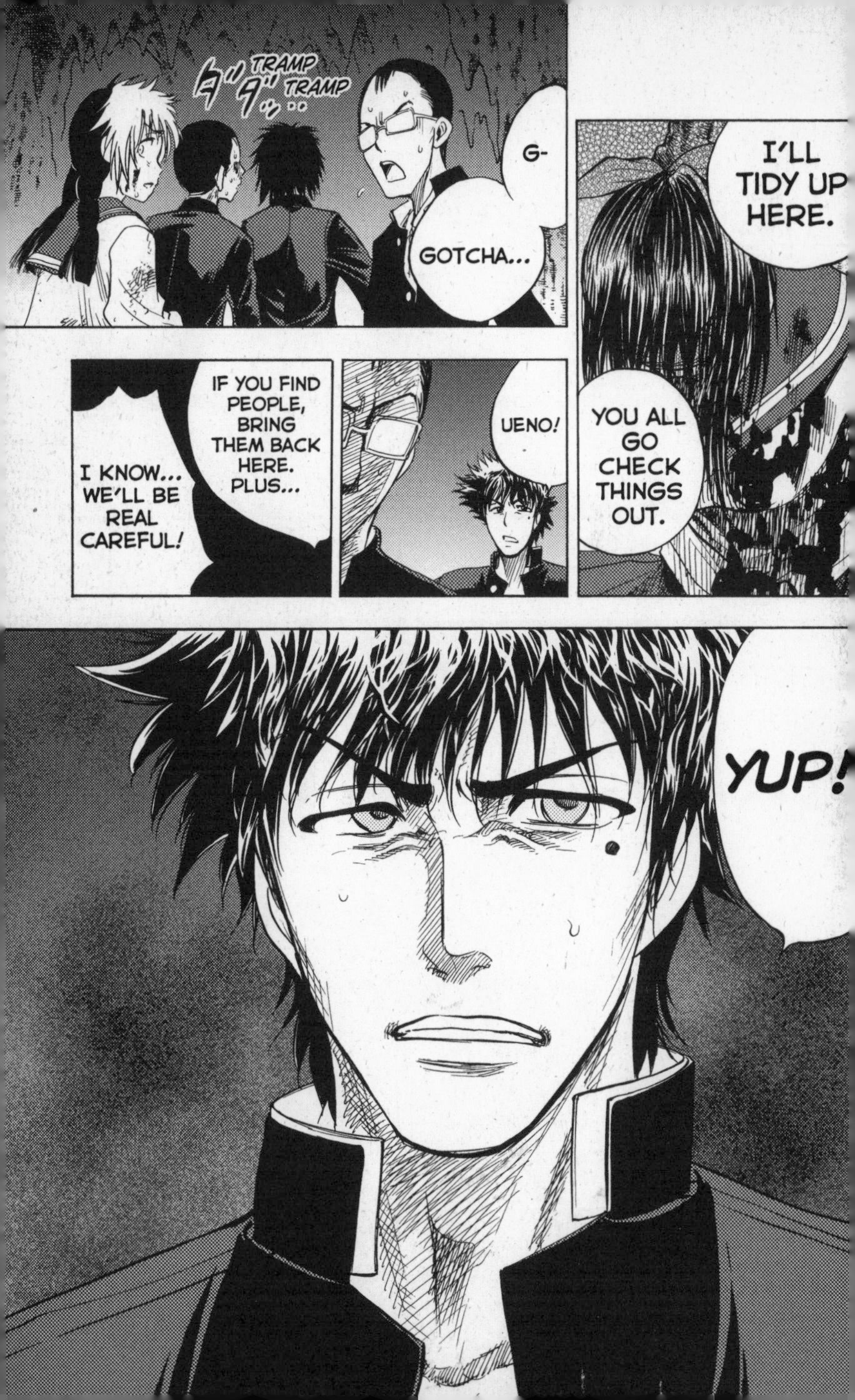
I'LL TIDY UP HERE.
YOU ALL GO CHECK THINGS OUT.
TRAMP TRAMP
G-
GOTCHA...
UENO!
IF YOU FIND PEOPLE, BRING THEM BACK HERE. PLUS...
I KNOW... WE'LL BE REAL CAREFUL!
YUP!

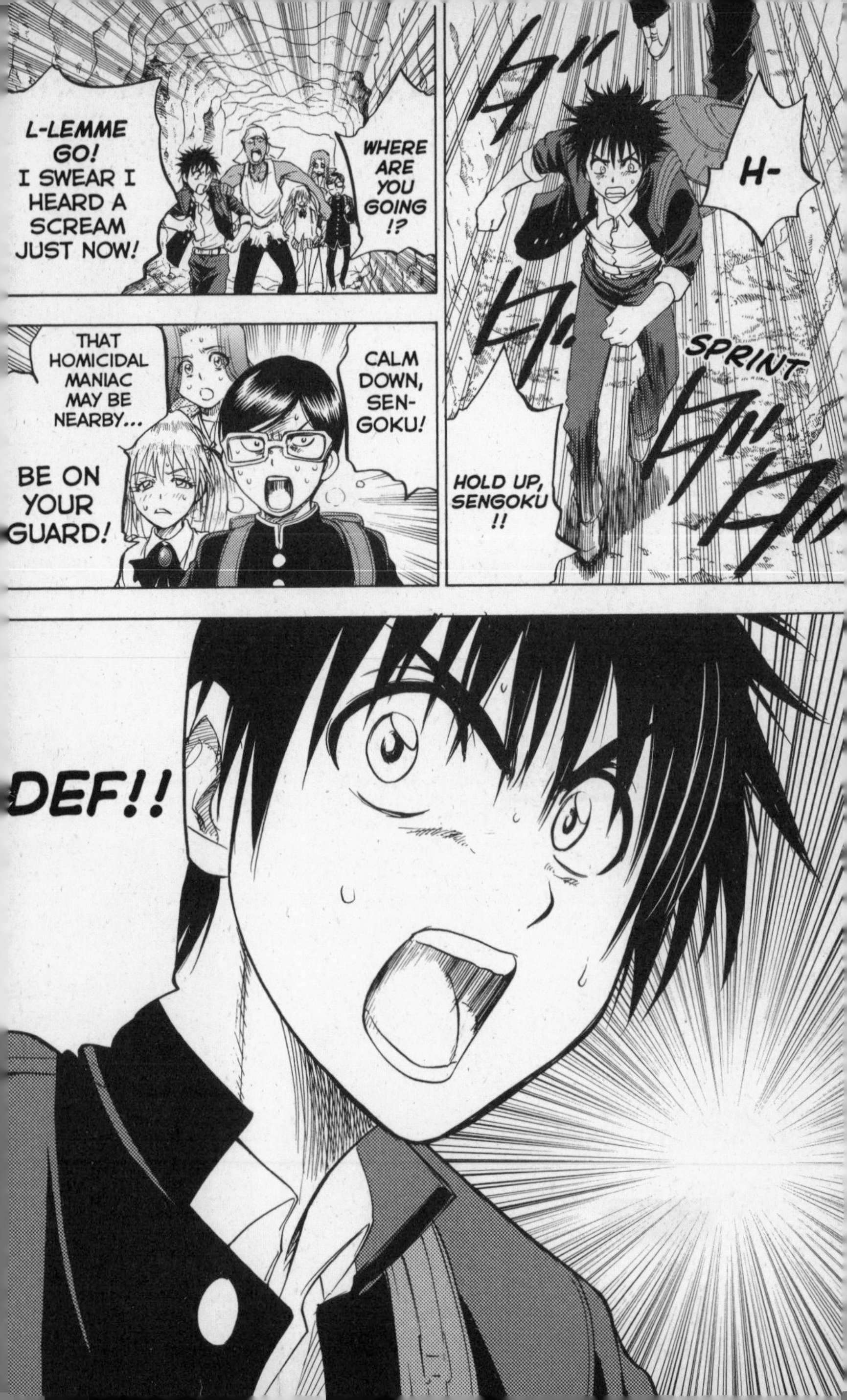
H-
SPRINT
HOLD UP, SENGOKU !!
WHERE ARE YOU GOING !?
L-LEMME GO! I SWEAR I HEARD A SCREAM JUST NOW!
CALM DOWN, SEN-GOKU!
THAT HOMICIDAL MANIAC MAY BE NEARBY...
BE ON YOUR GUARD!
DEF!!

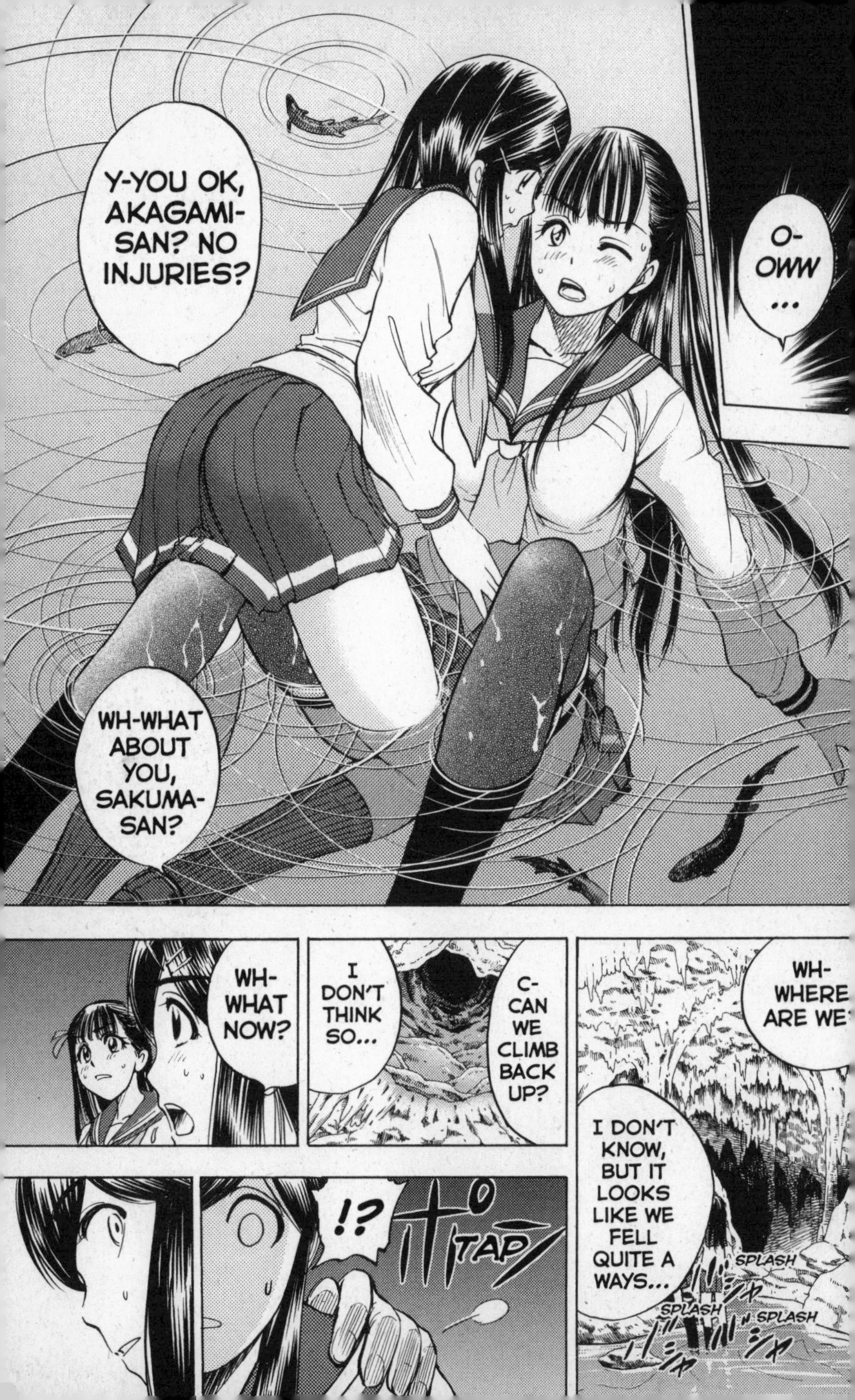
O-OWW ...
Y-YOU OK, AKAGAMI-SAN? NO INJURIES?
WH-WHAT ABOUT YOU, SAKUMA-SAN?
WH-WHERE ARE WE
I DON'T KNOW, BUT IT LOOKS LIKE WE FELL QUITE A WAYS...
SPLASH
SPLASH
SPLASH
C-CAN WE CLIMB BACK UP?
I DON'T THINK SO...
WH-WHAT NOW?
!?
TAP

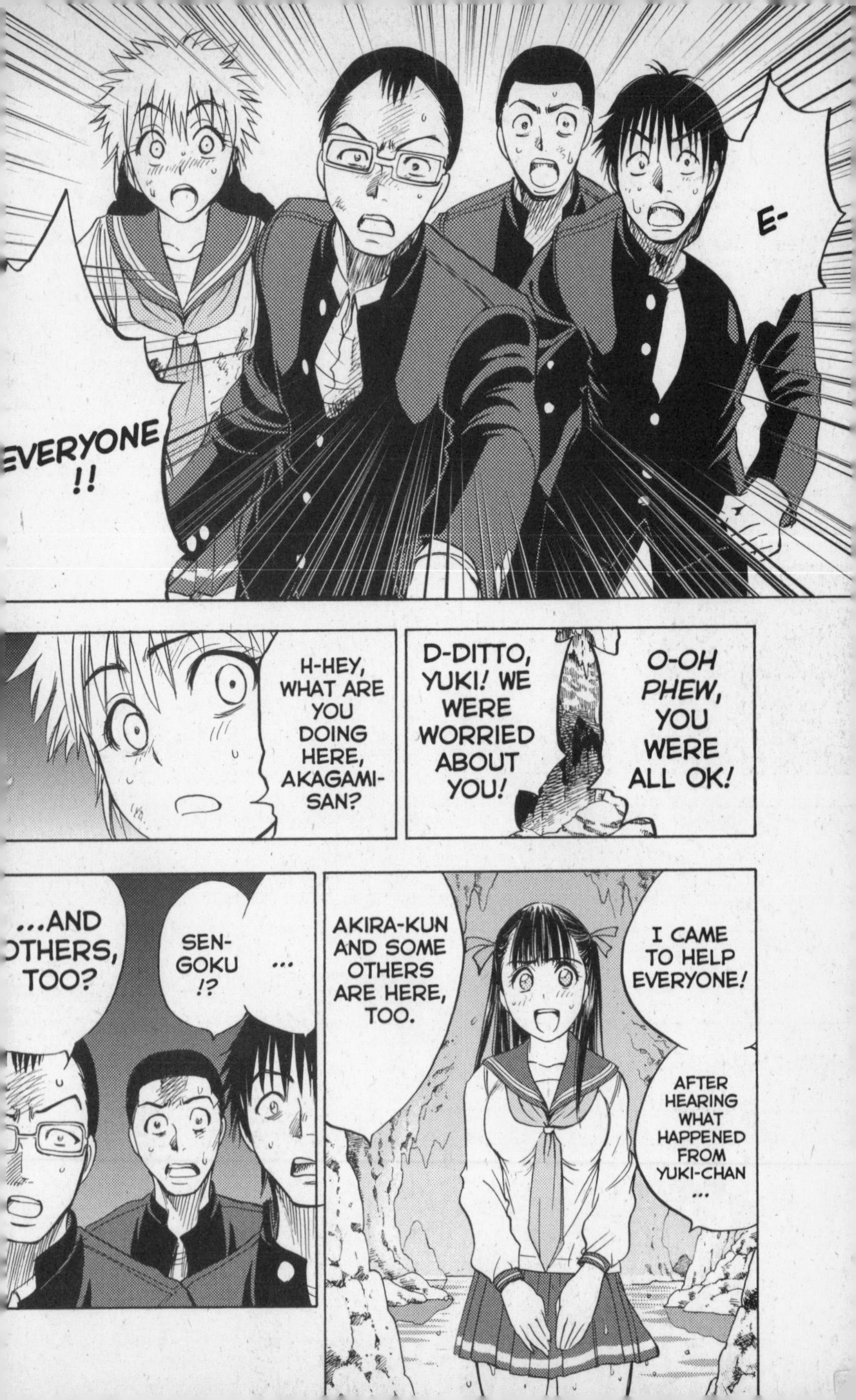
E-
EVERYONE !!
O-OH PHEW, YOU WERE ALL OK!
D-DITTO, YUKI! WE WERE WORRIED ABOUT YOU!
H-HEY, WHAT ARE YOU DOING HERE, AKAGAMI-SAN?
I CAME TO HELP EVERYONE!
AFTER HEARING WHAT HAPPENED FROM YUKI-CHAN ...
AKIRA-KUN AND SOME OTHERS ARE HERE, TOO.
...
SEN-GOKU !?
...AND OTHERS, TOO?

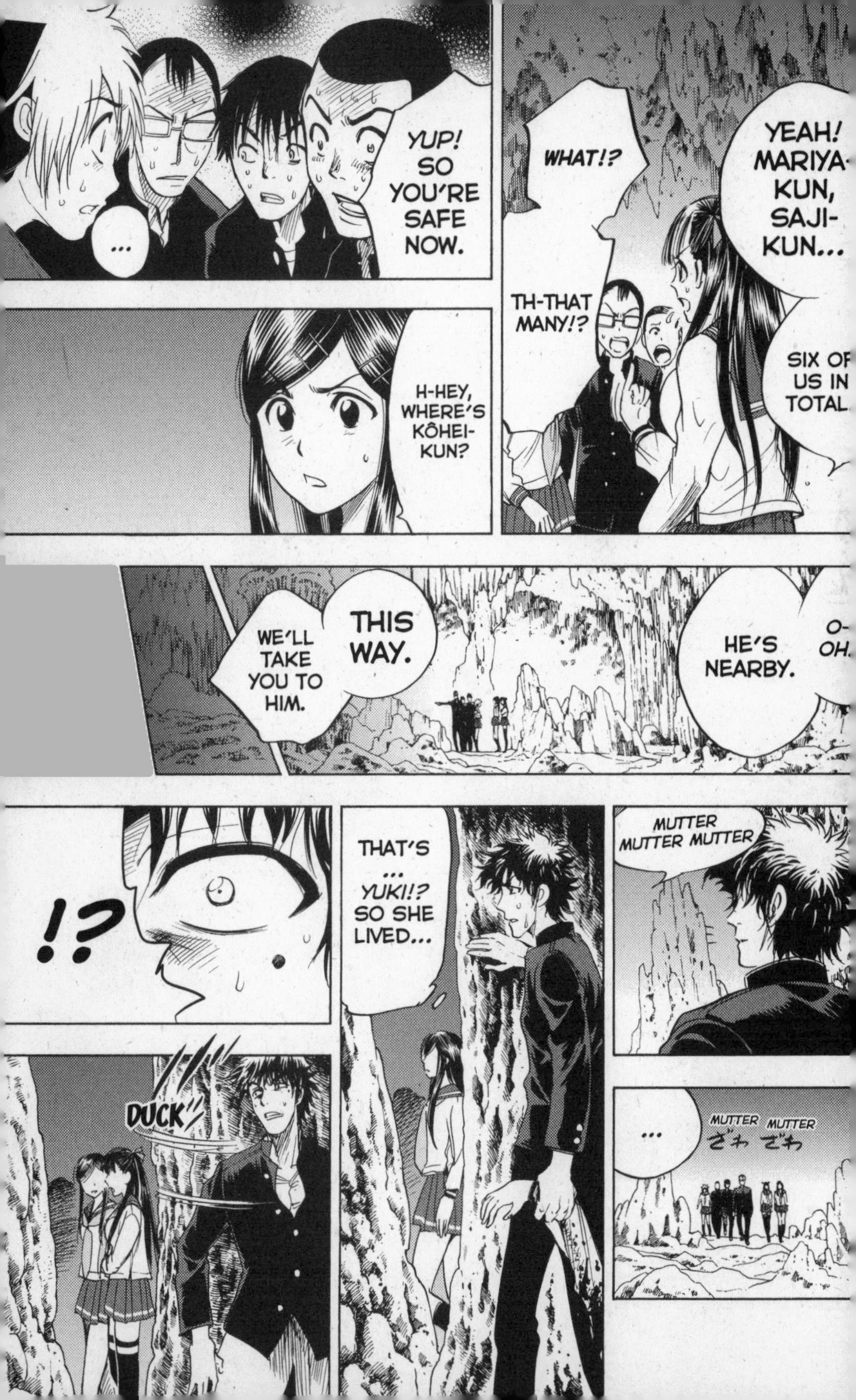
YEAH! MARIYA-KUN, SAJI-KUN...
WHAT!?
SIX OF US IN TOTAL.
TH-THAT MANY!?
YUP! SO YOU'RE SAFE NOW.
...
H-HEY, WHERE'S KÔHEI-KUN?
O-OH.
HE'S NEARBY.
THIS WAY.
WE'LL TAKE YOU TO HIM.
MUTTER MUTTER MUTTER
...
MUTTER MUTTER
ざわ ざわ
THAT'S ... YUKI!? SO SHE LIVED...
!?
DUCK

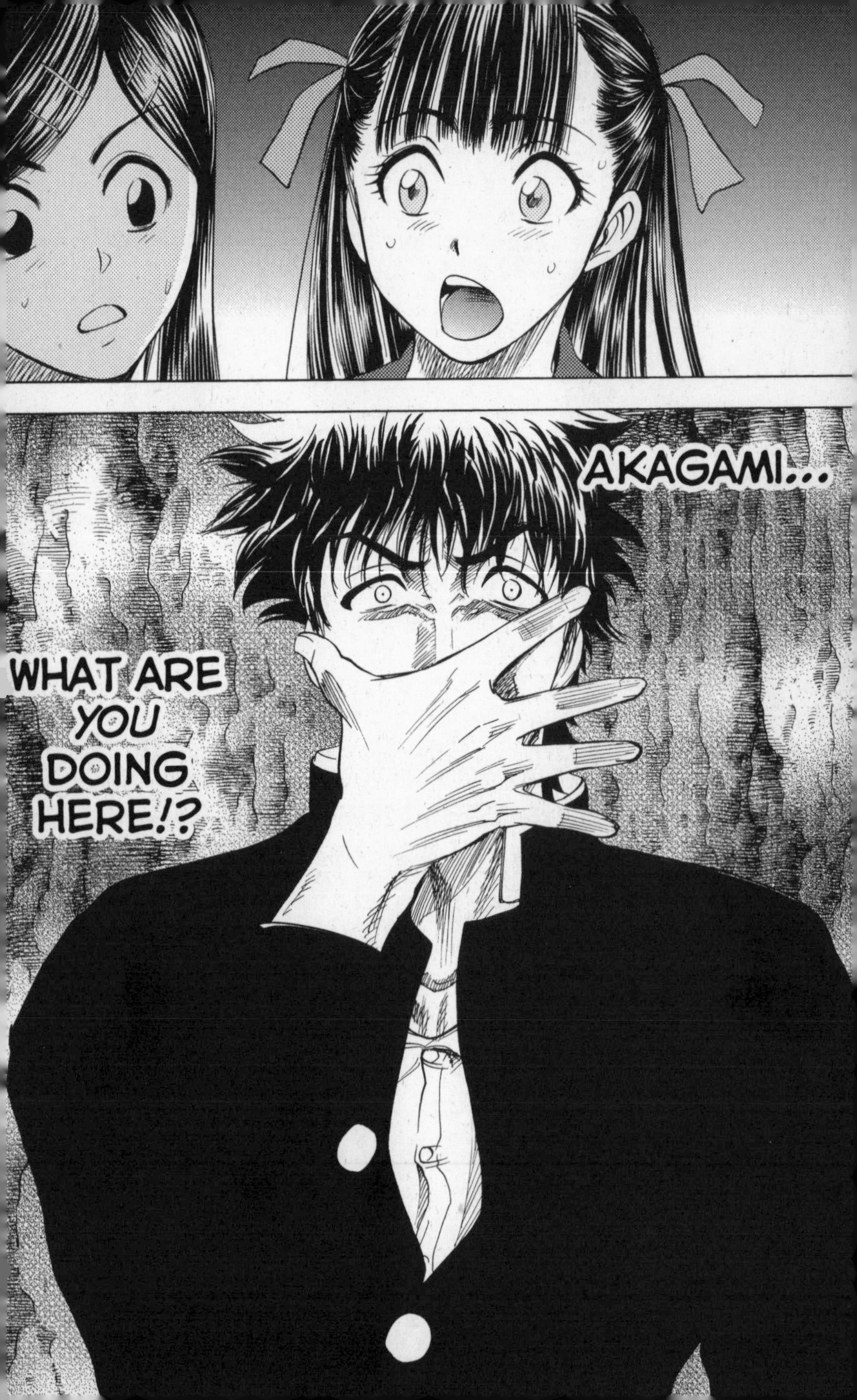
AKAGAMI...
WHAT ARE YOU DOING HERE!?

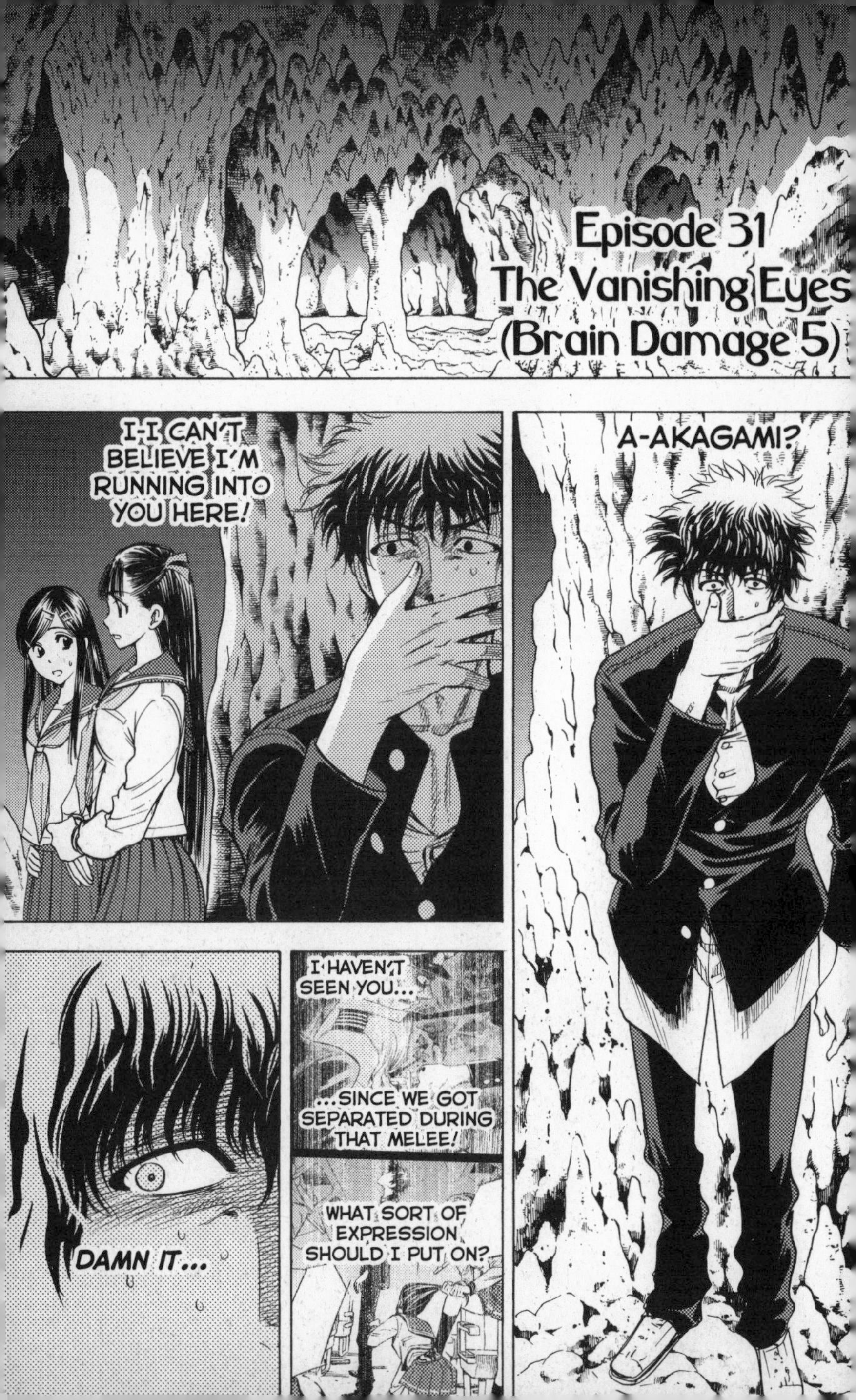
Episode 31
The Vanishing Eyes
(Brain Damage 5)
A-AKAGAMI?
I-I CAN'T BELIEVE I'M RUNNING INTO YOU HERE!
I HAVEN'T SEEN YOU...
...SINCE WE GOT SEPARATED DURING THAT MELEE!
WHAT SORT OF EXPRESSION SHOULD I PUT ON?
DAMN IT...

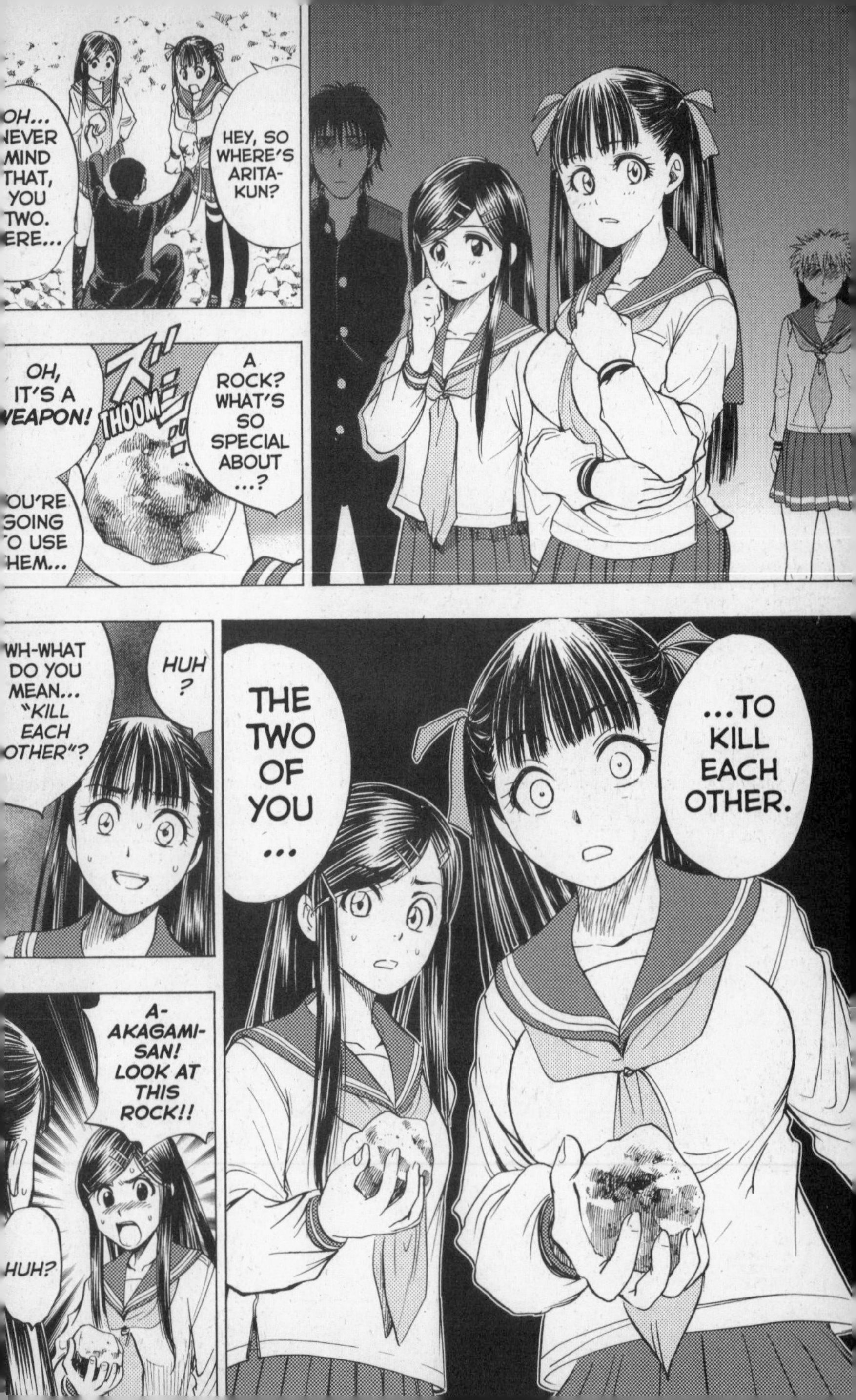
HEY, SO WHERE'S ARITA-KUN?
OH... EVER MIND THAT, YOU TWO. ERE...
A ROCK? WHAT'S SO SPECIAL ABOUT ...?
THOOM
OH, IT'S A EAPON!
OU'RE GOING O USE HEM...
...TO KILL EACH OTHER.
THE TWO OF YOU ...
HUH ?
WH-WHAT DO YOU MEAN... "KILL EACH OTHER"?
A-AKAGAMI-SAN! LOOK AT THIS ROCK!!
HUH?

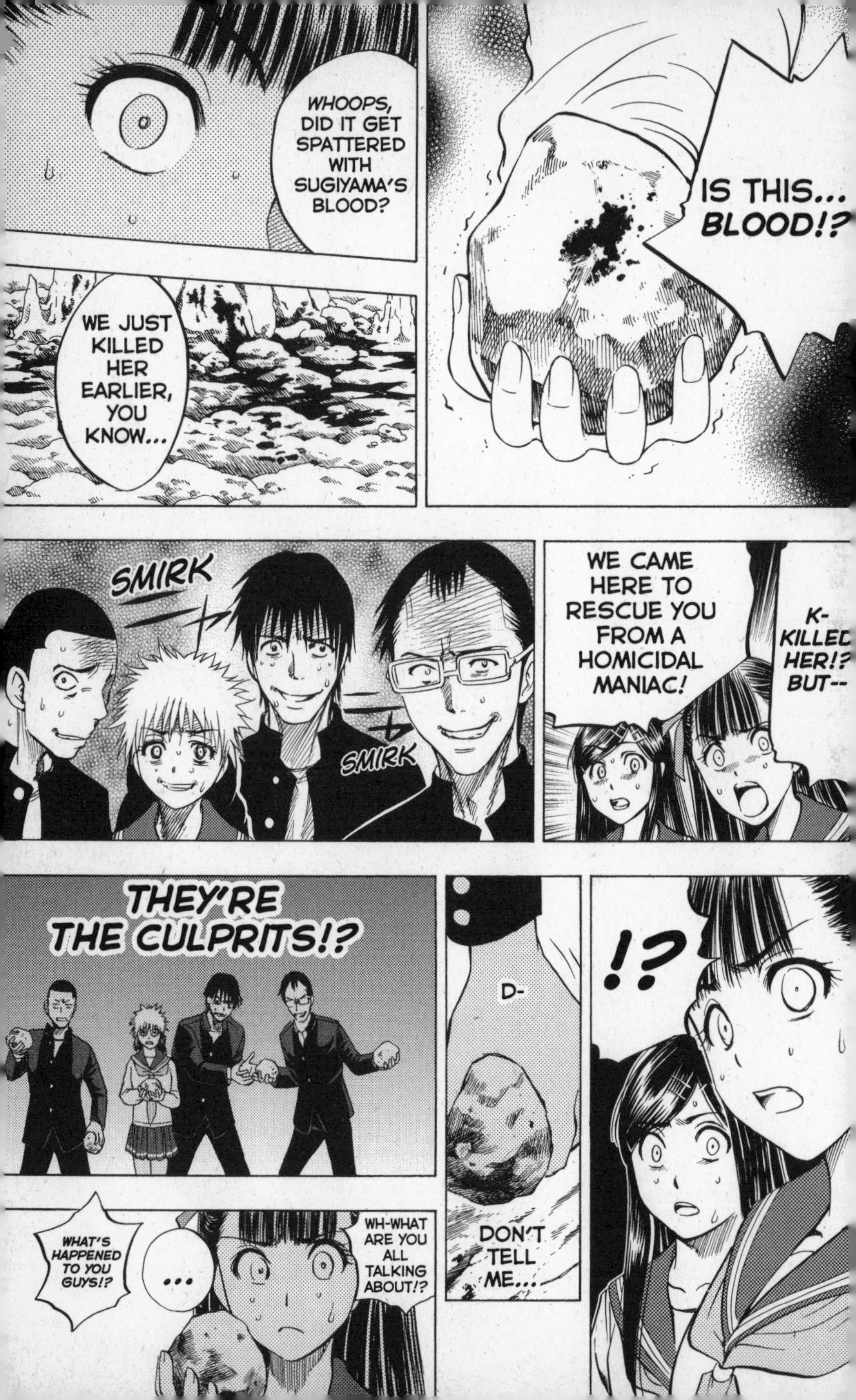
IS THIS... BLOOD!?
WHOOPS, DID IT GET SPATTERED WITH SUGIYAMA'S BLOOD?
WE JUST KILLED HER EARLIER, YOU KNOW...
K-KILLED HER!? BUT--
WE CAME HERE TO RESCUE YOU FROM A HOMICIDAL MANIAC!
SMIRK
SMIRK
!?
D-
DON'T TELL ME...
THEY'RE THE CULPRITS!?
WH-WHAT ARE YOU ALL TALKING ABOUT!?
...
WHAT'S HAPPENED TO YOU GUYS!?

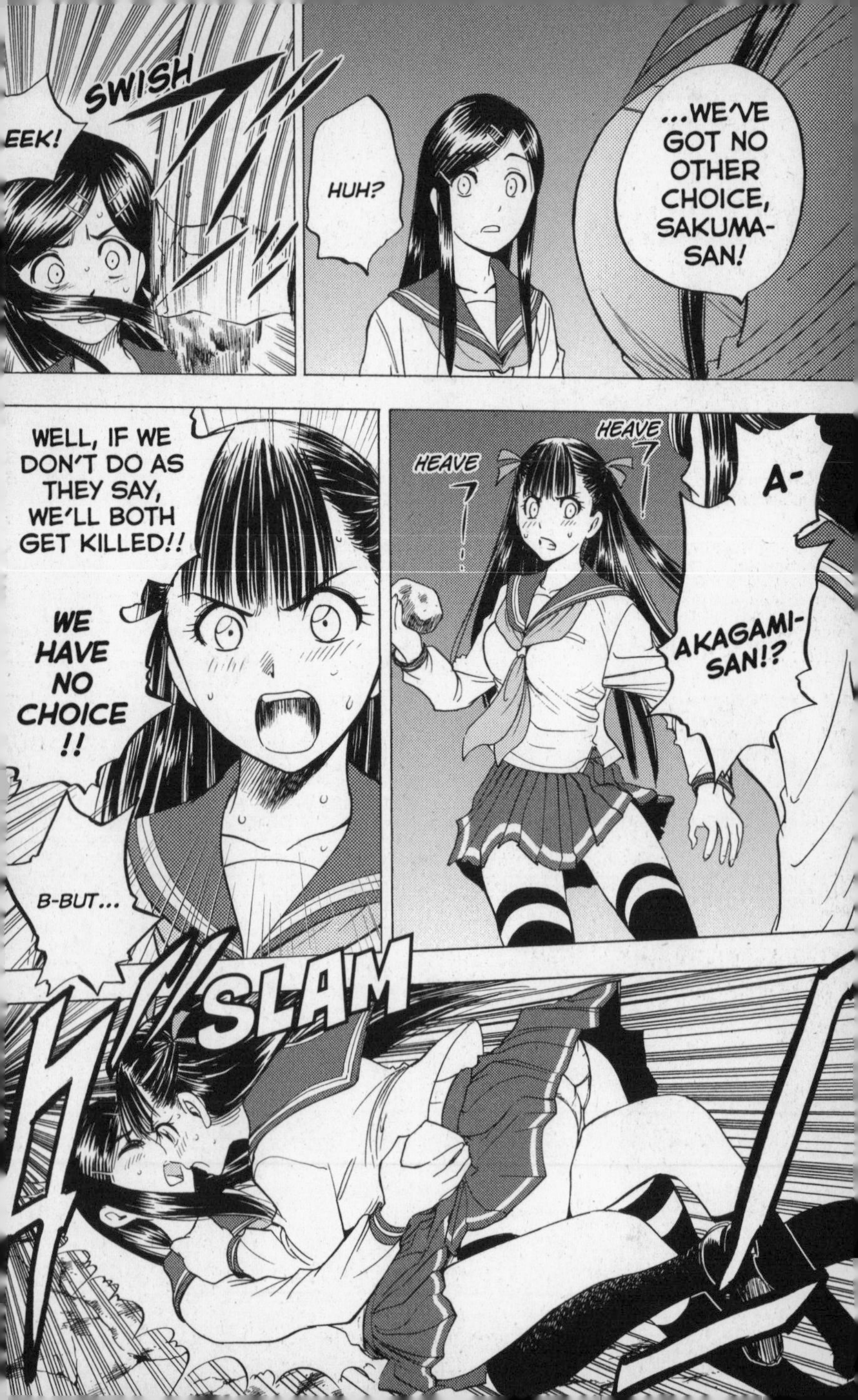
...WE'VE GOT NO OTHER CHOICE, SAKUMA-SAN!
HUH?
SWISH
EEK!
HEAVE
HEAVE
A-
AKAGAMI-SAN!?
WELL, IF WE DON'T DO AS THEY SAY, WE'LL BOTH GET KILLED!!
WE HAVE NO CHOICE !!
B-BUT...
SLAM

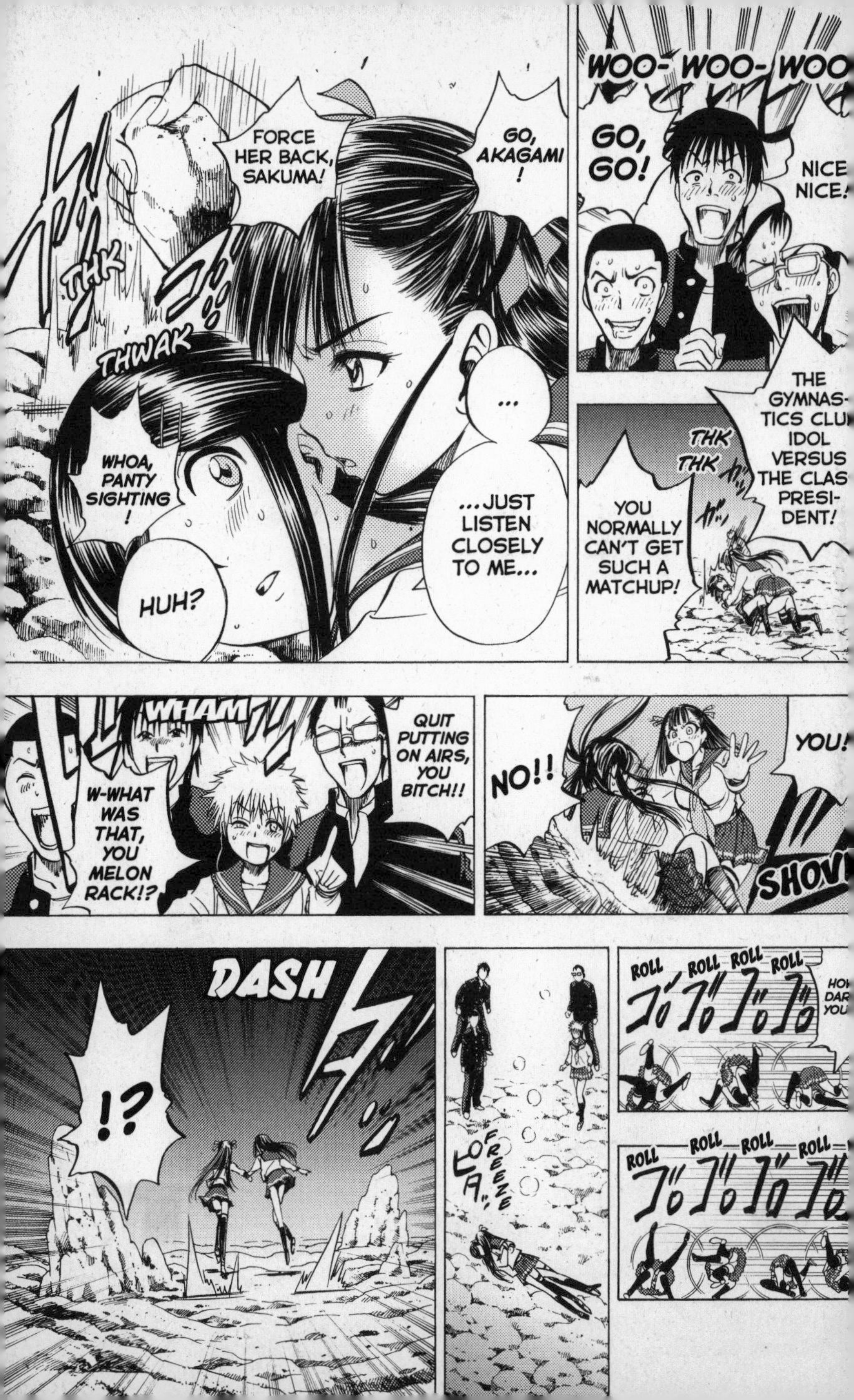
WOO- WOO- WOO
GO, GO!
NICE NICE!
THK THK
THE GYMNASTICS CLU IDOL VERSUS THE CLAS PRESIDENT!
YOU NORMALLY CAN'T GET SUCH A MATCHUP!
GO, AKAGAMI!
FORCE HER BACK, SAKUMA!
THK
THWAK
...
...JUST LISTEN CLOSELY TO ME...
WHOA, PANTY SIGHTING!
HUH?
YOU!
NO!!
SHOV
WHAM
QUIT PUTTING ON AIRS, YOU BITCH!!
W-WHAT WAS THAT, YOU MELON RACK!?
HOW DAR YOU
ROLL ROLL ROLL ROLL
ROLL ROLL ROLL ROLL
FREEZE
DASH
!?

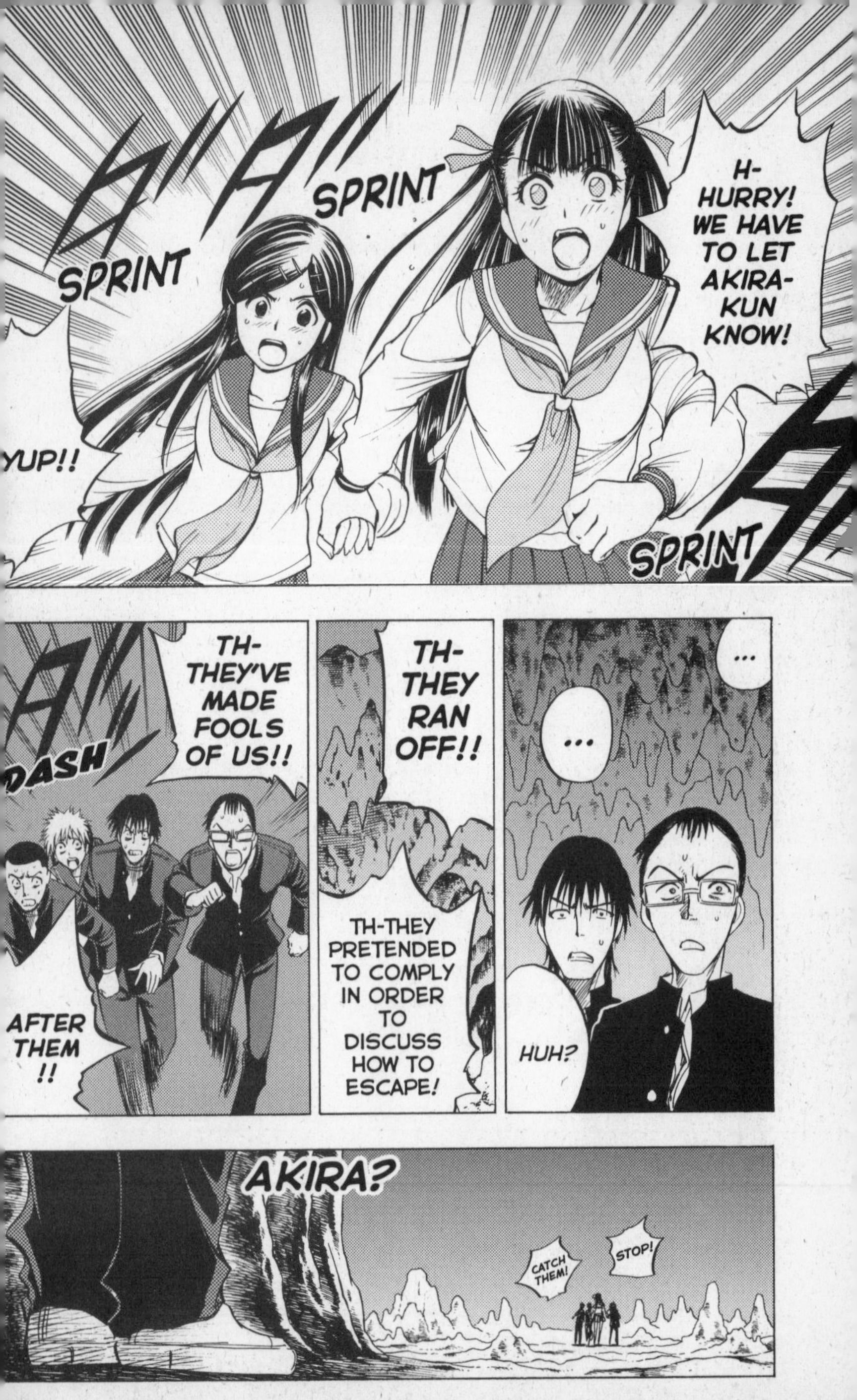
SPRINT
H-
HURRY!
WE HAVE
TO LET
AKIRA-
KUN
KNOW!
SPRINT
SPRINT
YUP!!
...
...
HUH?
TH-
THEY
RAN
OFF!!
TH-THEY
PRETENDED
TO COMPLY
IN ORDER
TO
DISCUSS
HOW TO
ESCAPE!
TH-
THEY'VE
MADE
FOOLS
OF US!!
DASH
AFTER
THEM
!!
AKIRA?
STOP!
CATCH
THEM!

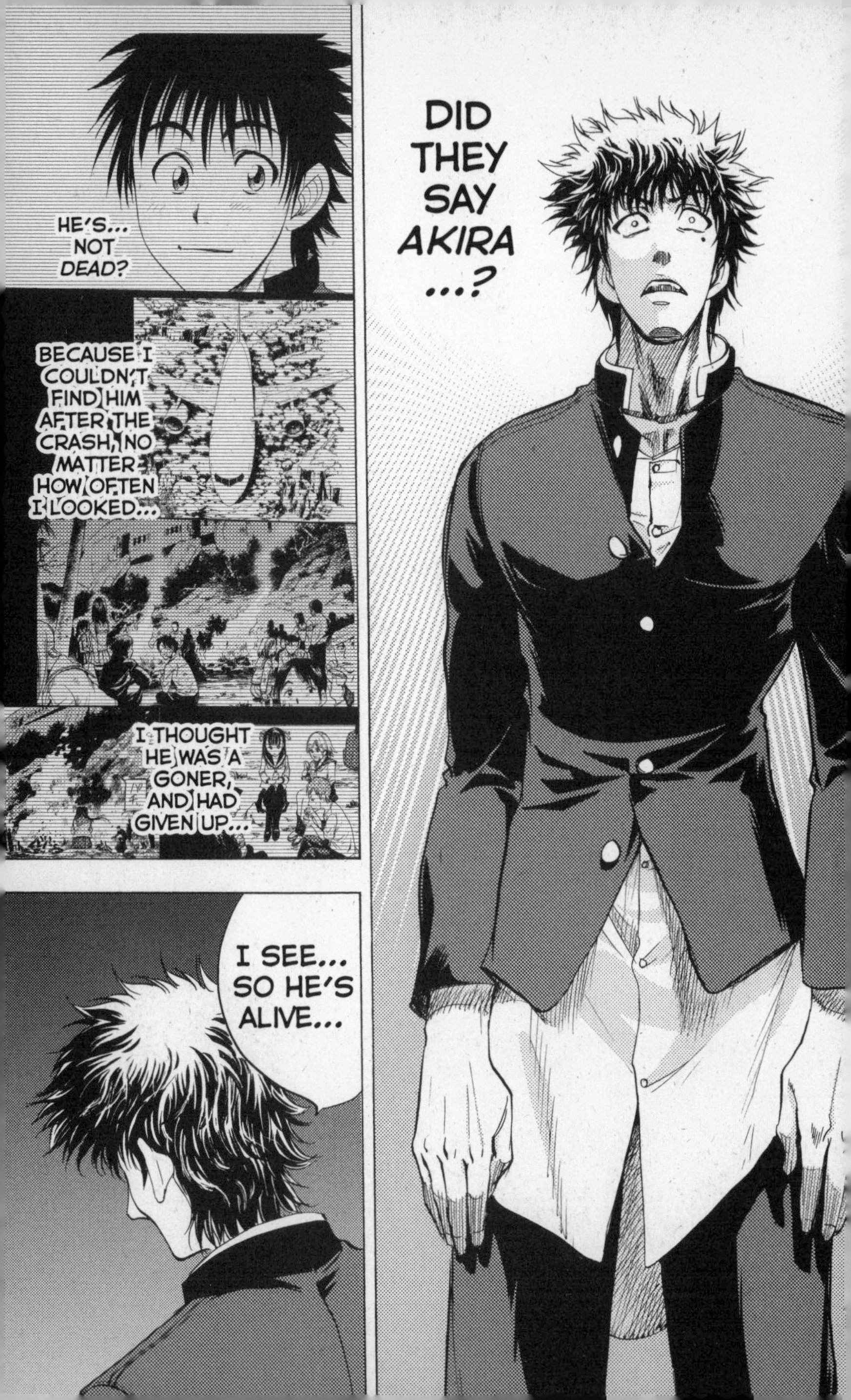
DID THEY SAY AKIRA ...?
HE'S... NOT DEAD?
BECAUSE I COULDN'T FIND HIM AFTER THE CRASH, NO MATTER HOW OFTEN I LOOKED...
I THOUGHT HE WAS A GONER, AND HAD GIVEN UP...
I SEE... SO HE'S ALIVE...

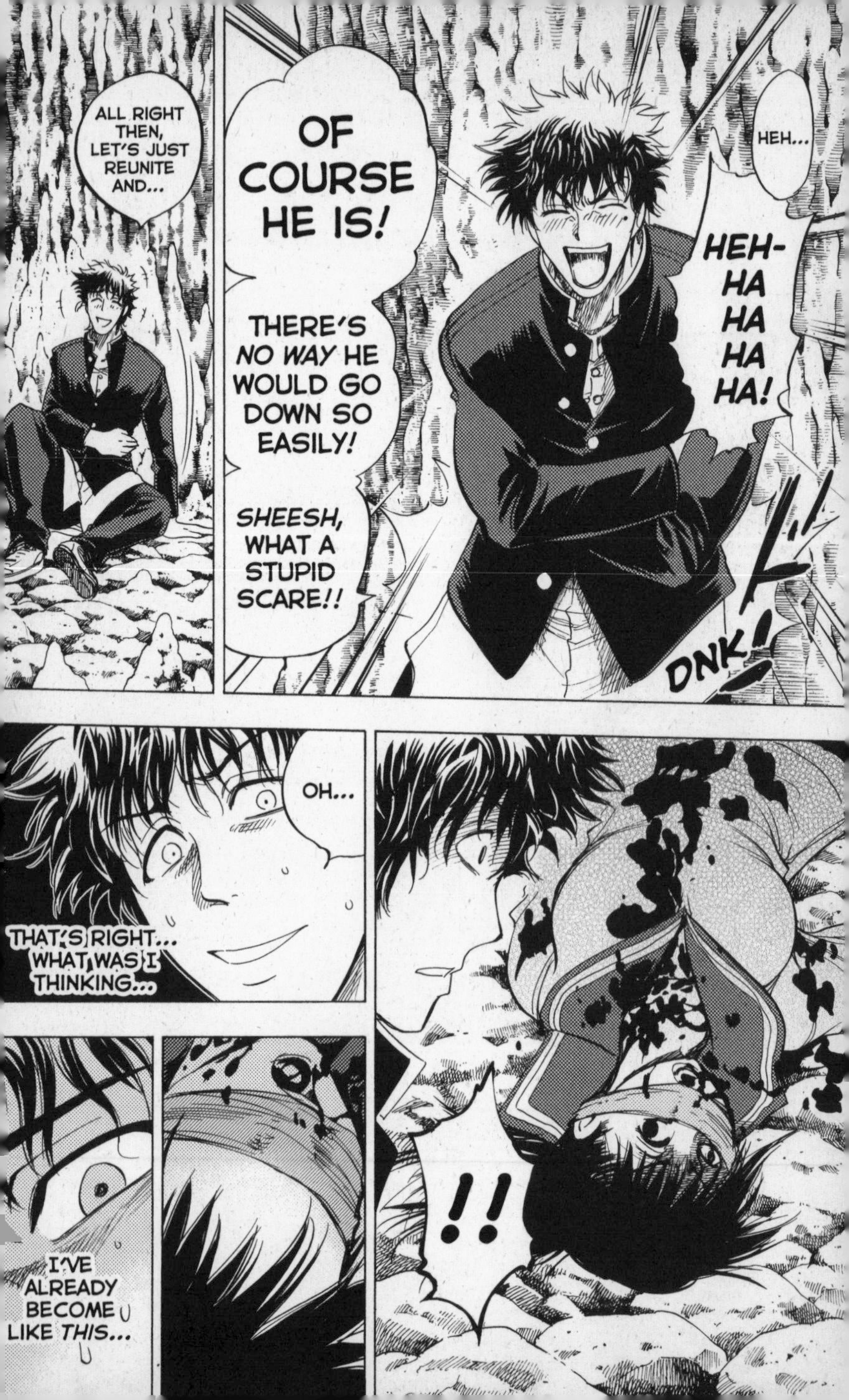
HEH...
OF COURSE HE IS!
HEH-HA HA HA HA!
THERE'S *NO WAY* HE WOULD GO DOWN SO EASILY!
SHEESH, WHAT A STUPID SCARE!!
DNK!
ALL RIGHT THEN, LET'S JUST REUNITE AND...
!!
OH...
THAT'S RIGHT... WHAT WAS I THINKING...
I'VE ALREADY BECOME LIKE *THIS*...

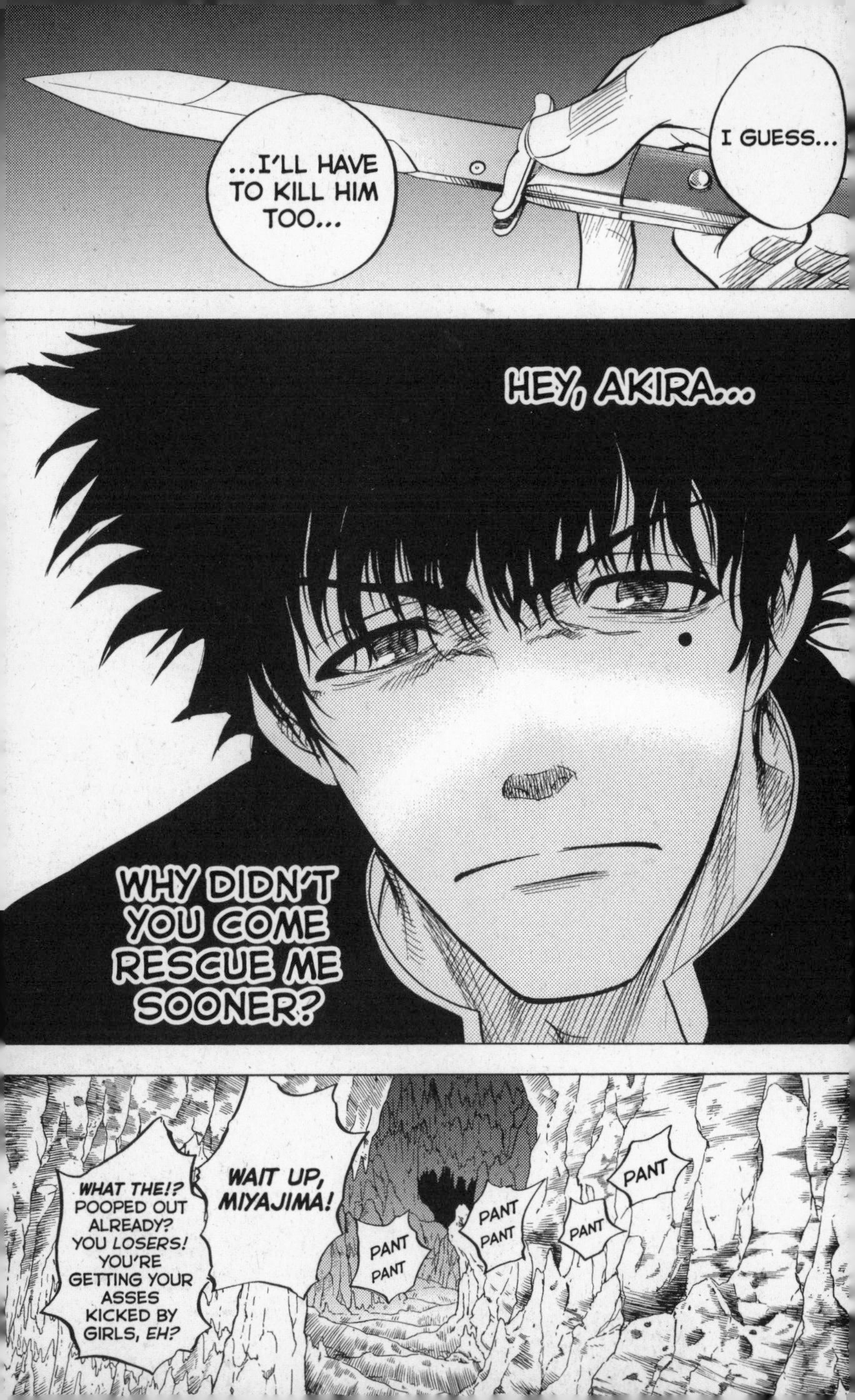
I GUESS...
...I'LL HAVE TO KILL HIM TOO...
HEY, AKIRA...
WHY DIDN'T YOU COME RESCUE ME SOONER?
PANT
PANT
PANT PANT
PANT PANT
WAIT UP, MIYAJIMA!
WHAT THE!? POOPED OUT ALREADY? YOU LOSERS! YOU'RE GETTING YOUR ASSES KICKED BY GIRLS, EH?

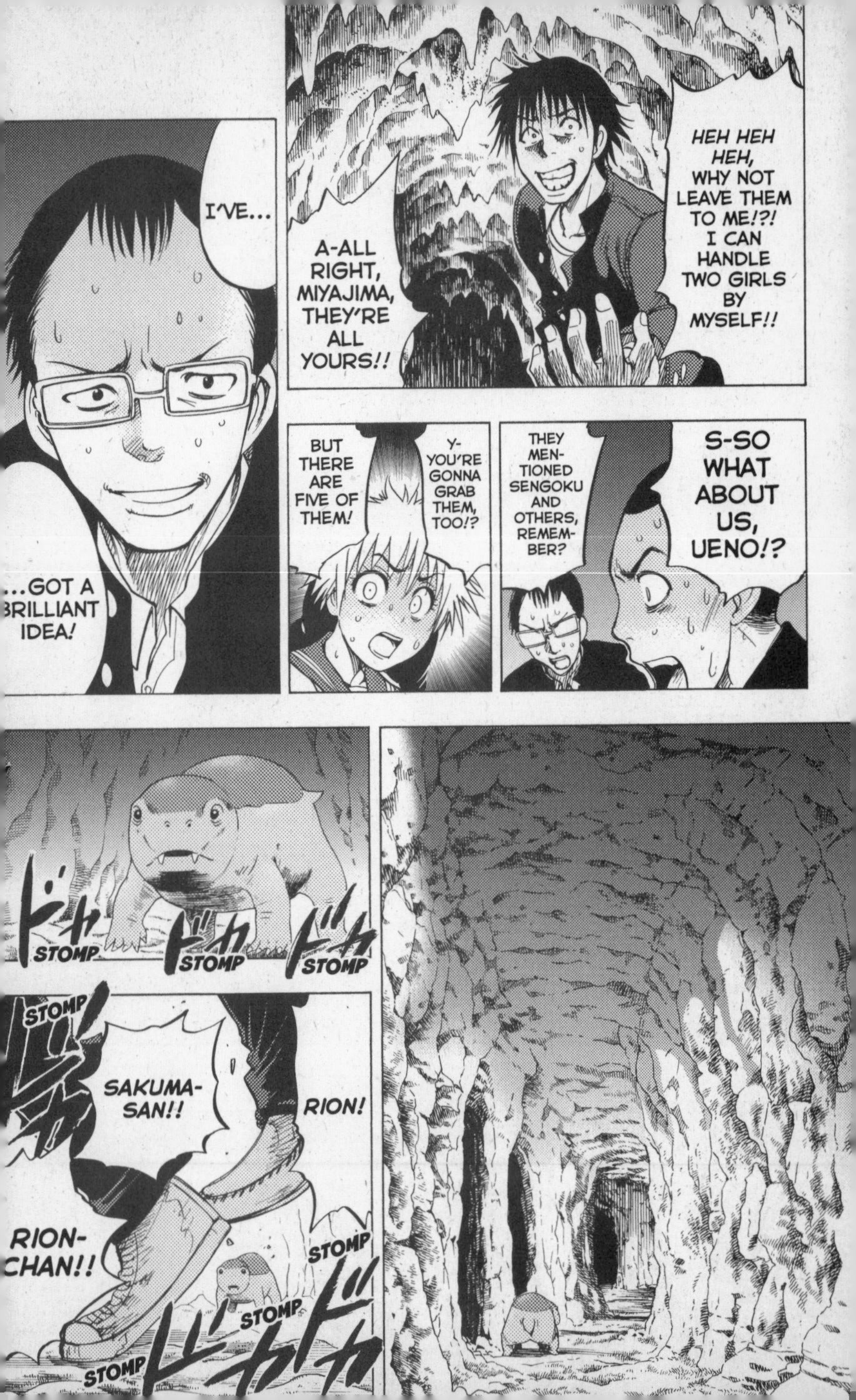
HEH HEH HEH, WHY NOT LEAVE THEM TO ME!?! I CAN HANDLE TWO GIRLS BY MYSELF!!
A-ALL RIGHT, MIYAJIMA, THEY'RE ALL YOURS!!
S-SO WHAT ABOUT US, UENO!?
THEY MEN-TIONED SENGOKU AND OTHERS, REMEMBER?
Y-YOU'RE GONNA GRAB THEM, TOO!?
BUT THERE ARE FIVE OF THEM!
I'VE...
...GOT A BRILLIANT IDEA!
STOMP
STOMP
STOMP
STOMP
RION!
SAKUMA-SAN!!
RION-CHAN!!
STOMP
STOMP
STOMP

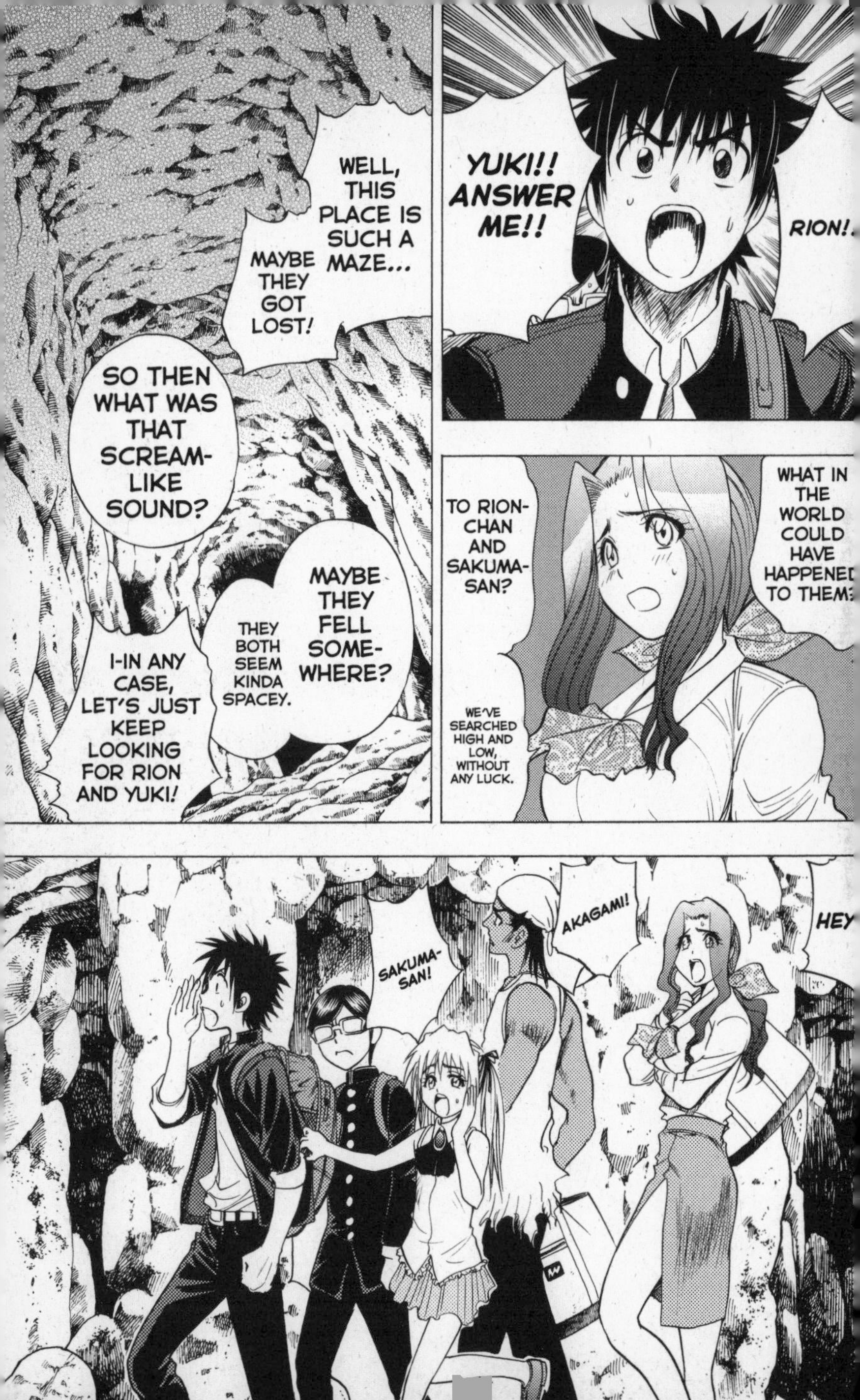
RION!!
YUKI!! ANSWER ME!!
WHAT IN THE WORLD COULD HAVE HAPPENED TO THEM?
TO RION-CHAN AND SAKUMA-SAN?
WE'VE SEARCHED HIGH AND LOW, WITHOUT ANY LUCK.
WELL, THIS PLACE IS SUCH A MAZE...
MAYBE THEY GOT LOST!
SO THEN WHAT WAS THAT SCREAM-LIKE SOUND?
MAYBE THEY FELL SOMEWHERE?
THEY BOTH SEEM KINDA SPACEY.
I-IN ANY CASE, LET'S JUST KEEP LOOKING FOR RION AND YUKI!
HEY
AKAGAMI!
SAKUMA-SAN!

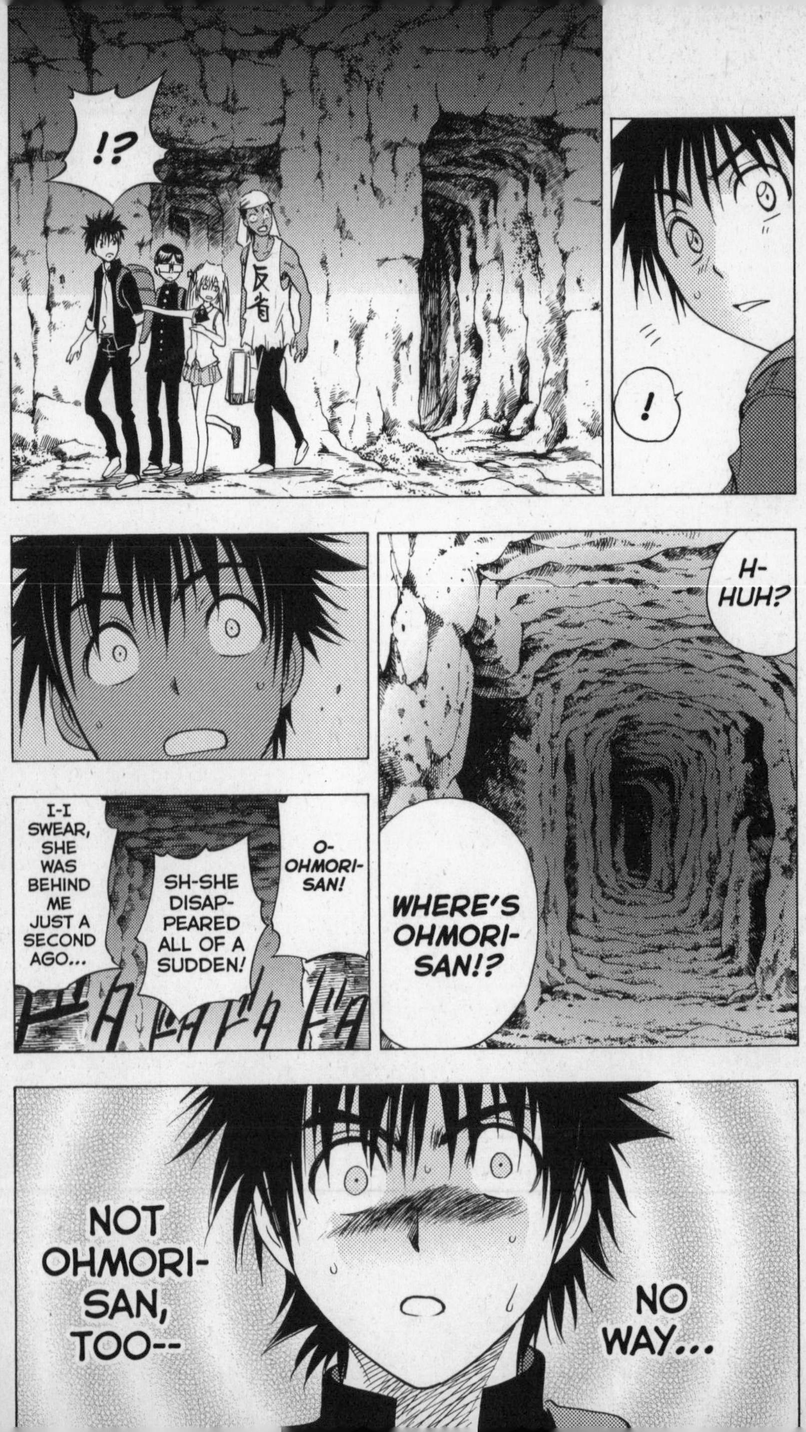
!
!?
H-HUH?
WHERE'S OHMORI-SAN!?
O-OHMORI-SAN!
SH-SHE DISAPPEARED ALL OF A SUDDEN!
I-I SWEAR, SHE WAS BEHIND ME JUST A SECOND AGO...
NO WAY...
NOT OHMORI-SAN, TOO--

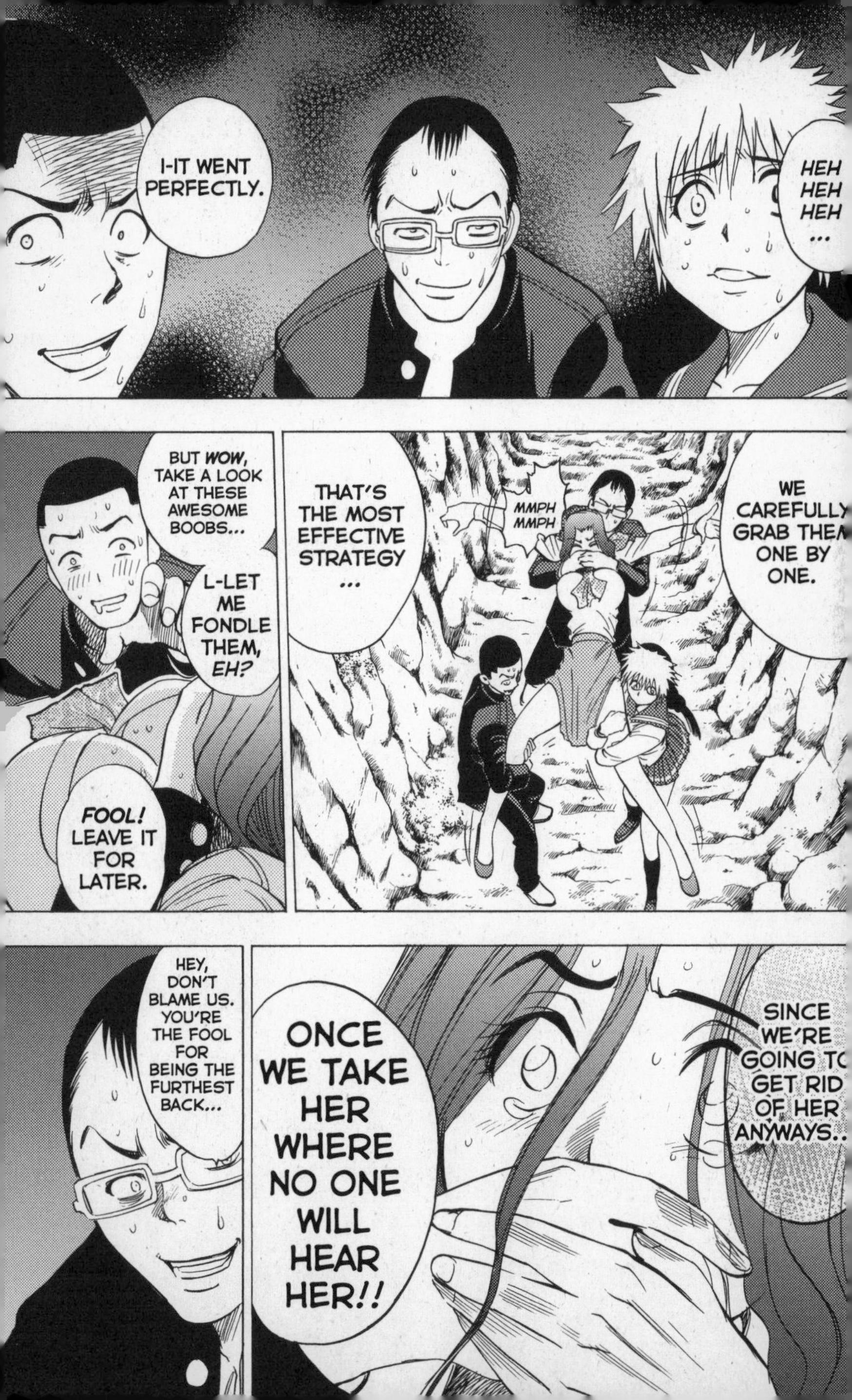
HEH HEH HEH ...
I-IT WENT PERFECTLY.
WE CAREFULLY GRAB THEM ONE BY ONE.
MMPH MMPH
THAT'S THE MOST EFFECTIVE STRATEGY ...
BUT *WOW*, TAKE A LOOK AT THESE AWESOME BOOBS...
L-LET ME FONDLE THEM, *EH?*
FOOL! LEAVE IT FOR LATER.
SINCE WE'RE GOING TO GET RID OF HER ANYWAYS..
ONCE WE TAKE HER WHERE NO ONE WILL HEAR HER!!
HEY, DON'T BLAME US. YOU'RE THE FOOL FOR BEING THE FURTHEST BACK...

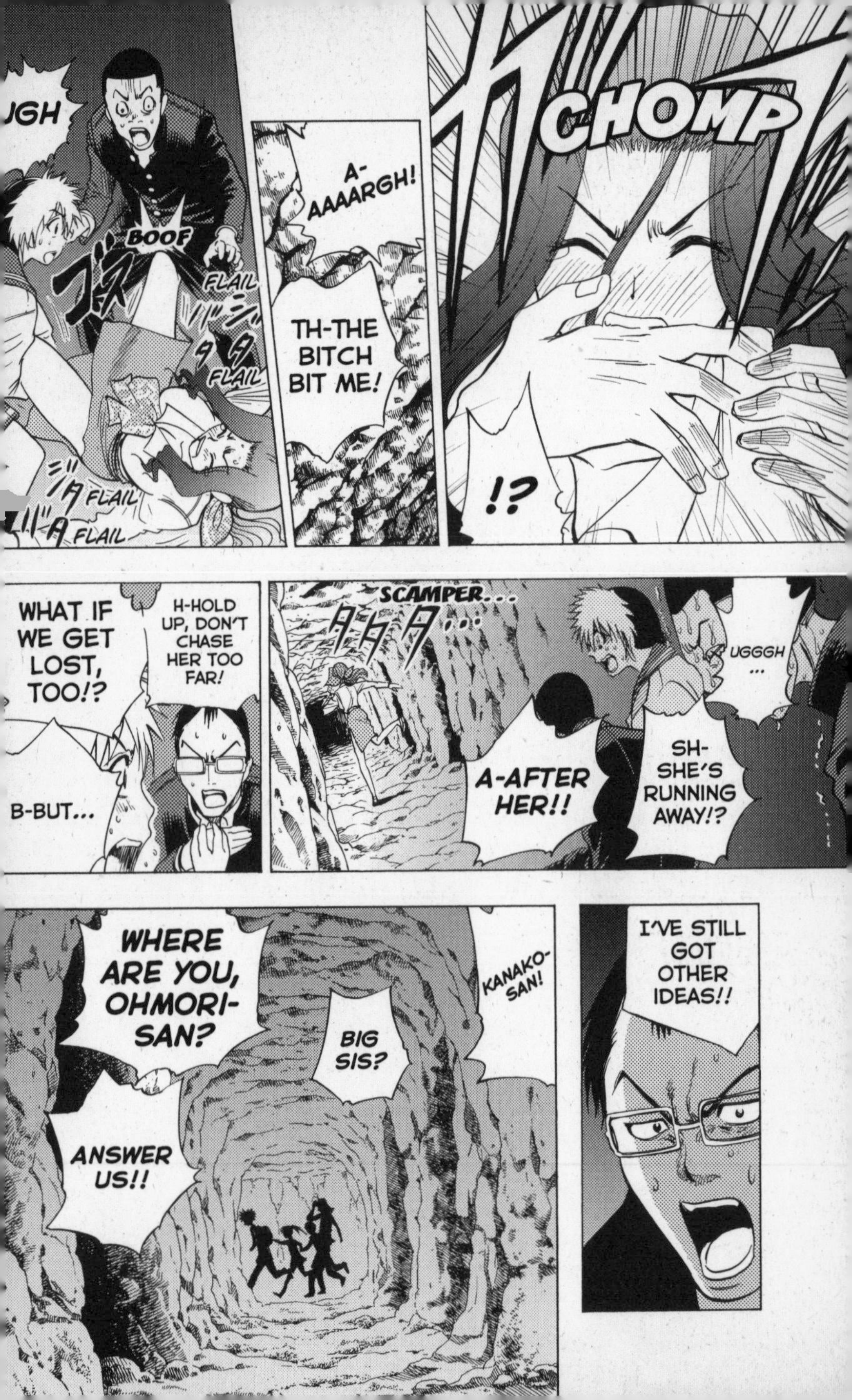
CHOMP
!?
A-AAAARGH!
TH-THE BITCH BIT ME!
UGH
BOOF
FLAIL
FLAIL
FLAIL
FLAIL
UGGGH...
SH-SHE'S RUNNING AWAY!?
A-AFTER HER!!
SCAMPER...
H-HOLD UP, DON'T CHASE HER TOO FAR!
WHAT IF WE GET LOST, TOO!?
B-BUT...
I'VE STILL GOT OTHER IDEAS!!
KANAKO-SAN!
BIG SIS?
WHERE ARE YOU, OHMORI-SAN?
ANSWER US!!

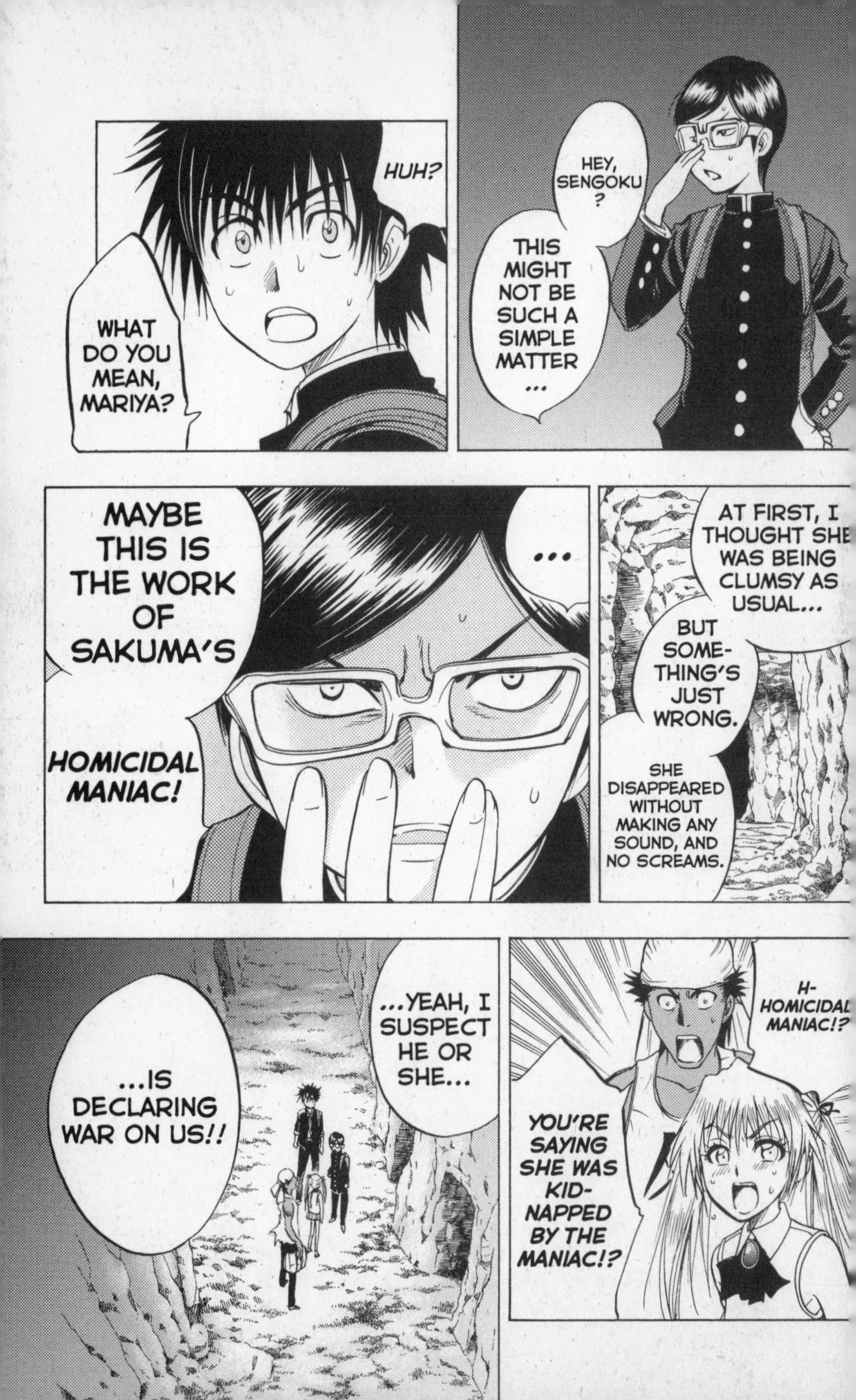
HEY, SENGOKU?
THIS MIGHT NOT BE SUCH A SIMPLE MATTER...
HUH?
WHAT DO YOU MEAN, MARIYA?
AT FIRST, I THOUGHT SHE WAS BEING CLUMSY AS USUAL...
BUT SOME-THING'S JUST WRONG.
SHE DISAPPEARED WITHOUT MAKING ANY SOUND, AND NO SCREAMS.
...
MAYBE THIS IS THE WORK OF SAKUMA'S
HOMICIDAL MANIAC!
H-HOMICIDAL MANIAC!?
YOU'RE SAYING SHE WAS KID-NAPPED BY THE MANIAC!?
...YEAH, I SUSPECT HE OR SHE...
...IS DECLARING WAR ON US!!

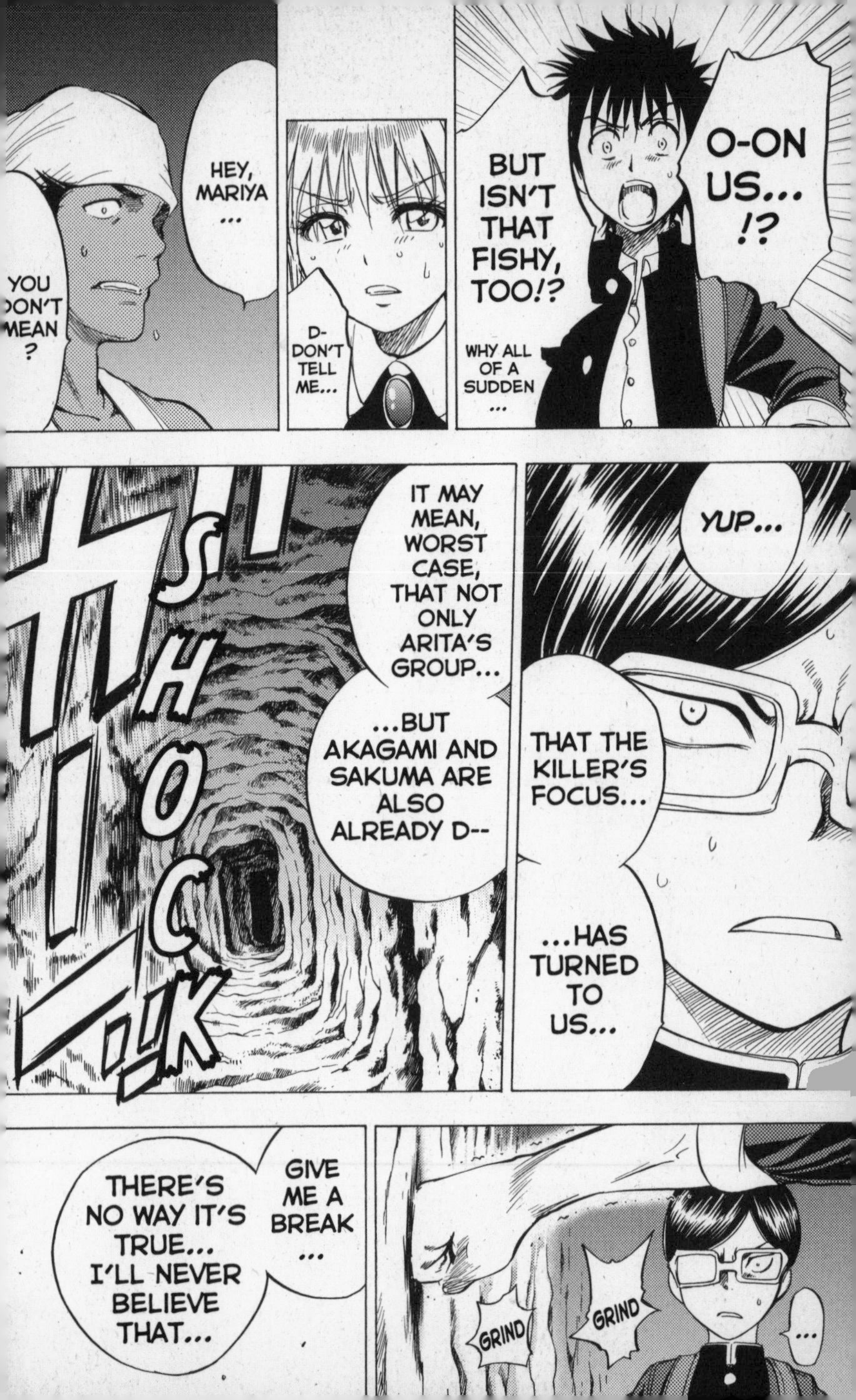
O-ON US... !?
BUT ISN'T THAT FISHY, TOO!?
WHY ALL OF A SUDDEN ...
D-DON'T TELL ME...
HEY, MARIYA ...
YOU DON'T MEAN ?
YUP...
THAT THE KILLER'S FOCUS...
...HAS TURNED TO US...
IT MAY MEAN, WORST CASE, THAT NOT ONLY ARITA'S GROUP...
...BUT AKAGAMI AND SAKUMA ARE ALSO ALREADY D--
SHOCK
...
GRIND
GRIND
GIVE ME A BREAK ...
THERE'S NO WAY IT'S TRUE... I'LL NEVER BELIEVE THAT...

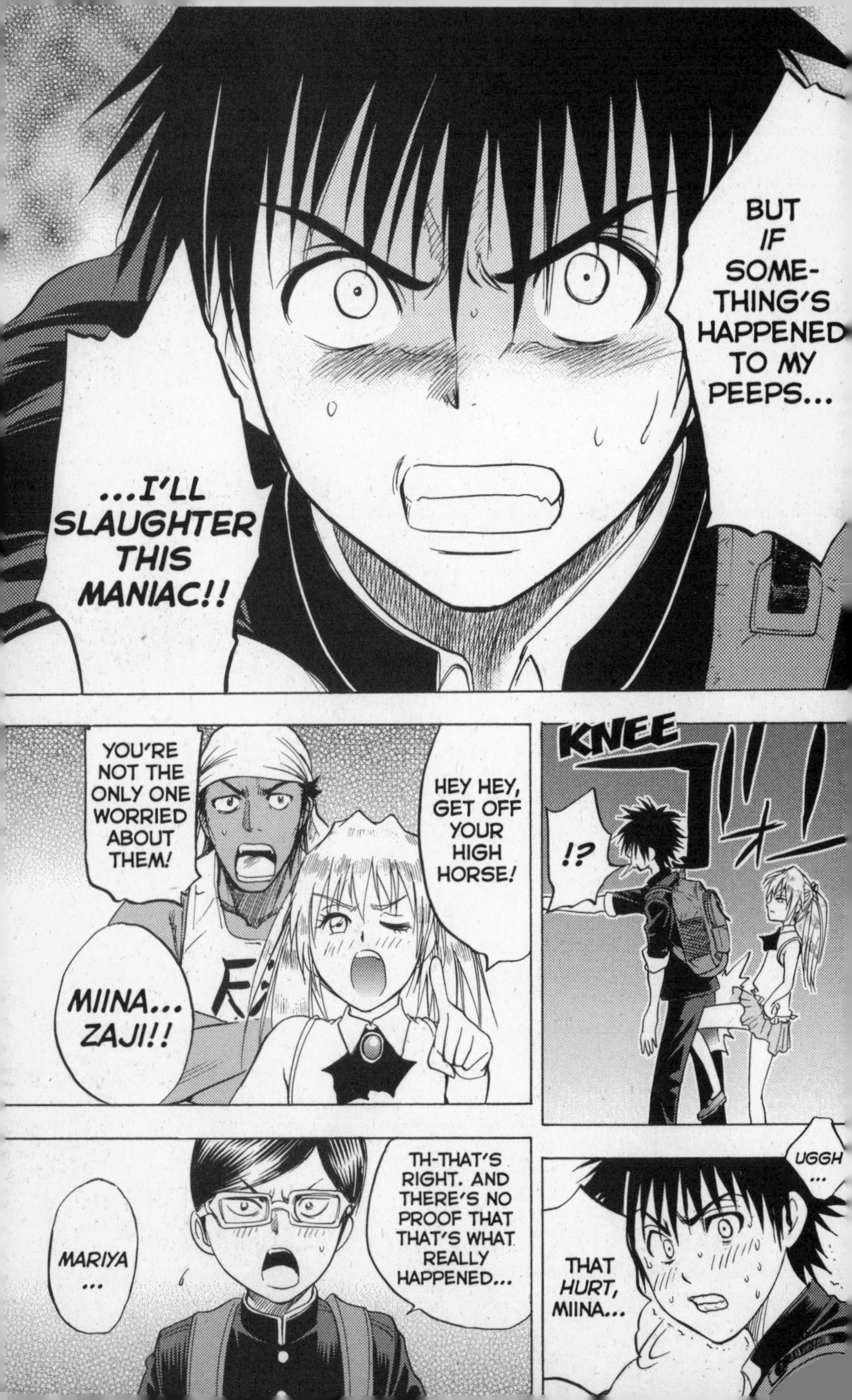
BUT IF SOME-THING'S HAPPENED TO MY PEEPS...
...I'LL SLAUGHTER THIS MANIAC!!
KNEE
!?
HEY HEY, GET OFF YOUR HIGH HORSE!
YOU'RE NOT THE ONLY ONE WORRIED ABOUT THEM!
MIINA... ZAJI!!
UGGH...
THAT HURT, MIINA...
TH-THAT'S RIGHT. AND THERE'S NO PROOF THAT THAT'S WHAT REALLY HAPPENED...
MARIYA...

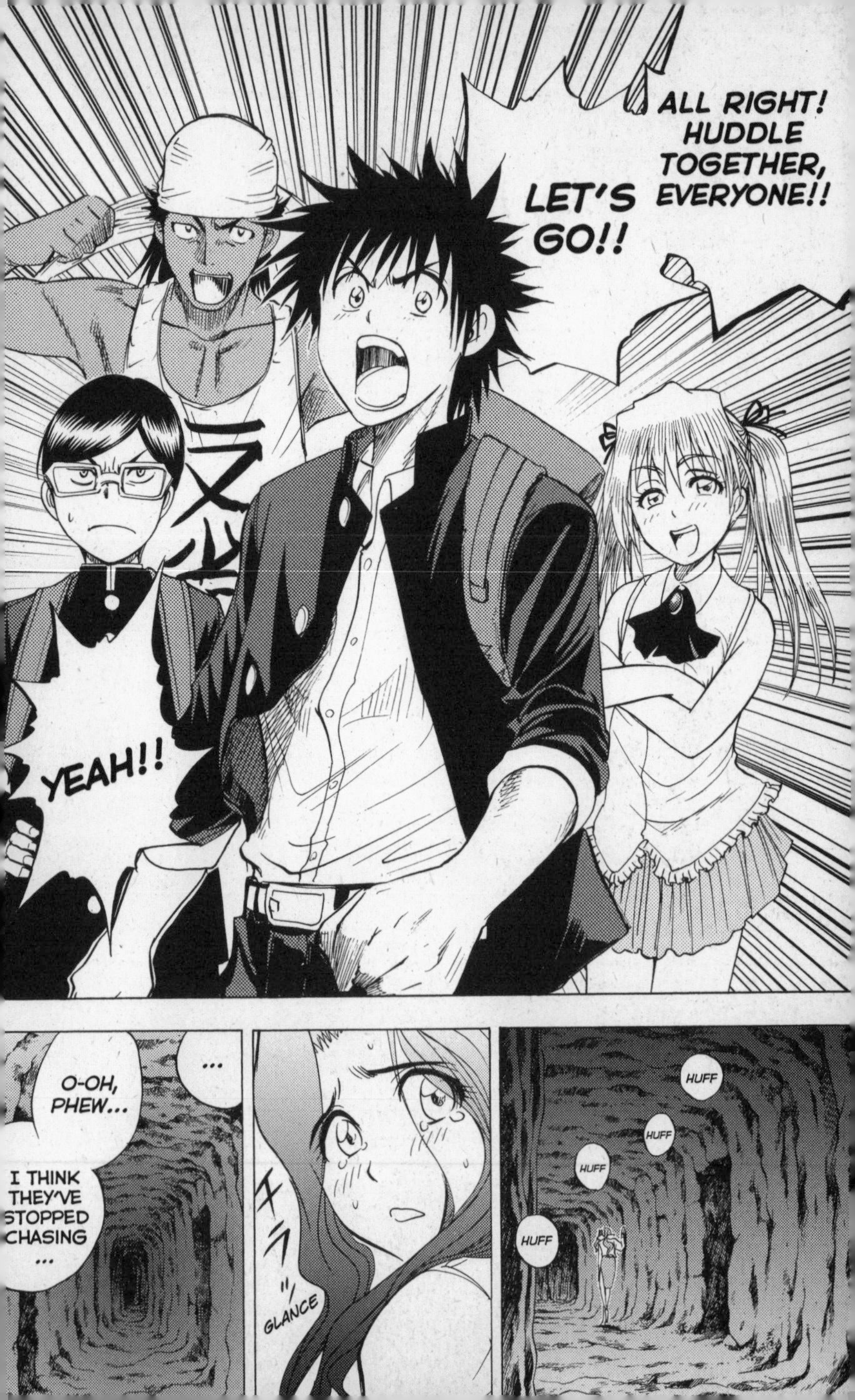
ALL RIGHT! HUDDLE TOGETHER, EVERYONE!!
LET'S GO!!
YEAH!!
HUFF
HUFF
HUFF
HUFF
GLANCE
...
O-OH, PHEW...
I THINK THEY'VE STOPPED CHASING ...

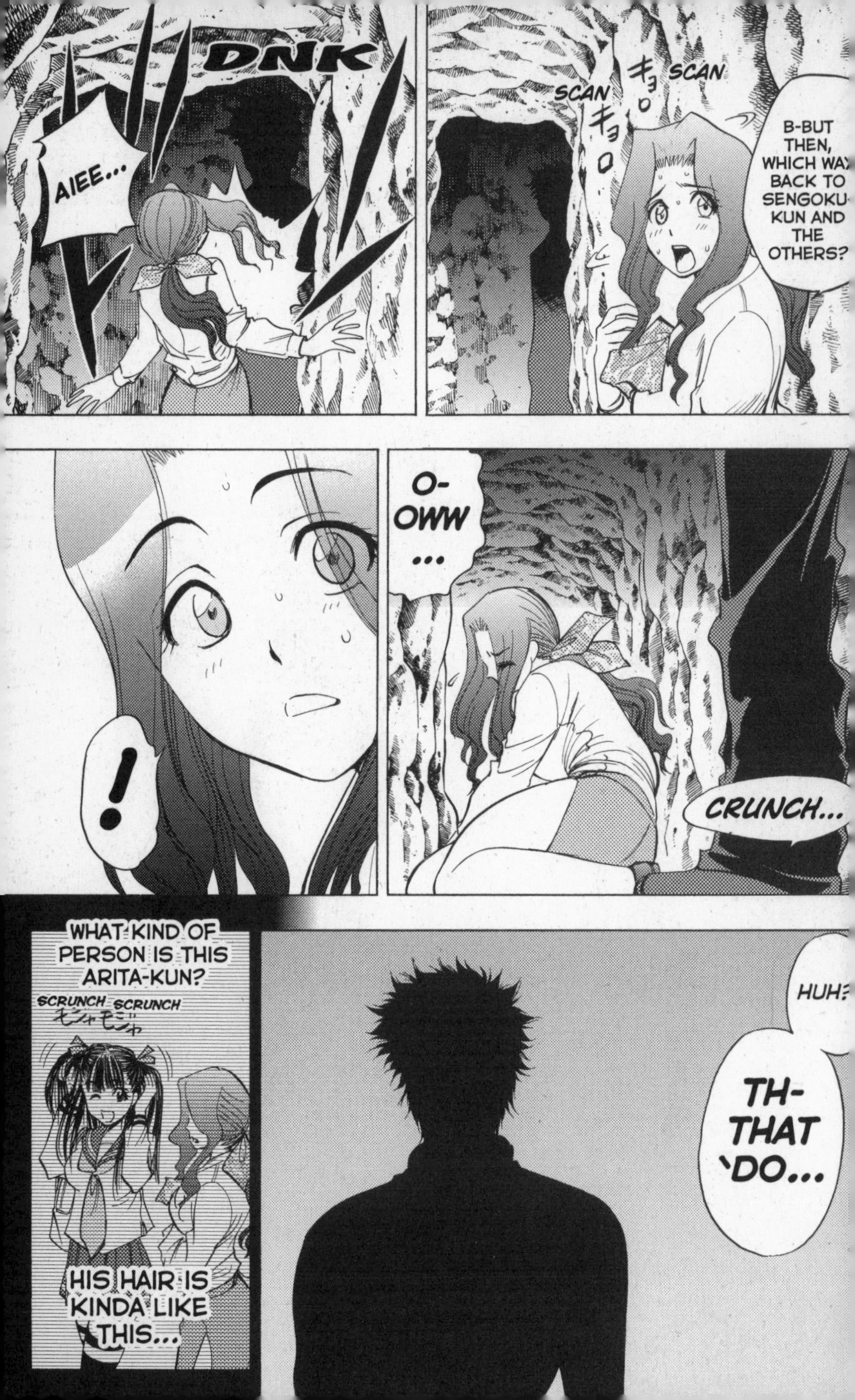

SCAN
キョロ
SCAN
キョロ
B-BUT THEN, WHICH WA BACK TO SENGOKU-KUN AND THE OTHERS?
DNK
AIEE...
O-OWW ...
CRUNCH...
!
HUH?
TH-THAT 'DO...
WHAT KIND OF PERSON IS THIS ARITA-KUN?
SCRUNCH SCRUNCH
モジャモジャ
HIS HAIR IS KINDA LIKE THIS...

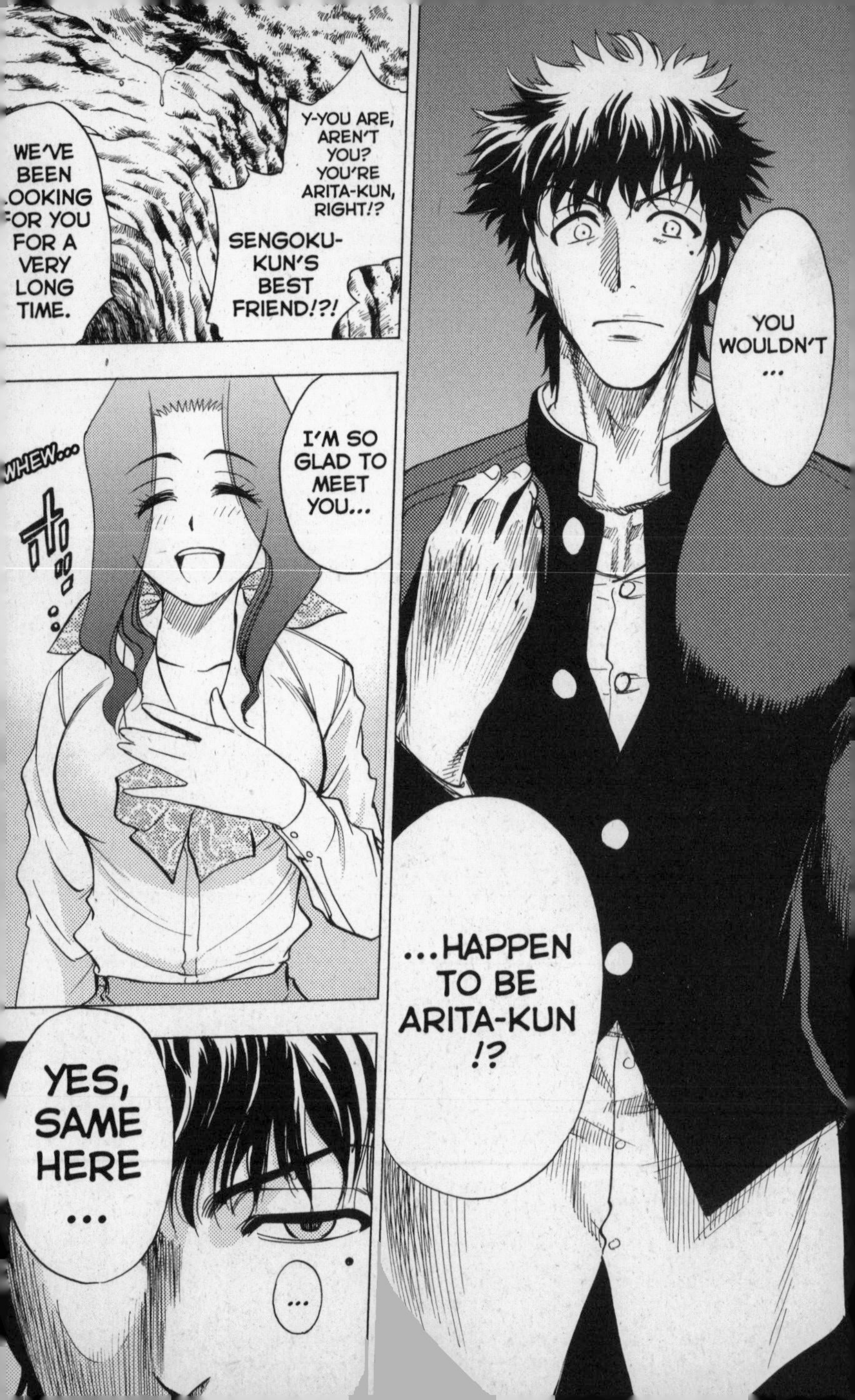
YOU WOULDN'T ...
...HAPPEN TO BE ARITA-KUN !?
Y-YOU ARE, AREN'T YOU? YOU'RE ARITA-KUN, RIGHT!?
SENGOKU-KUN'S BEST FRIEND!?!
WE'VE BEEN LOOKING FOR YOU FOR A VERY LONG TIME.
I'M SO GLAD TO MEET YOU...
WHEW...
...
YES, SAME HERE ...

To Be Continued...

Character Profile

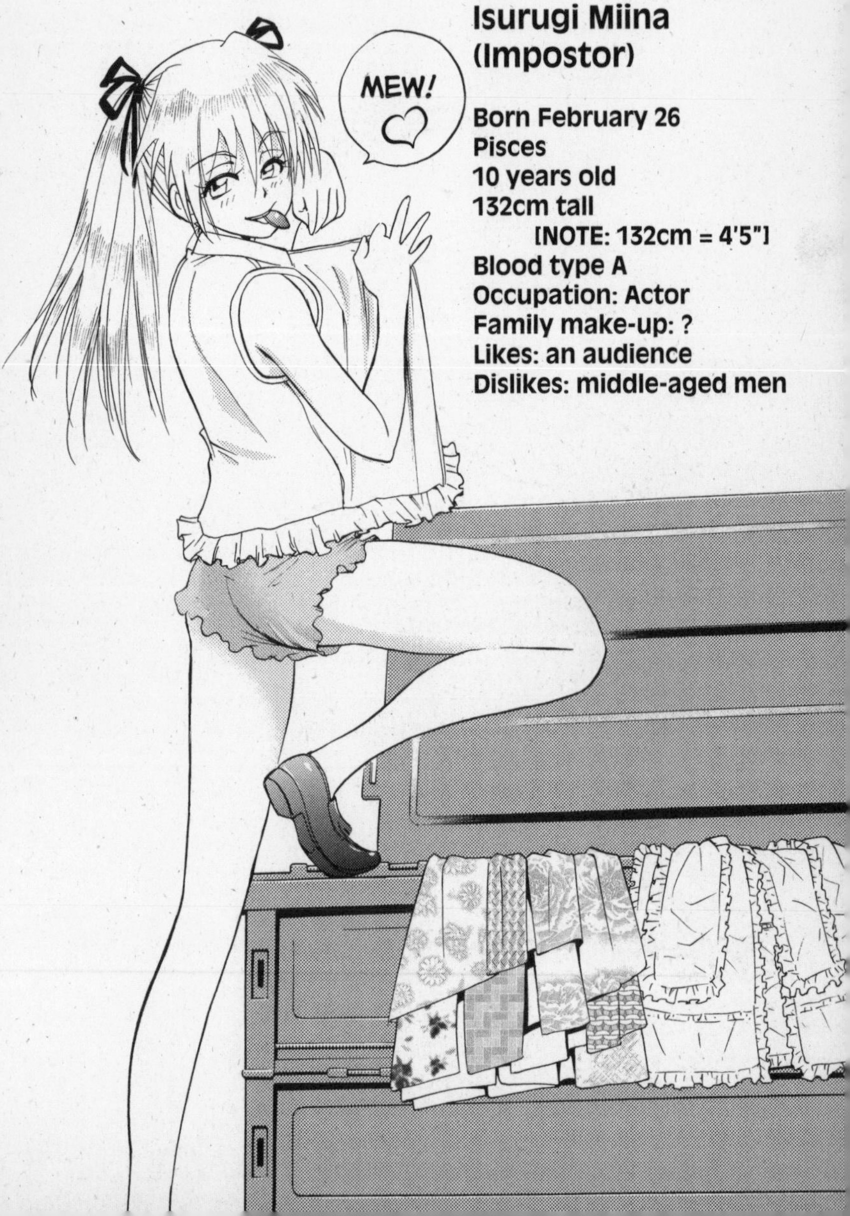
MEW!

Isurugi Miina (Impostor)

Born February 26
Pisces
10 years old
132cm tall
[NOTE: 132cm = 4'5"]
Blood type A
Occupation: Actor
Family make-up: ?
Likes: an audience
Dislikes: middle-aged men

Character Profile

Saji "Zaji" Kazuma

Born July 31
Leo
15 years old
170cm tall
[NOTE: 170cm = 5'8"]
Body weight 62kg
[NOTE: 62kg = 136.4 pounds]
Blood type O
Family make-up: father, mother, older sister, grandparents
Likes: manga
Dislikes: his father

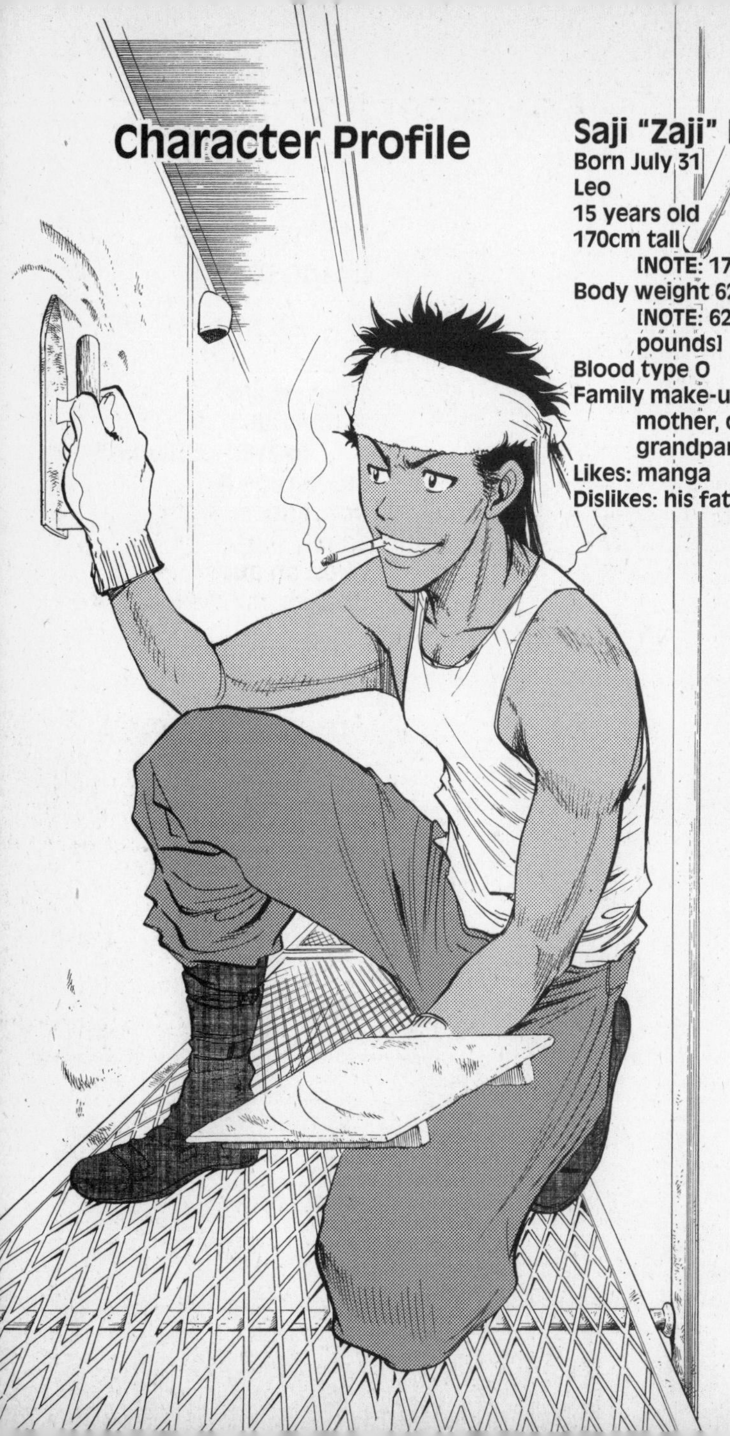

Mariya Shirô's Encyclopedia of Extinct Animals

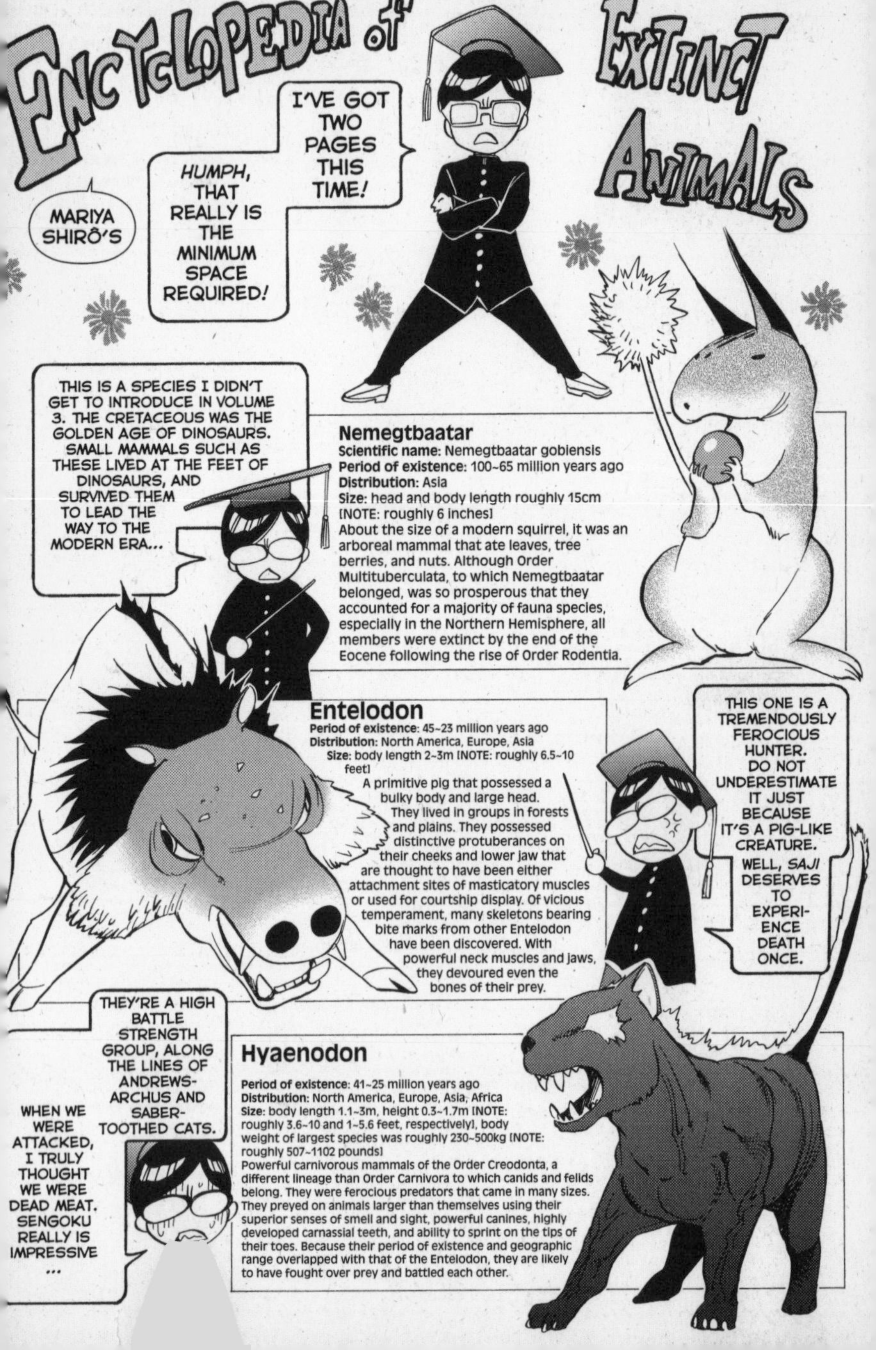
I'VE GOT TWO PAGES THIS TIME!
HUMPH, THAT REALLY IS THE MINIMUM SPACE REQUIRED!
THIS IS A SPECIES I DIDN'T GET TO INTRODUCE IN VOLUME 3. THE CRETACEOUS WAS THE GOLDEN AGE OF DINOSAURS. SMALL MAMMALS SUCH AS THESE LIVED AT THE FEET OF DINOSAURS, AND SURVIVED THEM TO LEAD THE WAY TO THE MODERN ERA...
THIS ONE IS A TREMENDOUSLY FEROCIOUS HUNTER. DO NOT UNDERESTIMATE IT JUST BECAUSE IT'S A PIG-LIKE CREATURE.
WELL, *SAJI* DESERVES TO EXPERIENCE DEATH ONCE.
THEY'RE A HIGH BATTLE STRENGTH GROUP, ALONG THE LINES OF ANDREWSARCHUS AND SABER-TOOTHED CATS.
WHEN WE WERE ATTACKED, I TRULY THOUGHT WE WERE DEAD MEAT. SENGOKU REALLY IS IMPRESSIVE ...

Nemegtbaatar

Scientific name: Nemegtbaatar gobiensis
Period of existence: 100~65 million years ago
Distribution: Asia
Size: head and body length roughly 15cm [NOTE: roughly 6 inches]

About the size of a modern squirrel, it was an arboreal mammal that ate leaves, tree berries, and nuts. Although Order Multituberculata, to which Nemegtbaatar belonged, was so prosperous that they accounted for a majority of fauna species, especially in the Northern Hemisphere, all members were extinct by the end of the Eocene following the rise of Order Rodentia.

Entelodon

Period of existence: 45~23 million years ago
Distribution: North America, Europe, Asia
Size: body length 2~3m [NOTE: roughly 6.5~10 feet]

A primitive pig that possessed a bulky body and large head. They lived in groups in forests and plains. They possessed distinctive protuberances on their cheeks and lower jaw that are thought to have been either attachment sites of masticatory muscles or used for courtship display. Of vicious temperament, many skeletons bearing bite marks from other Entelodon have been discovered. With powerful neck muscles and jaws, they devoured even the bones of their prey.

Hyaenodon

Period of existence: 41~25 million years ago
Distribution: North America, Europe, Asia, Africa
Size: body length 1.1~3m, height 0.3~1.7m [NOTE: roughly 3.6~10 and 1~5.6 feet, respectively], body weight of largest species was roughly 230~500kg [NOTE: roughly 507~1102 pounds]

Powerful carnivorous mammals of the Order Creodonta, a different lineage than Order Carnivora to which canids and felids belong. They were ferocious predators that came in many sizes. They preyed on animals larger than themselves using their superior senses of smell and sight, powerful canines, highly developed carnassial teeth, and ability to sprint on the tips of their toes. Because their period of existence and geographic range overlapped with that of the Entelodon, they are likely to have fought over prey and battled each other.

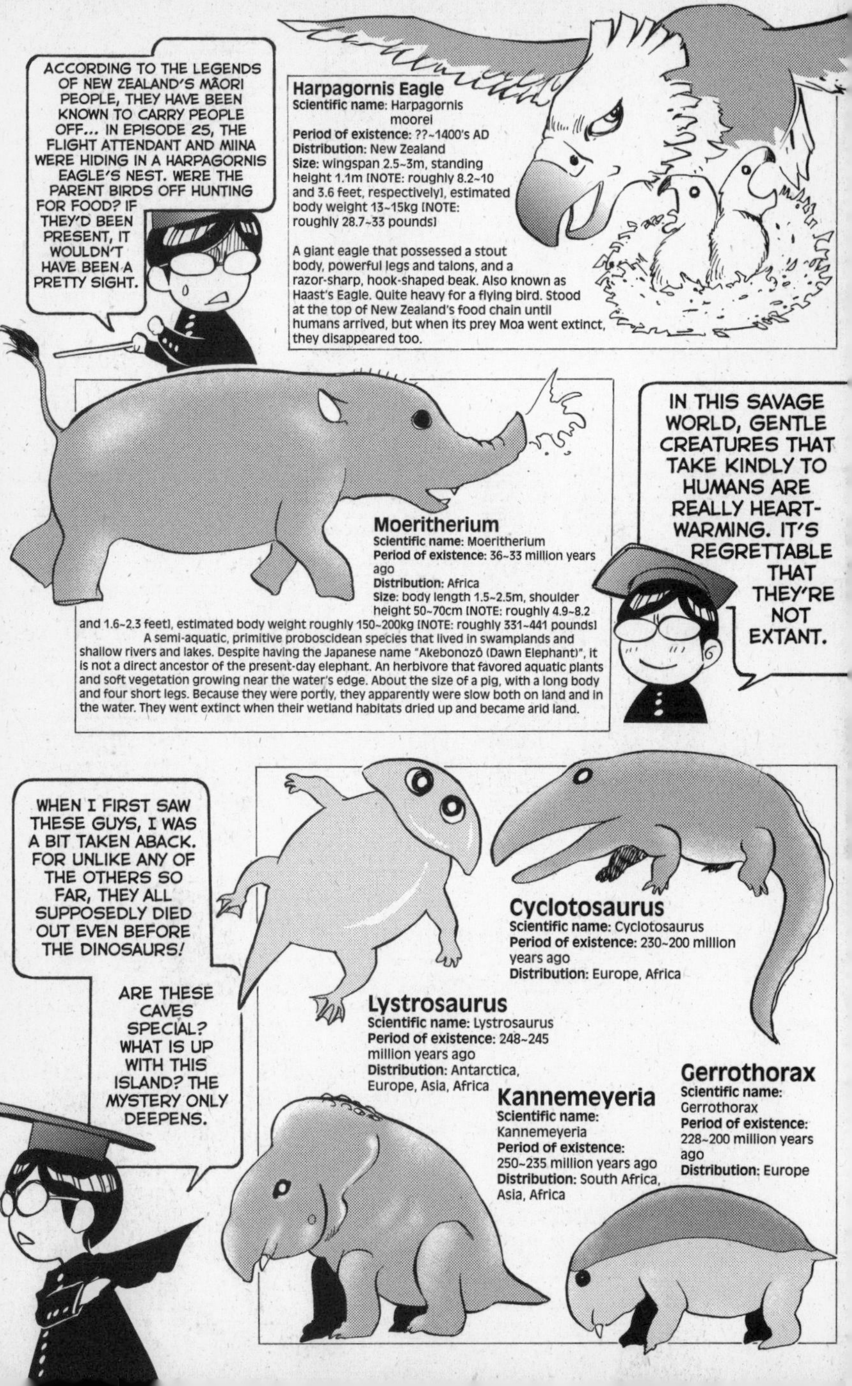
Harpagornis Eagle
Scientific name: Harpagornis moorei
Period of existence: ??~1400's AD
Distribution: New Zealand
Size: wingspan 2.5~3m, standing height 1.1m [NOTE: roughly 8.2~10 and 3.6 feet, respectively], estimated body weight 13~15kg [NOTE: roughly 28.7~33 pounds]
A giant eagle that possessed a stout body, powerful legs and talons, and a razor-sharp, hook-shaped beak. Also known as Haast's Eagle. Quite heavy for a flying bird. Stood at the top of New Zealand's food chain until humans arrived, but when its prey Moa went extinct, they disappeared too.
ACCORDING TO THE LEGENDS OF NEW ZEALAND'S MĀORI PEOPLE, THEY HAVE BEEN KNOWN TO CARRY PEOPLE OFF... IN EPISODE 25, THE FLIGHT ATTENDANT AND MIINA WERE HIDING IN A HARPAGORNIS EAGLE'S NEST. WERE THE PARENT BIRDS OFF HUNTING FOR FOOD? IF THEY'D BEEN PRESENT, IT WOULDN'T HAVE BEEN A PRETTY SIGHT.
IN THIS SAVAGE WORLD, GENTLE CREATURES THAT TAKE KINDLY TO HUMANS ARE REALLY HEART-WARMING. IT'S REGRETTABLE THAT THEY'RE NOT EXTANT.
Moeritherium
Scientific name: Moeritherium
Period of existence: 36~33 million years ago
Distribution: Africa
Size: body length 1.5~2.5m, shoulder height 50~70cm [NOTE: roughly 4.9~8.2 and 1.6~2.3 feet], estimated body weight roughly 150~200kg [NOTE: roughly 331~441 pounds]
A semi-aquatic, primitive proboscidean species that lived in swamplands and shallow rivers and lakes. Despite having the Japanese name "Akebonozô (Dawn Elephant)", it is not a direct ancestor of the present-day elephant. An herbivore that favored aquatic plants and soft vegetation growing near the water's edge. About the size of a pig, with a long body and four short legs. Because they were portly, they apparently were slow both on land and in the water. They went extinct when their wetland habitats dried up and became arid land.
Cyclotosaurus
Scientific name: Cyclotosaurus
Period of existence: 230~200 million years ago
Distribution: Europe, Africa
Lystrosaurus
Scientific name: Lystrosaurus
Period of existence: 248~245 million years ago
Distribution: Antarctica, Europe, Asia, Africa
WHEN I FIRST SAW THESE GUYS, I WAS A BIT TAKEN ABACK. FOR UNLIKE ANY OF THE OTHERS SO FAR, THEY ALL SUPPOSEDLY DIED OUT EVEN BEFORE THE DINOSAURS!
ARE THESE CAVES SPECIAL? WHAT IS UP WITH THIS ISLAND? THE MYSTERY ONLY DEEPENS.
Gerrothorax
Scientific name: Gerrothorax
Period of existence: 228~200 million years ago
Distribution: Europe
Kannemeyeria
Scientific name: Kannemeyeria
Period of existence: 250~235 million years ago
Distribution: South Africa, Asia, Africa

RANSLATION NOTES

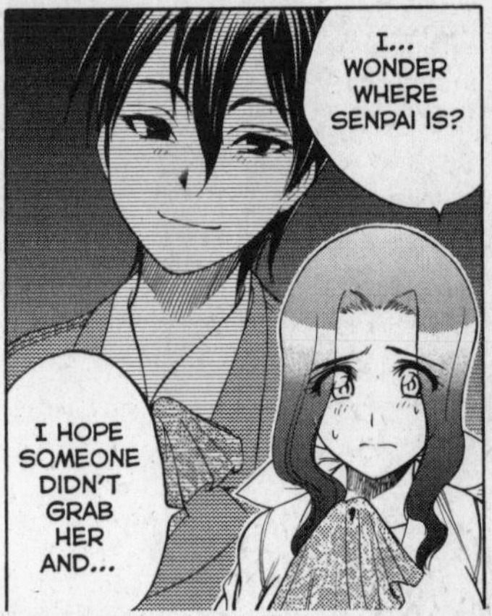
I... WONDER WHERE SENPAI IS?
I HOPE SOMEONE DIDN'T GRAB HER AND...

apanese is a tricky language for most Vesterners, and translation is often more rt than science. For your edification and eading pleasure, here are notes on some f the places where we could have gone in different direction with our translation f the work, or where a Japanese cultural eference is used.

Senpai, page 3

Senpai is a Japanese word that refers to someone senior to oneself in the context of academic year or office hierarchy, with some inference of a mentor-mentee relationship. It is the opposite or counter term to kôhai.

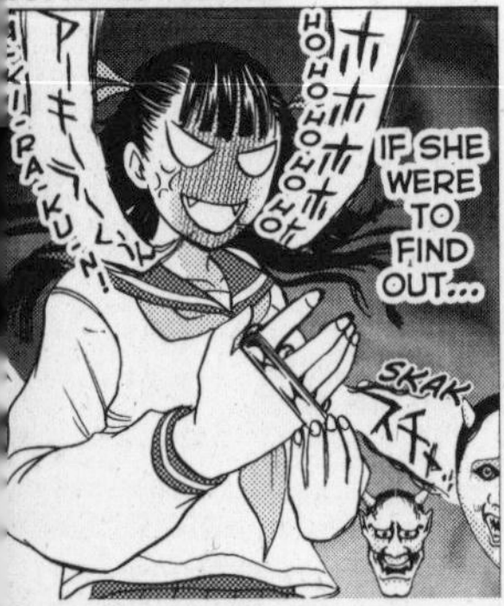
IF SHE WERE TO FIND OUT...
SKAK

Hannya Mask, page 009

A hannya is a type of female demon. Originally human, a woman becomes a hannya through extreme obsession or jealousy. Hannya masks are used in Japanese noh and kyôgen theater to portray such women, and with their distinctive features of two pointy horns, glaring eyes, and open leer displaying fangs, are some of the most recognizable Japanese masks. White masks indicate those who were of the nobility when human, while red masks indicate those who were lower class.

'akuza, page 11

'akuza are the most well-known and established rganized crime syndicates in Japan, and are often eferred to as the Japanese Mob or Japanese Mafia n the West.

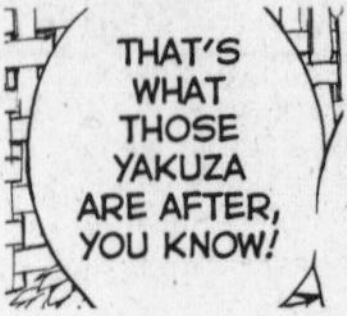
THAT'S WHAT THOSE YAKUZA ARE AFTER, YOU KNOW!

"Wild Boar Karino", page 019

Karino's nickname in his jurisdiction of Nishi-Kawasaki, there is a secondary gag in addition to the obvious one of the similarity of his facial features to that of a boar. The kanji that spell "Karino" can be translated as "hunting field", and Karino is a police officer by profession.

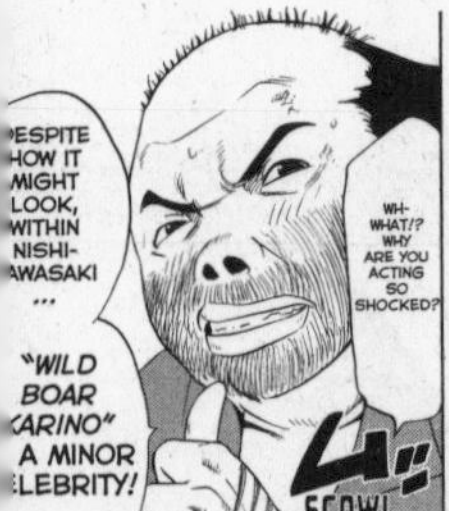
WH-WHAT!? WHY ARE YOU ACTING SO SHOCKED?
ESPITE HOW IT MIGHT LOOK, WITHIN NISHI-AWASAKI ...
"WILD BOAR KARINO" A MINOR ELEBRITY!
SCOWL

Zaji, page 58

Zaji is just the nickname this character goes by. His actual name is Saji (family name) Kazuma (given name).

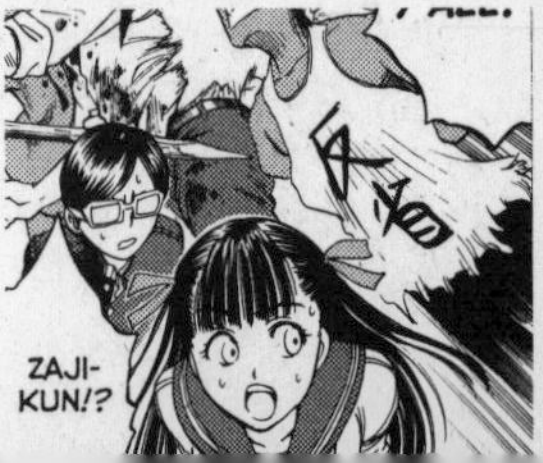
ZAJI-KUN!?

Kappa, page 107
Kappa are a type of freshwater aquatic creature or sprite that appears in Japanese folklore. Child-sized and humanoid, they are usually depicted with greenish scaly skin, webbed fingers and toes, beak-like mouths, and a concave bowl-like indentation on the top of their head that holds water. Although stories of benevolent or repentant kappa abound, they are most commonly known as malevolent monsters that drown humans and animals, especially children.

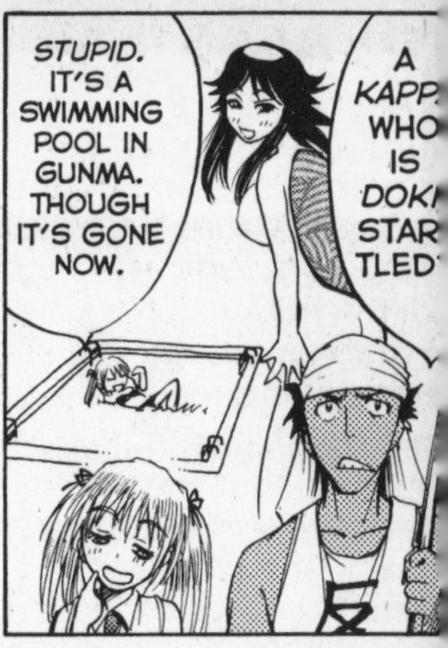
A KAPP WHO IS DOK STAR TLED
STUPID. IT'S A SWIMMING POOL IN GUNMA. THOUGH IT'S GONE NOW.

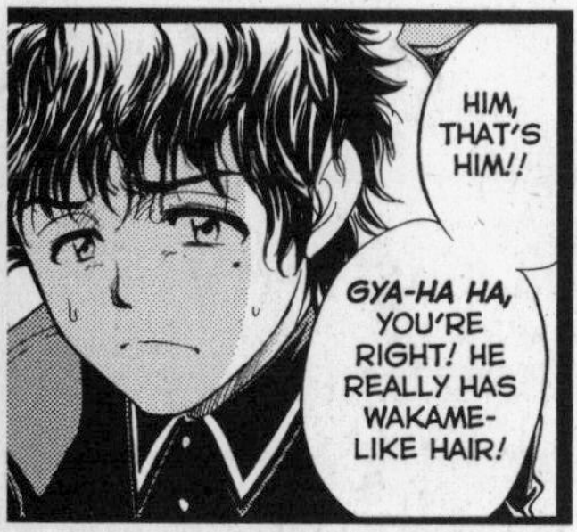
HIM, THAT'S HIM!!
GYA-HA HA, YOU'RE RIGHT! HE REALLY HAS WAKAME-LIKE HAIR!

Wakame, page 111
Wakame is the green, thin, flat-to-wavy edible seaweed used in Japanese soups and salad, especially miso soup.

Scheduled (school) check-up, page 153
At least once yearly, students undergo a required medical check-up at school, which consists of a physical examination, height and weight measurements (including sitting height), body condition score, and urine and stool exams. At co-ed schools, boys and girls report to separate rooms, as students must strip down to their underwear for the check-up.

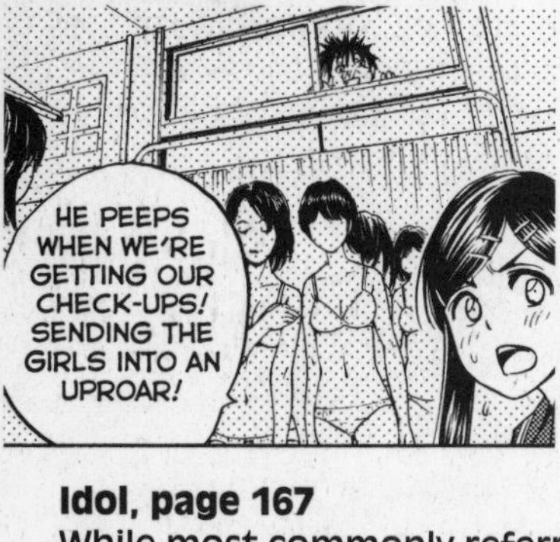
HE PEEPS WHEN WE'RE GETTING OUR CHECK-UPS! SENDING THE GIRLS INTO AN UPROAR!

Idol, page 167
While most commonly referring to young female media personalities, such as J-pop artists, actresses, and models (but occasionally also foreigners and young male stars), this Japanese phenomenon can extend to civilians as well, i.e. the prettiest student or junior employee.

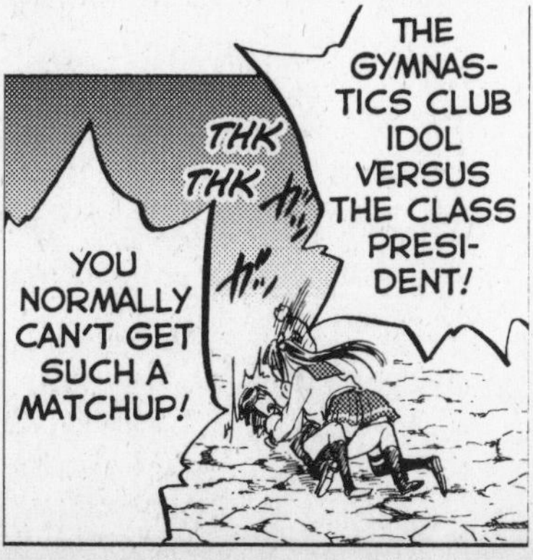
THE GYMNAS-TICS CLUB IDOL VERSUS THE CLASS PRESI-DENT!
THK THK
YOU NORMALLY CAN'T GET SUCH A MATCHUP!

TOMARE!

[STOP!]

You are going the wrong way!

Manga is a completely different type of reading experience.

To start at the *beginning*, go to the *end*!

That's right! Authentic manga is read the traditional Japanese way—from right to left, exactly the *opposite* of how American books are read. It's easy to follow: Just go to the other end of the book, and read each page—and each panel—from the right side to the left side, starting at the top right. Now you're experiencing manga as it was meant to be.